Firewalls For Dummies, 2nd Edition

W9-CEG-633

Private and Automatic IP Address Ranges

A	10.0.0.0	to	10.255.255.255	(10.0.0.0/8)
B	172.16.0.0	to	172.31.255.255	(172.16.0.0/12)
C	192.168.0.0	to	192.168.255.255	(192.168.0.0/16)
APIPA	169.254.0.0	to	169.254.255.255	(169.254.0.0/16)

Common TCP and UDP Ports

Protocol	Port	Name
TCP	20	FTP data
TCP	21	FTP control
TCP	23	Telnet
TCP	25	SMTP (E-mail)
TCP/UDP	53	DNS query
UDP	67/68	DHCP (Dynamic IP address configuration)
TCP	80	HTTP (Web)
TCP	110	POP3 (E-mail)
TCP	119	NNTP (Newsgroups)
TCP	143	IMAP4 (E-mail)
TCP	389	LDAP (Directory service)
TCP	443	HTTPS (Web SSL)
UDP	1701	L2TP (Virtual Private Networks)
TCP	1723	PPTP (Virtual Private Networks)

Common IP Protocols

Protocol	Name
1	ICMP (ping)
6	TCP
17	UDP
47	GRE (PPTP)
50	ESP (IPSec)
51	AH (IPSec)

52724838

For Dummies: Bestselling Book Series for Beginners

Firewalls For Dummies, 2nd Edition

Cheat Sheet

Web Sites to Visit

www.infosyssec.org	Security portal
www.sans.org	Many security-related resources
www.cert.org	Security advisories on discovered security threats
www.securityfocus.com	Latest information on security vulnerabilities
www.iana.org/assignments/port-numbers	Comprehensive listing of protocol port numbers

Firewall Shopping Checklist

- ✔ Is the firewall ICSA-certified?
- ✔ Is the firewall easy to configure?
- ✔ Are there remote management options?
- ✔ Does it match the current expertise of your firewall administrators?
- ✔ Which OS platform and what hardware does it require?
- ✔ Does it require client software?
- ✔ What are the licensing options and costs?
- ✔ Does it support application-level rules?
- ✔ Does it support NAT?
- ✔ Does it support a DMZ?
- ✔ Does it support VPN?
- ✔ Does it support new protocols and plug-ins?
- ✔ Does it detect common attacks and intrusion attempts?
- ✔ Does it have adequate logging options?
- ✔ Are real-time monitoring options available?

Copyright © 2003 Wiley Publishing, Inc. All rights reserved.

Item 4048-3.

For more information about Wiley Publishing, call 1-800-762-2974.

For Dummies: Bestselling Book Series for Beginners

Firewalls FOR DUMMIES®
2ND EDITION

by Brian Komar, Ronald Beekelaar,
and Joern Wettern, PhD

WILEY

Wiley Publishing, Inc.

Firewalls For Dummies®, 2nd Edition

Published by
Wiley Publishing, Inc.
909 Third Avenue
New York, NY 10022
www.wiley.com

Copyright © 2003 by Wiley Publishing, Inc., Indianapolis, Indiana

Published by Wiley Publishing, Inc., Indianapolis, Indiana

Published simultaneously in Canada

For general information on our other products and services or to obtain technical support, please contact our Customer Care Department within the U.S. at 800-762-2974, outside the U.S. at 317-572-3993, or fax 317-572-4002.

Wiley also publishes its books in a variety of electronic formats. Some content that appears in print may not be available in electronic books.

Library of Congress Control Number: 2003101908

ISBN: 0-7645-4048-3

Manufactured in the United States of America

10 9 8 7 6 5 4 3 2

2B/RT/QW/QT/IN

About the Authors

Brian Komar, B. Comm (Hons), a native of Canada, makes his living as a Public Key Infrastructure (PKI) consultant, speaker, author, and trainer. Brian speaks at conferences around the world on network design and security topics. His consulting practice focuses on PKI design and architecture projects and on research assignments specializing in interoperability between different vendors' security products. In his spare time, Brian enjoys traveling and biking with his wife Krista and sharing a fine bottle of wine (or more) with his good friends.

Ronald Beekelaar, M.Sc., a native of The Netherlands, makes his living as a network security consultant, author, and trainer. Ronald frequently trains network administrators on network design and enterprise security topics. He writes articles for several computer magazines, mostly about operating systems and security issues. Ronald lives in Utrecht, The Netherlands, with his wife Kim. They enjoy traveling abroad. If they find the time, they often travel to European cities, especially London, to see a theater show and visit museums.

Joern Wettern, Ph.D., a native of Germany, is a network consultant and trainer. Joern has also developed a range of training materials for a large software publisher, and these materials are used to train thousands of network administrators around the world. He frequently travels to several continents to speak at computer conferences. Joern is paranoid enough to use an enterprise-class firewall to connect his home network. Somehow, he still manages to enjoy the occasional sunny day and the many rainy ones in Portland, Oregon, where he lives with his wife Loriann and three cats. In his spare time, of which there is precious little, Joern and his wife hike up the mountains of the Columbia Gorge and down the Grand Canyon. You can also find him attending folk music festivals and dancing like a maniac. Joern's latest project is to learn how to herd his cats — without much success thus far.

The authors can be reached at FirewallsForDummies@hotmail.com.

Dedication

To Loriann, Krista, and Kim, and our parents.

Author's Acknowledgments

This second edition would not have been possible without a large number of people, especially the good folks at Wiley. We want to thank Byron Hynes for being an excellent technical editor, and especially the humor he contributed to the project. Melody Layne for pulling us together for another run at the content, Paul Levesque for his insights on the content, and Rebekah Mancilla for her editorial assistance.

Beyond the Wiley crew, we received help from firewall vendors who made it possible for us to cover a number of different products and helped us with issues that came up during the writing of the book. We would like to especially thank the ISA Server and PKI teams at Microsoft and Check Point for providing an evaluation copy of FireWall-1 NG.

Finally, not a single chapter of this book would have been possible without our spouses, who were willing to let us work on this project and thus are the real heroes in this story.

Publisher's Acknowledgments

We're proud of this book; please send us your comments through our online registration form located at www.dummies.com/register/.

Some of the people who helped bring this book to market include the following:

Acquisitions, Editorial, and Media Development

Project Editor: Paul Levesque

(Previous Edition: Linda Morris)

Acquisitions Editor: Melody Layne

Copy Editor: Rebekah Mancilla

Technical Editor: Byron Hynes

Editorial Manager: Leah Cameron

Media Development Manager: Laura VanWinkle

Media Development Supervisor: Richard Graves

Editorial Assistant: Amanda Foxworth

Cartoons: Rich Tennant, www.the5thwave.com

Production

Project Coordinator: Ryan Steffen

Layout and Graphics: Seth Conley, Carrie Foster, Lauren Goddard, Michael Kruzil, Tiffany Muth, Shelley Norris, Lynsey Osborn, Jacque Schneider

Proofreaders: Andy Hollandbeck, Angel Perez, Kathy Simpson, Charles Spencer, Brian Walls, TECHBOOKS Production Services

Indexer: TECHBOOKS Production Services

Publishing and Editorial for Technology Dummies

　　Richard Swadley, Vice President and Executive Group Publisher

　　Andy Cummings, Vice President and Publisher

　　Mary C. Corder, Editorial Director

Publishing for Consumer Dummies

　　Diane Graves Steele, Vice President and Publisher

　　Joyce Pepple, Acquisitions Director

Composition Services

　　Gerry Fahey, Vice President of Production Services

　　Debbie Stailey, Director of Composition Services

Contents at a Glance

Table of Contents

Introduction

*W*elcome to *Firewalls For Dummies,* a book written to help the average Joe understand how firewalls work and how to configure a firewall. This book meets the needs of the person just finding out about computers, as well as the network administrator who needs to implement his or her first firewall.

But what is a firewall, you may ask? The quick-and-dirty definition is that a firewall is a boundary network device that resides between a private network and the Internet. The firewall is configured to inspect the network traffic that passes between the Internet and your network and only allows the network protocols that you desire to pass through the firewall. If a protocol isn't included in the approved list, the firewall discards the packets of data and prevents them from entering the network.

Firewalls bring to mind visions of the computer geek at the office, sitting in a darkened closet with his router and handy toolkit, warding off hackers as they attack from the Internet. This book attempts to shed some light on the subject by breaking down the myths around the firewall so that you can understand what a firewall does and how it's configured.

This book explains firewalls in normal, everyday language so that you can learn about them. In addition, you can laugh along with us as we relate stories from the trenches where we have configured firewalls. After you read the book, you'll have the confidence to configure your firewall to allow applications such as e-mail or Web servers to securely interact with the Internet.

In addition to firewalls, we also look at intrusion detection software meant for the at-home user, such as ZoneAlarm and Norton Personal Firewall, which help detect network attacks as they happen. The sooner you know an attack is taking place, the sooner you can react to the attack and minimize the damage that an attacker inflicts.

We want you to feel that installing a firewall is no big deal when you understand the purpose that a firewall serves and the basics of configuring a firewall.

About This Book

We try to provide you with a book that can act as a reference guide for firewalls. We don't expect you to read the book from cover to cover but to look at specific topics that meet your needs. Twenty chapters and an appendix cover all topics of firewalls and their implementation. Just turn to the chapter that catches your attention and start reading. Each chapter has been designed so that you can read it on its own.

How to Use This Book

This book is easy to drive, and doesn't require a manual. Simply turn to the Table of Contents, find a topic that interests you, and go to that chapter.

If you're looking for configuration details for specific firewalls, jump to Part IV where we provide detailed steps on how to install and configure popular firewall products used today. If you're just looking for tips on how to configure a firewall for specific protocols, Parts II and III look at simple and advanced protocol rules in standalone and Demilitarized Zone (DMZ) configurations.

What You Don't Need to Read

You don't have to read every single word in this book to find out about firewalls. Sidebars and extra information included in the book provide additional information that can help you, but you don't need to read them to use firewalls. This additional information is marked with the Technical Stuff icon.

However, if you want that extra technical information, you now know where to find it!

Foolish Assumptions

When we sat down to come up with the outline for this book, we drew up a short list of assumptions about you, the reader. We assume that:

1. You have seen, heard, touched, or know someone who owns a computer.

2. You have read an article in a magazine or newspaper that covers security issues involving computers.

3. You are scared (or at least concerned) and want to secure your network with a firewall.

How This Book Is Organized

Inside this book, you will find the chapters divided into five parts. Each part addresses a specific issue involved in designing and implementing firewall solutions. The book is modular enough that you aren't forced to read each chapter in order. Feel free to find the part that catches your interest, and dig in from there!

Part I: Introducing Firewall Basics

You have to start somewhere! The chapters in this part help you to identify the threats and risks to your network when it's connected to the Internet and how firewalls help mitigate those risks. If you've read articles about the latest hacking attempts, you may wonder how those attacks work and why your network may be vulnerable. This part helps you to understand how those attacks take place and what measures you can take to protect your network from the attack.

In addition to looking at various attacks, this part also goes over the basics of the TCP/IP suite so that you can get a grasp on the rules implemented by today's firewalls.

Part II: Establishing Rules

So, you're sitting at your desk, minding your own business, and your boss walks in. The boss sees your copy of *Firewalls For Dummies* lying on your desk and says, "Can you help the network geek with the firewall?" This is the part for you! Part II helps you design firewall rules to protect networks and home offices.

Not only does this part show you how to configure firewall rules, it also describes the process of determining what protocols to allow in and out of your network. If you don't have guidelines for securing your network, coming up with a configuration for your firewall is almost impossible!

Part III: Designing Network Configurations

Put on your helmets for a trip to the world of Demilitarized Zones (the computer kind, not the combat kind). Part III puts it all together by showing you common firewall configurations that are used to protect a network.

This part looks at firewall configurations that use one or more firewalls to protect both your private network and resources that you expose to the Internet.

Part IV: Deploying Solutions Using Firewall Products

After reading this book, you will know how to configure some of today's popular firewalls to protect your network. This part describes the steps required to secure Microsoft Windows and Linux desktops, gives you the dirt on common intrusion detection systems, and studies the configuration of two popular firewalls: Microsoft Internet Security and Acceleration (ISA) Server and Check Point FireWall-1.

Part IV closes with a useful discussion on how to choose a firewall. Think of it as a buying a new car. When you buy a new car, you come up with a list of features that you want in your car, such as a CD player or power windows. This chapter covers the features that you may want to have in the firewall you select.

Part V: The Part of Tens

No *For Dummies* book would be complete without the Part of Tens. We include tips on security configuration, tools you may want to acquire, and Internet sites that can keep you up-to-date with security issues.

In addition to the Part of Tens, the Appendix provides a comprehensive listing of IP Protocol numbers, ICMP type numbers, and a TCP/UDP port listing that you can use to aid your firewall configuration.

Icons Used in This Book

Feel like geeking out with us? This is where we insert the pocket protectors and really go under the hood to look at security. Expect to find references to Internet resources and highly detailed configuration information when you see this icon. Don't be afraid: We explain this technical stuff without using a lot of computer jargon.

Houston, we have a problem! This icon advises you of potential dangers that exist with specific protocols or security configurations. If you take the wrong route, you could be in mortal danger, or least have a security issue that could compromise your network.

Sometimes you see topics over and over. We all hate to memorize things, but sometimes you need to memorize a topic related to firewalls.

Tips provide you with inside information on how to quickly configure a rule or get past a common hurdle when designing firewalls.

Where to Go from Here

You have the book in your hand, and you're ready to get started. Feel free to turn to any topic in the book that interests you! Look in the Table of Contents for the topic that drew your interest to firewalls. If you're not curious about any specific topic but just want an overview, turn the page and start with Part I. Either way, enjoy yourself and let us help you learn about firewalls!

Part I

Introducing Firewall Basics

The 5th Wave   By Rich Tennant

RocketSoft
Design and Construction

"The feeling is, we may not have all the Internet security we should."

In this part . . .

Firewalls — who needs 'em? Well it turns out, most of us do. If you or your company is connected to the Internet, you may want to protect yourself from all the threats and risks to which your network is exposed. The chapters in this part help you to understand why a firewall is needed to safely connect to the Web.

This part discusses the basics of the network protocol that makes the Internet happen: TCP/IP. It also explains how hackers use TCP/IP and the Internet connection to your computer to attempt to break into your network. You discover the basics (and the not-so-basics) of how a firewall can be used to separate the good from the bad.

Chapter 1

Why Do You Need a Firewall?

*I*f you want to find out about firewalls, you bought the right book. Before we start exploring the gory details of how firewalls work and how to configure them, we use this chapter to lay the groundwork. If you are already familiar with how the Internet works and how you connect to it, and if you have a basic understanding of firewalls, then you can skip this chapter. If these topics are new to you, if you want to refresh your knowledge of any of these topics, or if you want to get an overview of what a firewall is, then read on.

Defining a Firewall

A *firewall* is a piece of software or hardware that filters all network traffic between your computer, home network, or company network and the Internet. It is our position that everyone who uses the Internet needs some kind of firewall protection. This chapter tells you what a firewall does and sets down the basic questions that you should ask as you are evaluating specific firewalls.

Not too long ago, only construction workers and architects asked the question, "Why do we need a firewall?" Before the term *firewall* was used for a component of a computer network, it described a wall that was designed to contain a fire. A brick and mortar firewall is designed to contain a fire in one part of a building and thus prevent it from spreading to another part of the building. Any fire that may erupt inside a building stops at the firewall and won't spread to other parts of the building.

A firewall in a computer network performs a role that is very similar to that of a firewall in a building. Just as a firewall made out of concrete protects one part of a building, a firewall in a network ensures that if something bad happens on one side of the firewall, computers on the other side won't be affected. Unlike a building firewall, which protects against a very specific threat (fire), a network firewall has to protect against many different kinds of threats. You read about these threats in the papers almost every day: viruses, worms, denial-of-service (DoS) attacks, hacking, and break-ins. Attacks with names like SQL Slammer, Code Red, and NIMDA have even appeared on the evening news. Unless you haven't read a newspaper or watched the news in the last year, you surely have heard at least one of these terms. It's no secret: *they* are out there, and *they* are out to get us. Often we don't know who *they* are, but we do know where possible intruders are and where we don't want them to penetrate. Hackers are roaming the wide expanses of the Internet, just like the outlaws of the Old West roamed the prairies, and we don't want them to enter our network and roam among the computers in it.

You know that you need to protect your network from these outlaws, and one of the most efficient methods of protecting your network is to install a firewall. By default, any good firewall prevents network traffic from passing between the Internet and your internal network. "Wait a second," you may be thinking. "I just spent a lot of time, effort, and money to get my network connected to the Internet so that I can send e-mail to business partners, look at my competitor's Web site, keep up-to-date on sports scores, and check the latest fashion trends. And now you're telling me that a firewall blocks network traffic. How does this make sense?"

The answer is easy. Keep in mind that separating the Internet from your internal network traffic is the default behavior of most firewalls. However, the first thing that you will probably do after installing the firewall is to change the defaults to allow selected traffic network through the firewall. This is no different from a building inspector who allows fire doors in a physical firewall. These doors are designed to provide an opening while still guaranteeing safety for all occupants. When you configure a firewall, you create some controlled openings that don't compromise your network's safety but that allow selected network traffic to pass through.

As you are designing your protection against attacks from the Internet, never rely on a single form of protection for your network. Doing so can give you a false sense of security. For example, even if you completely disconnect your network from the Internet to prevent a computer virus from entering your network, an employee can still bring to work a floppy disk that has been infected with a virus and inadvertently infect computers in your network.

Just because you're paranoid . . .

"Aren't you a little paranoid?" is a question that we're often asked. Thus far, we haven't consulted a medical professional because to us, the answer is clear: You bet we're paranoid. We know that *they* are out to get us. Sometimes we think that there are millions of people out on the Internet who want to break into the computers on our networks. If only the Trojans had been as paranoid, they would have looked more carefully at the horse that they were given. When dealing with computer networks, a moderate amount of paranoia is a very healthy trait — the more you are concerned about possible risks, the more likely you'll be in a position to provide adequate protection for your network. As the saying goes, "Just because you're paranoid doesn't mean that they're not really out to get you."

The Value of Your Network

Before you look in more detail at what threats you face and how you can protect yourself against these threats by using a firewall, take a minute to look at your network and establish how much it is worth to you. The best way to establish the value of something is to evaluate the cost of a loss. Take a look at some different types of damage and consider the cost of each:

- ✔ **Lost data:** How important is the data on your corporate network? To answer this question, try to estimate what would happen if the data disappeared. Imagine that someone managed to break into your network and deleted all your accounting data, your customer list, and so on. Hopefully you have methods in place to restore lost data from a backup — no matter how you lose it. But, for just a second, imagine that all your corporate data is gone and you have to reconstruct it. Would your company still be in business if this happened to you tomorrow?

- ✔ **Confidential data:** If anyone were to break into your network and get access to confidential data — for example, the secret plans for the perpetual motion machine that you are developing — imagine what could happen. What would an intruder do with the data? Because you don't know, you have to assume the worst. If the secret plans end up in the hands of a competitor, he or she may beat you to the market with a miracle machine, and the profits and the Nobel Prize in Physics go to that person instead of you. The damage may even be worse if the data that is stolen is your entire customer list, including complete contact and billing information.

- ✔ **Downtime:** Have you ever called a company to order an item or to complain about something, and you were told, "I can't help you, the network is down." If so, you probably remember your reaction. The excuse sounded cheap, and you felt like taking your business somewhere else.

However, network outages do happen, and often the best thing that employees can do is twiddle their thumbs and tell customers to call again later. Preventing intrusions from the Internet may cost a little bit of money, but the amount of money lost due to downtime caused by such an intrusion could cost a lot more.

✔ **Staff time:** Each time an attack on your network is successful, you must take time to fix the hole and to repair any damage. For example, if a virus infects the computers in your company, you may have to go to each computer to remove the virus and repair any damage. The time that you spend doing this adds up quickly, and — as the saying goes — time is money. Don't expect to fix a large-scale problem quickly; that is, unless you are in the information technology department of an organization that we know. After a recent virus outbreak, they solved the problem by erasing the hard drives of every single computer and reinstalling everything from scratch. When the employees came to work the next morning, they realized that all of their data was lost, and they had to start the arduous task of reconstructing it from scratch. The IT people were nowhere to be found; for them the problem had been solved — the virus was gone. For everyone else the problem had just started.

✔ **Hijacked computer:** Imagine that someone broke into your computer and used it for his own purposes. If your computer is not used much anyway, this may not seem like a big deal. However, now imagine that the intruder uses your computer for illegitimate purposes. For example, a hacker uses your computer to store stolen software. When law enforcement personnel, who have partially traced the hacker's tracks, come knocking on your door, you have some explaining to do.

✔ **Reputation:** Do you want to be the company that is mentioned in the local or national news as the latest victim of a computer attack? Imagine what this would do to your company's reputation. The potential damage from such publicity has even caused some companies to sweep network intrusions under the table.

Get Yourself Connected

Not too long ago, you only had a choice between two types of connections to the Internet: a slow modem dial-up connection for individuals and smaller organizations, or a fast and very expensive connection for larger companies and institutions. Things have changed. In many parts of the world, you now have a choice among several different types of Internet connections, each of them providing different access speeds and different security risks. Increasingly, these choices are becoming available in many parts of the world. In this section, we examine the different types and assess the benefits that they provide and the risks that they pose. As you will see, an important factor here is the bandwidth — the amount of data you can transfer across a network connection. Bandwidth is directly related to the connection speed.

Network and modem transfer speeds are normally measured in bits per second (bps). Computers keep track of data using a binary system in which all characters are translated to zeros and ones. A *bit* is a single one or zero. Most characters in the alphabet, including digits and special characters, can be expressed using eight bits; this is often referred to as a *byte*. So, if your network connection allows for data transfer at 8 kilobits per second (that's 8,000 bits per second), or 8 Kbps, your computer will transfer about 1,000 characters per second — minus a few because of the overhead to keep track of the connection. You may also have heard the term *baud,* which used to be a common measurement for modem speeds. A baud is a measurement for the number of electrical signals that are sent per second. At low transfer rates, the baud number is identical to the bps rate, but at higher rates the two differ. Because of this difference, you don't see the term *baud* used much anymore. When comparing modem speeds you only have to look at the bps numbers. These numbers are easy to interpret and compare: The higher the number, the faster the connection. Another good thing to remember is that a kilobit per second (Kbps) is about 1,000 bps, and a megabit per second (Mbps) is about 1 million bps.

Modem dial-up connections

Most dial-up connections use a modem to connect to the Internet. You connect a modem to your telephone line and all data between your computer and the Internet service provider (ISP) is transmitted using POTS (plain old telephone service), also referred to as PSTN (public switched telephone network).

Current modem technology allows you to connect at speeds of up to 56 Kbps — blazing fast compared to the speeds that were available just a few years ago, but agonizingly slow compared to most other technologies available. To make things worse, a 56 Kbps modem can connect at this speed only under ideal circumstances, which almost never happen. Poor line conditions, too many telephone switches, and regulatory limitations can all contribute to limiting the actual bandwidth that you can attain. After you are connected, you can transmit data only at the maximum speed in the downstream direction, from your ISP to your computer. Current technology limits upstream connections from your computer to your ISP to 33.6 Kbps. Still, because of their low cost, modems are still what most individuals use to connect to the Internet.

Some modems don't even operate at 56 Kbps. Modems and line conditions can have an effect on the actual data throughput. For example, one of the authors of this book went on a recent vacation to a small, remote island in Malaysia. There he discovered that the only Internet connection on the island was via a satellite phone connection, which limited connection speeds to 9,600 bps — furthermore, that limited bandwidth was shared by the two computers on the island.

Modem connections have one feature that can be both an advantage and a disadvantage. With a modem you have to establish a new connection each time you want to connect to the Internet. Connecting takes only a minute, but when you stare at your computer screen while the modem is dialing, this minute can seem like an eternity. From a security point of view, though, this characteristic of a dial-up connection is a good thing. Your computer is only connected to the Internet while you are dialed in. During all other times, nobody on the Internet can contact your computer and break into it.

ISDN connections

The ISDN line and dial-up connection have one major similarity: They're both used for both voice communications and data transmission. (By the way, ISDN stands for Integrated Services Digital Network, but almost everyone uses the acronym.) One main difference between the two technologies is that using an ISDN line enables you to have a voice call and a data transfer at the same time. The other main difference is that an ISDN enables you to transfer data at higher speeds than dial-up connections allow. Depending on the exact ISDN implementation, speeds of up to 128 Kbps are possible. Installing and configuring ISDN takes more skill and effort than plugging a modem into a telephone line, but many people find it worth the extra effort to get a faster connection.

Like a regular telephone dial-up connection, an ISDN connection is only active while you are dialed into the Internet.

DSL connections

The newest type of connection that telephone companies are offering is called a Digital Subscriber Line (DSL). DSL is a nifty enhancement to your telephone service that allows high-speed data transmissions over regular telephone lines, while enabling you to also use your telephone line for a voice call at the same time. This almost sounds like ISDN, but read on for some big differences.

You'll find much to like about DSL:

- **Speed:** DSL comes in many flavors, each with a different acronym, such as ADSL (Asymmetric Digital Subscriber Line), and each gives you much better bandwidth than a dial-up modem or ISDN connection. DSL bandwidth ranges from 256 Kbps all the way up to 7 Mbps or more. Some types of DSL feature different upload and download speeds, and sometimes the actual speed depends on how many other people are surfing the Internet at the same time. However, independent of what type of DSL you use, the transmission speeds are very fast. Most people who move from a dial-up connection to a DSL connection are amazed by the speed difference and have a hard time imagining ever going back to a modem.

✔ **Cost:** DSL costs more than a dial-up connection, but most subscribers find it well worth the cost. Most types of DSL feature an "always on" connection, which means that you don't need to establish a dial-up connection each time you start using the Internet. Instead, you are always connected and your Web browser displays a Web page immediately each time you open it.

So, what's not to like about DSL?

✔ **Availability:** DSL is not available everywhere. Not all local telephone companies have installed the required hardware, and DSL is only available if you live within a certain distance from your telephone company's central office.

✔ **Telephone requirements:** The telephone line to your house has to be in good condition, and telephone companies often have other technical limitations. In addition, some telephone technicians are not familiar with DSL and have a hard time configuring it. The good news is that service is getting better as telephone companies are getting used to supporting DSL.

✔ **The always-on connection:** Although you never have to wait for an Internet connection to be established, anyone who can connect to your computer from the Internet can do so anytime that he or she wants to. Hackers like targets that are always there and predictable, such as computers that use DSL to connect to the Internet. Hackers are not so thrilled by targets that are disconnected from the Internet for most of the day, such as computers that use dial-up connections.

Although DSL has some disadvantages, it is an amazing technology. If it is available in your area, then you should definitely evaluate it as an option to connect to the Internet, but keep in mind that this type of connection increases the importance of using the protection that a firewall provides.

If you want to know more about DSL, we recommend the book *DSL For Dummies* by David Angell, published by Wiley Publishing, Inc.

Cable modems

Cable modems provide an Internet connection over cable television wiring. In addition to connecting your television to this cable, you also connect a cable modem to the wiring, and you suddenly have a high-speed Internet connection. Although the technology itself is distinct from DSL technology, the benefits are similar: You get a very fast Internet connection that's always on. Just like DSL, cable modem availability is still spotty, but it's getting better all the time as cable TV providers are upgrading their equipment and adding this service.

How fast is a cable modem? The answer is: It depends on the technology, but also on how many other users are currently connected to the Internet and are sharing the cable that connects your cable modem to your cable TV provider's office. Many cable modem users find that initially their connection is blazing fast, as much as 1 Mbps or more. However, as more and more subscribers are added, everyone has to share the same bandwidth, and soon every subscriber's share of the bandwidth becomes less. However, when everyone except for you is asleep or at the beach, you will find that a cable modem lets you surf the Internet faster than a DSL connection would.

Cable modems have the same security issues as DSL, and then some. Like DSL, cable modems are always on. This means that whenever your computer is running, an intruder could break in; that is, unless you have taken proper precautions to secure your computer. Computers with always-on connections are a favorite target of hackers. Some computers — especially Windows-based computers with shared resources, such as shared folders or printers — announce themselves on the local network so that other users can easily find these shared resources and connect to them. This is great in a home network, but with a cable modem, these computers announce their shared resources to everyone on the same cable segment. This means that your neighbor's printer may show up as a resource as you look for the shared printer on your spouse's computer. Although a cable modem connection does not present a danger to a securely configured computer, many people don't take the proper security precautions and suddenly find that a stranger has connected to their computer or has sent a mystery message to their printer.

T1 and T3

T1 and T3 are telephone company terms for very fast connections. A T1 line can carry 1.544 Mbps; a T3 line carries 43 Mbps. These types of connections are usually too expensive for individuals and small companies. However, they provide reliable connections for medium-sized and large companies. Very large companies may even need multiple T3 lines.

T1 and T3 lines (and the similar E1 and E3 lines in Europe) are always on and present the same security challenges as a DSL line. In addition, although DSL connections are often utilized by a single home computer, T1 and T3 lines are almost always used by an entire corporate network to which multiple computers are connected.

Address types

Another important security consideration, which applies to each type of connection, is the type of network address that your computer is assigned. This is the IP address, which we cover in more detail in the next chapter. Some types of connections, such as dial-up modem connections, give your computer a new network address each time that you connect, which is referred to as a *dynamic* address. Dynamic addresses make it difficult for a hacker to initiate any extended effort to break into your computer. Because your computer doesn't use the same address for a long time, it's like a moving target for hackers.

Some Internet connections use *static* addresses. Using a static address means that your computer is assigned the same address each time it connects to the Internet. T1 and T3 connections almost always use static addresses; some DSL and cable modem connections do, too. Even if addresses do change with these connections, those changes may not happen frequently. When a hacker knows that he or she can connect to a single address and connect to the same computer every single time, the hacker is able to launch long, sustained attacks.

Although static addresses represent a risk, they provide you with a predictable method to access your computer from the Internet, including connections that are legitimate. For example, if you run a Web server, people need to be able to find your computer. At the same time, static addresses make life easier for hackers.

The need for speed and security

To enable you to easily compare and contrast the options covered in this chapter, Table 1-1 presents a comparison of the Internet connection methods that we cover in this section.

Table 1-1	Comparing Connection Options	
Connection Type	*Speed*	*Security Considerations*
Dial-up modem	Up to 56 Kbps downstream; up to 33.6 Kbps upstream	No permanent connection, uses dynamic address
ISDN	Between 56 Kbps and 128 Kbps in both directions	No permanent connection, uses dynamic address

(continued)

Table 1-1 *(continued)*

Connection Type	Speed	Security Considerations
DSL	Speeds vary; common speeds range from 256 Kbps to 1.4 Mbps	Often permanent connection, uses dynamic or static address
Cable modem	Speeds vary and depend on number of concurrent users; average speed up to 1 Mbps	Permanent connection, uses dynamic or static address
T1	1.544 Mbps	Permanent connection, uses static IP addresses
T3	43 Mbps	Permanent connection, uses static IP addresses

TCP/IP Basics

To understand how firewalls work, you have to know a little about how computers communicate and what language they speak. Just like people communicate on different levels, such as with spoken language, gestures, and intonation, computers also use different languages at the same time. As far as Internet connections and firewalls are concerned, the most important such language is TCP/IP (Transmission Control Protocol/Internet Protocol).

TCP/IP is a collection of *protocols,* each of which defines the rules for how computers communicate across the Internet. In Chapter 2 of this book you can find out a lot more about TCP/IP and how it works. For now, simply think of TCP/IP as a language that is used between computers on the Internet. One of the most important elements of TCP/IP is its addressing scheme. Computers that use TCP/IP use a unique number, called an IP address, to identify themselves. All data that is sent from one computer to another using TCP/IP includes information on what IP address the data comes from and what IP address it is being sent to.

TCP/IP defines the methods that computers connected to the Internet use to transmit information. This includes dividing this information in small manageable chunks called *packets.* Each packet contains header information and data. Most firewalls examine the packet header to determine whether the packet should be allowed to enter or leave a network behind a firewall. The header contains valuable information about where a packet comes from, what computer is the intended recipient of the packet, and even what program on the destination computer should process the information in the packet. This program could be a Web server or a mail server application. Some firewalls can also examine the inside of a packet or the insides of multiple packets, such as all packets that comprise an e-mail message or a Web page, and then decide how to handle this traffic.

What Firewalls Do

So what exactly does a firewall do? As network traffic passes through the firewall, the firewall decides which traffic to forward and which traffic not to forward, based on rules that you have defined. All firewalls screen traffic that comes into your network, but a good firewall should also screen outgoing traffic.

Normally a firewall is installed where your internal network connects to the Internet. Although larger organizations may also place firewalls between different parts of their own network that require different levels of security, most firewalls screen traffic passing between an internal network and the Internet. This internal network may be a single computer or it may contain thousands of computers.

The following list includes the most common features of firewalls:

- **Block incoming network traffic based on source or destination:** Blocking unwanted incoming traffic is the most common feature of a firewall.

- **Block outgoing network traffic based on source or destination:** Many firewalls can also screen network traffic from your internal network to the Internet. For example, you may want to prevent employees from accessing inappropriate Web sites.

- **Block network traffic based on content:** More advanced firewalls can screen network traffic for unacceptable content. For example, a firewall that is integrated with a virus scanner can prevent files that contain viruses from entering your network. Other firewalls integrate with e-mail services to screen out unacceptable e-mail.

- **Make internal resources available:** Although the primary purpose of a firewall is to prevent unwanted network traffic from passing through it, you can also configure many firewalls to allow selective access to internal resources, such as a public Web server, while still preventing other access from the Internet to your internal network.

- **Allow connections to internal network:** A common method for employees to connect to a network is using virtual private networks (VPNs). VPNs allow secure connections from the Internet to a corporate network. For example, telecommuters and traveling salespeople can use a VPN to connect to the corporate network. VPNs are also used to connect branch offices to each other. Some firewalls include VPN functionality and make it easy to establish such connections.

✔ **Report on network traffic and firewall activities:** When screening network traffic to and from the Internet, it's also important to know what your firewall is doing, who tried to break into your network, and who tried to access inappropriate material on the Internet. Most firewalls include a reporting mechanism of some kind or another.

What Firewalls Look Like

When you look at the graphics in this book, you see a firewall represented by a little brick wall. If you are a structural engineer, you know right away that this is not a real firewall, because a real firewall in a building must have structural reinforcements. Whether you are an engineer of any kind or not, though, you probably realize that a computer firewall doesn't look like a brick wall, anyway. Take a look at what computer firewalls look like.

A firewall that fits

Clothing salespeople want us to believe that there is a size that fits all. As a smart consumer and a fashionable dresser, you know that there is no such thing as one size that fits all. Similarly, there is also no size firewall that works well for every organization. Firewalls usually fall into one of the categories in the following list. The type of firewall that you install depends on your exact requirements for protection and management.

✔ **Personal firewall:** A personal firewall is most often installed as a piece of software on a single computer and protects just that computer. Personal firewalls also come as separate hardware components, or they may be built into other network devices, but they all protect a single computer or a very small number of computers. Personal firewalls also normally have very limited reporting and management features.

✔ **Departmental or small organization firewall:** These firewalls are designed to protect all the computers in an office of limited size that is in a single location. Firewalls in this category have the capacity to screen network traffic for a limited number of computers, and the reporting and management capabilities are adequate for this function.

✔ **Enterprise firewall:** Enterprise firewalls are appropriate for larger organizations, including organizations with thousands of users that are geographically dispersed. The reporting capabilities include consolidated reports for multiple firewalls; the management tools enable you to configure multiple firewalls in a single step.

As you are evaluating firewalls, keep in mind that some firewall products can work well in more than one setting. However, few firewalls — if any — work well in all three settings: personal, departmental, and enterprise.

Network router

One of the basic network connectivity devices is a *router*. A router transfers network packets between two different networks. In order for network traffic to get from one computer to another on the Internet, this traffic normally has to traverse a number of routers. Some router manufacturers have enhanced the functions of their products by including firewall features.

If you already have a router that connects your network to the Internet, you should explore whether it can perform packet filtering or other firewall functions. Most likely, you will find that your router provides some rudimentary firewall capabilities but that it doesn't give you any advanced features.

Appliance

Some firewalls consist of a piece of hardware with integrated software that provides a number of firewall functions. Such a device is often referred to as a *firewall appliance*. Just like a refrigerator that simply works when you plug it into an outlet, a firewall appliance starts working the moment you plug it in — there's no separate software to install. However, you still may have to do some configuration, which most often entails using a Web browser that's running on another computer. If you use such a firewall, the device is fairly simple to administer. You don't have to worry about configuring a separate operating system, and most often the device has no other functions that may interfere with the firewall's operations.

Software-only firewalls

Software-only firewalls run on a computer that can also perform other functions. Most personal firewalls that protect a single computer fall into this category. After all, the reason you get a personal firewall is to protect your computer while you are using the Internet — not to make your computer a dedicated firewall. Some enterprise firewalls are also software-based.

All-in-one tools

An increasingly popular type of network device is the all-in-one tool. One vendor, for example, offers a small box that promises to act as a cable modem, router, network hub, wireless networking base station, and firewall. If it did the laundry and cooked dinner, it would be close to perfect — at least according to the specifications on the box. We have not tested this particular type of device, but often when we evaluate multifunction devices that include a firewall, we find that the manufacturer excludes some functions that we consider important. The device performs several functions reasonably well, but not necessarily well enough. There are a few exceptions to this rule, so don't dismiss a product just because it performs several functions; however, be skeptical as you evaluate such products.

When evaluating an all-in-one product, make sure that you pay special attention to the firewall features. The cost of the damage that can be done by hackers that are able to break through a firewall that doesn't work well is normally much more than what you can save by buying an all-in-one tool.

Rules, Rules, Everywhere Rules

Life has more than its share of rules. We just can't seem to get away from them. When it comes to firewalls, rules play an important part, too. A firewall enforces rules about what network traffic is allowed to enter or leave your personal computer or network. Most firewalls come with some preconfigured rules, but most likely you will have to add more rules. After the rules are in place, a firewall examines all network traffic and drops the traffic if the rules prohibit it. A large part of administering a firewall consists of configuring rules, such as the following:

- ✔ Allow everyone to access all Web sites.
- ✔ Allow outgoing e-mail from the internal mail server.
- ✔ Drop all outgoing network traffic unless it matches the first two rules.
- ✔ Allow incoming Web requests to the public Web server.
- ✔ Drop all incoming network traffic except for connections to the public Web server.
- ✔ Log all connection attempts that were rejected by the firewall.
- ✔ Log all access to external Web sites.

Configuring rules for a home network can be very easy. You may merely have to define a rule that allows all outgoing network traffic and another one that allows no connections to be established from the outside. Setting up the rules for a large corporation with many Web servers, thousands of users, and many departments (each with different needs for accessing the Internet) can be much more complicated.

Chapter 2

IP Addressing and Other TCP/IP Basics

*M*ost people who use the Internet have heard of TCP/IP, which stands for Transmission Control Protocol/Internet Protocol, and know that it has something to do with how the Internet works. If you are an expert on network protocols, you can skip this chapter, but if you want to know more about what makes the Internet work, keep reading.

To understand how a firewall processes network traffic, you have to know just a little about TCP/IP. TCP/IP is the language that computers speak when they communicate with each other over the Internet. Fortunately, TCP/IP is much easier to learn than any foreign language, and only computers need to understand all the nuances of TCP/IP. However, just as it's important to know a few sentences in another language when traveling abroad, you have to know a few basics about TCP/IP in order to understand firewalls.

This chapter covers the basics of TCP/IP. Major topics include a short history of TCP/IP and an architectural overview of the network protocols that comprise TCP/IP. You discover how different types of addresses work to allow computers to find each other on the Internet and what some of the major network protocols that are used on the Internet do.

How Suite It Is: The TCP/IP Suite of Protocols

TCP/IP is a *suite* of protocols, which means that it is a bunch of protocols that work together. *Protocol suite* sounds much more sophisticated than *protocol bunch,* doesn't it?

A *protocol* is a collection of rules that computers use to communicate with each other. Sometimes, multiple protocols are needed to communicate, which is not much different from the real world. Suppose that the president of France wants to talk to the president of the United States. Before the discussion takes place, both presidents must agree on a number of issues. For example, they have to decide on whether to use a telephone or meet in person. If they use a telephone, they have to decide which particular aide of the French president will initiate the call to which particular aide of the American president. After that issue is settled, they need to agree on which language to use. They also must decide on the tone of the conversation: Will it be a formal talk or an informal exchange of ideas? And finally, they have to decide on the meaning of what they say: If the U.S. president says that he doesn't like snails, will the French president understand this as a subtle hint about the menu for the next state dinner or as an attack on the French way of life? As you can see, protocols have several layers, too. For example, the lower layer in this example is the question about whether to use a telephone. Only when that has been sufficiently resolved can the presidents get to the higher layer — the meaning of snails.

Like the presidents of the two countries, computers need to agree on some standards, and it is the protocols that define these networking standards. Furthermore, just as in diplomacy, protocols exist at each level. Starting at the hardware level, an agreement must be made about what voltage to use to signal data on a network wire. If no standard is determined, some computers may use 10,000 volts, whereas others expect a signal that uses 1 volt. The result may be entertaining for an observer, but destructive for the computer.

Sizing up the competition

TCP/IP is not the only game in town. Other network protocols are available, such as IPX/SPX (Internetwork Packet Exchange/Sequenced Packet Exchange, used primarily by Novell) and AppleTalk (used primarily by Apple for Macintosh computers). However, these protocols and others are being used less and less as TCP/IP is replacing them. Why? Because all major networking vendors support TCP/IP, and it's the protocol used by the Internet to connect millions of computers around the world with each other. The keyword is *interoperability,* which means that TCP/IP lets your computer talk to almost all other computers.

TCP/IP and carrier pigeons

TCP/IP supports many transmission media. Indeed, a part of the TCP/IP specifications actually covers how to use it over a transport system made up of carrier pigeons. The fact that this part of the standards was published on April Fool's Day should give you an indication that this specification is not meant to be taken very seriously, though. You can read this fine example of geek humor, called "RFC 1149: A Standard for the Transmission of IP Datagrams on Avian Carriers" at www.rfc-editor.org/rfc/rfc1149.txt.

TCP/IP doesn't really concern itself with the physical signaling characteristics of the transmission media — the cable type and electrical voltages stuff. Indeed, it works over a number of transmission media, such as Ethernet cabling, telephone lines, and satellite links. Instead, TCP/IP deals with how data is put into *packets,* which are chunks of data with additional information that is needed to deliver the data correctly. Think of a data packet as a letter that you drop into the mailbox: You write information about the sender and recipient on the outside, add information about special delivery options, and put whatever you want to send into the envelope. In the same manner, a network packet contains information about the recipient and the sender, special options, and the data that needs to be delivered. And, just as the postal service doesn't care about the contents of your envelope, TCP/IP doesn't care about the contents of the packet. For example, if you send e-mail, TCP/IP is concerned only with delivering the packets that make up the mail message; it doesn't care about the mail message itself.

Networking for the Cold War: A very short history of TCP/IP

TCP/IP was originally developed in 1969 by a U.S. government agency known as DARPA (Defense Advanced Research Projects Agency). The goal was to develop network protocols that would allow communications between military computers over an unreliable infrastructure. The idea was that if part of the communications capabilities of the United States were destroyed in a war, the rest of the network would not be affected. For example, if a direct link between two computers became unavailable and there was still an indirect link via a third computer, TCP/IP should be flexible enough to allow automatic rerouting of network traffic via this alternate connection. Because of the links between DARPA (later renamed ARPA) and leading universities, TCP/IP also became the network protocol of choice for many university networks, and eventually it became the protocol suite used for the Internet.

Being a good host

In the world of TCP/IP, more types of computing devices exist than actual computers. Traditionally, only computers were connected to networks, but today it seems that everything from game consoles to cellular phones can connect to the Internet. Now even refrigerators can use the Internet to order milk when your milk carton is near empty. Because all the devices that connect to the Internet do so by using TCP/IP, a generic term is needed to refer to any device that has an Internet address and is connected to a network. In the world of TCP/IP, such a device is referred to as a *host*. Just keep in mind that most Internet hosts won't invite you to dinner.

Most of us are not too concerned about how the U.S. military infrastructure will survive a large-scale nuclear war. However, because of the roots of TCP/IP, the Internet today uses a set of protocols that can function well in an environment in which there is no centralized control and there is constant risk of partial network outages. For example, suppose that construction workers dig a trench and accidentally destroy a buried network cable that connects two parts of the country. As a result, some computers may not be able to communicate with each other. However, most of the Internet will continue to function, and most network traffic will get rerouted automatically.

TCP/IP also allowed the Internet to grow at a rapid rate. The Internet started out with only five computers; today it encompasses millions of computers and other devices. During the 1990s, the military pulled out of the business of managing the Internet. For a while, the National Science Foundation ran it, but the government quickly turned over most management and infrastructure tasks to private companies. At the same time, people outside military and academic institutions became aware of the Internet and realized that it could be used for a whole range of things, from sending e-mail to shopping — even for listening to radio stations on the other side of the world. Although the TCP/IP protocol is showing signs of strain in dealing with this growth, overall it has held up very well to the tremendous growth of the Internet. In technical terms, it has scaled rather well.

Peeling Away the Protocol Layers

When we looked at protocols earlier in this chapter, we used the analogy of a conversation between the presidents of two nations. We saw that multiple layers of communication are involved and that protocols exist for each.

TCP/IP also involves several layers of protocols. Different parts of the networking software or applications on your computer are responsible for processing the information inside each of the layers. As far as TCP/IP protocols are concerned, there are four layers:

- ✔ **Network Interface layer:** This layer, which is sometimes also called the Network Access layer, deals with all the protocols that determine how a network packet is sent across a given physical network structure. The TCP/IP protocol specifications cover only portions of this layer. Basically, you can use any network structure that you want, such as Ethernet or a satellite connection (or even pack animals, if you can figure out how to make it work). If TCP/IP were the postal service, the Network Interface layer protocols would define how the letter carriers load their vehicles, what kinds of trucks transport the letters, and so on.

- ✔ **Internet layer:** This layer is concerned with giving each computer in a large network a unique address and being able to route all packets to a computer based on this address. If TCP/IP were the postal service, the Internet layer protocols would define the format for envelopes and how postal codes and street addresses are used to deliver a packet.

- ✔ **Transport layer:** Protocols at this layer are responsible for data integrity. One of the functions of such a protocol is to ensure that all the packets for a given transmission are received. If not, the protocol may request that the originating computer send them again. If TCP/IP were the postal service, the Transport layer protocols would be responsible for keeping track of registered mail, ensuring that letters are received intact, and notifying the sender if a letter did not arrive.

- ✔ **Application layer:** Protocols at this layer are responsible for implementing specific applications or programs. For example, e-mail protocols define what command a mail program sends to a mail server to retrieve e-mail messages. If TCP/IP were the postal service, Application layer protocols would define what you are allowed to place inside an envelope and perhaps even the language in which a postcard must be written.

Several models are used to describe the functions of networks. In addition to the four-layer TCP/IP model, a seven-layer OSI model, developed by the International Organization for Standardization, also describes the functions of networks. It's not important which model we use here, as long as it helps us to understand how networks function. After all, a model is just a method for classifying things, just as we can classify creatures as fish, mammals, reptiles, and so on. Just keep in mind that if you hear someone referring to a given layer, you have to know which model he or she is referring to before the layer reference can make sense.

When you send an e-mail message to a mail server, a mail protocol defines how the message should be formatted and what commands the mail server understands. This mail protocol operates at the Application layer. Before this mail message is sent out, a Transport layer protocol takes the message and divides it into different parts, called *packets*. Each of these parts is then sent across the network using an addressing scheme that is defined by Internet layer protocols. Network Interface layer protocols define how the packets are sent out across the physical network medium. Just to make things a little more complicated, at this level the information is sent in chunks of data that are referred to as *datagrams,* which are nothing more than packets by another name. At the receiving side, protocols at each layer determine how the message is received, how the address is confirmed, how packets are reassembled into a mail message, and how the mail server interprets the mail message.

How is using layers to understand the nature of a network related to better understanding how firewalls work? Most traditional firewalls focus on the Internet and Transport layers. These layers define where network packets come from, for whom they're intended, and whether a packet fits correctly into a sequence of related packets. More advanced firewalls, however, also operate at the Application layer. Inspecting traffic at the Application layer means that a firewall understands how packets combine to form a larger data exchange, such as an entire e-mail message, and the structure of that e-mail message. Before we explore this further, we want to cover in a bit more depth how computers send network packets to each other.

The Numbers Game: Address Basics

Just as you need telephone numbers and addresses to send messages to your friends, computers need addresses to reliably communicate with each other. Take a look at some of the addressing schemes and how they are used:

  ✔ **Hardware addresses:** Each network adapter that is used on an Ethernet network (the cabling scheme used in most office networks) is identified by a unique hardware address that is contained in the electronics of the network adapter. The adapter's manufacturer ensures that the hardware address is unique and not a duplicate of the hardware address of any other computer in the world. The uniqueness of the hardware address is designed so that network traffic for a computer is always received by that particular computer. This addressing scheme works well on a small network, but it has severe problems in a larger environment. Without a worldwide directory of all network cards that have ever been produced and the location where they are operating, there is no way to route information to the correct card. After all, even though the hardware addresses of two network cards may be very similar, one could be in the Antarctic and the other one in New York City.

- ✔ **IP addresses:** With TCP/IP, each computer is assigned at least one IP address. Unlike hardware addresses, IP addresses are not guaranteed to be unique, but a good network administrator will make sure that they are. After all, just as having several houses with the same address makes mail delivery impossible, using the same IP address for multiple computers causes problems in delivering network packets. An IP address is comprised of two parts: a network address and a host address. This IP address is just like a postal address that contains a street and a house number. All computers on the same network segment share the network address. The host portion is unique to a computer on that segment. *Routers,* which are devices that move network packets between different network segments, have enough knowledge about Internet addressing to move a packet to the correct network segment based on the network portion of the IP address. After the packet arrives on the correct network segment, it can be easily sent to the recipient. IP addresses are normally written in *dotted decimal format,* which means that they are comprised of four numbers with dots in between; for example, 192.168.1.200. Each of these numbers can be between 0 and 255, which are all the decimal numbers that you can create with eight bits.

- ✔ **DNS names:** Computers like addresses that are comprised of numbers, especially because an IP address can also be expressed in binary numbers, which is the numbering system that computers are built upon. However, binary numbers are not so easy for people to remember. For example, if we told you to connect to a Web site at the address 208.215.179.139, you would likely immediately forget this address. However, there is a better way. To help people like us, the DNS (Domain Name System) was developed. DNS is a large directory of names, such as `www.dummies.com`. DNS names are much easier to remember than IP addresses. However, when you connect to a Web site, your computer looks up the DNS name and finds the corresponding IP address. It works like telephone directory assistance in looking up a name. Keep in mind that even when you type a DNS name, your computer will eventually connect to the remote computer using an IP address.

You can get more information about an IP address or a DNS name in many ways. One of the best is available on the Internet at `www.samspade.org`. This site allows you to type a DNS name or IP address and then tells you details about the owner of this address.

DNS names are actually very easy to understand. Take a look at `www.dummies.com` to see what this address means. Start by looking at the address from the right (the .com) and move to the left (the www). DNS is made up of *domains,* which are portions of all the possible DNS names. For example, the .com domain includes all names that end with .com. Domains can be further divided into smaller subdomains. Dummies.com is a subdomain of the .com domain and includes all names that end with dummies.com, such as `www.dummies.com`.

✔ The letters to the right of the last period, or dot, are referred to as the *top-level* domain. Every organization that wants to use a DNS domain has to register the domain as a subdomain within a top-level domain. Depending on the type of organization or the country you are in, you can register your DNS domain as a subdomain of one of several domains. The list of top-level domains is slowly being increased. Two-letter domains indicate a country, such as .ca for Canada and .fr for France. Top-level domains with more than two letters are not country-specific. Table 2-1 shows some popular domains and their meaning. Keep in mind that anyone can register within the .com, .net, and .org domains, so their meaning is just a rough guideline. A complete list of top-level domains that are not specific to a country is available at `www.iana.org/gtld/gtld.htm`.

Table 2-1	Popular Top-Level Domains
Domain	*Meaning*
.com	Commercial (companies)
.net	Network (anyone involved in maintaining the Internet)
.edu	Educational (colleges and universities)
.mil	Military (branches of the U.S. military)
.gov	Government (any U.S. government agency)
.org	Organization (any nonprofit organization)
.int	International organization (probably the most exclusive domain; it can be used only by organizations that are established under a multinational treaty)
.info	Anyone who wants to provide any information on the Internet
.name	An individual's name
.ca	Canada
.uk	United Kingdom
.au	Australia
.nl	Netherlands
.de	Germany
.tv	Tuvalu (A small island nation in the South Pacific of just over 10,000 people. In 2000, the government of Tuvalu negotiated a contract leasing its .tv domain for $50 million in royalties over the next 12 years.)

The root of all DNS

One more domain exists above the top-level domain; it is referred to as the DNS *root* domain. The root domain contains information about all top-level domains, but it is normally not included in DNS names, which just map the path from the top-level domain to the computer.

✔ The next component is referred to as a second-level domain. This is a subdivision of a top-level domain. For example, both the wiley.com domain and the dummies.com domain are second-level domains within the .com top-level domain. An organization can register a second-level domain and divide it even further to match its administrative requirements.

✔ If an organization does not further subdivide its domain, it places the name of a specific computer that belongs to the domain in front of its domain name to specify the computer's full DNS name. For example, if the name of the computer on the U.S. president's desk were `bitforce1`, its full DNS name would be `bitforce1.whitehouse.gov`. Often, the computer's name is descriptive of the role that it plays. For example, a common convention is to use the name www in front of a domain name (such as in `www.dummies.com`) to indicate that the computer that the address refers to is a Web server. However, this is simply a convention. You can name your Web server after your cat Fluffy if you want. Although this may confuse everyone, DNS would still allow people to connect to your Web server.

As you are exploring the Internet, you may run across the term *fully qualified domain name,* or FQDN, which is simply the entire DNS name of a computer, including the path from the computer name back to the top-level domain, such as `www.dummies.com`.

Consider how all these names work together. When you type `www.dummies.com` in your browser, the browser tries to send one or more network packets to the computer that has the DNS address `www.dummies.com`. To do this, your networking software first contacts a DNS server to find the IP address for this Web site. The DNS server may not know the address, but it will be able to contact a DNS server that does. After one or more referrals, your computer will receive the answer that the IP address of `www.dummies.com` is 208.215.179.139. Your computer forwards each network packet to the next router, which is normally a computer that your ISP (Internet Service Provider) has set up. You probably configured this router as your computer's default gateway. This router then forwards the packets to one or more routers on the

Internet until it arrives at a router that is attached to the same network segment as the computer that runs the Dummies Web site. The routers use the network address portion of the IP address to get the packets there. The last router then uses a broadcast (the technical equivalent of yelling "Where is the computer with this address?") to find out the hardware address of the Dummies Web server. After it has received an answer, the router sends the packets to the Web server, using both the IP address and the hardware address as the packet is moved to its final destination. Pretty amazing, isn't it, especially considering that all of this may take only a fraction of a second? So, the next time you're looking at the Dummies Web site, thank the hard-working routers and DNS servers that made this possible for you.

While configuring a firewall, you may configure rules that deny users access to certain Web sites that some people deem inappropriate. When you configure such a rule, remember that your users may be able to bypass rules that use a DNS name by using the corresponding IP address instead. Therefore, you should make sure that for each rule that uses a DNS name, you also create a corresponding rule that applies to the IP address for that DNS name. Some firewalls, such as Microsoft Internet Security and Acceleration Server 2000 (see Chapter 16), automatically look up the DNS name when someone uses an IP address and apply rules correctly. However, most firewalls don't do this unless you define rules for both DNS names and the corresponding IP addresses.

URLs: How to Reference Resources

Another method of referring to Internet resources that you should be familiar with is the Uniform Resource Locator, or URL. Unlike DNS addresses, which are used to refer to computers, URLs are used to refer to specific resources on computers. A URL is comprised of three components. The first component is the protocol that you use to access the resource. Next, following a colon and two forward slashes, is the computer on which the requested resource is located. Finally, following another forward slash is the name of the resource on the target computer. For example, typing this

```
http://cda.dummies.com/WileyCDA/Section.rdr?id=100051
```

into the address box of your Web browser tells it to use the HyperText Transfer Protocol (HTTP) to connect to the computer with the DNS name `cda.dummies.com` and retrieve a Web page called `WileyCDA/Section.rdr?id=100051`.

Understanding IP Addresses

When you administer a firewall, you have to define rules about what network traffic is allowed to pass through the firewall. Often, these rules are based on IP addresses. For example, if your Web server's IP address is 23.10.10.7, you may want to create a rule that allows network traffic to that Web server. In order to use IP addresses, you should understand at least the basics of how they work. Understanding how they work is much easier when you understand a little about binary math because that's what computers use when analyzing IP addresses. Don't be scared, though; we won't take you back to algebra class. If you made it through second-grade math, you'll be able to understand how binary math works.

1 and 1 is 10

Binary math isn't much different from regular decimal math; it's just not something that most of us are accustomed to using. When we use the decimal system, we have ten number symbols. We start counting from 1 to 9, but at that point, there is no separate symbol for the next number. Instead, we add a 1 to the front to form the number 10. In essence, 10 means one times ten plus zero times one, 25 means two times ten and five times one, and so forth. When we reach 100, we again set all digits to 0 and then add another one to the front. When we refer to 250, we mean two times one hundred, plus five times ten, plus zero times one. Because we use the decimal system every day, we don't even think about this anymore, but this is how we learned numbers in school.

To understand binary math, go back to the point where you learned numbers, except in this case, forget all about the numbers 2 to 9. Binary math only uses two symbols, 0 and 1. Just as in decimal math, as you count, you run out of symbols, and you simply add another digit. Start counting with 1, which in binary is also 1. However, when we get to 2 (decimal), there's no symbol for that in binary math, so we set the last digit to 0 and add a 1 to the front. The number 2 (decimal) thus becomes the number 10 (binary). When we add one more to this, we end up with the number 3 (decimal), but the number 11 (binary). For the next number, we have to add another digit to the front and set the other digits to 0, and we end up with 100 (binary). As you can see, counting in binary is as easy as 1, 10, 11, and so forth.

Take a look at how the TCP/IP software on your computer — which in many cases is a part of the operating system — handles IP addresses. You have seen that IP addresses are most frequently expressed in dotted decimal format, such as 192.168.1.200. However, your computer internally converts this number into decimal format. You can take a look at Table 2-2 to follow along as we perform this operation. The number 192 can be represented as 128 plus 64, thus its binary equivalent is 11000000. The number 168 can be represented as 128 plus 32 plus 8; thus, the binary equivalent is 10101000. Converting the entire IP address to binary (and adding leading zeros to make each number eight digits long), we end up with 11000000.10101000.00000001.11001000.

Table 2-2	Decimal Equivalents of Binary Numbers
Binary	*Decimal*
1	1
10	2
100	4
1000	8
10000	16
100000	32
1000000	64
10000000	128

When talking about binary math, each digit is referred to as a *bit*. A complete IP address consists of 32 bits.

If using binary math doesn't get you excited, don't feel bad. You are in good company because most everyone we know doesn't get excited about binary math either. Instead of learning how to convert numbers from binary to decimal or vice versa, you can use the Calculator application included with Windows. To do this, you first have to change the Calculator's mode to Scientific by selecting this option on the View menu. Next, make sure that the Dec (Decimal) radio button in the top left is selected and type a number. When you select the Bin (Binary) button to change the display to binary, the Calculator converts the number to binary. To do the same thing in reverse, click Bin first, type the binary number, and then click the Dec button.

What IP addresses mean

An IP address has several characteristics. First, it is unique on the Internet, at least if it's correctly configured. This means that no two computers share the same IP address. Second, each IP address is comprised of two components:

the network address and the host address. This is like a mailing address, which has a street name and a house number. Just as all houses in the same street share a street name, all computers on the same network segment share a network address. And just as a house number is unique to each house on a street, the host address is unique to each computer on a network segment. Routers use the network address to move network packets to the correct network segment, and the host address is then used to route packets to the correct host on that network segment.

IP addresses differ from mailing addresses in one important aspect, though. With a mailing address, you always know which part is the street name and which part is the house number. With IP addresses, it's not obvious which part is the network address and which is the host address. The only thing we know is that the first part is used for the network address and the last part for the host address, but from looking at an IP address alone, we don't know where the network address ends and the host address begins. To provide support for very big networks as well as very small networks, we can change how many bits are used for each part of the address. For example, we could use only the first 8 bits for the network address. This would give us 256 possible networks (256 is how many unique binary numbers that you can create with 8 bits). Each of these would have 16,777,216 separate hosts (16,777,216 is how many unique binary numbers that you can create with the remaining 24 bits). On the other hand, by using the first 24 bits for the network address and the remaining 8 bits for the host address, you would end up with 16,777,216 networks, each of which can have 256 unique hosts.

If you find all this stuff about how to figure out a network address confusing, that's understandable. It's confusing without a remaining piece of information — the indicator of where the network address ends and the host address begins. This piece of information is called the *subnet mask*. Expressed in binary numbers, a subnet mask always has ones in the beginning and zeros in the end. When you line up a subnet mask with an IP address, the location of the ones shows you the part of the IP address that specifies the network, and the location of the zeros shows you which part is the host address. For example, consider the IP address 192.168.1.200 and the subnet mask 255.255.255.0. When you convert these to binary, you end up with the following:

```
192.168.1.200   11000000.10101000.00000001.11001000
255.255.255.0   11111111.11111111.11111111.00000000
```

To get the network address, you use the part of the IP address that lines up with the ones in the subnet mask and replace the remainder with zeros. In our example, the network address is 11000000.10101000.00000001.0000000. When you convert this back to decimal numbers, you end up with a network address of 192.168.1.0. The host portion of the IP address is the part that doesn't belong to the network address. In our example, this is 11001000 (binary), or 200 (decimal).

Whenever you are referring to an entire network, such as when you configure firewall rules that refer to a network, you have to specify the IP address of the network in conjunction with its subnet mask. Sometimes you can take a shortcut by adding a forward slash and the number of ones in the subnet mask to the IP address itself. For example, you can use 192.168.1.0/24 to refer to the network 192.168.1.0 with a subnet mask of 255.255.255.0 (which begins with 24 ones).

In the early days of the Internet, network addresses were divided into several classes, each of them with fixed subnet addresses. A Class A address starts with a number of 0 to 127 and always has a subnet mask of 255.0.0.0. A Class B address starts with a number of 128 to 191 and always has a subnet mask of 255.255.0.0. A Class C address starts with a number of 192 to 223 and always has a subnet mask of 255.255.255.0. This rather inflexible convention has been largely replaced with CIDR (Classless Inter-Domain Routing), which allows you to slice and dice networks any way you want. Because the system of using address classes is largely outdated, we base our description of IP addressing in this chapter entirely on CIDR concepts.

Private IP Addresses

Some ranges of IP addresses are reserved and not assigned to any computers connected directly to the Internet. These addresses are allocated for use only on private networks and between computers that aren't connected to the Internet. These private IP address ranges are 10.0.0.0–10.255.255.255, 172.16.0.0–172.31.255.255, and 192.168.0.0–192.168.255.255. Using addresses from these ranges for the computers within an organization's networks means that you don't have to allocate any of the increasingly sparse regular addresses for all computers. You also increase security because a hacker can never send network packets directly from the Internet to a computer that's inside a network that uses private addresses.

A similar type of address is one that's assigned by Automatic Private IP Addressing (APIPA). APIPA is a feature of some operating systems, such as recent versions of Windows, which randomly assign an IP address between 169.254.0.0 and 169.254.255.255 to a computer when this computer is not configured with an IP address and can't acquire a valid IP address from a Dynamic Host Configuration Protocol (DHCP) server on the network. Such IP addresses allow computers in a small network to communicate with each other even without any IP configuration.

What about legitimate incoming network traffic? And what about people inside your network who want to establish a connection to a computer on the Internet, such as a Web server? You can allow for both of these scenarios by using a technique called Network Address Translation (NAT). NAT keeps track of all Internet connections and changes the headers of IP packets to allow them to travel to and from a network that uses private IP addresses. You can read more about how NAT works in Chapter 3.

Dissecting Network Traffic: The Anatomy of an IP Packet

All traffic that uses TCP/IP utilizes IP (Internet Protocol). As you saw when we examined the different protocol layers, the Internet layer is responsible for addressing network packets and getting them to the correct destination. The protocol that is used for this is IP. Just as every letter has an envelope with address information, each IP packet has a header that contains information about the recipient and the sender. Unlike envelopes, though, IP packets don't need postage to be delivered, so you never have to worry about running out of stamps. Take a look at some of the information in an IP header.

Source address

The source address is the IP address from which the packet originates. It's like the return address on an envelope sent by postal mail. Generally, you can find out where the packet originated by looking at the source address. However, just as you can't absolutely trust the return address on an envelope that you receive in the mail, source addresses may not reveal the correct sender.

When does an IP packet not contain the correct IP address? Here are a benign and a not-so-benign reason:

- ✔ **Network Address Translation (NAT):** A technique that is used to send all traffic from an internal network to the Internet by using a single public IP address. Many firewalls employ NAT to hide the actual IP addresses of internal computers. Although NAT may prevent you from tracing the origin of a packet to its original source, you can at least trace the packet back to a legitimate source.

- ✔ **Spoofing:** A technique that is used by the bad guys. Hackers may send IP packets with a forged IP address to hide their location. For example, if you were a hacker and intended to crash someone's computer, you wouldn't want your victim to trace the attack back to your computer's IP address.

Most of the time, you don't have to be too concerned about whether an IP address represents the correct sender. Just keep in mind that an IP source address may not always tell the full story.

Destination address

A destination address is like the address on an envelope. Each router on the Internet through which the packet passes looks at this address and dutifully delivers it to its final destination. Just as with the source address, NAT may translate the address on its way to the final recipient. However, you normally don't have to be concerned that a hacker may spoof the destination address. After all, the result would be that the packet doesn't arrive at its intended destination, which would be rather pointless.

Transport layer protocol

An IP packet contains information about the Transport layer protocol that the packet should be routed to after it arrives at its destination. This information is needed by the *TCP/IP protocol stack* (a fancy term for a part of the networking software on your computer that processes all TCP/IP requests) to determine how the packet should be further processed. The most commonly used protocols in this category are TCP and UDP, and you will find out more about them later in this chapter.

Other stuff

An IP packet header also contains some other information. Most of the time, you don't have to worry about this information. For example, a field for the length of the packet tells your computer's TCP/IP stack where one packet stops and where the next one begins. The TCP/IP stack does need to know about this, of course, but you could live a perfectly happy life without ever worrying about a packet length.

The other Internet layer protocol: ICMP

Internet Control Message Protocol (ICMP) is an Internet layer protocol that is used to confirm that two hosts can communicate with each other. Devices that use TCP/IP also use ICMP to inform other devices of potential problems.

For example, the ICMP source quench message is the TCP/IP equivalent of telling another computer: "I can't keep up with all the traffic you're sending me — slow down, please."

Transport Layer Protocols

Most IP packets contain data that is specific to a Transport layer protocol. A Transport layer protocol defines additional information in the packet. For example, whereas the IP protocol is responsible for getting packets to another computer, a Transport layer protocol may contain sequence information that is used to assemble multiple packets (that were jumbled up in transit) back into the right order. The Internet Assigned Numbers Authority (IANA) maintains a list of these Transport layer protocols at `http://www.iana.org/assignments/protocol-numbers`. This list currently contains 134 protocols, but most of the time, you have to be concerned only with a few of them. The Appendix of this book also contains a list of the most frequently used protocols. Because the vast majority of traffic on the Internet uses either the TCP or the UDP protocols, we will concentrate on these protocols here.

Staying connected: UDP and TCP

The main difference between UDP (User Datagram Protocol) and TCP (Transmission Control Protocol) is that UDP is connectionless, whereas TCP is connection-oriented. What does this mean? A connectionless protocol doesn't make sure that all packets that are sent are also received. UDP is like an answering machine recording: When you reach an answering machine, the recording starts playing. The answering machine makes no attempt to confirm that you are indeed listening or that you understood the message. After you leave a message on the answering machine, you can't confirm that the answering machine did indeed receive your message, or that it received it in its entirety. You just have to trust the machine. Similarly, a computer sends UDP packets, but the UDP protocol has no provisions for checking whether all packets really arrive at the destination. Because of this, UDP is sometimes referred to as an unreliable protocol.

TCP is similar to a telephone conversation that you have with someone. Before you start talking, you establish that each participant in the conversation can hear the other one. You also ensure that the other participant in the conversation can understand you. If one person doesn't hear part of the conversation, he will ask the other person to repeat the part that was lost.

Like a telephone conversation, TCP has provisions for session setup and session maintenance. Both hosts that are part of a TCP connection keep track of the conversation. The first step is a three-way handshake — a succession of three network packets that are used for session setup. During this three-way handshake, both hosts agree on a number of communications parameters, such as how to number all other packets so they can make sure that packets can be reassembled in the correct order. Also, if packets get lost in transit, one host can inform the other about this and request retransmission. Because TCP keeps track of the transmission and ensures that all parts of the transmission are successful, TCP is sometimes called a reliable protocol.

When is UDP used, and when is TCP used? UDP is sufficient for many types of network traffic. For example, when you're listening to a live radio program over the Internet, UDP is the perfect protocol. Suppose that one of ten packets from the Internet radio station gets lost because of some severe congestion on the Internet. Because every tenth packet is lost, you will hear short breaks in the radio program. However, the listening experience would be even more disturbed if the missing pieces would have to be retransmitted; nothing would come out of the loudspeaker until each missing packet had been received, maybe five to ten seconds after they were intended to be heard.

TCP, on the other hand, is more appropriate for network traffic that requires the integrity of the information that is sent. For example, if you are downloading a file from the Internet, your main concern is that the file arrives intact. If portions of the file don't make it, you want to take advantage of TCP's ability to automatically retransmit packets that were lost in transit and to assemble all packets in the right order.

Ports are not only for sailors

When dealing with TCP or UDP packets, you often hear the term *port*. No, this doesn't mean that these protocols are designed for mariners. Instead, a port is a number that identifies where a packet came from on the sending host, and where it should go to on the receiving host. If you compare an IP address to a street address for mail delivery, the port number is like an apartment number.

When a server application, such as a Web server, runs on a computer that uses TCP/IP, it reserves a port on that computer. This reservation is nothing more than telling the networking software that any packet that is addressed to this port should be forwarded to the server application. Any application that sends TCP or UDP packets also sends them from a port. This way, the TCP/IP stack knows what application should receive return packets. In addition to source and destination addresses, IP packets also contain source and destination ports.

Some ports are well known

Many server applications use standard ports so that client applications know what port on a target host to address a packet to without querying the target host first. For example, most Web servers respond to client requests that are addressed to TCP port 80. Numbers can be registered, and most server applications use the port that has been registered for this type of application. Ports under 1024 are the most exclusive ports and are known as *well-known ports*. You can view a list of well-known ports and other registered ports that the Internet Assigned Numbers Authority maintains at `www.iana.org/assignments/port-numbers`. Each application running on a computer has to have its own port so that incoming packets can be sent to the correct application. Web requests should end up with your Web server application, e-mail should end up with your e-mail server application, and so on.

Consider the following example: A client computer running a Web browser tries to connect to a Web server. As soon as the Web browser requests a connection, the TCP/IP stack springs to action and sends a packet to the Web server. This packet is addressed to port 80 at the destination (the standard for Web servers) on the Web server. The client's TCP/IP stack also includes a source port number. For client requests, this is normally an unused number between 1024 and 65535. This number is used as part of the address when the Web server returns packets to the client. In our example, the client picks port 1028. The resulting packets that are sent to and from the Web server are shown in Table 2-3. The inclusion of the port number allows both sides to keep track of which application needs to process incoming packets. Because each conversation uses a unique set of port numbers, multiple programs on both computers can communicate with each other simultaneously.

Table 2-3	Properties of TCP Traffic in Sample Connection				
Direction	*Transport Protocol*	*Source IP*	*Source Port*	*Target IP*	*Target Port*
To Web server	TCP	172.16.1.200	1028	172.16.1.1	80
To client	TCP	172.16.1.1	80	172.16.1.200	1028

How do you know what ports an application uses? You need to know some rules regarding ports. Any application that expects other computers to connect to it, such as a Web server, normally uses the port that has been set aside for that type of application. Unless you want to hide your Web server, you configure it to answer incoming requests from clients. Client applications, however, normally use the next available port above 1023 to establish a connection. Because other computers don't initiate connections with programs running on a client computer, the port that a program on the client uses doesn't have to be predictable.

Application Layer Protocols

You may think that we spent a lot of time in this chapter talking about how to get network traffic to the right destination and getting it there intact. However, we haven't talked about what is contained in this IP traffic. This is what Application layer protocols define. Some of these protocols define how files are transferred, and some of them deal with e-mail messages, but each of them defines how data is passed from one program, or application, to another. After you strip the IP and UDP or TCP information from an IP packet, what remains is the information that is passed to the Application layer protocol and that tells the program using this protocol how to perform a specific action, such as transferring data.

HTTP

As protocols go, HTTP (HyperText Transfer Protocol) is a relative newcomer, but for most Internet users, it's the protocol that matters the most. Web clients request this protocol to request Web pages and other Web objects, such as graphics that appear on Web pages, from a Web server. By default, Web servers listen on TCP port 80 for requests from clients, but you can also configure a Web server to listen on a nonstandard port. If you do this, the clients need to specify this port when connecting.

When you use a Web browser to connect to a Web server on the Internet, you normally use a URL (Uniform Resource Locator). A URL contains the following components: protocol://address:port/content. The protocol can be one of several protocols that the Web client understands, but most often it is HTTP. The address is either the IP address of the server that you want to connect to, or a DNS name for which your computer finds the corresponding IP address. The colon and the port are optional, and you only have to use them if you are using a nonstandard protocol. For example, if you use HTTP as the protocol and don't specify a port, your Web browser will connect to port 80 on the server because this is the default port for Web requests. Finally, the content may be a specific file on the server. For example, if you are requesting a Web page and you don't specify a specific object, the Web server will normally send its home page to the client browser.

SMTP

SMTP is the Simple Mail Transport Protocol. SMTP is used to send e-mail messages to an SMTP server. Some packets to SMTP servers come from client computers, but you can also configure multiple mail servers to send e-mail to each other for further delivery. The SMTP protocol uses TCP port 25 on the server.

POP3

POP3 (Post Office Protocol Version 3) is another e-mail protocol. Whereas SMTP is used for sending e-mail, POP3 is the protocol that your mail program uses to retrieve mail messages from your mail server. Clients connect to the server on TCP port 110.

DNS

The DNS (Domain Name System) protocol is used to convert DNS names to IP addresses. Normally, client computers need to convert a DNS name to an IP address quite often. To do this conversion, a client computer may send a request to a DNS server, which, by default, allows connections on UDP port 53. This DNS server then may have to contact other DNS servers to help with the name resolution request. These servers also listen on UDP port 53. If a DNS transaction involves more data than what fits into a UDP packet, DNS may automatically switch to using TCP port 53 instead. Also, DNS servers may transfer data between each other that consists of entire DNS zones using a process called *zone transfer.* Zone transfers also use TCP port 53.

Telnet

Telnet is an application that allows you to remotely connect from a Telnet client to a Telnet server and get a remote terminal session, such as a command prompt window, on the server. A Telnet server listens for incoming connections on TCP port 23. All communications between a Telnet client and a Telnet server use this port on the server.

Windows includes a Telnet program that you can use to establish a Telnet session. However, using the Telnet program to connect a nonstandard port can also be a great troubleshooting and firewall-testing tool. You can specify any port on the command line to see whether you receive a reply on the port that you specify. For example, to see whether the Web server for `www.dummies.com` responds, type the following command inside a command prompt window and, when connected, press Enter a few times to see the response from the Web server:

```
telnet www.dummies.com 80
```

Complex protocols

In this chapter, you have encountered a number of protocols that use a single port. Keep in mind that some protocols, such as FTP (File Transfer Protocol), use more than one port. When you configure a firewall for those ports, you have to make decisions about how the firewall will handle multiple connections that are part of the same conversation.

FTP

FTP (File Transfer Protocol) is a protocol that is used to transfer files. Most operating systems include a simple FTP client program, and many more-capable FTP programs are available. Most server operating systems also include an FTP server application. FTP is used to transfer files from a server or to a server.

Unfortunately, FTP is a moderately complex protocol. An FTP server listens on TCP port 21 for incoming connections. When a client establishes a connection on this port, it can do either of the following:

- ✔ Tell the server which client port it expects the actual data of the file transfer to arrive on (in which case the server uses TCP port 20 to send the data)

- ✔ Ask the server which port on the server that the client should connect to in order to initiate the data transfer

A firewall needs to decide whether to allow packets to pass through it; you define the rules for this when you configure the firewall. If you want FTP traffic to pass though the firewall, you basically have two choices: allow FTP data traffic only on TCP port 20, thus preventing clients from requesting nonstandard ports, or allow data transfer using any possible port, which also allows potentially lots of unknown traffic through the firewall. This isn't always an easy decision. Fortunately, some firewalls know enough about a protocol, such as FTP, that they can inspect the contents of the initial control connection between client and server and use this to find out what port the client and server negotiate for the data transfer. After the firewall has determined the port that is used for the data transfer, it can allow traffic between the client and the server that uses this port. For more information about how firewalls handle the FTP protocol, see Chapter 7.

Future protocols

Table 2-4 lists some protocols that are not part of the TCP/IP protocol suite because the protocols have not been designed yet. However, we think that these protocols are overdue, and hope that someone will invent them soon.

Table 2-4	Protocols Not Yet Invented
Protocol	*Usage*
RITSP	Remote Instant Technical Support Protocol. Fixes your computer automatically over the Internet.
WWW	Why Why Why Protocol. Tries to explain the purpose of strange Web sites.
Telnut	Allows remote access to peanuts and other similar snacks.
TVSIPTDE	The Very Simplified Internet Protocol That Does Everything. Who needs any other protocol when we have this one?
ECDP	Emergency Caffeine Delivery Protocol. This is useful when you can't stay awake while configuring your firewall.
MIWNP	Make It Work Now Protocol. Especially useful when you don't want to deal with configuring or troubleshooting something.
BMUSP	Beam Me Up Scotty Protocol. We use this when we have to get out of here quickly.

The Keeper of the Protocols

Most of the protocols that comprise TCP/IP are defined in one or more RFCs (Request for Comment). RFCs are the primary specifications for the Internet.

They dictate how things should work. Some RFCs deal with very technical aspects of one or more protocols; others are only informational and may recommend certain practices. Proposing RFCs and giving feedback on any RFC that someone else proposed is an open process. You can find out more about this process, as well as search for RFCs, at the Web site of the RFC Editor at www.rfc-editor.org.

Putting It All Together: How a Request Is Processed

Now that you know how the TCP/IP suite of protocols works, put all that knowledge together and see how a request for a Web page is processed from beginning to end. When you type www.wiley.com in your Web browser, the following process takes place:

1. Your computer sees the request and sends out a query to a DNS server to determine the IP address of the Web server.

2. The DNS server, possibly after contacting other DNS servers for assistance, returns the IP address 208.215.179.146 to the client computer.

3. Because you specified HTTP as the protocol on the URL, your computer tries to establish a connection to TCP port 80 on the Web server.

4. Your computer uses its own IP address and subnet mask to determine that the Web server is not on the same network segment. It forwards a packet that is addressed to TCP port 80 on the computer with the IP address 208.215.179.146 to the next router.

5. Routers on the Internet pass the packet along until it reaches the Web server.

6. After the Web server receives the client's packet, it responds to the client. Several packets are exchanged at this point to establish some TCP communications parameters, such as sequence numbers for packets. The resulting packet or packets originate from port 80 on the Web server and are addressed to the same port from which the request originated.

7. After the connection has been established, additional packets are sent. In this example, they contain a requested Web page. The resulting packet or packets originate from port 80 on the Web server and are addressed to the same port from which the request originated.

8. The TCP stack on your computer passes all packets along to your Web browser, which renders the resulting Web page and displays it on your computer's screen.

Chapter 3

Understanding Firewall Basics

●●●

In This Chapter

▶ What a firewall does

▶ Firewall strategy

▶ Packet filtering

▶ Network Address Translation (NAT)

▶ Application proxy

▶ Monitoring and logging

●●●

*W*hen you connect your computer or your computer network to the
Internet, you are connecting it to millions of other computers. People
who may be trying to get to the private data on your computer network may
be using some (or even a lot) of those computers.

To keep unwanted intruders off your computer network, you should install
and configure a firewall to separate the untrusted outside world from the
trusted inside computer network. The firewall should inspect all network
traffic and decide which traffic should be allowed to pass and which traffic
should be blocked.

In order for all this to work, you have to tell the firewall what is acceptable
network traffic by specifying policy rules. Every firewall has different methods of specifying what traffic is allowed to pass, and every firewall has different inspection possibilities. However, the basics of most firewalls are the same.

In this chapter, you explore the basics of firewalls, including a filtering strategy,
packet filters, Network Address Translation (NAT), and application proxies.

What Firewalls Do (And Where's the Fire, Anyway?)

The term *firewall* doesn't accurately describe its function. A real firewall is a barrier to prevent fires from spreading from one room or building to another. A real firewall blocks fires completely. On the other hand, the firewalls discussed in this book should inspect all "fires" and let some pass through while blocking others. Sure, the Internet is hot, but who came up with this term?

A term that more accurately describes the function of the Internet firewall products is *doorman*. The firewall (or doorman) is the security guard that sits behind a desk near the front entrance of a large office building and screens everybody who wants to come inside. Depending on the type of office, the guard may also screen or inspect people who are leaving the building.

Many basic concepts of an Internet firewall can be well described by using the doorman example. We'll use Doorman Sam, a hard-working security guard at corporate headquarters of the fictitious law firm, Legal Inc., to illustrate many of the firewall basics. Consider this chapter to be *Doormen For Dummies*.

Basic functions of a firewall

If you ask several people what constitutes a firewall, you are bound to receive several different answers. Different firewall vendors use the term with different definitions. In its simplest form, a firewall is any device or software product sitting between your network and the Internet that blocks some network traffic. However, most people agree that a true firewall should have at least the following four basic functions:

- **Packet filtering:** The headers of all network packets going through the firewall are inspected. The firewall makes an explicit decision to allow or block each packet.

- **Network Address Translation (NAT):** The outside world sees only one or more outside IP addresses of the firewall. The internal network can use any address in the private IP address range. Source and destination addresses in network packets are automatically changed (or "translated") back and forth by the firewall.

- **Application proxy:** The firewall is capable of inspecting more than just the header of the network packets. This capability requires the firewall to understand the specific application protocol.

✔ **Monitoring and logging:** Even with a solid set of rules, logging what happens at the firewall is important. Doing so can help you to analyze a possible security breach later and gives feedback on the performance and actual filtering done by the firewall.

Because firewalls are a single point of entry for network traffic entering or leaving your internal network, the firewall is an excellent location to perform additional security tasks. Many firewalls support the following advanced functions:

✔ **Data caching:** Because the same data or the contents of the same Web site may pass the firewall repeatedly in response to requests from different users, the firewall can cache that data and answer more quickly without getting the data anew from the actual Web site every time.

✔ **Content filtering:** Firewall rules may be used to restrict access to certain inappropriate Web sites based on URLs, keywords, or content type (video streams, for example, or executable e-mail attachments).

✔ **Intrusion detection:** Certain patterns of network traffic may indicate an intrusion attempt in progress. Instead of just blocking the suspicious network packets, the firewall may take active steps to further limit the attempt, for example, by disallowing the sender IP address altogether or alerting an administrator.

✔ **Load balancing:** From a security standpoint, a single point of entry is good. But from an availability standpoint, this single point of entry may lead to a single point of failure as well. Most firewalls allow the incoming and outgoing network request to be distributed among two or more cooperating firewalls.

These four basic functions are discussed in this chapter. The advanced functions are described in Chapter 4.

It's interesting to compare the list of functions with our Doorman Sam. If you equate network packets with employees or visitors going in and out the corporate headquarters building and compare Sam to a firewall, you'll see that many of the same principles apply and help in understanding the reasons behind those functions.

Although the data-caching function is hard to translate to Sam's job description, the security guard is exceptionally good at detecting intrusions and acting upon them, probably even much better than most firewall products. You only have to walk up to the front desk and ask to see an unknown employee three times in five minutes to get a strong reaction from Sam.

What a firewall can't do

A security guard can't prevent all security problems, and neither can firewalls prevent all security problems.

In a way, trying to protect a building is not much different from trying to protect a computer network. Both the building and the network contain employees who are trying to get their work done without interference or hindrance from security measures. Yet most people realize the necessity of the security personnel and abide by the security rules. Similarly, users on the network should also understand that installing modems, bringing in virus-infected diskettes, or opening and executing e-mail attachments of unknown origin may jeopardize security measures.

Security threats that a firewall can't protect you from are

- ✔ **Inside attack:** Users on the internal network have already passed the firewall. The firewall can do nothing to stop internal network snooping or intrusion attempts from within. Other security measures, such as configuring restricted permissions on workstations and servers, and enabling the auditing of network access, should be implemented to protect against these kinds of attacks. (Although you can deploy firewalls between your corporate servers and your internal users as well.)

- ✔ **Social engineering:** This is the term used to describe attacks in which hackers obtain information by calling employees and pretending to be a colleague at the front desk, a member of the security staff, or just somebody from the firm doing routine checks. This person asks for privileged information, such as server names, IP addresses, or passwords. Employees should be aware of these tactics and know that certain information should never be given.

- ✔ **Viruses and Trojan horse programs:** Firewalls attempt to scan for viruses in all network traffic, but these wicked programs change constantly. Distinguishing between acceptable e-mail attachments and malicious content continues to be a problem for computer users. Good precautions should be taken to prevent the spread of viruses and to minimize the damage that a virus can do. Trojan horse programs are perhaps even harder to spot, because they don't attempt to spread to other files or computers like their virus sisters. A very small Trojan horse program that is run once by an unsuspecting user can open up a back door to his computer. A good example of the kind of damage that these programs can do is a Trojan horse program that sends out all collected keystrokes at password prompts once a week.

✔ **Poorly trained firewall administrators:** The firewall doesn't know what is acceptable and what is not unless an administrator tells it. Competent firewall administrators should correctly specify which network traffic should be blocked. Doorman Sam has the intelligence to understand that a naked man who claims that his clothes and shoes already arrived and he is supposed to join them in the third floor conference room is clearly crazy, even though Sam's security instructions may not have a naked-man-meeting-his-clothes-upstairs clause. Most firewalls, however, can easily be confused by fragmented IP packets and should be explicitly configured to handle such fragments.

New network protocols and services are introduced constantly. New vulnerabilities and software bugs in firewalls are also discovered constantly. Administrating a firewall is not a one-time task. You should stay alert and constantly maintain the firewall rules, update and install vendor-supplied patches, and check the generated firewall log files.

Unfortunately, you can't just install a firewall and forget about it.

General Strategy: Allow-All or Deny-All

One of the first things that you must decide when you configure your firewall is the general strategy on how to specify what network packets and protocols you allow inside your network, and which network traffic that you want to block.

The two major possibilities are

✔ **Allow-all strategy:** Allows all network packets except those that are explicitly denied.

✔ **Deny-all strategy:** Denies all network packets except those that are explicitly allowed.

At first sight, the Allow-all strategy appears to be the easiest — requiring only that you create an exception list of network protocols or Web site content that is explicitly forbidden. This strategy is also in line with how other components work on your network, such as non-firewall routers, network cards, and basically all computers that allow all traffic to pass except when explicitly denied.

The Allow-all strategy may sound enticing, but you should always use the second strategy — Deny-all, which is much more secure.

If you use the Allow-all strategy, you have to list every possible method that someone can use to intrude on your network and then come up with the rules to block related network traffic. Doing so results in a lot of rules, and even then you are bound to miss one, two, or several methods that can be used to exploit your network. (Not to mention that your list of deny rules would not include newly discovered methods or services that allow an intruder to enter your network.) This is akin to Doorman Sam locking only the ground-floor windows that were previously used for illegal entrance into the building. Clearly, this is not a safe approach.

The Deny-all approach is much easier to administer. No traffic is allowed, except for a small number of explicitly defined protocols and services. The Deny-all approach has two advantages:

- ✔ You have to maintain only a small list of allowed network traffic rules. The smaller the list, the easier it is for you to verify that the configuration of the firewall is correct.

- ✔ You don't have to constantly add new rules to exclude newly discovered problems.

Note that your firewall may even use the Deny-all approach automatically. Of course, this means that if you haven't added any of the "Allow" rules yet, the firewall effectively blocks all network traffic. Somebody we knew participated in the test program of a new firewall product and was surprised at how many participants reported that the firewall seemed broken because they lost all network connectivity with the Internet after installing the product. They failed to realize that they had not yet added any "Allow" rules. (These were probably typical Allow-all people.)

Normally, the firewall policy that you want to express with firewall rules may actually be a combination of both Deny-all and Allow-all ingredients. The following firewall policy listing illustrates this point. In this example, the policy specifies what content network users can access on the Internet.

1. Deny network traffic on all IP ports.

2. Except, allow network traffic on port 80 (HTTP).

3. Except, from all HTTP traffic, deny HTTP video content.

4. Except, allow HTTP video content for members of the Trainers group.

5. Except, deny Trainers to download HTTP video content at night.

Notice that this firewall policy listing swings between "Deny-all, except" and "Allow-all, except" when expressing which network traffic should be allowed or blocked. This listing serves only as an example to give you an idea of how the Deny-all/Allow-all strategy works. Actual firewall rules for the same example on a firewall that defaults to Deny-all may look like the rules shown in Table 3-1.

Table 3-1	Example Firewall Rules (Deny-All Strategy)		
Port/Content	*Users*	*Time*	*Action*
Port 80/except video	All	Always	Allow
Port 80/video	Trainers	Day	Allow

If we expressed the same rules on a firewall that could be configured to use the Allow-all approach, the rules from this sample firewall policy may look like the rules shown in Table 3-2.

Table 3-2	Example Firewall Rules (Allow-All Strategy)		
Port/Content	*Users*	*Time*	*Action*
All ports, except 80	All	Always	Deny
Port 80/video	All, except trainers	Always	Deny
Port 80/video	Trainers	Night	Deny

Notice how much more complex the Allow-all strategy rules in Table 3-2 are in comparison to the Deny-all strategy rules in Table 3-1.

An administrator needs to create firewall rules to implement a firewall policy. Many theories exist on what is the most intuitive way to represent a list of rules. Many firewalls use a combination of the following three techniques to process firewall rules:

- ✔ **In order:** The firewall rules are processed top to bottom. The rule that matches the current IP packet is used. The remaining rules in the list are not considered. The administrator should take care when specifying the correct order of the rules. An incorrect order can have drastically different results.

- ✔ **Deny first:** Firewall rules that explicitly deny certain packets are processed first. A matching rule blocks the current IP packet. If no Deny rule matches, the Allow rules are processed next.

  ✔ **Best fit:** The firewall uses its own methods to determine the order in
    which the list of firewall rules is processed, which usually means going
    from detailed rules to general rules.

Make sure that you know which technique or combination of techniques that
your firewall uses to process the rules. For example, look at Table 3-3. It contains three simple firewall rules. Imagine that user Kim, who is a member of
the Temps group, attempts to connect to a Web site on the Internet. Depending
on the rule processing technique that the firewall uses, different results may
occur. The outcome may be Allow if the firewall uses "In order" (due to rule
A); it may be Deny, if the firewall uses "Deny first" (due to rule B); and it may
be Allow, if the firewall uses "Best fit" (due to rule C).

Table 3-3	Processing Order of Firewall Rules		
Rule	*Port*	*Users*	*Action*
Rule A	80 (HTTP)	All	Allow
Rule B	80 (HTTP)	Temps	Deny
Rule C	80 (HTTP)	Kim	Allow

Packet Filtering

The first firewall products used only packet filtering to protect the internal
network from outside users. The firewall inspected the IP header of each
packet that entered the network and made a decision to allow or to block the
packet based on the IP addresses used and the specific port number in the
TCP or UDP header.

Although this functionality is still the cornerstone of firewall products, packet
filtering used this way is not enough to secure the network. Packet inspection
needs to be smarter about which inbound network packets are expected in
response to a legitimate request from an internal network user, and which
inbound network packets are unsolicited and should therefore be blocked.
When a firewall sees an outgoing network packet, it should remember that an
incoming response is due soon, and only allow those expected incoming network packets. The remembered information is called *state*. This smarter form
of packet filtering is called *stateful* packet filtering, as opposed to the original
stateless packet filtering, which did not remember the state of expected
return packets.

Even with stateful packet filtering, networks still have a couple of vulnerabilities that should be addressed:

✔ The outside world can learn the IP addresses used on the internal network. The firewall should use Network Address Translation (NAT) to solve this problem.

✔ Packet filters have limited decision capabilities because they look only at a small portion of the network packet. The firewall should use application proxy functionality to further inspect the packet.

Filtering IP data

Packet filters are rules that inspect the information in the packet header of every network packet arriving at the firewall, so that they can decide whether the packet should be allowed in or out or whether it should be dropped.

If the packet is allowed to pass, it continues on its merry way. But note that an IP packet never passes any router or firewall without undergoing some modifications. Before the IP packet is sent on its way, the router or firewall reduces the numerical value of the Time-To-Live (TTL) information in the IP header by at least 1. If the TTL value, which the sender of the packet probably set at 128, ever reaches 0, the packet is discarded. Discarding the packet prevents endless looping of IP packets in cyberspace, due to router misconfiguration or similar causes. Because the TTL field in the IP header changes, the value of the Header checksum field must be recalculated and is changed as well.

The IP packet may be modified even more when passing through the firewall. Later in this chapter, we show you how to add Network Address Translation (NAT) to the firewall. In NAT, the IP numbers and port numbers that are used in the packet are substituted with other numbers before the packet continues. When the firewall also performs application proxy functionality, the network packet may not pass at all, and instead, be rebuilt from scratch and sent along.

You can create packet filter rules that check the following fields in a network packet that arrives at the firewall:

✔ **Source IP address:** This is the IP address that the packet lists as its sender. This field doesn't necessarily reflect the true original computer that sent the packet. The field may have been changed for legitimate reasons by a NAT machine between the sender and the firewall, or hackers may have changed the field, which is known as *IP spoofing*.

✔ **Destination IP address:** This is the IP address to which the packet is being sent. Make sure you list the actual IP address in the packet filter rule and not the Domain Name System (DNS) name, such as `server3.dummies.com`. Otherwise, a hacker that takes over a DNS server can immediately pass all packet filters undisturbed.

✔ **IP protocol ID:** An IP header can be followed by different protocol headers. Each of these protocols has its own IP protocol ID. The best-known examples are TCP (ID 6) and UDP (ID 17). Others that you will encounter are ICMP (ID 1), GRE (ID 47) — which is used for PPTP connections — and ESP (ID 50) and AH (ID 51), which are both used for the IPSec protocol.

✔ **TCP or UDP port number:** The port number indicates to which service this packet is destined. You should allow only ports that are associated with allowed services, such as HTTP (port 80) or FTP (port 20/21). The Appendix contains a list of many well-known port numbers and their associated services.

✔ **ICMP message type:** ICMP is the housekeeping protocol of the TCP/IP protocol suite. Some of the ICMP types are very useful messages; others are very dangerous and should not be allowed to pass through the firewall.

✔ **Fragmentation flags:** IP packets can be broken into smaller packets to accommodate network segments that can only handle smaller-sized packets. Unfortunately, as is discussed a later in the chapter, this functionality can be misused.

✔ **IP Options setting:** Optional functions of TCP/IP can be specified in this field. Hackers can exploit the Source Route option in particular. These options are only used for diagnostics, so the firewall should drop network packets with IP Options set.

Besides checking the fields mentioned in the preceding list, packet filters can also make a distinction between packets that are outbound from the internal network to the Internet, and inbound from the Internet to the internal network. The network interface on which a packet arrives is an important criterion by itself. Because a hacker can easily forge the sender IP address in a network packet, the firewall can't really trust that information. However, if the packet arrives at the external network interface using a sender IP address that belongs to the internal network, the firewall should recognize the IP spoof immediately, just by noticing that it arrives at the external network interface.

In the next few sections, we give you further details on how packet filters can inspect the information in the packet headers.

ICMP

Many ICMP packets are useful in diagnosing network connectivity. The best-known example is the PING application that sends an ICMP Echo Request to another machine. If that machine is available, an ICMP Echo Reply packet is returned to the PING application. Other useful ICMP types are TTL Exceeded and Destination Unreachable, which indicate that the packet did not reach the final destination.

ICMP also has message types that can be dangerous. The ICMP Redirect can be used to tell the firewall to use a different route to send packets to certain recipients. You should not allow this type. This is like Mr. C. Rook telling Doorman Sam to forward all legal documents pertaining to the big Chemical Plant case to him instead, because it's "a quicker route." This ICMP Redirect functionality clearly shows that TCP/IP was designed in a time where all computers on the network were supposed to cooperate with each other in a friendly and constructive way. Actually, the original RFC777 document that defines ICMP is dated April 1, 1981. Go figure.

The Echo Request/Echo Reply types also create a vulnerability if used by outside hackers to learn which computers and which IP addresses are available on the internal network. The firewall should block this outside-initiated use of the PING functionality. If the firewall implements NAT, this vulnerability won't be present.

Table 3-4 shows sample ICMP packet filters that allow PING from the internal network.

Table 3-4	ICMP Packet Filters		
Protocol	*Type*	*Direction*	*Action*
ICMP	Echo Request	Outbound	Allow
ICMP	Echo Reply	Inbound	Allow
ICMP	TTL Exceeded	Inbound	Allow
ICMP	Destination Unreachable	Inbound	Allow
ICMP	Echo Request	Inbound	Deny
ICMP	Echo Reply	Outbound	Deny
ICMP	Redirect	Inbound	Deny

The direction in the packet filter is important because it distinguishes between the PING command that is initiated on the internal network (Allow) and the externally initiated PING command (Deny).

Fragments

IP network traffic travels over all kinds of network segments between the sender and the destination. Not all of these segments or links may allow the same maximum packet size. The maximum packet size is called the Maximum Transmission Unit (MTU) of the network. If a larger IP packet has to cross a network link that allows only a smaller size, the original IP packet can be broken into smaller IP packets and continue. These smaller packets are called IP *fragments* and are shown in Figure 3-1. Each of these IP fragments has its own IP header that contains the source and final destination IP addresses, as well as a fragment position number, but only a small part of the original TCP information.

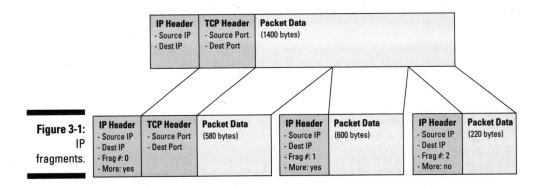

Figure 3-1:
IP
fragments.

Two aspects of fragments are important:

- ✔ To speed up things after crossing the network link that allows only a smaller size, the IP fragments are not reassembled again at the other side but travel independently to the final destination. There, they are reunited again in order to form the original IP packet.

- ✔ Each IP fragment contains only a part of the original TCP information. Therefore, only the first fragment contains the TCP part that shows the TCP port number. The other fragments carry the remaining TCP information but not the TCP port number.

What's the poor firewall to do? The arriving IP fragments, except the first one, contain no indication of a TCP port number, so the packet filters can't make a decision based on that. Blocking the second and subsequent fragments disallows all network packets that have passed a network link with a small maximum packet size. Reassembling the packet itself and making a decision based on the complete IP packet means that the firewall is accepting all these fragments and storing them until all fragments have arrived and then continue. This opens up a strong possibility that a hacker can make the firewall do a lot of intensive work, especially if the hacker never sends the last packet. The firewall may be so busy with sorting out all these small packets that it can't focus on other tasks. This is called a *denial-of-service attack.* This attack is like sending Doorman Sam a card that says "See other side for instructions" printed on both sides. He's not going to fall for that.

Letting the second and subsequent fragments pass the firewall may be the solution, but this strategy also has a disadvantage. The first fragment can be inspected and is possibly blocked. The final-destination computer on the internal network knows that if the first fragment never arrives, it should not reassemble the fragments that did come through and use the fragment anyway. Some implementations of TCP/IP make the mistake of reassembling the fragments, and hackers capitalize on this mistake by sending a complete IP packet that is disguised as a fragment. The firewall allows the packet to pass through, thus relying on the absence of the first fragment. The final-destination computer receives this self-advertised fragment and processes it as a complete IP packet! Because the firewall doesn't block second and subsequent fragments, the hacker is able to send packets to computers on the internal network unchecked.

Verify that all computers on the internal network correctly discard IP fragments when the first fragment never arrives before allowing the firewall to pass IP fragments.

We're sure that when you were young, you never got into the movie theater by claiming that your mom already went ahead with the tickets. Somehow, when we were kids, we always ran into Doorman Sam when he still had his previous job as a ticket-taker at the movies.

IP spoofing and source routing

Just as you can use a fake return address on an envelope and a fake From address on outgoing e-mail messages, a hacker can use a fake Source IP address in the IP packets that he sends to your firewall. This is known as *IP spoofing.*

The firewall should not rely on the Source IP address alone to make the decision to allow the packet to pass. By the same token, it's not useful to have the packet filters block packets based on the Source IP address. Because the Source IP address can't be trusted to be true, the firewall must be able to distinguish on which network interface the IP packets arrive. Packets arriving on the external network interface but claiming to come from an internal IP address should be blocked right away. You may actually get away with this with Doorman Sam. "Hi, good morning again, my security badge is still inside, I was merely checking the lights on my car."

Why would a hacker do this, and how could he possibly gain any advantage by doing this? After all, if he spoofed the sender IP address, he will have a hard time receiving the possible response packets sent in return to the fake address.

You'd be surprised. Here are several good reasons (from a hacker's stand-point, that is) to send a spoofed IP packet:

- ✔ The internal network may already contain a malicious Trojan horse application installed on one of the computers. The hacker may merely want to signal the application to start doing its lowly deed, which is sim-ilar to sending a coded message to spy on the inside: "The blue sparrow will see an early spring tonight." No need to confirm.

- ✔ The hacker may want to stage a denial-of-service attack against one of the internal computers.

- ✔ The hacker may have temporarily disabled the computer that legiti-mately uses the spoofed sender IP address and is pretending to answer the now lost return packets at carefully timed intervals. This resembles those irritating voice-mail outgoing messages that some people seem to enjoy, where you think that the person you called actually picked up the phone, but instead the voice-mail message contains deliberate pauses and pretends to respond to what you said.

- ✔ The IP packet with the spoofed IP address may actually contain a rout-ing slip that contains IP addresses that the return packet should visit on its way to the Source IP address. This is called the Source Route option. Obviously, the hacker would list an IP address that he is monitoring on the Source Route list.

To prevent the Source Route option exploit, the firewall should be configured to drop all packets that have the Source Route option turned on. This is one of the options in the IP Options field of an IP packet. All of the options are for diagnostics purposes only, so the firewall packet filters can drop any packet that has any option set.

Stateful packet filtering

So far we have only looked at stateless packet filtering. Modern firewalls use a more robust version, which is called *stateful packet filtering*.

With stateful packet filtering, the firewall remembers "state" about expected return packets. Any unexpected packet arriving at the firewall claiming to be a solicited response is blocked immediately.

When an IP packet is a request for information, such as an HTTP (port 80) request to a public Web site, the IP packet lists its return IP address and an unused return port number greater than 1023 (for example, 2065) to which to deliver the response. If the firewall knows only stateless packet filtering, it doesn't know that a packet will arrive shortly on port 2065. The only choice that a stateless packet filter firewall has is to leave all ports greater than 1023 open for all traffic. A hacker can easily use this opening to initiate communication with internal computers on ports greater than 1023. The firewall will pass this unsolicited traffic.

Stateful packet filtering blocks all traffic on ports greater than 1023 and allows only network traffic that matches the response port of a previously sent IP packet. The firewall internally maintains a table of information on which ports it may expect traffic. If the firewall determines that a communication exchange is finished, it removes that information from the table. In cases where the firewall is unable to detect that the communication has ended, it automatically removes that information after a short time period.

The doorman guarding the headquarters at Legal Inc. is stateful, too. Rarely is a visitor allowed to enter without an appointment. Doorman Sam will most likely have a dated list of expected visitors and not rely on a spoofed appointment confirmation letter carried by the visitor himself. Movies make you believe that wearing coveralls and pretending to be a toilet repairman seems to do the trick. Wearing balloons and implying that you came to do a surprise serenade is also a classic.

Think of the delivery guy rolling in ordered supplies. He doesn't know who ordered it; he just knows to deliver it at the front desk, which is similar to the Network Address Translation (NAT) functionality that we look at next.

Dynamic packet filtering

Because a temporary packet filter allowing network traffic on the return port is automatically created, stateful packet filtering is a form of dynamic packet filtering. The temporary packet filter is usually the reverse of the manually created packet filter but is only valid for the duration of the communication.

Stateful packet filtering is often called *dynamic packet filter mirroring*, or even *stateful inspection*.

Some firewalls allow you to create a packet filter that specifies which additional return ports should be opened in the temporary packet filter.

Network Address Translation (NAT)

Originally, Network Address Translation, or NAT, was introduced to save IP addresses in use on the Internet. An IP address is 32 bits long and with that number of bits, you can have only about four billion different IP addresses. Because many companies have claimed large blocks of IP addresses, the available IP numbers were quickly becoming depleted. In May 1994, RFC1631 suggested what was then thought to be a short-term solution — NAT. As it turned out, NAT offered several unexpected advantages, as you'll soon discover.

With NAT, all computers on the internal network can use a private range of IP addresses, such as 10.0.0.0/8, which is not in use on the Internet. When they make a connection to the outside world, the NAT computer replaces the private IP address, for example, 10.65.1.7 — listed as Source IP address in the IP packet — with its own public IP address, 23.1.8.3, and sends the packet on its way. The destination computer on the Internet thinks the original sender is 23.1.8.3, and sends a return packet back to this IP address. The NAT computer receives a packet for 23.1.8.3 and replaces the Destination IP address with the original 10.65.1.7 to travel the last leg on the internal network, as shown in Figure 3-2. NAT may as well have been called Network Address Replacing.

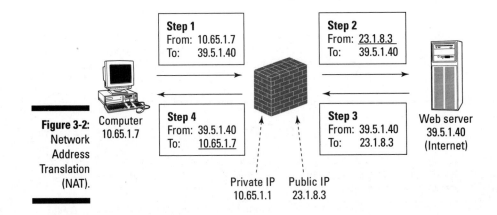

Figure 3-2: Network Address Translation (NAT).

Step 1
From: 10.65.1.7
To: 39.5.1.40

Step 2
From: 23.1.8.3
To: 39.5.1.40

Step 4
From: 39.5.1.40
To: 10.65.1.7

Step 3
From: 39.5.1.40
To: 23.1.8.3

Computer
10.65.1.7

Web server
39.5.1.40
(Internet)

Private IP   Public IP
10.65.1.1   23.1.8.3

Why does NAT save IP addresses? Because NAT never exposed the 10.0.0.0/8 IP address on the Internet, many companies can use the same internal private range of IP addresses and only need a single (or a few) public IP addresses. The computer on the internal network never noticed that NAT took place. The destination computer on the Internet didn't notice NAT was involved either. Brilliant.

REMEMBER

Private IP addresses

RFC1918 specifies that the following IP addresses are reserved for private use and won't be used on the Internet.

- 10.0.0.0–10.255.255.255 (=10.0.0.0/8)
- 172.16.0.0–172.31.255.255 (=172.16.0.0/12)
- 192.168.0.0–192.168.255.255 (=192.168.0.0/16)

How did the NAT computer know to send the returning packet addressed to 23.1.8.3 back to the original sender 10.65.1.7? Just as stateful packet filtering keeps a list of expected return packets, NAT also keeps a list of which addresses to replace with which original address. These are called *NAT mappings.*

Finally, what if more than one computer on the internal network wants to use the NAT computer to communicate with the Internet? The 1994 RFC1631 document proposed to solve this by letting the NAT computer have multiple public IP addresses and using one for every concurrent connection from the internal computers to the Internet. In every modern implementation of NAT, this can just as easily be solved by not only changing the Source IP address to 23.1.8.3, but by replacing the source port number with an unused port number above 1023 as well. All the NAT computer has to do is keep a list of which port number temporarily belongs to which requesting internal network computer.

Technically, the technique to replace ports is called *Network Address Port Translation* (NAPT), but everybody just says NAT. Nearly 65,000 port numbers are available, so in theory, one NAT computer can handle thousands of internal network computers.

Security aspects of NAT

Although saving IP addresses is cool, NAT also has a security aspect. As a by-product of replacing the original IP address, NAT hides the true IP numbers in use on the internal network, which is a big advantage.

The possibility of hiding the actual IP addresses is also the reason that almost all firewalls can do NAT. The outside world will only see the outside public IP address of the firewall and will never learn the internal IP addresses. Even if a hacker knows the internal private IP addresses, they are not nearly as interesting to him as the internal public IP addresses that would have been used without NAT. Private IP addresses, such as those in the 10.0.0.0/8 range, can't be routed over the Internet. ISPs actively block those addresses if used on the Internet. Thousands of companies use 10.65.1.7 internally, so it isn't possible to decide where an IP packet with that address needs to go on the Internet.

In firewall circles, people tend to see NAT more as a security precaution than as a method of saving IP addresses. The term *IP masquerading* is often used for NAT, which emphasizes the hiding aspect of NAT.

NAT does nothing to protect the computer on the internal network. If the computer is tricked into making a connection to an untrusted computer on the Internet, the NAT component happily shuttles the intruding packets back and forth. A firewall should always combine NAT with stateful packet filtering.

You normally don't have to do a lot to let NAT do its work. Unlike packet filters, which have to be defined for every protocol or service that you want to allow, NAT is largely an automatic function of a firewall.

In the description of NAT, we concentrated on network traffic that was initiated by computers on the internal network. It's also possible to use NAT when computers on the Internet initiate the network requests. (This can be done with static address mapping and is discussed in the next chapter.)

Consequences of NAT

The use of NAT has some drawbacks, and although they don't outweigh the advantages of using NAT on our firewall, it's worthwhile to point them out.

- ✔ The NAT computer is effectively doing IP spoofing, although we usually don't call it that if it is the firewall that does the spoofing as opposed to a malicious hacker. A hacker in a NAT-protected network is harder to pinpoint from the outside. It appears that all traffic is coming from the firewall doing NAT. The log files created by the firewall may help to determine who was using which port at what time, but this is certainly harder than having directly obtained the unique IP address of the hacker computer. Masquerading IP addresses has its disadvantages.

- ✔ Some network protocols list the original Source IP address or source port number in more places than the IP packet itself. This is normally not a problem, but if the firewall wants to automatically replace all the occurrences of the numbers that should be hidden, it should know exactly where these protocols list the numbers and change them accordingly.

Most NAT implementations support changing the IP numbers in a couple of well-known protocols that need this change. The best-known examples are the FTP protocol and the ICMP protocol. For other protocols that are not supported, you either have to install routines that do this — the so-called *NAT editors* — or you are unable to use them through the NAT firewall.

✔ If the sending computer encrypts the IP header of a packet, or if the data of the packet itself is encrypted and contains the IP address as well, the firewall may not be able to make the necessary changes to the IP header or the data inside the packet. Encryption is used to protect the IP packet from deliberate changes made by intermediate snoopers on the network. It makes sense that the firewall won't be able to make those changes, either. Solutions for this problem are not readily available. Installing additional NAT editors won't help much. Of course, those routines won't know how to decrypt those packets, either. Ongoing work on standards for allowing IPSec-encrypted data through a NAT firewall is almost finished.

✔ Some multimedia or conferencing protocols want to create independent back channels to the sender of a request. Doing so causes problems with stateful packet filtering, but NAT may have trouble with these kinds of protocols as well. Depending on the firewall, you may be able to create packet filters that specify the expected ports for the return channel, or you can install a special application proxy, as discussed in the next section.

Just as stateful packet filtering has to remove information from the list of return packets that it expects to receive, the NAT function should remove temporary mappings between external ports and internal IP addresses. If the firewall is unable to detect that a communication session has ended, it removes the mappings automatically after a short period of time.

During the entire period that the NAT mapping exists, hackers may try to send packets to the still open return port. If the Source IP addresses match, the firewall may pass the packet to the internal network computer. However, it is unlikely that the internal network computer is still expecting network packets on the port that it used. Even a temporary packet filter and a temporary NAT mapping may be exploited if the hacker knows enough information and times his intrusion attempt correctly.

Application Proxy

Besides stateful packet filtering and NAT, another function of a good firewall is the application proxy service, sometimes called *application gateway*. Consider an application proxy as an elaborate version of a packet filter.

Whereas a packet filter is capable of inspecting data only in the lower levels of an IP packet, such as the IP address or port number, an application proxy is capable of inspecting the entire application data portion of an IP packet.

An example is an FTP application proxy that can scan FTP packets for certain file names and block the requests if needed.

An application proxy plays the role of a liaison officer. The internal network computer sends a particular Internet request to the firewall. The application proxy on the firewall picks up on the request, inspects the entire packet against rules configured by the firewall administrator, and then regenerates the entire Internet request before sending it to the destination server on the Internet. The firewall appears to have sent the request. The returned result will again be inspected, and if the rules allow the result to pass, the firewall will build a response packet and send it to the internal network computer.

The following are two important distinctions between packet filters and application proxies:

- ✔ A packet filter inspects only the packet header, whereas an application proxy can scan the entire application data in the packet.

- ✔ A packet filter passes an allowed packet. The same packet travels from the internal computer to the server on the Internet. An application proxy regenerates an allowed packet. A new packet is built and sent from the firewall to the server on the Internet. A similar strategy is used on the return packet.

The application proxy maintains two separate connections. One connection is between the application proxy and the internal computer, and the other connection is between the application proxy and the Internet server.

An application proxy service on a firewall offers several advantages:

- ✔ The application proxy can inspect the entire application portion of the IP packet. This inspection happens both when the Internet request is sent and when the reply packet from the Internet server is returned.

- ✔ Because the application proxy understands the application protocol, it can create a much more detailed log file of what is sent through the firewall. Packet filter log files know only about the IP packet header information.

- ✔ The internal computer and the server on the Internet never have a real connection. Instead, the firewall regenerates every packet that is sent between the two. This means that problems or attacks associated with buffer-overflows or illegal conditions in the packets never reach the internal computer.

✔ An application proxy actively sends newly created packets on behalf of the original sender. It doesn't route packets between the network interfaces. If the application proxy or firewall were to crash, the communication connection would cease to exist. With just a packet filter approach, a crash of the firewall may result in any packets being allowed to route through.

✔ An application proxy can inspect network traffic that uses multiple connections. Packet filters don't recognize that separate connections to the same application belong together.

✔ Because the application proxy looks at the entire application data, it can store return results, such as content of Web pages, in a cache. Subsequent requests for the same information can be fulfilled from the cache instead of having to fetch the same content repeatedly. Although many people associate a proxy with this caching function, it is a secondary function from a security standpoint.

Unfortunately, application proxies have some distinct disadvantages, as well:

✔ **Proxy per application:** The application proxy service needs to understand the application protocol used. This means that the firewall should have a specific application proxy for every network application. Most firewalls support a proxy for common applications, such as FTP and HTTP, but for other network applications, you may not find a suitable application proxy. In that situation, you can't use the application proxy function for these network applications.

✔ **Required proxy configuration:** For some application proxies, the internal network computer may need to be aware that it is actually connecting to the application proxy instead of directly connecting to the server on the Internet. Internal network computers that want to use these application proxies require a configuration change. This is called a *classic application proxy* by RFC1919. If a computer on the internal network can use the firewall application proxy without doing any special configuration, RFC1919 calls this a *transparent application proxy.*

Because application proxies are application-specific, firewall software usually lets you configure individual settings per application proxy supported by the firewall.

Doorman Sam, still on guard at Legal Inc., can be a proxy as well. In the evening, when the legal team is working late, they call down to the front desk and have Sam order pizzas on their behalf. When a pizza delivery guy from Proksie Pizza arrives at the front desk with a stack of pizzas a little later, Sam checks to see if the delivered pizzas match the order. The pizza place never knew who exactly ordered the pizzas; as far as they are concerned, they just received an order from Legal Inc. Doorman Sam takes the pizzas and has somebody else deliver them to the legal team on the fourth floor. We're not sure whether the legal team would really appreciate it if Sam tried to implement some sort of caching when they order pizzas the next day as well.

Monitoring and Logging

Why would you need to do extensive logging if you configured a firewall with packet filters, made sure that NAT is hiding the private IP addresses, and implemented application proxies that separate the internal network from the Internet?

Good question. It's true that a carefully configured firewall provides security for your internal network, but you still need to be sure that you didn't overlook anything. That's one of the reasons why you want to have the firewall log every connection it makes and every packet it blocks. You want to verify whether the firewall is really as secure as you believe it to be.

Here are four good reasons to let the firewall create extensive logs of everything it does:

- **Report usage:** You want to aggregate the information in generated logs to have an indication of the firewall's performance, usage, and statistics and perhaps even do accounting and charge users for the service.

- **Detect intrusion:** It is bad enough if a hacker infiltrated your network. It would be worse if you didn't know about it. The longer a hacker can linger on the network, the more damage he can do. Frequent inspection of the log files can reveal suspicious patterns or even show the evidence of a successful intrusion of your network.

- **Discover attack method:** Even if you detect an intrusion, you still need to be sure that the hacker is stopped and that he can't repeat the attack that he staged before. This requires a careful analysis of all the log files. Hopefully, you will spot how the hacker was able to enter your network and also when he first entered your network. Such information reveals possible Trojan horse applications that may have been left behind earlier or the invalidity of backups made after the fact.

- **Legal evidence:** An extensive log file may even be needed as evidence, if an intrusion of your network leads to legal prosecution. The log files form a factual account of when the intruder first attempted to contact your network and what subsequent actions he took after that.

A firewall should log all access. You may use the auditing capabilities of the operating system as well. The more information you can gather, the better.

Although it may be boring to review large files with boring lines of log information, regular attention may detect a possible intruder before he can do a lot of damage. (Chapter 4 covers intrusion detection — having the firewall detect suspicious activities.)

To help you analyze the log files, you can use one of several software programs available that help you detect patterns, summarize totals, and aggregate logs.

Try to avoid the temptation to save on hard drive space by deleting log files or configuring the firewall to log less. And if you're serious about securing your network, you should keep the generated log files for a long time. Keep them for at least as long as you want to look back to find out when a certain condition first appeared.

Often, the first thing a hacker will attempt to do is to delete or modify your log files to cover up his tracks or prevent detection. To battle that scenario, you may want to store the log files on another computer or store the log files on a write-once device.

Chapter 4

Understanding Firewall Not-So-Basics

*T*he primary function of a firewall is clear: To protect the internal network from the (sometimes) hostile outside network known as the Internet. Because you want to communicate on the Internet, the firewall should allow some network traffic to pass, while blocking unwanted traffic. However, you may want Internet users to initiate communication with your network, so the firewall should let in some outside network traffic.

In this chapter, you look at some advanced functions of firewalls that can be used to further define a firewall's inspection possibilities, optimize its performance, or even alert you to suspicious network traffic patterns.

Not all firewalls have all these advanced functions. Some support only limited versions of these functions, and some even use different names for these functions. Using different names makes it hard to determine what a particular firewall can and cannot do. Luckily, an organization called ICSA conducts a certification process for firewall products, a sort of firewall exam. In Chapter 18, you find out more about how you can use the information from the ICSA.

If you haven't done so already, be sure to read Chapter 3 about firewall basics. The not-so-basic firewall functions described in this chapter are

✔ **Static address mapping:** If an Internet-accessible server is located on a private network protected by a firewall, the outside world will know only the public firewall address. Static address mapping allows access attempts to the public firewall address to be redirected to the internal server.

✔ **Content filtering:** Unlike packet filters, application proxy services inspect the entire application data portion of an IP packet. This technique is used to define elaborate firewall rules, based on Web site addresses (URLs), keywords, Web content type — such as video streams — or executable mail-attachment types. Not all firewalls support all these filtering options, of course.

✔ **Intrusion detection:** A firewall may block particular network packets, but it can also play a more active role in recognizing suspicious network activity. Certain patterns of network traffic may indicate an intrusion attempt in progress. Instead of just blocking the suspicious network packets, the firewall may take active steps to further limit the attempt, such as disallowing the sender IP address altogether or alerting an administrator to take notice.

✔ **Data caching:** Because the same data or the contents of the same Web site may pass through the firewall repeatedly in requests to different users, the firewall can store that data in a temporary cache and answer a user's request more quickly without actually retrieving the data every time. Caching is one of the methods firewalls employ to handle Web requests more quickly.

✔ **Load balancing:** Another method used to improve the performance of Internet requests is using more than one firewall — handy reinforcements that provide the same functionality and are set up with the same firewall policy rules. These firewalls can work together and share the cached results, or they can be independent from each other and just divide the network traffic load between them.

✔ **Encryption:** Encryption techniques are used first and foremost to prevent others from intercepting and reading information sent on the network; as an added benefit, they also serve to prevent modifications of IP packets while they travel on the network. The use of these encryption techniques, such as Secure Sockets Layer (SSL), IP Security (IPSec) and Virtual Private Networks (VPN), has consequences for the use of the firewall as well. For example, the firewall will lose its ability to inspect the contents of encrypted network traffic and may not be able to perform its NAT function on the encrypted IP packets.

Making Internal Servers Available: Static Address Mapping

The actual IP address of an Internet-accessible server on a firewall-protected private network is not known to the outside world. Users on the outside know only the public firewall IP address. Configuring static address mappings on the firewall allows access attempts to the public firewall IP address to be redirected to the internal server.

Static address mappings can also be used for outbound network traffic. In this case, you want the NAT component of the firewall — the function of the firewall that replaces (or "translates") private IP addresses on the internal network to public IP addresses when connecting to the Internet — always to use the same public IP address for connections from a particular computer on the internal network to the Internet.

When we described NAT for outbound Internet traffic in Chapter 3, we assumed that the NAT component of the firewall would automatically use the firewall's own external IP address and dynamically select an available source port to use. For example, if a computer with IP address 10.1.65.2 on the internal network wants to connect to a server with IP address 39.4.18.13 on the Internet, the firewall with external IP address 23.1.4.10 will dynamically create the address mapping similar to the example shown in Table 4-1.

Table 4-1	Outbound Dynamic Address Mapping		
Protocol	*Internal IP: Port*	*Firewall IP: Port*	*External IP: Port*
TCP	10.1.65.2:4305	23.1.4.10:6004	39.4.18.13:80

Note that firewalls normally do not let you see the list of current dynamic address mappings.

In this example, port 4305 is chosen by the internal computer, whereas port 6004 is chosen by the firewall. Network traffic returning from the external server and arriving at firewall port 6004 is sent back to the original sender 10.1.65.2. This dynamic address mapping is done only when the internal computer actually makes a connection to the Internet. After the connection is finished, the mapping will be removed by NAT.

However, there are two situations where the NAT address mappings should be less dynamic:

- ✔ **Static IP address assignment:** If your Internet Service Provider (ISP) has provided you with multiple public IP addresses for use on the firewall, you can assign specific public IP addresses to certain private IP addresses from computers on the internal network. This static address mapping can be used for both outbound and inbound network traffic.

- ✔ **Static inbound translation:** When you want to make a server with a private IP address available to connections from users on the Internet, you have to tell the firewall to forward certain inbound ports on the public IP address of the firewall to the server on the internal network. This is also called *port forwarding* or *server publishing.*

Static IP address assignment

Your ISP may provide you with a range of IP addresses, such as 23.1.4.8 through 23.1.4.15. You can assign all eight of these IP addresses to the external network card of the firewall. Without static address assignment, the NAT component can just use the first external IP address, 23.1.4.8, as the source IP address for all Internet requests from all computers on the internal network. Because port numbers range from 1 to 65535, the firewall has thousands of ports available as translated source ports, so it can easily handle all internal computers with just one public outside IP address.

However, you may have applications running on the internal computers that require a distinct public IP address to be used for Internet connections. An example of such an application is an Internet game that may require different IP addresses for different game players. Or for logging purposes, you may want certain internal computers always to use the same public IP address when connecting to the Internet. In those situations, you have to configure the firewall to use a specific public IP address, such as 23.1.4.12, for all the outbound Internet requests made by a specific computer on the internal network.

Note that the outside world can never see the internal computer's own IP address, such as 10.1.65.7, but always sees it use 23.1.4.12. Other computers on the internal network use one of the other public IP addresses when connecting to the Internet.

In this example, the NAT component on the firewall contains the static address mapping that is shown in Table 4-2. (The * in the table stands for any port number or IP address.)

Table 4-2	Static IP Address Mapping		
Protocol	*Internal IP: Port*	*Firewall IP: Port*	*External IP: Port*
TCP/UDP	10.1.65.7:*	23.1.4.12:*	*:*

Static IP address mapping can be used for outbound network traffic initiated by internal computer 10.1.65.7, or it can be set up to allow inbound network traffic initiated on the Internet. In that case, network traffic for all ports on 23.1.4.12 are forwarded to 10.1.65.7. Note that normal packet filters are still used to determine which ports are actually forwarded to the internal computer.

Static inbound translation

Instead of statically mapping all ports of a specific public IP address to an internal private IP address, most firewalls also allow you to specify that only specific ports from the public IP address should be mapped to the internal private IP address. This is commonly referred to as *port forwarding* or *server publishing* and is shown in Figure 4-1.

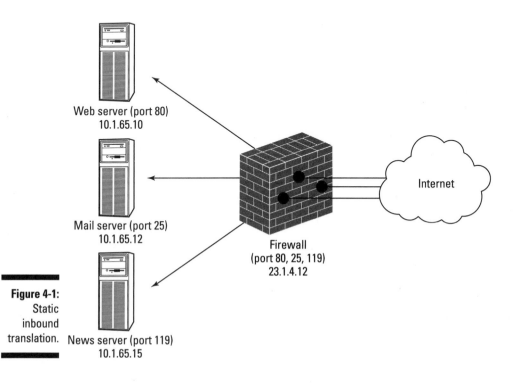

Web server (port 80)
10.1.65.10

Mail server (port 25)
10.1.65.12

Firewall
(port 80, 25, 119)
23.1.4.12

Internet

Figure 4-1:
Static
inbound
translation.

News server (port 119)
10.1.65.15

Because only a specific port is mapped to an internal IP address, the same public IP address can be used to offer several different services on several different internal servers by using different port-forwarding rules on the same IP address. Table 4-3 shows an example that forwards inbound traffic on port 80 (HTTP protocol), port 25 (SMTP mail protocol), and port 119 (NNTP news protocol) to different internal servers.

Table 4-3	Static Inbound Port Translation		
Protocol	*Internal IP: Port*	*Firewall IP: Port*	*External IP: Port*
TCP	10.1.65.10:80	23.1.4.12:80	*.*
TCP	10.1.65.12:25	23.1.4.12:25	*.*
TCP	10.1.65.15:119	23.1.4.12:119	*.*

Note that the static address mappings in Table 4-3 describe only the inbound mapping of a particular port on the public IP address of the firewall (23.1.4.12:80) to a port on the server on the internal network (10.1.65.10:80). When a computer on the Internet actually makes a connection to access the server, NAT adds the temporary dynamic mapping to correctly return the network traffic to the computer on the Internet.

Some firewalls allow you to map a port (for example, 8030) on the public IP address of the firewall to a different port on the internal server, which allows for "secret" ports to your internal server. For example, you can tell select out-side customers that, to test your new Web site, they can connect to www. dummies.com:8030. The static mapping on the firewall can be set up to forward network traffic on port 8030 to an internal Web server, which most likely uses standard http port 80.

Static address mappings that are used to allow inbound network traffic can be combined with additional rules at the firewall to further restrict which traffic is allowed in.

Filtering Content and More

Application proxy services can inspect the entire application data portion of an IP packet, unlike packet filters, which can look only at the header of a packet. The application proxy service must understand the application protocol used. However, using an application proxy service allows you to create much more extensive rules on what network traffic is acceptable or not acceptable at the firewall.

Many firewalls support these kinds of extended rules. Some example rules are given in Table 4-4.

Table 4-4	Advanced Filter Rules				
Name	*Action*	*Type*	*Site*	*Keywords*	*From*
No music video	Deny	HTTP/ video	mtv.com	—	—
No warez	Deny	HTTP or FTP	—	warez, filez	—
No spam	Deny	SMTP	—	—	getrich@ hotmail.aol

The first rule blocks HTTP video content that is obtained from the MTV Web site. The second rule blocks downloaded information that contains the word "warez" or the word "filez" — the weird spellings here are explained in the "Hack3r'z sp3ak" sidebar. The last rule blocks all e-mail that appears to come from an e-mail address that has sent unsolicited spam-style e-mail.

Table 4-4 expresses the extended filtering capabilities as one-line filter rules. Because of the complexity of the filtering combinations and their dependency on specific application protocol options, most firewall products display a special application-specific representation of these rules instead of the one-line style used in Table 4-4.

Firewalls may be able to filter traffic based on the following application-specific aspects:

- ✔ **HTTP content type:** Even though network traffic on port 80 (HTTP) may be allowed, you can restrict the list of acceptable content types. Examples of content that you may want to disallow are video files or audio files.
- ✔ **File names:** The firewall can block certain files from entering the internal network. Of course, this filter is useful only if the file is not renamed to something else.
- ✔ **File content/virus:** A filter may be able to inspect the contents of files that are downloaded. Objectionable content may be blocked. The most useful example is the detection of viruses in those files.
- ✔ **Keywords:** Certain keywords can be placed on a block list. Packets that contain keywords from the block list are disallowed.

✔ **SMTP e-mail inspection:** Besides the scanning of viruses or keywords on the block list, special e-mail filters may disallow certain attachments or deny certain sender domains or addresses.

✔ **FTP get/put, SNMP get/set:** Application protocols may be filtered to only allow "read" actions and block "write" operations. Examples are restrictions on the File Transfer Protocol (FTP) or the Simple Network Management Protocol (SNMP).

Some of these filtering options may be better performed by dedicated filtering software. Examples are using antivirus programs for virus-scanning or using parental access control programs for maintaining a blocked list of inappropriate keywords. Software vendors of filtering software often sell their products as plug-ins for well-known firewalls.

Besides filtering application-specific data, firewalls can also restrict network traffic based on aspects that are independent of the particular protocol used. Examples of these are

✔ **Site name/site IP address:** Packet filters are already capable of determining the external source IP address or external destination IP address. This functionality may be extended by specifying a filter that restricts access based on a site's DNS name, such as www.bad.com. The advantage of this approach, besides improved readability, is that the filter blocks network traffic to all the IP addresses that the name resolves to. A site's name may resolve to two or more IP addresses. Note, however, that a firewall may not endlessly match names and IP addresses back and forth. If you have a rule that disallows access to the Web destination 197.2.3.66, the firewall may not notice that 197.1.7.13 actually refers to the same Web site.

✔ **Time of day:** Rules can be expressed that include the time of day, which allows different restrictions for daytime, nighttime, and weekends, for example.

✔ **User name:** Instead of defining rules that apply to everyone, filters may be restricted to apply only to certain users or groups of users. Of course, this restriction requires that the firewall be able to authenticate the user who is making the Internet request. The firewall may have a special rule that applies to unauthenticated users or anonymous connection attempts.

✔ **Connection quota/data quota:** Filtering options that are based on accumulative previous Internet connections are much harder to implement. An example is a filter that limits data transfer through the firewall to a maximum of 1000MB per user per month. This filter requires the firewall to collect and remember information per user over time and must include mechanisms for coordinating the information if multiple firewalls are used for the same purpose.

Hack3r'z sp3ak

To establish its independence as a group and to facilitate easier automatic finding of hacker-related information, the hacker community adopted alternate spellings of certain letters and words. Most notable is the use of z instead of s and the numeral 3 for e. Illegally obtained software can be found by searching the Internet or newsgroups for "warez"; other related materials are called "filez."

Of course, excessive use of this lingo makes it difficult to read hacker-style text. But that may well be a side effect that the hack3r d00dz intended.

When setting up the advanced rules mentioned in this section, make sure that you fully understand how rules are processed. A deny rule that is too specific — about whom it applies to, at what time, for which protocol and content type, and from which site on the Internet — may be easy to circumvent by just changing one aspect of the Internet request. You may have intended that a request be blocked when any of several conditions match, but the rule only applies when all conditions in the rule match.

On the other hand, a particular rule may unnecessarily block otherwise perfectly acceptable network traffic. For example, a firewall should not just block any packet that contains the word "warez." While this no-warez firewall rule may make it harder to download illegally obtained software, it also has the unwanted effect that an e-mail discussion about "warez" is impossible as well.

Detecting Intrusion

Filtering packets and inspecting the application portion of an IP packet may do an adequate job in deciding which network traffic should be allowed in and which should not. However, modern firewalls are capable of taking a more active role. The firewall can monitor the packets arriving at the firewall and analyze them for signs of security problems — sort of like a burglar alarm for your firewall. This is called an intrusion detection system.

Just analyzing the packets at the firewall for telltale signs of intrusion attempts is not enough, of course. Intrusion detection systems must also include a reporting or alerting mechanism. You may even have the firewall page you at 2 a.m. to alert you that an incident is in progress.

In this section, we take a look at the analysis that a firewall may perform to detect an intrusion, and if an actual intrusion is detected, how the system should respond. Finally, we discuss how firewall administrators should react when an intrusion is reported.

Detecting an intrusion in progress

Intrusion detection systems exist in many different forms. We are only look-ing at the intrusion detection that can occur at the firewall by analyzing the stream of packets arriving at the firewall. Other systems may detect things such as unusual RAM or CPU uses, unexpected changes in file dates or sizes, or statistically noticeable anomalies in a user's usage patterns.

The major difference between packet filtering and intrusion detection at the firewall is that packet filtering decides which network traffic is allowed to enter the internal network (mostly based on one packet a time), whereas inspection-based intrusion detection doesn't control the network traffic but attempts to recognize patterns or conditions in one or several packets, blocked or allowed, in order to spot an intrusion in progress.

Intrusion detection systems actually work a lot like virus-scanning software. They use a list of signatures that specifies what constitutes a possible usage pattern an intruder may attempt. Sometimes this list of signatures is update-able with newly discovered attacks.

The following list describes common events or patterns that an intrusion detection system may detect:

- **DNS zone transfer:** There are several documented ways that a hacker may exploit the DNS service running on the firewall. Obtaining DNS naming information by doing a reverse query on all IP addresses in a given range or by initiating a DNS zone transfer, are two examples that may be detected by the intrusion detection system.

- **Address scans:** An attacker may scan a range of IP addresses to see which one is responsive to its queries. The intrusion detection system should recognize the repetitive nature of the IP addresses scan.

- **Port scans:** Perhaps the most common tactic a hacker may use is the enumeration of open TCP/IP ports on the firewall's external network interface. The hacker attempts to connect to ranges of ports to find out which numbered ports appear open and subsequently can be used to mount another attack. The intrusion detection system should recognize the sequential scanning of ports. Some hackers use a random port order in an effort to outsmart the intrusion detection system.

- **Ping-of-death/Teardrop/Land/Winnuke:** These are all names of various types of malformed IP packets that can cause older TCP/IP implementa-tions to misbehave or even crash. Especially the ping-of-death attack, where an ICMP ping packet with an unusually large data portion is sent, was notorious, if not for its inspiring name.

Responding to an intrusion

The real value of an intrusion detection system is determined by how effective the response to a detected intrusion attempt is. In general, four types of responses are possible:

- **Log or record the problem:** This is the most passive response. The firewall makes an entry in its log files noting the detected attempt.

- **Report or trigger an alarm:** This may include sending an e-mail to the firewall administrator or even paging a security officer. Not all intrusion attempts should invoke this reaction. You wouldn't want hackers to somehow find out that an otherwise harmless port scan wakes you up in the middle of the night, every night.

- **Modify the firewall configuration:** The response to a detected condition may be to change the configuration of the firewall automatically. This can involve changing what analysis is performed or increasing what information is logged. It could also mean that the firewall will automatically block all traffic on a particular port, or all traffic coming from the intruder's source IP address. Although this "autohardening" of the firewall sounds really effective, it can be very counterproductive and is not usually advised. An attacker may use this behavior to trigger the firewall into shutting itself down or, if the attacker is spoofing the source IP addresses used in the attack, shutting out other users who are using those IP addresses legitimately. An automatic response by the firewall to block traffic from the source IP address that appears to stage a denial-of-service attack may actually help the attacker reach his goal!

- **Strike back!** This is the most aggressive response. The firewall traces the source of the attack and takes action to disable the attacker's machine. This take-charge kind of response appeals to a lot of people, but is really not advisable. First, the attacker is most likely either using a spoofed source IP address or a previously hacked system from an innocent victim as a platform to attack your computers. Second, you may provoke a full-scale escalation of the attack. And most importantly, depending on the local laws, this response may be illegal, and you may expose yourself to criminal charges or damages.

Because the two active responses mentioned earlier have serious drawbacks, intrusion detection systems still rely on alerting human administrators to monitor the situation and decide on further action.

Reacting to a security incident

Your response to a security incident depends on the nature of the attempted attack. Some attempted attacks require no action at all, whereas other continuing attacks may require that you contact law enforcement authorities.

The Internet is very large and houses many would-be attackers. With the help of automated tools and scripts, it's easy for a bored hacker to routinely scan large blocks of IP addresses for interesting ports. This means that on any given day, your firewall may report hundreds of port scans from different IP addresses from around the world. This "knob-rattling" is nothing to be alarmed about.

Other attacks may be more worrisome. If a continuous stream of malformed IP packets targeted at your site interrupts normal operation of the firewall, or if possible intruders appear to have already entered your network, you may have to take some action.

Hopefully, your intrusion detection system or the generated reports of the firewall logs alert you that something is up. Depending on the severity of the situation, here is what you should do in these cases, in order:

1. Do not panic!

2. Document!

Not panicking is the kind of advice you can randomly insert in any list of "what-to-do" tips on any topic, but when you detect an intrusion of your network, it's particularly important that you not react hastily. If you notice that the attacker is still accessing your network while you watch, you may feel the need to immediately do something. If you panic and therefore take the wrong action, such as adding a firewall rule that mistakenly allows more network traffic in or deleting a log file instead of copying it, the attacker may actually benefit from your reaction.

Resolving an intrusion attempt may take a while. To be honest, you may have to add "order pizza" to the preceding list.

Documenting everything you do is important to be able to restore a previous situation later and to make it easy to involve other people during the incident-in-progress. You may even need the chronological documentation as proof if law enforcement authorities get involved.

During a serious attack, you won't have much time to think about whom to contact (management, staff, security personnel, users, pizza place, the firewall vendor, Internet service provider, other sites, and so on), in which order, and what damage-control actions should be taken. You should create a notification plan beforehand. The plan should include all relevant phone numbers, an inventory of needed materials, such as spare hard disks, and policies on crucial steps, such as which machines to disconnect and when to notify which people. You may even agree on a scheme about how to communicate with others in the organization without divulging to the intruder that you are aware of the attack and that a response is underway. Your response may look like this: "Attention all users: The surprise birthday party for Alice is commencing in Room 4 at 7 p.m. Bring your own disks. — Bob."

Immediately disconnecting everything may be the easiest approach, but taking snapshots of the current situation and trying to understand how the attack could have been possible is another useful tactic. Of course, if the intruder is actively destroying things, people may not appreciate your allowing it to continue while you find out what's going on.

Your plan should also include how to restore normal operation after the incident has ended. This plan might entail reinstalling the firewall and related software from scratch to avoid the danger of leaving a Trojan horse–style program or another backdoor created by the intruder.

Many fascinating books, such as *The Cuckoo's Egg* by Clifford Stoll, recount classic stories of how a brave firewall administrator (usually the author of those books), followed every step of the attacker, hunted down the intruder in the following months, and eventually got the bad guy arrested, which finally restored peace in town. Don't expect to gain a book deal out of your brush with a hacker, but such accounts are certainly an entertaining and interesting source to find out about tactics hackers use.

Improving Performance by Caching and Load Balancing

You want to make the firewall a single point of control for all the network traffic going to and from the Internet, which means that all traffic is funneled through this one entity, possibly affecting response times. To make matters worse, the firewall is actively inspecting all packets flowing through it, and at the same time has to update log files describing the network traffic. The operating speed and the capacity of a firewall are important aspects to consider.

In general, two approaches can be taken to improve the performance of the firewall:

✔ **Serve results from cache:** Previously obtained results are cached locally in order to fulfill equivalent requests more quickly later.

✔ **Balance the load:** The same service is provided by several machines that either work together to divide the total load or work independently.

Both solutions can be used when employing firewalls. Requested Web pages can be saved temporarily at the local disk of the firewall and can be used later when a request for the same Web page arrives at the firewall. Several machines may also be configured identically to provide the same firewall function but share the load between them. Several firewalls may even share one larger Web request cache.

In your network design, you may choose to separate the caching function from the firewall function by using separate caching server computers behind the firewall computers. In this section, we assume the caching of Web requests occurs on the firewall computer itself.

Caching Web results

A Web proxy service that is handling the Web requests from client computers can store the returned results (that is, Web page elements, such as graphics and text) locally on the disk. Subsequent queries for the same content can then be returned using the locally stored copy instead of going out to the Internet Web site again, which has two advantages:

✔ **Improved performance:** The firewall can return results to the requesting clients quicker.

✔ **Lower connection costs:** The connection to the Internet is used less often, which could mean cost savings on connections that have costs associated per used megabyte. You may even decide that a smaller bandwidth connection is sufficient.

Of course, the advantage from caching the results will be obtained only if users frequently access the same Web site.

An HTTP page can specify an expiration date in its code. The header of an HTTP page can also contain special information, called *meta tags,* that specify whether a specific page should or shouldn't be cached. The Web proxy service should obey those indications, which is especially important on Web pages that change frequently.

Certain Web pages will not normally be cached, including those that are encrypted by Secure Socket Layer (SSL and also HTTPS) or that contain user authentication data.

Many firewalls expand on the basic caching mechanism and try to improve the number of times a Web request can actually be served from the cache instead of having to go out to the Internet to get the content and making the user wait longer for a response. Some techniques that are used to improve caching hits are

- ✔ **Active caching:** The caching service actively downloads or refreshes content in the cache when the data is about to expire during times when the firewall is experiencing low activity. The decision to refresh the data in the cache can be based on how often the specific object was requested by users during the previous period. A firewall that does not actively refresh the contents is said to use passive caching.

- ✔ **Prefetch cache contents:** Instead of waiting for the users to initiate the request to get Web pages from the Internet, the caching service may prefetch content from frequently accessed Web sites and store those in the cache. Prefetching can be arranged to happen every morning before the users arrive at work. The firewall administrator must specify which Web sites should be prefetched. The content should be data that changes infrequently so it will still be valid when served from the cache during the day.

- ✔ **Hierarchical caching:** Several caching servers can form a hierarchy where the central firewall has a supercache that responds to queries from other firewalls. A common example is branch offices that each have a caching server. When the local cache of the branch office is unable to fulfill the Web request, it is forwarded to the central firewall, which has access to the Internet. Returned results are stored at the central cache for the benefit of other branch offices but are also stored at the cache of the local branch office.

- ✔ **Distributed caching:** This is perhaps the most important technique for improving cache performance. Instead of using a single cache of a certain size on one firewall, several firewalls work together to benefit from each other's cache. Unlike hierarchical caching, all participating firewalls play the same role but may not necessarily have the same cache size. Two well-known distributed caching mechanisms, Internet Cache Protocol (ICP), and Cache Array Routing Protocol (CARP), are described in the following sections.

Internet Cache Protocol (ICP)

The ICP caching mechanism assumes that each cache server in a group of cache servers works independently. When a request for a Web page arrives at a particular cache server, it first tries to fulfill the request from its own cache. If that fails, the cache server asks the other servers in the group *(siblings)* whether they have the requested object in cache. If the cache servers have the object in cache, the data is sent to the original cache server, which stores the result in its own cache and subsequently answers the user's request. If all cache servers in the group indicate that they do not have the object, the original cache server forwards the request to a higher cache server *(parent)* or obtains it directly from the Internet. In either situation, the results are cached at the original cache server.

The essential difference between an ICP request to a sibling cache server and a parent cache server is that the sibling may just answer "miss" if the object is not in its cache, whereas the parent goes out and gets the object itself if it is not present in the parent cache.

Cache Array Routing Protocol (CARP)

The CARP caching mechanism works differently than ICP. Instead of sending queries to all sibling cache servers in the group to determine who has the requested object in cache and then duplicating the returned object from the sibling cache server in the cache of the original cache server, CARP knows which sibling might contain the requested object or will contain the object after caching has occurred.

A cache server that uses CARP performs a mathematical calculation on the requested URL to determine which cache server in the group should handle and cache the request. That particular cache server is contacted and then gets and caches the object if it was not present in its cache already. The result is returned to the original cache server, where it is not being cached, but immediately forwarded to the requesting client computer. In this way, each object will only be in the total cache once, and the mathematical calculation can predict which cache server will contain the object for each URL used.

Web browsers at the client computer may even know the mathematical calculation itself and send the Web request to the correct cache server in the group directly.

The same caching mechanism used to cache content from Web pages on the Internet can be used for Web pages from Web servers behind the firewall being requested by users on the Internet. This is called *reverse caching*.

United we stand, dividing the load

Using a cache to store previously requested Web pages is one method that improves the performance of a firewall. Another method that fulfills the requests of users more quickly is to use more than one firewall in a group and let them work together by sharing the load of users' requests among them.

Grouping firewall computers and letting them work together has two benefits:

- ✔ **Improved performance:** The total number of users' requests is divided over the firewalls in the group. Each firewall is capable of processing its share of work more quickly than if only one firewall is handling all the users' requests.

- ✔ **Fault tolerance:** The redundancy of using more than one firewall to provide identical firewall functionality makes the system less dependent on one particular firewall computer. If one of the firewall computers is unavailable for some reason, the other firewall computers in the group take over its work.

In the previous section, we discuss ICP and CARP as mechanisms to share the caching load on cache servers in a group. The other methods used to share the total load on the firewall are

- ✔ **DNS round robin:** The DNS server is capable of registering several IP addresses for the same DNS name, for example 10.4.1.1 through 10.4.1.5. If a client computer asks the DNS server to resolve that DNS name to an IP address, the DNS server cycles through the list of IP addresses registered for that name and responds with a different IP address every time. Client computers that ask to resolve the computer name each connect to a different IP address. Each IP address should belong to a firewall server. The total number of connections to the DNS name are divided equally over the IP addresses listed in DNS. However, this scheme doesn't take into account how busy the firewall using that IP address actually is. In fact, when one of the firewalls is unavailable, the DNS server will happily refer a portion of the requested connections to the unavailable firewall.

- ✔ **Software load balancing:** Either implemented on the firewall servers itself or on a router just before the group of firewalls, the load-balancing software divides requested connections among the available firewalls. The software may even sense how busy a firewall is at a particular moment and divide the load based on this information.

If two or more firewalls are grouped together, they need to automatically divide the connections between them, and they need to be configured identically. This configuration should be done manually or by some sort of automatic synchronization mechanism. Most firewalls allow for automatic configuration. If firewalls are grouped, this automatic configuration should be repeated for each firewall.

Using Encryption to Prevent Modification or Inspection

Firewalls protect the inside network from the outside network by carefully inspecting the network traffic that travels between those two networks. If the firewall is configured correctly, no unwanted network traffic gets in from the outside network or leaves from the inside network, just like company policy wants it. So why do we need to introduce encryption?

The answer is simple. The firewall may do a good job of separating networks, but it cannot control or protect the network packets that travel on the internal network or the external network itself. Only when packets arrive at the firewall can the firewall inspect the traffic and either drop or allow the specific network packets. Encryption techniques are used to protect the network packets while they travel on the entire network. In this section, we look at the consequences these encryption techniques have on the functionality of the firewall.

Encryption and firewalls

You may think that encryption is used only to securely transfer information from one location to another, while preventing anyone who eavesdrops on the connection to read and understand what you send. This is the traditional view of encryption. However, encryption techniques are used for other purposes, all of which are relevant to firewalls.

- ✔ **Data confidentiality:** The classic use of encryption. The sender uses a secret combination of numbers — the key — to make normally readable information unreadable by anyone except for the people who know the specific key used to make the information readable again.

- ✔ **Authentication:** Data may be encrypted if it travels over the network, but if you are unsure who sent it, you may still not be able to trust the information. Authentication protocols establish the identity of the other party. Encryption techniques used by those authentication protocols make sure that identifying aspects, such as passwords, are not intercepted or merely recorded and replayed to gain access.

- ✔ **Data integrity:** Sometimes it's not important that everybody can read the information that is sent, but you want to be certain that the data that you receive is not changed by any intervening party. An encryption technique called *digital signatures* can be used to verify the integrity of receiving data. An example of this usage is a digitally signed device driver that you obtain from a download site on the Internet. As long as you can verify that the driver data was not modified after the vendor created it, it doesn't matter where you downloaded it from.

Several different encryption techniques (called *encryption protocols*) exist, implementing the functions mentioned earlier. Understanding the finer mathematics underlying each of those encryption protocols is not necessary.

Encryption may have the following effects on your firewall:

- ✔ **It renders your firewall unable to inspect data:** If you encrypt the information that you send so that other participants on the network are not able to read the data on its way to the destination, the firewall cannot decipher the content either when the network packets pass through the firewall. This is especially important when the firewall is supposed to make decisions based on the information in the packets.

- ✔ **Your firewall is unable to perform NAT:** Depending on the specific encryption protocol used to ensure the integrity of the data, the firewall may not be able perform network address translation on the packets. Normally, it replaces the source or destination IP addresses in the IP header and changes the TCP or UDP ports, which may break the integrity checksums used by the encryption protocol. The destination computer subsequently rejects the packet because it discovers that the packet has changed after it left the source computer.

  Another reason that the firewall may be unable to perform NAT is that some network protocols include the source or destination addresses in the application portion of the IP packet. If that portion is encrypted, the firewall can't find the addresses and replace those during the NAT process.

- ✔ **Your firewall can now provide a start or end point for VPN:** Because the firewall is the border between the internal network and the untrusted external network, it is a convenient place to initiate a Virtual Private Network (VPN) connection, or to be the receiving end point of a VPN connection. A VPN is an encrypted connection between two computers that allows private information to travel securely over an otherwise untrusted external network, such as the Internet. An example is a VPN connection over the Internet between two firewalls at different branch offices.

The actual firewall rules needed to allow authentication and VPN network traffic to, from, or even through a firewall are discussed in Chapter 8.

Who are you: Authentication protocols

Authentication protocols are used to tell a firewall which user is making a connection. If no authentication is done, the user is connected anonymously. Authentication is mandatory if you want to use firewall rules that apply to specific users or groups of users.

Because authentication involves "proof" in the form of a password or another secret that must not be known to others, encryption techniques are used to protect this authentication data.

Several well-known authentication protocols exist. Which protocol is used depends on the operating system and on the application that makes the connection to the firewall. Some authentication protocols, such as Basic Authentication, make use of the standard HTTP protocol; others, such as Kerberos, require special ports to be open.

The firewall may not be able to inspect authentication traffic that passes through the firewall. This is normally not a problem because it is commonly accepted that authentication traffic, such as a logon to a computer, is not supposed to reveal any passwords or other secrets that are coming from the user when the traffic passes the firewall. Of course, if the authentication is to the firewall itself, the firewall will be able to check the passwords or other secrets supplied by the user.

The use of encryption techniques to establish a user's identity is unrelated to the encryption of subsequent data transfer after the connection is made. In a normal situation, the authentication packets are encrypted in some form, while the subsequent data connection is unencrypted. Secure Sockets Layer (SSL), IPSec, and VPNs, which we discuss later in this chapter, involve encrypting the data portion of IP packets as well.

The S in HTTPS

Secure connections to the Internet can be established by using Secure Sockets Layer (SSL), or its very similar standardized variant, Transport Layer Security (TLS). This is an encryption protocol that can be combined with many conventional network protocols. The most common example is the use of SSL for HTTP connections. In the Web browser's address box, the use of SSL is indicated by URLs that start with `https://` rather than `http://`.

An HTTPS connection from a client on the internal network to a computer on the Internet can pass the firewall. SSL is an application-level network protocol, so the IP and TCP/UDP header of an IP packet are not encrypted and may be changed by the firewall without affecting the SSL-encrypted portion of the IP packets. The protocol does not store address information in the SSL-encrypted portion, so using NAT at the firewall should be no problem for SSL.

Because only the IP and TCP/UDP header of an SSL packet are not encrypted, the firewall can't inspect the application data portion of the packet. It can't store the returned results in the cache either, because it's impossible to determine whether the data portion (for example, the HTTP data) contains instructions for how long the data is valid or instructions not to cache the result at all. The information is probably encrypted for a good reason — it might contain credit card numbers as part of an e-commerce transaction, which is not data you want to place in the firewall cache.

IP and security: IPSec

The TCP/IP protocol was not designed with security in mind. When the protocol was originally designed, it was more important to provide working connectivity between university researchers and government agencies than to burden the design of TCP/IP with complicated encryption and security aspects. Remember that the initial designers did not set out to create the Internet from the get go but just a private network among friends to facilitate the quick exchange of research results.

When security and the use of TCP/IP became an issue (probably pretty soon after its conception), many application-level solutions to provide encryption support for authentication and data protection were developed. SSL for HTTP is one of those application-level protocols. Other solutions, such as Pretty Good Privacy (PGP) and Security Multipurpose Internet Mail Extensions (S/MIME) — both used for the encryption of e-mail messages — are tied in with other applications.

A more recent development is the use of the IP Security (IPSec) protocol. This protocol is not tied to a specific application but instead is implemented in the TCP/IP protocol itself. Any application network traffic or network protocol can be encrypted with IPSec.

IPSec supports two different methods to protect the IP packets. The Authentication Header (AH) method does not encrypt the data in the packet but only adds a cryptographic verification number, known as a checksum, to the IP packet, so that the destination computer can verify that the entire packet has arrived unchanged. The Encapsulating Security Payload (ESP) method encrypts almost the entire packet. The IP header is not encrypted, so routers can still read the destination IP address. The two methods can also be used together.

IPSec uses its own set of rules to determine what network traffic should be encrypted. Connections that start or end at the firewall itself are governed by the IPSec rules defined at the firewall. They should not cause a problem with the firewall's filtering or NAT capabilities.

Marriage of IPSec and NAT?

IPSec is well received among Internet connoisseurs. The protocol has become a standard and is described in many RFC documents. The fact that IPSec is application- and user-independent, has a flexible rule-based configuration, and can be used with many existing standard encryption methods has caused many software vendors and firewall vendors to replace other encryption techniques and implement IPSec support.

At the same time, NAT is really cool, too. It enables internal networks to conveniently use private IP addresses and provides security by not revealing the internal IP address structure. Unfortunately, IPSec's protection methods cannot be combined with NAT's IP and port translation work.

Well, never fear. This is about to change. Work is underway to let these two useful IP technologies work together.

Windows XP and Windows Server 2003 already contain a solution for combining IPSec and NAT. The IPSec protocol is extended to detect the presence of NAT between the client and the server and, if detected, to use a smart trick to let the IPSec-encrypted data pass through the NAT firewall.

What happens is that the original IPSec packet, whose IP address and port information cannot be changed, is placed inside another packet. This other packet is not protected by IPSec, and so can pass through a NAT firewall without harm. When the packet gets to the other side, the receiving end obtains the original IPSec packet — unchanged — from the arriving packet.

This only works if both sides of the IPSec conversation know this trick, which is called NAT Detection (NAT-D) and NAT Traversal (NAT-T). The NAT firewall in between does not need to know about this extension to IPSec.

However, IPSec connections that are intended to pass through the firewall are different. The firewall can't inspect IP packets that are encrypted by IPSec ESP. IP packets protected by IPSec AH can be read by the firewall.

The AH method protects the source and destination IP address in the IP header of a packet, so firewalls that perform NAT can't handle IPSec AH traffic. The ESP method does not protect the IP header, but the TCP or UDP portion that contains the port information is encrypted. Normally NAT changes the port information, so firewalls cannot perform NAT on IPSec ESP traffic either.

Virtual Private Networks (VPNs)

IPSec is one method to encrypt the contents of data that is sent from one computer to another. A similar approach is the use of a Virtual Private Network (VPN). A VPN is an agreement between two computers, separated by a public network, such as the Internet, to encrypt all IP packets destined for the internal network behind the other computer.

Three VPN scenarios are related to firewalls:

- A VPN connection between two firewalls. A typical usage is a VPN connection between two branch offices.

- A VPN connection from a computer on the Internet to the firewall. This is the situation where a laptop user on the road uses a VPN connection over the Internet to dial into the office.

- A VPN connection from a computer on the internal network or the Internet connecting through the firewall. This is often put in place when a user on the internal network needs to create a connection to a VPN server on the Internet.

VPN between two firewalls

A common scenario is a VPN connection between two firewalls at different branch offices of a company. All network traffic from one branch office to the other branch office is encrypted at the firewall and sent securely to the other firewall over the public Internet. The two internal networks are connected as if a dedicated private link between the two branch offices is used. In reality, a true private link is not in place, but instead, an encrypted connection over a public network is used, hence the name, *virtual private network*.

In the scenario of a VPN between two firewalls at different branch offices, a client computer with private IP address 10.80.7.5 in one office may use a private IP address, such as 10.65.1.2, to address a computer in the other branch office. Of course, those private source and destination IP addresses cannot be used when the IP packet travels over the Internet. The NAT component at the firewall can replace a private source IP address on outbound network traffic and substitute the original IP address on the returned response, but it can't handle the situation when both the source and destination IP address are of the private kind. This is where the VPN agreement between the two branch office firewalls comes into play. Instead of using NAT, the VPN software adds another IP header with a public address of the other firewall in front of all IP packets destined for the other branch office. At the other end of the VPN connection, the additional IP header is removed again, and the original IP header with destination IP address 10.65.1.2 is used to travel the last leg on the other branch office's internal network. A similar procedure is performed when the response is sent back.

Adding an IP header in front of an IP packet is called *encapsulation*. All packets traveling over the VPN connection are wrapped with this additional IP header.

A VPN connection is also called a *VPN tunnel* and is shown in Figure 4-2.

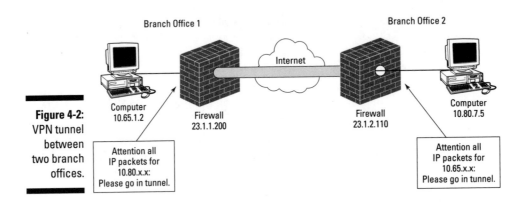

Figure 4-2:
VPN tunnel
between
two branch
offices.

In contrast with the way IPSec works (various IPSec rules specify which encryption method is used for different IP packets), a VPN solution looks only at the destination IP address of a packet and uses the same encryption on all packets that are wrapped with an additional IP header and sent using the VPN connection.

Because the firewalls are start and end points of the VPN connection in this scenario, the normal IP packet inspection at the firewalls can still occur. Firewall rules can be set up to specifically allow only VPN network packets from the other branch office.

Creating such an open VPN tunnel to another branch office extends the size of the internal network on both branch offices. If the other network is broken into, the attacker can essentially jump through the VPN tunnel and attack all branch offices as if he were inside each internal network already. Additional restrictive packet filters or even intrusion detection triggers on the VPN connection can minimize this risk.

VPN from the Internet to the firewall

Very similar to the two connecting branch offices is the scenario in which a computer on the Internet, such as a company user on the road with his laptop or a telecommuter using her home computer, creates a VPN connection to the company firewall (see Figure 4-3). The purpose of the VPN connection is to dial in securely to the office over the Internet.

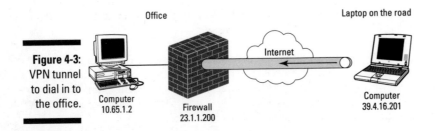

Figure 4-3:
VPN tunnel
to dial in to
the office.

In this situation, the VPN connection will not be initiated by the firewall but by the computer on the Internet without a fixed IP address. This means that firewall rules cannot be as specific as was the case when two branch offices created a VPN connection. On the other hand, it is even more important now to realize that the internal network is extended by this newly created VPN connection. The laptop computer on the Internet or the home computer dialing in to the office are now part of the internal network! This creates a specific vulnerability where attackers may use the current Internet connection of the laptop or home computer to connect to those computers and then use the VPN tunnel to jump right into the company network. Additional firewall configuration, such as restrictive firewall rules, is a must here.

VPN through the firewall

In the third scenario, the firewall is not the start or end point of the VPN tunnel, but instead the VPN connection runs through the firewall. (See Figure 4-4.) Examples of this situation are a computer on the internal network that creates a VPN connection to a VPN server on the Internet. This can be done to create a secure connection to a business partner.

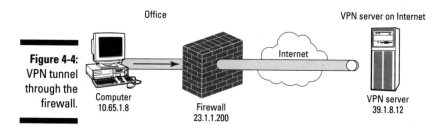

Figure 4-4:
VPN tunnel through the firewall.

Office   VPN server on Internet

Internet

Computer
10.65.1.8

Firewall
23.1.1.200

VPN server
39.1.8.12

One major difference between the other two scenarios and this scenario is that the firewall is unable to inspect the network traffic that passes in the VPN tunnel through the firewall. This is similar to the restrictions that are caused by other encryption techniques, such as SSL connections through the firewall.

If the firewall uses NAT, another important distinction between the earlier scenarios is present. When NAT is used, the start and end point of the VPN tunnel can no longer just route IP packets though the tunnel but needs the help of the NAT component of the firewall to translate the source and destination IP address of the IP packets. Not all VPN protocols allow this translation to occur.

The two main VPN protocols are Point-to-Point Tunneling Protocol (PPTP) and Layer Two Tunneling Protocol (L2TP). PPTP does not protect the IP header and therefore allows IP address translations when the packets pass the firewall. L2TP uses IPSec to protect the packets. IPSec may not allow NAT changes to the packets when they pass the firewall.

However, if both the client computer and the server computer understand the IPSec over NAT extension described in the "Marriage of IPSec and NAT" sidebar earlier in this chapter, then they can also use L2TP, which uses IPSec for encryption, through a NAT firewall.

The actual firewall rules needed to allow VPN network traffic to, from, and through a firewall are discussed in Chapter 8.

Chapter 5

"The Key Is under the Mat" and Other Common Attacks

*H*ackers — we all know they're out there, and we also know that they're out to get us. Every week it seems we hear something about yet another network attack or a new virus spreading over the Internet and causing computer problems.

You know that you have to protect yourself, but before you can do anything, you have to know exactly what the dangers are. The better informed you are, the easier it will be for you to assess each threat that you encounter and protect yourself against these threats. This chapter helps you to understand the most common types of attacks. Don't worry — we don't get into the gory technical details of each type of attack, but we do examine each of the most common attack types. Armed with this knowledge, you can assess what type of defense may be best suited for each attack.

Intrusion Attacks: A Stranger in the House

The most feared type of attack is an intrusion from outside the organization, where someone breaks into your network and gets access to your computers. An intrusion is also the most obvious type of attack, and almost everyone who considers installing a firewall initially does so to prevent unauthorized access to the internal network. Before you look at *who* would want to get unauthorized access to your computers, look at *why* an intruder might want access to your computers:

✔ **Confidential data:** This includes anything from sensitive financial data to the blueprints of your next confidential engineering project. You'd be surprised to know who might be interested in this information. For example, this person may be a competitor or a hacker who plans to sell the data about your new perpetual motion machine. Sometimes hackers try to access confidential data just to show off their technical prowess — to show their friends that they went where they weren't supposed to go. Cases have also been reported of foreign intelligence services trying to garner confidential data about projects that might help companies in their country. Although only a few companies need to worry about a snoop from a foreign country robbing them of their intellectual property, remember that interest in confidential data may come from expected as well as unexpected sources.

✔ **Customer data:** Many companies store data about their customers on their corporate network. Obviously, this information could be useful to the company's competition. It may also prove useful to a hacker who doesn't care much about your customer list per se but rather about information related to customer payments — primarily, credit card numbers. Some hackers have been known to go on shopping sprees using credit card numbers that were stolen from company sites via the Internet. And some hackers specialize in stealing credit card information from company Web sites and extorting money from these companies in exchange for not telling the affected customers that this company neglected to secure their customer data sufficiently.

✔ **Computer resources:** Hackers may be interested in taking over your company's resources for their own use. The computing power of your computers may be just what the hackers want because their computer is not sufficient for a task that they are trying to perform.

✔ **A way to hide their tracks:** Hackers may actually want to break into someone else's computer (not yours), but they don't want to get caught. A good way to perform this type of intrusion is to launch that attack from someone else's computer (yours). After a hacker has taken control of one of your computers, he is able to launch the next attack from there. If he gets caught, all the tracks point to you, and you will probably have to do some explaining when attacks on another computer system appear to originate from your network.

If you detect someone breaking into your computer systems, and you are able to track down the source of this attack, remember that this source may be a computer that has been commandeered by a hacker located somewhere else.

Regularly audit the activity on all your computers to detect whether illegitimate activity occurs on any of them. Although many network administrators log activity on computers, doing an accurate audit involves actually reviewing those logs on a regular basis and investigating any unusual activity or unexpected configuration changes.

Joyriding

A few years ago, a car belonging to one of the authors of the book you're holding in your hands was stolen, and a day later it was found a short distance from his house with no damage to it other than broken locks. The police told him that, apparently, someone just stole it to ride around in it for an hour or two. It was a classic case of joyriding. Similarly, some hackers break into corporate networks for joyriding. Breaking into a computer system presents a challenge, and if the hacker successfully breaks into a secured network, he may feel like he has accomplished something, and he can brag to his friends about his accomplishments. Breaking into computer systems as a sport may seem relatively harmless, but it is akin to a burglar entering your house without stealing anything — it is still illegal, and it still violates the rights of the owner.

Denial-of-service Attacks

A denial-of-service attack makes a service that a computer provides unavailable. For example, in early 2001, users all over the Internet were unable to connect to Microsoft's Web servers. Many people were wondering what happened. Actually, all of the Web servers were up and running, but nobody was able to connect to them. The problem had multiple causes, including the fact that a hacker or a group of hackers attacked the network that contained Microsoft's Domain Name System (DNS) servers. Because users could not connect to the DNS servers, these servers were unable to direct anyone to Microsoft's Web site, which caused legitimate users to be denied access.

Any type of attack that is designed to prevent the legitimate use of a computer resource is referred to as a denial-of-service attack; sometimes it is abbreviated as DoS. Some types of denial-of-service attacks include preventing users from making a connection, crashing a computer, or overloading a computer with so many connections that it can't answer any legitimate connection requests.

Denial-of-service attacks can even be unintentional. A computer worm, known as SQL Slammer, rapidly spread around the world one Saturday morning in January 2003. This worm was designed to do only one thing: spread as rapidly as possible. In the process of doing this, it also created so much network traffic that it slowed down all other Internet traffic and even prevented people from using ATMs that depend on communicating with a central computer.

A denial-of-service attack comes in many variations. It may target a single computer, or it may prevent access to an entire network of computers. DoS may mean shutting down a Web server or overloading a network connection with too much traffic. No matter how large the scope of a denial-of-service attack, in each case, it is intended to prevent legitimate users from accessing network resources that they are allowed to access.

Don't forget to protect yourself against the ultimate denial-of-service attack: theft of equipment. Imagine the surprise of a network administrator whose users can't access the e-mail server because someone broke into the office and stole the server. In your haste to implement high-tech security solutions, such as a firewall, don't forget old-fashioned, low-tech solutions, such as locks on your doors.

When everyone is out to get you: Distributed DoS attacks

A distributed denial-of-service (DDoS) attack takes the denial-of-service attack one step further. Sometimes a denial-of-service attack involves overwhelming the target computer with so much network traffic that it can't respond to legitimate connection requests. As you can imagine, generating enough network traffic to do this can be a challenge. However, if enough hackers band together and coordinate their actions, or if a hacker is able to commandeer enough computers, then the hackers may be successful in generating enough traffic to make it impossible for the target of the attack to keep up with it. Because such an attack is launched from multiple computers that are most likely distributed all across the Internet, such an attack is called a distributed denial-of-service, or DDoS attack.

How Hackers Get In

Hackers have a number of ways to get into computers and networks. Most operating systems and other programs have vulnerabilities, and it is only a matter of time before someone discovers them. This section explores some of the most common techniques that hackers use to attack computer systems.

The key is under the mat: Insecure passwords

Before looking at some of the more sophisticated techniques that hackers use to break into your network, you should realize that most intrusions are made possible by simple carelessness. Just as burglars find it easy to break into a house whose occupant has placed the key under the doormat, breaking into a network is easy if you use passwords that are easy to guess, such as the word *password,* a blank password, or the default password provided by a standard software installation. Before you start worrying about sophisticated high-tech methods that hackers can use to break into your network, you should consider all the simple flaws in your system, such as insecure passwords, that may represent even greater vulnerabilities. This should go without saying, but *never* write down a password anywhere. If you have, please correct this habit immediately because it presents a severe security risk.

You can follow many guidelines for selecting secure passwords. A good rule is to choose a password that is easy to remember but difficult to guess. A good password may be based on a combination of the name of a childhood pet and the phone number of a distant relative. Both of these facts are difficult for people to guess, but you remember the components of the password quite readily.

You also have to consider what automated password-cracking programs can do. Hackers may intercept a network transmission that contains data that has been encrypted with a password, or they may intercept logon traffic to a computer that includes a user name and corresponding password. After a hacker has this information, he will try to "crack," or guess, the password. Often this process involves using a program that tries to guess the password, first by trying every word in the dictionary, then by trying any possible combination of characters. Because computers can guess hundreds or even thousands of passwords per second, automating this procedure is much more efficient than manually typing in a large number of guessed passwords.

The only way to protect yourself against a brute-force password-cracking attack is to select a password that is sufficiently complex so that the password can't be found in a reasonable amount of time. You can do this by selecting a long password (seven characters or longer) and by using a combination of different characters (uppercase and lowercase characters, numbers, special characters). You should also change all your passwords on a regular basis in order to minimize the amount of time that a hacker has to crack a password and the amount of time that he or she can use the password.

Default configurations

Surprisingly, many software default configurations contain potential security vulnerabilities. One reason for these vulnerabilities is that software vendors often place a priority on making their products easy to use, and as a result, security may take a back seat. Also, vendors often feel pressure to get new software or hardware to the market, whether it has been sufficiently checked for security flaws or not.

Another problem with default configurations is that they are easy to predict. For example, some database programs ship with a default user account and password to administer the database. Because this username and password are the same for everyone who installs such a program, they are easy to predict. Unless you specifically change such settings, hackers can use these predictable settings to attack most instances of this database. Sometimes you can protect yourself against weaknesses in default installations by changing some defaults, such as a blank password that is used for an administrative account. Sometimes you need to apply security fixes that a vendor has made available after the product was released. You can get information about security fixes from software vendors. You can also refer to some of the resources listed in Chapter 20.

Bugs

In a perfect world, all software would be flawless. Unfortunately, we don't live in a perfect world, and built-in errors, or *bugs,* in computer software or hardware are a fact of life. If you've ever had a program crash while you were in the middle of doing some important work, you know how annoying bugs are. With the complexity of today's software, it is almost unavoidable to have any software without bugs. Hackers can use bugs in programs to get these programs to crash — which constitutes a denial-of-service attack — or to get unauthorized access to a computer.

A real-life DDoS attack: Meet Mafiaboy

One morning in February 2000, many people who tried to go to some high-profile Web sites, such as Yahoo.com or CNN.com, could not connect to these sites for about four hours. The Web sites simply didn't respond. For most people, this was simply an annoyance, but the cost to the Web sites' owners was significant. Not only did they lose revenue because customers took their business elsewhere, but they (and the companies that maintain the Internet's infrastructure) also had to assign a large number of employees to track down the problem. Companies ended up spending thousands of hours and hundreds of thousands of dollars trying to stop this attack. Over the next few days, the details of this story emerged: These companies were victims of a distributed denial-of-service attack. Several weeks later, investigators identified the culprit, a Canadian teenager who calls himself Mafiaboy when communicating with other hackers on the Internet.

Mafiaboy had spent several months breaking into computers all over the Internet. On each of these computers he installed a program that, when he started it, went out to the Internet and flooded a Web server with a large number of requests. Although a single one of these computers can't generate enough traffic to accomplish a denial-of-service attack, a large number of them attacking simultaneously can — and Mafiaboy had commandeered hundreds or thousands of them. After boasting to his friends that he could single-handedly bring down a number of Web sites, Mafiaboy activated the program on all the computers he had commandeered, and within hours his attack had become one of the top news stories of the day.

Ironically, Mafiaboy's boastings of his deeds in hacker forums on the Internet led the Royal Canadian Mounted Police and the FBI directly to him, resulting in a sentence of eight months in juvenile detention for his attack.

What color is your hat?

Hackers come in all kinds, and it is difficult to classify them. However, over the years, a distinction has developed that tries to separate the "good hackers" from the "bad hackers." Hackers with benign intentions are referred to as the *white hats,* and hackers with sinister intentions are referred to as the *black hats* — evoking images of the *Mad* magazine *Spy vs. Spy* comic strip. The black hats are what we commonly think of when we refer to hackers. These are the people who break into other people's computers, either to access data illegitimately or to joyride. The white hats, on the other hand, are the ones who study security vulnerabilities in order to learn how to protect computer systems. These white-hat hackers may be security professionals at corporations and government agencies who stay up-to-date on security vulnerabilities. White hats study hacking techniques to keep hackers out of computer systems. While most white-hat hackers have the same desire to find new security vulnerabilities that black-hat hackers have, white hats use the knowledge that they gain to protect computer systems, not to attack them. Sometimes, however, it can be difficult to distinguish a black hat from a white hat; in fact, it looks gray. For example, what color is the hat of a hacker who destroys another hacker's data in order to protect the innocent?

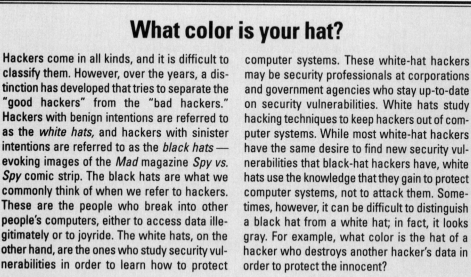

One type of bug that hackers exploit is a *buffer overflow*. A buffer-overflow condition can exist when a program allows a user to enter data and set aside a limited amount of space for the data that the user enters. This temporary holding area for data is referred to as a *buffer*. A well-written program checks the length of the data that is entered and rejects any user-entered data that is longer than the buffer. A badly written program accepts data that exceeds the maximum allowed length. When a user enters data into a badly designed program and the data exceeds the maximum allowed data length for the buffer, the program overwrites data that is located in the computer's memory that is adjacent to the buffer. Writing arbitrary data to your computer's memory can have a number of results, from crashing your computer to inserting another program into your computer that could give an intruder unlimited access to the computer. For example, you may be able to send an extremely long command to a Web server that causes a buffer overflow on that server. Hackers have found ways to exploit buffer overflow bugs in order to crash or take control of computers. Fortunately, most software vendors nowadays are much better at checking their software for buffer overflows than they used to be, but buffer overflows still occur on a regular basis.

Bugs are a fact of life, but most reputable software and hardware vendors review their products based on customer feedback and their own testing, and then release bug fixes shortly after a vulnerability has been detected. Of course, there is no guarantee that a hacker has not found the bug before the vendor has released a fix, but by promptly applying any newly released security fixes, you can preempt most hackers. Most successful intrusion attacks take advantage of known security flaws for which fixes are available but not implemented because administrators of the affected systems were too busy or too uninformed to do so. Virtually every computer attack over the last few years that you have read about could have been prevented if people had updated their computers. Code Red, Nimda, SQL Slammer, and many other attacks exploited computer bugs for which fixes were available when the attacks occurred.

Most people in the security community who look for vulnerabilities for academic purposes or to stay ahead of hackers abide by an unwritten rule: Anyone who discovers a bug in a product should always contact the product's vendor first and give the vendor an opportunity to develop a fix for the bug before announcing it publicly. This means that the details of a security flaw are often announced only after a fix has been made available. However, unscrupulous hackers won't share flaws that they discover with the vendor but try to exploit such flaws for their own gain.

Back doors

Some software developers have been known to leave *back doors* in their products. A back door is a way to get into the program by bypassing certain security features; for example, by including a hidden user account with a high level of privileges. A back door may be used during the software development process to bypass some security settings and to get easy access to some program features that should be restricted during normal operations. Unscrupulous programmers may leave a back door for themselves so they can get unauthorized access to the program after a customer is running it. Some unscrupulous programmers have been known to leave a back door in a program they developed for a client so that they can disable the program in the event of a dispute with the client. After a programmer has created a back door, a hacker may discover it and use it to access a computer system. Fortunately, such back doors are becoming increasingly rare.

Another kind of back door is also becoming increasingly widespread. Programs such as NetBus and BackOrifice are essentially remote-control programs that allow a hacker to gain complete access to your computer over the network without you knowing about it. Such programs may record every keystroke on your keyboard, or network traffic to and from your computer. You may wonder how such back-door programs get on your computer in the first place. In most cases, a computer virus or a Trojan horse program places them there. The next section explains how these types of programs operate and why they create serious security dangers.

Hard-to-crack passwords

How complex does a password have to be? The answer to this question really depends on the possible characters that comprise the password, and how many characters the password contains. If you only use the 26 characters of the English alphabet and your password is only 2 characters long, then you have only 676 (26 to the power of 2) possible passwords. A password-cracking computer program can guess any password of this length that you create from two letters in a fraction of a second. If you choose your password from both lowercase and uppercase characters, numbers, the ten number keys, and the 32 special characters on your keyboard, such as the comma and the asterisk, then the number of distinct passwords increases to 9,216 (96 to the power of 2), which is still a low number. However, if you make sure that the password consists of at least 7 characters, then the number of possible combinations increases to over 75 trillion, or to be exact — 75,144,747,810,816 (96 to the power of 7). It would take a hacker over 2,300 years to try every possible combination if the password-cracking program tried 1,000 possible passwords every second. Using a very powerful computer that tried one million passwords every second, it would still take 2.3 years. If you change your password every month or two, the password will most likely be different by the time the hacker has cracked it.

It's a zoo: Viruses, worms, and Trojan horses

It seems that not a day goes by that we don't hear about a new computer virus. It sounds scary — and indeed it is. Before we explore the dangers of viruses, worms, and Trojan horses, take a closer look at what exactly these animals are.

- ✔ **Viruses:** A virus is a computer program that is designed to spread itself from one file to another. The effect can range from benign to catastrophic. A virus may just spread itself and never have any other effect. More likely, a virus makes itself noticed in a variety of ways, ranging from displaying a message from the virus's creator to destroying data on your disk. Viruses have a variety of ways to spread from file to file. A few years ago, the most common method of spreading a virus was by sharing floppy disks. If the floppy disk contained an infected program and the recipient ran the program, the disk infected other programs or the system area of a floppy disk. The file or the disk may then be shared with other individuals and infect files on their computers. With the advent of the Internet and the popularity of e-mail, floppy disks are no longer the most common means of virus transmission. Files can be exchanged much more easily and sent to a much larger number of people in e-mail or via file downloads. These new ways to spread viruses have made them a much greater threat than they used to be.

- ✔ **Worms:** Worms are similar to viruses. They also spread, but instead of spreading from file to file, they spread from computer to computer. Worms also have a method of copying themselves to other computers, either by connecting to other computers over a network or by e-mail. Sometimes worms even do so without any human intervention, and sometimes the main purpose of a worm is actually to infect as many computers as possible and to spread as rapidly as possible, rather than to destroy data. Nimda, Code Red, and SQL Slammer are some of the most well-known worms.

- ✔ **Trojan horses:** A Trojan horse, just like the wooden creature in the old Greek saga, comes as a gift that contains something unexpected. Just as the Trojans were too excited about their gift horse to look it in the mouth, all of us tend to be trusting — too trusting at times. Someone who designs a Trojan horse program preys on this trust by packaging a nasty surprise inside a program that looks interesting to someone who receives it. Suppose that someone sends you a program that plays a funny cartoon on your computer. After you get a good laugh out of it, you forward this program to your friends, who forward it even further. However, while you were laughing at the cartoon, the program also modified your computer. Not only did it install a back-door program that allows others to access and control your computer over the Internet, it also announced the availability of your computer to the author of the program by sending a message to him. The much-publicized "Love Bug" virus and a virus named after the Russian tennis star Anna Kournikova are examples of Trojan horses.

Viruses, worms, and Trojan horses have one thing in common: Someone created them by writing a computer program. Although users can spread these critters inadvertently, they are created on purpose. The purpose may be to prove programming prowess, vandalism, or a number of other things.

Do you have an antivirus program installed on your computer? How about your mail server or your firewall? You should screen for viruses in all of these locations. A number of programs are available to do this. You can find information about these programs on the Web sites of vendors that provide these solutions, such as Symantec (www.symantec.com), McAfee (www.mcafee.com), or Trend Micro (www.antivirus.com). No matter what antivirus software you use, make sure that you regularly update the virus definitions. If the definitions on your computer are outdated, the antivirus program can't detect the newest viruses.

Who are you? Man-in-the-middle attacks

One type of network attack, referred to as a *man-in-the-middle attack,* involves intercepting a legitimate connection between two computers and then hijacking this connection. Often, after a user has established a connection to a server, the server assumes that all network traffic that arrives over this connection originates from the user who established the connection. When a file or other resource is accessed, access is granted based on that user's privileges. Some network attacks involve listening in on the connection and then sending network packets to the server. In these network packets, the hacker's computer impersonates the original computer. If such an attack is successful, the intruder gets all the access that the original user was granted. Fortunately, man-in-the-middle attacks require significant technical sophistication and are not easily accomplished.

Impersonation

Impersonation involves a computer or a Web site that is run by a hacker but that appears to be another Web site. For example, a hacker may create a Web site that looks like a popular shopping Web site that collects users' names and payment information as users are entering them on the Web site. Other impersonation attacks may involve the collection of usernames and passwords. Redirecting a user to a different Web site can be accomplished by changing information on DNS servers, by getting someone to click an innocent-looking link on a Web site, or by a number of other methods. Fortunately, successfully impersonating other computer systems is not easily accomplished and requires a lot of effort.

Eavesdropping

One technique that intruders use to attack you involves eavesdropping on network traffic. Network protocols that use cleartext transmission to send a password, such as the File Transfer Protocol (FTP), are most susceptible to eavesdropping. Most networks rely on shared media, in which any computer connected to the network cable can potentially listen in on all network traffic that goes across the network cable. Unless this network traffic is encrypted, anyone with sinister intentions can record the network packets that are exchanged between other computers. This allows anyone with physical access to a network segment to eavesdrop on the network traffic that flows across this segment. This may include users inside your organization or someone who can plug a computer into a network connection that's located in unattended locations, such as a lobby or an unoccupied conference room.

Outside intruders may also get access to your network in order to eavesdrop. Often, outside access occurs by getting a legitimate user to inadvertently run a program that sends recorded network traffic to the hacker. In many cases, the employee is not even aware that this is happening. A virus or a Trojan horse program installed the listening program.

Even out on the Internet, someone may be listening in on network traffic between your computer and a computer on the Internet. Because of the distributed nature of the Internet, you have no guarantee that someone else does not intercept an e-mail message or an interaction with a Web server. The only way to guarantee that no stranger is eavesdropping is to encrypt the conversation. Encryption techniques depend on the technology used, such as a Web server or e-mail. If you ever send confidential information, it's worth investigating the encryption solutions that are available.

Eavesdropping becomes even more of a risk when wireless networks are involved. Companies have found hackers parked in cars in the company's parking lot eavesdropping on wireless network traffic. Wireless networks are easy prey to hackers with a laptop computer and a Pringles potato chip can that has been converted into a cheap but effective antenna. We know someone who was able to receive wireless transmissions more than a mile away from the building where they originated; his setup utilized a baby-formula container as an antenna. Companies that install wireless networks without implementing encryption and access control lose valuable data every day.

Whenever you send any confidential information across the Internet, encrypt your confidential network traffic by using one of the methods described in Chapter 4 or by using an encryption program to encrypt the information before sending it. You can also use an alternative to transmitting this information over a network, such as using the telephone or hand-delivering a printed document. Unless you know for sure that you are using encryption to send information, assume that someone else may read this information. Although it is unlikely that this will really happen, it is a good practice to assume the worst, especially when the information that you are sending can cause monetary damage or embarrassment if it ends up in the wrong hands.

Inside jobs

Firewalls are a great way to protect your network from dangers that originate from the Internet and to keep intruders out. However, relying on a firewall as your only protection can give you a false sense of security. Remember that your network faces other kinds of threats, and one of these threats comes from legitimate users who are doing illegitimate things. This could be someone trying to look into a co-worker's files without being allowed to do so. It could also be a user who brings in a program from home that — unbeknownst to the user — creates a back door into your computer network. As important as it is to have a firewall that protects your network, just remember that even a well-designed firewall can't protect against some threats.

Other techniques

Hackers can use a wide range of other techniques to get into your network, and some of them are not as obvious as others. No matter how well you understand certain types of threats, remember that numerous others exist, including some that have not even been discovered yet.

I Love You!

Don't worry; this is not a confession of love from us to you. It is the name of a worm that spread like wildfire across the Internet within a matter of just a few hours on May 4, 2000. After being set loose by a student in the Philippines, the I Love You worm infected hundreds of thousands of computers on the Internet with unprecedented speed. Users found a message with the subject line ILOVEYOU in their e-mail inbox. Inside the message was an attachment entitled LOVE-LETTER-FOR-YOU.TXT.vbs. When a recip- ient who used Outlook to read the message opened the attachment, the worm proceeded to overwrite files on the user's computer. Moreover, the worm used Outlook to send copies of itself to all addresses in the affected person's address book. In addition to the damage to the affected computers, the I Love You worm, sometimes also called the Love Bug virus, created enough e-mail traffic to clog up many corporate mail servers.

Social engineering, for example, is a term that refers to tricking people into giving access when they shouldn't or getting people to share information that they shouldn't share. Suppose that you are doing your desk job at MegaCorp, and one day you get a call from Fred Smith, who identifies himself as a manager in the Information Technology department. According to Fred, someone broke into MegaCorp's user account database and stole some passwords. Unfortunately, your password was one of them, and Fred needs you to change your password right away. To make sure that the new password is complex enough to provide sufficient security, Fred suggests a new password for you. Of course you are happy to help Fred secure your company's network. You change your password to the one that Fred suggests, and you soon forget about this call. At the same time, a hacker across town tells his friends about how he pretended to be Fred Smith to get a password from an unsuspecting user at MegaCorp. He then proceeds to use this password to dial into MegaCorp's network and dig for data that interests him.

Some hackers have found that they can hide their tracks by creating false alarms. Many organizations have methods to detect intrusion attempts and to alert a network administrator. Some hackers have found weaknesses in such systems and perform activities to create thousands of "false positives," thus hiding their activity among the many false alarms. The challenge for the network administrator is to find out which attack is the real one.

Can a Firewall Really Protect Me?

Does a firewall protect you against the threats we described in this chapter? The answer is not straightforward. A firewall is indeed a very effective method of protection against many of these threats, but not all of them. Remember that a firewall is placed between your internal network and the

Internet. A correctly configured firewall can prevent unauthorized traffic from entering your network and keep data from leaving your network. These two functions can prevent hackers from accessing computers on your network and from stealing data from your network, and they may even prevent computer viruses from making it into your network. However, a firewall does not protect you against attacks that bypass your firewall, such as a hacker who walks into your office building or an employee who inadvertently brings a computer virus to work on an infected floppy disk.

Are You Scared Yet?

Are you scared after reading about all the ways that can be used to attack your computer network? You should be — but don't be paralyzed by fear. With the knowledge that you gain from this book, you are well prepared to anticipate dangers to your network. Now that you know the dangers, you can prepare to protect yourself against attacks that hackers may launch against your network and create defenses against break-ins and other dangers. Just knowing the dangers that you face is the first step in developing a strategy to defend your network from an attack. The next step is to plan your defenses. The remainder of this book guides you in implementing a firewall solution. As you implement a solution, don't neglect to protect your network from attacks that a firewall can't prevent.

Legitimate eavesdropping: Listening in on your own conversations

Sometimes it makes sense to record network traffic on your own network for troubleshooting purposes. Other times, you may have to closely examine network traffic to find out exactly how a network protocol is working. Tools that allow you to do this are called *protocol analyzers* or *packet sniffers.* Chapter 19 introduces several of these tools. If you need to use a protocol analyzer, make sure that you do it on your own network or, if you use it on another network (including the network at your workplace), make sure that the owner of that network has given you permission to use such a tool. Serious privacy concerns are involved in sniffing network traffic, and most network administrators treat any instance of unauthorized sniffing as a serious attack on their network. A few years ago, we installed a protocol analyzer on a computer that was connected to a test network. By mistake, we connected this test network to the main corporate network. Within a few hours, one of us received a call from a network administrator who quizzed him about why he was eavesdropping on the corporate network. After he explained to the network administrator that we were using this tool for legitimate purposes and convinced the administrator that we connected it to the corporate network by mistake, the administrator let us off the hook, but only after we promised to read the entire corporate Security policy.

Part II
Establishing Rules

The 5th Wave — By Rich Tennant

"Yes, I know – 'Fire, BAD!'. However, that's not entirely why I'm building a firewall."

In this part . . .

Rules rule! That's a quick summary of this part. A firewall by itself doesn't do much. You have to tell it what kind of network traffic is allowed to come into your network from the Internet, and what traffic is allowed to go out.

This part shows you how to set up the firewall rules that describe what the firewall should do. Do you want to send e-mail through the Internet? Do you want to surf the Web, but don't want hackers to surf your computer? Create the correct firewall rules to specify what you want.

Chapter 6

Developing Policies

●●●

In This Chapter

▶ Creating an Internet Acceptable Use policy

▶ Creating a Security policy

▶ Using the policy documents to configure your firewall

●●●

*Y*ou can't configure a firewall to protect your company network unless you know what network traffic is allowed and what is disallowed. A good way to identify these security concerns is by creating two policy documents:

✓ **Internet Acceptable Use policy:** This policy identifies what actions are considered acceptable when users access the Internet. More specifically, the Internet Acceptable Use policy spells out for users the do's and don'ts for Internet access.

✓ **Security policy:** This policy defines the resources that a company deems important enough to secure. The security policy describes the company's plan of action for security. It should define what needs to be protected and what actions must be taken in order to protect the resources. For employees, the security policy defines what is important to the company and what therefore must be secured from attackers.

The Internet Acceptable Use policy document and the Security policy document serve three major purposes:

✓ For network users, the policies define what is and isn't allowed on the network. Understanding these policies is essential in order to avoid a lot of problems with Internet usage. Possible issues include sending out company-sensitive information or the consequences of opening suspicious e-mail attachments.

✓ For the company, the policies constitute an agreement between the company and the users about allowed actions and consequences, and serve as a defense in case the use of Internet access leads to legal problems. Examples of legal problems that may arise are using illegally downloaded software or distributing sexually offensive material. A company may have to use policy documents to prove that they performed due diligence in attempting to prevent such actions.

✔ For firewall administrators, the policies are a guideline to define incoming and outgoing firewall rules to ensure that the firewall enforces the company's policy as much as possible. Firewall rules should always reflect a company's Security and Internet Acceptable Use policies.

A firewall is a tool for enforcing company rules regarding how employees can use the Internet. So before the company can set up an effective firewall, it first must decide its policies. This chapter defines how to set up these policies for Internet access.

Defining an Internet Acceptable Use Policy

A firewall protects your network by enforcing what network traffic is allowed for both inbound and outbound traffic. Appropriate types of traffic can be determined from the Internet Acceptable Use policy.

The Internet Acceptable Use policy not only contains security-related policies, it may also specify rules about what is considered unacceptable Web content, for what purposes the Internet may be used, and how to represent the company in Internet newsgroups or mailing lists.

Although personal telephone calls are generally treated as acceptable employee behavior, an employee's personal use of company Internet access is another matter entirely because it can easily lead to legal issues and cause a financial loss to a business. Therefore, clearly describing what kinds of Internet access are acceptable and what kinds of access are unacceptable is important. If you create a policy that's too restrictive, users may not be able to do their jobs, or may try to circumvent the policy. On the other hand, if your policy is loose, users' productivity may suffer due to too much private Internet use or incidents such as sending excessive e-mail chain letters. The network may even face software viruses. You have to balance between being too restrictive and too loose.

If your job is to define the Internet Acceptable Use policy for your company, be sure to do the following when you write the policy:

✔ **Define all available services:** The Internet Acceptable Use policy must define what programs and protocols that company employees can use when they access the Internet. This section allows users to understand what programs they can use, and perhaps prevent requests for new protocols to be implemented. For the firewall administrator, this section gives a good idea of what "approved" protocols should be configured to pass to the Internet.

✔ **Determine who can access the Internet:** Not everyone requires access to the Internet or should be allowed to access it. By describing who, or better yet, what company positions need Internet access, you can prevent a lot of conflicts over Internet access. A firewall administrator can use authentication at the firewall or at the proxy server in order to limit access to defined groups. In addition, groups can be limited to specific protocols when they access the Internet.

✔ **Define ownership of resources:** When you write the Internet Acceptable Use policy, you must ensure that you define who owns the files on the network. Defining ownership allows a company to inspect employee computers in the event of a security breach. In addition, ownership may allow the company to identify improper behavior that affects the security of the network. Make sure that the resources that you describe include the data on the employees' computers and the contents of e-mail as well.

Privacy laws of different countries can make it difficult to implement strict rules about scanning employee files and e-mails. Make sure that your company's legal department reviews the Internet Acceptable Use policy to ensure that the contents adhere to local laws. Privacy laws can be very complex.

✔ **Establish the responsibilities of the employees:** You must include the responsibilities of the users in the Internet Acceptable Use policy. By defining responsibilities, you familiarize the employee reading the policy with the company's expectations regarding use of company network resources. You may include best practices for employees for protecting passwords, such as keeping passwords confidential, reporting suspicious behavior on the network, or reporting any actions by their account that did not follow the Internet Acceptable Use policy.

✔ **Define all unauthorized use of the Internet:** This is probably the most important part of the Internet Acceptable Use policy. If you don't spend the necessary time on this section, you may hear, "But I didn't know I wasn't allowed to do that." Some of the areas that you may want to address in this section include:

- **Define for what purposes e-mail is expressly disallowed:** When you design this, think of what e-mails you receive that you wish never existed. This should at least include chain letters and spam e-mail. Be sure to specify what e-mail practices are not allowed when using the company's e-mail system.

- **Define which protocols and applications can't be used when accessing the Internet:** When drafting the list of protocols, you need to consider a few different categories. For example, many protocols, such as Telnet or FTP, have known security weaknesses due to their use of cleartext passwords. Cleartext passwords allow an attacker who intercepts network traffic to view the user's password and account information in cleartext as it is transmitted on the network. You also may want to prevent protocols that may have legal implications, such as peer-to-peer music sharing applications like KaZaa. KaZaa and many other such applications allow you to search the Internet for MP3s (music files) and download them to your computer. The music industry has taken the makers of these applications to court because their users are not paying for these MP3 data files. A company may want to prevent the use of these file-sharing applications to ensure that illegally obtained music isn't stored on company servers.

- **Define what Web content may not be accessed:** Be sure to address this topic in your Internet Acceptable Use policy. Typically, a company won't want its employees to access Web sites that contain pornography, nudity, violence, or profanity.

- **Define what types of files can't be downloaded from Internet sites:** The last thing you want is for your company to be charged with using pirated software because an employee downloaded it from a Warez site. Warez sites typically provide pirated software and software keys to unlock the software. (Warez is a hacker-style term for pirated software. Hackers like to use the letter *z* instead of *s*.) By explicitly stating that the use of software acquired in this manner isn't allowed, the company can easily delete any software it finds that was obtained in this manner.

- **Define unacceptable Internet access attempts:** Employees who have restricted Internet access at work but not at home may try to bypass the company's security mechanisms. For example, an employee may want to download MP3s using her laptop. Finding that the firewall prevents the use of KaZaa, she could attempt to dial-in to her personal ISP by using a company computer. By clearly stating that attempts such as this are unauthorized, the company can prevent such attempts, or at least discourage them.

- **Define what actions may not be performed on the Internet:** This is kind of a catchall category. It allows you to restrict employees from misrepresenting the company on the Internet. This part of the policy should include elements that ensure that an employee does not send or post content that reflects badly on the company.

I always include a disclaimer in any newsgroup posts that I create stating that the opinions in my posts are mine alone and do not reflect the opinions of the company for which I work. It enables me to answer questions honestly, and without fear that a mistake I may make in a post reflects poorly on my company.

✔ **Define all authorized use of the Internet:**

You can't dwell on what's disallowed. You also must include what is allowed when users access the Internet. For example, you can include the following information:

- **Define the maximum size for e-mail attachments:** With faster Internet connections becoming more widely available, people are sending larger and larger attachments. Who among us hasn't sent a Christmas-time video clip or a large MP3 attachment to a friend? These large attachments can rapidly use up disk space on the company's mail server.

- **Define what purposes e-mail can be used for:** You should be sure to specify what purposes are allowed for company-owned e-mail services. Typically, you include all business purposes, but exclude most personal purposes.

- **Define acceptable Web usage:** In the policy, be sure to specify what sites are considered acceptable for business. This can depend on your company's type of business. Acceptable Web sites may be defined either by content or by rating systems. Of course, you don't have to spell out a list of every acceptable Web site.

✔ **Define what can be downloaded from the Internet:** We all download various programs, utilities, documents, videos, or music from the Internet. Each download exposes the network to potential hazards, such as virus infection. The policy must define what can be downloaded. In addition, virus scanning should be implemented to reduce the chance of computer viruses.

✔ **Define the actions that are taken if the Internet Acceptable Use policy is not followed:** This is the tough part of the policy. You, or the company, must decide what the punishment will be if the Internet Acceptable Use policy is broken. Be careful not to be too harsh on small transgressions. The punishments that you set up must match the crime. The actions may include revoking Internet access from the employee, termination of the employee's employment with the company, or informing local legal authorities.

By defining the Internet Acceptable Use policy, the company can ensure that the firewall is configured to reflect the policy when you configure firewall rules. The Internet Acceptable Use policy acts as a guide to the firewall administrator to enable that person to design firewall rules that reflect the policy of the company.

After you determine the content of the Internet Acceptable Use policy, be sure to produce an Internet Acceptable Use policy document that must be signed by both the employees and management. This document ensures that both parties agree to the content and actions defined by the policy.

Defining a Security Policy

In addition to an Internet Acceptable Use policy, a company should also define a Security policy. A Security policy articulates the company's attitudes on security. Without a clear Security policy, configuring a firewall to meet the security expectations of the company is impossible.

For a home office, it may be useful to consider the same issues faced by a corporation to determine what you want your firewall to protect.

Although the firewall administrator can use the Internet Acceptable Use policy as a guideline to define rules at the firewall, the Security policy provides even more comprehensive information by identifying the necessary security configuration to secure each resource exposed to the Internet.

Setting a Security policy

You must take several steps to define a Security policy for a company.

1. **Establish a project team to develop a Security policy.**

2. **Identify what resources require protection.**

3. **Identify what potential risks exist for each resource.**

4. **Decide the probability of each risk.**

5. **Create mitigation plans that address each risk.**

Periodically, you must review the existing Security policy to determine whether the security needs of the company are still met by the Security policy. If your answer is "no," then you must redesign the Security policy to meet the current needs of the company.

The following sections describe the tasks involved in the Security policy development process.

Establishing a project team

You can't create a Security policy for your company on your own. Unless you get the right people involved with the project, the rest of the company may never accept the resulting Security policy.

So, who should make up the project team? The following people must be involved:

✔ **Experts in the technologies that you must deploy:** This may require help from consultants if your company doesn't have individuals with the needed expertise on staff.

✔ **Member of management:** If company management doesn't support the security policy, it won't be accepted as a company standard.

✔ **Representative from each area of the company:** Don't just include members from the necessary technology areas. If one part of the company isn't represented on the project team, that part of the company may not accept the findings of the team because their opinions were not represented.

Identifying resources to secure

After you decide on the members of the project team, you must identify the company resources that require protection. These resources may include hardware, software, and data.

In addition to identifying the resources that must be secured, the project team should also identify where these resources are located within the company. Your security plan should include whether the resources can be secured at the current location, or whether they should be moved to another location.

Finally, you must assign a value to each resource. You use the value to rank the resources in order of importance. If the resources all had the same value, it would be impossible to identify key resources that must be protected at all cost versus other resources that you merely would like to protect.

Identifying the risks to the resources

You must identify all risks facing the resources. Identifying risks helps you to determine what type of protection you need to implement in order to reduce those risks.

When considering potential risks, you sometimes have to think creatively. Some risks have a higher probability assigned than others. Some of the generic risks that may exist for a resource include:

✔ **Unauthorized access to the resource:** The resource may require limited access. If an attacker can connect to the resource over the Internet, or physically access the resource, the security of the resource may possibly be compromised.

✔ **Unauthorized disclosure of information:** After a resource is accessed, even more harm can be done if the information is publicized. The disclosure of sensitive data may lead to the company's image being tarnished, or potential loss of business for the company.

✔ **Unavailability of the resource due to denial of service attacks:** Denial of service attacks prevent access to the resource by attacking either the resource itself or the hardware that provides access to the resource.

In addition to these generic risks, individual risks must be identified for each resource. These risks can include risks related to the placement of the resource on the physical network and risks related to the specific protocols used to access the resources.

Many protocols, such as File Transfer Protocol (FTP), use cleartext authentication methods that send passwords in cleartext across a network connection. This should always be considered a risk for the resource.

Determining the probability associated with risks

A project team needs to predict the probability of the threat associated with each risk occurring. Developing a security strategy to address a threat that's unlikely to occur and that would cause only minor damage is senseless. Your time and money are better spent in providing security against threats that are more likely to take place.

After you have determined the probabilities, you can then prioritize the resources that you must secure. In general, you can determine the costs that you face if the resources are compromised by multiplying the cost of the resource by the probability of the damage occurring. Obviously, you want to prevent the highest cost risks from occurring.

Mitigating the risks

The actions that you take to reduce risk can range from placing the resource in a physically secure location to implementing a secured area of your network that limits what protocols are allowed to connect to a resource from the Internet.

The definition of the mitigation techniques will serve as the guidelines for the firewall rules. The Security policy defines what actions the company sees as appropriate to mitigate specific risks.

Chapter 7

Establishing Rules for Simple Protocols

*T*his chapter examines the firewall rules that allow both inbound and outbound access for commonly used protocols. The network shown in Figure 7-1 serves as the sample network for our discussion.

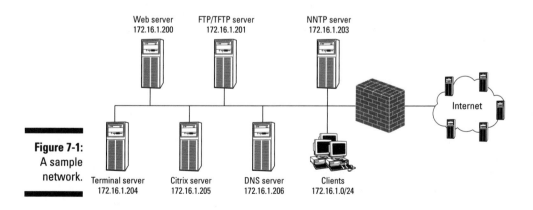

Figure 7-1: A sample network.

Web server
172.16.1.200

FTP/TFTP server
172.16.1.201

NNTP server
172.16.1.203

Internet

Terminal server
172.16.1.204

Citrix server
172.16.1.205

DNS server
172.16.1.206

Clients
172.16.1.0/24

Although these rules may seem monotonous, they are the essence of firewall configuration. After you get the hang of configuring firewall rules, you can easily extend the scenario and create more sophisticated rules to meet your security requirements for new protocols. These rules can be simple or complex, as the next sections make clear.

This chapter looks at the firewall rules required to allow the following protocols to pass through the firewall:

- ✔ **Web access:** Many organizations host their own Web sites and require a firewall to limit access to the Web server to only those who use approved protocols. In addition, internal users of the organization require access to Web servers on the Internet.

- ✔ **Name resolution:** When you access the Internet, you enter the fully qualified domain name (FQDN) of an Internet site in your browser. For example, when you enter www.dummies.com, name resolution resolves the FQDN to the IP address 208.215.179.139. Most organizations require their firewall to allow both inbound and outbound name resolution.

- ✔ **File copy protocols:** File copy protocols allow the transmission of large data files between organizations. Firewalls must be configured to allow both inbound and outbound traffic flows.

- ✔ **Messaging, chatting, and conferencing:** With increased bandwidth, more users are utilizing Internet messaging, chatting, and conferencing services to increase productivity and accessibility to other users on the Internet. A firewall must be configured to allow outbound access to these services.

- ✔ **Thin client solutions:** Thin client solutions allow terminals and older client operating systems to connect to a central server running terminal service sessions. All processing takes place at the back-end terminal server, and only screen and input information is sent between the client and the server. Firewalls must be configured to allow both forms of access.

- ✔ **Other business protocols:** Organizations may require access to news services, or want to allow users to PING hosts on the Internet while blocking PING access to internal resources. This chapter looks at configuring inbound and outbound firewall rules for these services.

All of the firewall rule listings in this chapter assume that your firewall will monitor traffic by inspecting packets and automatically allowing response packets to pass through the firewall without explicitly defining rules for the response packets. This is sometimes called *stateful inspection,* and is common in most current firewall products. If your firewall doesn't support this, you have to enter corresponding rules for the returning traffic or consider upgrading to a better firewall.

For Starters, Some Default Rules

Before we delve into tables and more tables of firewall rules, we need to describe some of the more common default firewall rules that are implemented on today's firewalls:

- ✔ **Default strategies:** A firewall will deploy either a *deny-all* or a *permit-all* strategy. What this refers to is how the firewall deals with a packet that doesn't match any of the defined rules at the firewall. If a deny-all strategy is implemented at the firewall, a packet that doesn't match any of the defined firewall rules is prevented from traversing the firewall. Likewise, if a permit-all strategy is implemented at the firewall, a packet that doesn't match any of the defined firewall rules is allowed to pass through the firewall.

  For most firewall products, you don't have to create a deny-all or permit-all firewall rule. Instead, the firewall product either allows you to define the strategy, or it implements one of the two strategies as its default behavior.

- ✔ **Inbound versus outbound rules:** When you define firewall rules, direction is an important characteristic. The traffic that you want to allow *outbound* from your network may not be the traffic that you want to allow *inbound.* For example, although your organization may want to allow users to connect to *any* Web site from the internal network, you may find it in your best interest to limit inbound connections only to the organization's public Web server.

- ✔ **Block obvious IP address spoofing:** This one is easy. When IP addresses are assigned to your network, you will know the IP addressing scheme used on the internal network. A firewall can be configured to block packets if they arrive at the external interface of the firewall but have an internal IP address as their source address. Likewise, if the source address is a private network address as defined in RFC 1918, the firewall can block these obvious IP address spoofing attacks.

  For more information on private network addressing, see Chapter 2.

Allowing Web Access

Web access is the most common form of traffic that passes through an organization's firewall. The two most common applications used to access the Web are Microsoft Internet Explorer and Netscape Navigator. From a firewall's perspective, it doesn't matter which browser you use because both browsers utilize either HTTP or secure HTTP (HTTPS) protocols.

Securing data with SSL

SSL provides Application layer security to transmitted data. In order for SSL to work, the Web server must have a certificate installed that provides the Web server with a private/public key pair. When a connection is made to an SSL-protected Web site, the SSL session is established, as shown in the figure below.

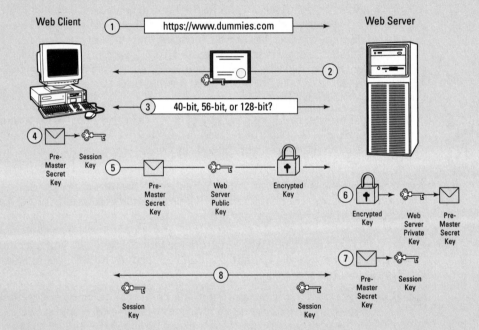

The SSL session is established in the following manner:

1. The Web client attempts to connect to the Web server by using a URL that starts with HTTPS, representing HTTP protected by SSL encryption.

2. The Web server sends its certificate to the Web client. The Web server's public key is contained in the certificate as an attribute of the certificate.

   Only the public key is transmitted on the network; the private key is never transmitted, protecting the private key from interception.

3. The Web client and the Web server enter into a negotiation to determine the strongest level of encryption that is supported or required by the Web server or Web client.

4. The Web client generates a pre-master secret key of the length negotiated between the client and the Web server. The Web client uses a designated algorithm to derive the session key. This session key is used only for the existing session and is never reused.

5. The client computer then encrypts the pre-master secret key by using the Web server's public key and transmits the encrypted key to the Web server.

6. The Web server decrypts the pre-master secret key by using the Web server's private key.

7. The pre-master secret key is used to derive the session key at the Web server by implementing the same algorithm implemented at the Web client.

8. All data transmitted between the Web client and the Web server for the current session is encrypted by using the derived session key.

HTTP connections use a random client port above port 1023 at the client computer and normally connect to Transmission Control Protocol (TCP) port 80 at the Web server. When additional security and encryption are required, Secure Sockets Layer (SSL) encryption can be configured at the Web server to encrypt all transmitted data between the client and the server. When SSL is implemented, the Web server normally accepts connections on TCP port 443 instead of TCP port 80.

A random client port above port 1023 is not limited to HTTP sessions. In fact, almost all client applications that establish a connection to a server use a random port between ports 1024 and 65535 for the source port. When you look at a protocol listing and see a specific port related to the protocol, it generally refers to the server-side port that is used.

Configuring inbound firewall rules

Inbound rules are required only when you are hosting a Web server that is accessible on the Internet. The firewall rules ensure that access to the Web server is limited to only HTTP or HTTPS connections.

Table 7-1 shows the firewall rules that are required to provide access to the internal Web server located at IP address 172.16.1.200 from any client on the Internet. The table assumes that the firewall uses a *deny all except those listed* methodology, which means that if a firewall receives traffic for a protocol that isn't in the list of firewall rules, the packet is dropped at the firewall.

Table 7-1	Firewall Rules to Access an Internal Web Server					
Protocol	Transport Protocol	Source IP	Source Port	Target IP	Target Port	Action
HTTP	TCP	Any	Any	172.16.1.200	80	Allow
HTTPS	TCP	Any	Any	172.16.1.200	443	Allow

The address that is listed in the firewall rules listing is always the true IP address of the server that is hosting the Web service. If private network addressing is used for the private network or if the firewall is configured to use NAT to hide the true addressing used by the internal Web server, then the firewall must perform a static mapping to allow the packets to be redirected to the internal Web server. For example, the Web server may be advertised on the Internet as being located at IP address 23.20.10.14. Therefore, the firewall must be configured to redirect any connection attempts to port 80 and port 443 at IP address 23.20.10.14 to IP address 172.16.1.200 on the internal network.

SSL encryption can be redirected to an internal server, even though the data is encrypted, because the source and destination address fields in the packets can be modified by the firewall without losing the integrity of the SSL encrypted data. SSL is different from Internet Protocol Security (IPSec), which is discussed in the next chapter.

Configuring outbound firewall rules

In addition to inbound Web access, chances are good that the users of your network want to access Web resources on the Internet. Table 7-2 shows the firewall rules that are required at the firewall to allow internal network users on the 172.16.1.0/24 network to access any Web server on the Internet by using HTTP or HTTPS.

Table 7-2	Firewall Rules to Access Internet-Based Web Servers					
Protocol	**Transport Protocol**	**Source IP**	**Source Port**	**Target IP**	**Target Port**	**Action**
HTTP	TCP	172.16.1.0/24	Any	Any	80	Allow
HTTPS	TCP	172.16.1.0/24	Any	Any	443	Allow

If a Web server on the Internet uses anything other than the default TCP ports of 80 and 443, this firewall rule would prevent internal users from accessing these Web resources. This includes all of the cool content, such as chat, video, and streaming audio, that could be imbedded in a Web page.

Finding Internet Resources

All Internet access depends on resolving a fully qualified domain name (FQDN) to an IP address. The Internet service that provides this resolution is known as the Domain Name System (DNS). DNS uses a distributed database, spread across the Internet, to resolve FQDNs to IP addresses.

How XML, DHTML, ASP, Java, and ActiveX affect the firewall

When you see articles written on Web development, you probably see several acronyms bounced around. All of these acronyms refer to methods of creating rich Web content. EXtended Markup Language (XML), Macromedia Shockwave Flash objects, Dynamic HyperText Markup Language (DHTML), Active Server Pages (ASP), Java, and ActiveX controls all allow Web developers to develop pages that come alive with content. The good news for a firewall administrator is that the content doesn't make a difference. All Web connections to a Web server use either HTTP or HTTPS. The content of the Web page doesn't change the transmission protocol used to connect to the Web servers. The download of this content, however, can be affected by the security settings defined in the client's Web browser. For example, security settings can be configured to prevent the download and installation of ActiveX controls.

The benefit of using DNS is that rather than telling someone to connect to the IP address 208.215.179.139, which he or she will promptly forget, mix up, or just give up on out of frustration, you can tell the person to connect to www.dummies.com, which is more intuitive and by far much easier to remember.

The DNS protocol uses two different ports for connection attempts. A request sent to a DNS server uses either a connection to UDP port 53 or a connection to TCP port 53. Typically, DNS resolution requests are sent to the UDP port because the request requires a simple response packet containing the answer from the DNS server. TCP port 53 is typically used when DNS servers exchange zone information through a zone transfer. The zone transfer requires that a session be established and that all data transmitted between the two DNS servers be verified to ensure that no information is omitted.

When configuring a firewall to allow DNS traffic, you may have to provide access to Internet-based clients as well as access to internal clients. The following sections outline the firewall rules that are required at a firewall in order to allow these traffic patterns to pass through the firewall.

Providing name resolution to Internet-based clients

When you register a name for use on the Internet, you are required to provide the IP addresses of at least two DNS servers that are authoritative for the zone on the Internet. By "authoritative," we don't mean that the DNS servers take charge of the zone, but that these servers always have the most up-to-date information about the zone and that all name resolution requests in the zone are directed to those DNS servers.

When the authoritative DNS server is located behind a firewall, the firewall must be configured to allow DNS connections to the DNS server from any host on the Internet. If you exclude any host from connecting to your DNS servers, it will be unable to resolve hosts containing your domain name to IP addresses, which is another way of saying that it will prevent others from connecting to your Internet resources.

Table 7-3 shows the firewall rules that are required to allow access to the DNS server located at IP address 172.16.1.206 on the private network.

Table 7-3	Firewall Rules to Access an Internal DNS Server					
Protocol	**Transport Protocol**	**Source IP**	**Source Port**	**Target IP**	**Target Port**	**Action**
DNS	UDP	Any	Any	172.16.1.206	53	Allow
DNS	TCP	Any	Any	172.16.1.206	53	Allow*

* Connections to TCP 53 are only required for zone transfers where the internal DNS server is the master server for the zone for an external DNS server. To tighten the security further, consider adding separate firewall rules for each specific external DNS server, rather than allowing any IP address to connect to the internal DNS server's TCP 53 port.

Providing Internet name resolution to internal clients

Your firewall has to allow Internet-based clients to query your DNS server, and you must provide a way for your internal network users to resolve FQDNs on the Internet (or face their wrath).

If the company has internal DNS services, the internal clients will send their Internet DNS queries to the internal DNS server. The internal DNS server can use one of two strategies to resolve FQDNs on the Internet:

- **Use root hints:** The internal DNS server will find the authoritative DNS server for the FQDN by querying the DNS root servers.
- **Forward DNS queries to an Internet Service Provider (ISP):** The internal DNS server will forward all unresolved DNS queries to the ISP's DNS server for resolution.

If the company doesn't have internal DNS services, you could instead configure the internal clients to use the ISP's DNS server as their configured DNS server.

Configuring DNS firewall rules when using root hints

When a DNS server is configured to use root hints, it queries one of the DNS root servers to determine which DNS server it should query to resolve the DNS request (see Figure 7-2).

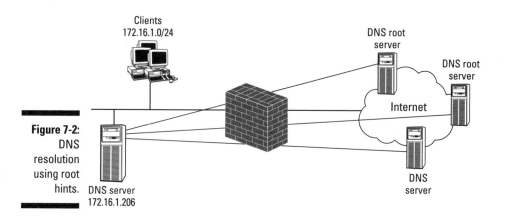

Figure 7-2: DNS resolution using root hints.

Specifically, the DNS server will query the DNS root server that's responsible for the top-level domain being queried, such as the .com DNS root server. The DNS root server will return a referral to a DNS server that is authoritative for your DNS query. The internal DNS server will then query the DNS server included in the referral. This process will repeat, until either the DNS information that the servers are querying is found cached at a queried DNS server, they are referred to the DNS server that is authoritative for the DNS zone where the DNS resource record is stored, or a response that the DNS information is not available or does not exist is returned.

When root hints are used for DNS resolution, the firewall must be configured to allow the internal DNS server (172.16.1.206) to send DNS queries to any DNS server on the Internet, as shown in Figure 7-2. Due to the uncertainty of which DNS servers the internal DNS server must contact, firewall rules must be established that allow the internal DNS server to query any DNS server on the Internet using DNS protocols, as shown in Table 7-4.

Table 7-4	Firewall Rules for DNS Access Using Root Hints					
Protocol	**Transport Protocol**	**Source IP**	**Source Port**	**Target IP**	**Target Port**	**Action**
DNS	TCP	172.16.1.206	Any	Any	53	Allow
DNS	UDP	172.16.1.206	Any	Any	53	Allow

Forwarding DNS packets to an ISP

Some firewall administrators find that allowing an internal DNS server to communicate with any DNS server on the Internet is a security risk and are unwilling to allow DNS connections to any DNS server on the Internet. In this scenario, as shown in Figure 7-3, DNS resolution traffic is restricted to a single Internet-based DNS server. Configure the internal DNS server to forward DNS requests to a specific DNS server if the internal DNS server can't resolve FQDNs.

After your internal DNS server forwards the DNS request to the ISP's DNS server, you have no control over how the DNS query is resolved. The ISP may use root hints, or it may forward the DNS request to another DNS server on the Internet. The point is, you really don't care. For your firewall, all you have to do is configure firewall rules that allow your DNS server to forward DNS requests to the ISP's DNS server.

Based on Figure 7-3, the firewall rules in Table 7-5 must be established at the firewall to allow the internal DNS server located at IP address 172.16.1.206 to forward DNS queries to the ISP's DNS server located at IP address 39.200.14.56.

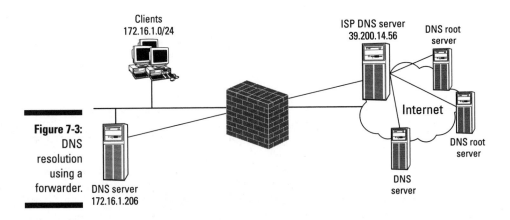

Figure 7-3: DNS resolution using a forwarder.

Table 7-5	Firewall Rules for DNS Access Using a Forwarder					
Protocol	Transport Protocol	Source IP	Source Port	Target IP	Target Port	Action
DNS	TCP	172.16.1.206	Any	39.200.14.56	53	Allow
DNS	UDP	172.16.1.206	Any	39.200.14.56	53	Allow

To provide redundancy, consider providing more than one external DNS server to which you will forward DNS requests. This ensures that if the first DNS server is unavailable, the request can be forwarded to a different DNS server.

If your DNS server supports *conditional* forwarding, you must create both a TCP and a UDP firewall rule for each target DNS server. The conditional forwarding feature forwards requests for a specific DNS domain to a designated DNS server. As far as a firewall is concerned, each conditional forwarding target is just another target for outbound DNS requests.

File Transfer Protocol (FTP)

Another common use of the Internet involves downloading files, such as drivers and applications, from the Internet. Typically, the File Transfer Protocol (FTP) is used to download files from the Internet. FTP provides the ability for either anonymous or authenticated users to access a designated FTP server for the purpose of downloading or uploading files.

Just because an application supports authentication doesn't mean that the authentication is secure. FTP does support authentication, but it uses clear-text authentication. This means that a *packet sniffer* can read the packets and determine the password that was used. Packet sniffers are either software programs or hardware devices that are able to inspect the actual content of packets transmitted on the network. Any protocols that transmit data without encryption can result in the packet sniffer capturing confidential data, such as passwords. Ensure that internal network users are informed of this vulnerability and recommend that they never use their network password for accessing resources on the Internet.

FTP uses two separate connections between the FTP client and the FTP server to support transfer of data, as shown in Figure 7-4.

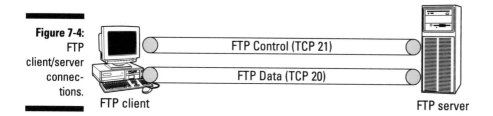

Figure 7-4:
FTP
client/server
connec-
tions.

The control channel is used to send all commands between the FTP client and the FTP server. These commands can include FTP-GET and FTP-PUT commands for the transfer of data. In response to an FTP-PUT or FTP-GET command, a separate channel is established to transfer the data between the client and the server, with the FTP server initiating the connection.

In addition to the two channels, your firewall configuration may also have to support the use of *passive* FTP clients. A passive FTP client negotiates with the FTP server to determine what port is used for the data connection, rather than the FTP server initiating the data connection from TCP port 20. After the data port is negotiated between the client and the server, the client will then establish the data connection to the FTP server, connecting from a port above TCP port 1023 at the client to the chosen port at the FTP server.

Some people, including us authors, consider the use of passive FTP clients to be a security hazard because a firewall rule must be established that allows external clients to connect to any port on the FTP server. Unless your firewall implements an FTP application proxy, which is able to analyze the commands issued by the FTP data session in order to ensure that the FTP session is taking place as required, don't allow passive FTP clients to connect to your FTP server.

Table 7-6 shows the firewall rules that must be established at the firewall in order to allow Internet-based clients to connect to an internally located FTP server. This set of firewall rules allows any host on the Internet to connect to the FTP server located at IP address 172.16.1.201.

Table 7-6		Firewall Rules to Access an Internal FTP Server				
Protocol	*Transport Protocol*	*Source IP*	*Source Port*	*Target IP*	*Target Port*	*Action*
FTP	TCP	Any	Any	172.16.1.201	21	Allow
FTP Data	TCP	172.16.1.201	20	Any	Any	Allow
FTP PASV*	TCP	Any	Any	172.16.1.201	Any	Allow

*FTP Passive clients require that the FTP server be able to return FTP data using a port requested by the client, rather than using TCP port 20 as in an Active FTP transfer.

If you have internal clients that require access to FTP resources on the Internet, the firewall must also be configured to allow outbound FTP packets. Table 7-7 shows the firewall rules that must be established to allow clients on the 172.16.1.0/24 network to connect to any FTP service on the Internet.

Table 7-7	Firewall Rules to Access an Internet-Based FTP Servers*					
Protocol	Transport Protocol	Source IP	Source Port	Target IP	Target Port	Action
FTP	TCP	172.16.1.0/24	Any	Any	21	Allow
FTP Data	TCP	Any	20	172.16.1.0/24	Any	Allow

*This table assumes that passive FTP clients are not used on the private network.

As you can see in Table 7-7, in order to allow internal clients to transfer data to and from an external FTP server, you have to allow all traffic that originates from TCP port 20 on any external computer. Because this allows external computers to establish a connection to any port on an internal computer, this can be a severe security risk. Some firewalls address this by only allowing the incoming FTP data connection *after* an internal client has initiated an FTP session. If your firewall doesn't support this, consider denying outgoing FTP connections so you don't have to configure Table 7-7's potentially dangerous FTP Data rule.

Messaging and Conferencing

Many people have fallen in love with instant messaging. Instant messaging is for the Type A personality. It enables you to determine if someone is connected to the Internet and get him or her to respond immediately to a question. Instantly. As you may have guessed, we are big believers in instant messaging.

This section describes the firewall rules that are required to use the available instant messaging, chatting, and conferencing software that is available today. Specifically, this section takes a look at the firewall rules necessary to use America Online (AOL) messaging, Microsoft Network (MSN) Messenger and Windows Messenger, and Microsoft NetMeeting.

America Online (AOL) Messaging

America Online was one of the first instant messaging services offered on the Internet. With AOL Messaging, you can determine whether friends are online and chat with them using the AOL Messaging software.

If you want to use AOL Messaging, your firewall must be configured with the firewall rule shown in Table 7-8.

Table 7-8		Firewall Rules to Allow AOL Messaging				
Protocol	Transport Protocol	Source IP	Source Port	Target IP	Target Port	Action
AOL	TCP	Any	Any	Any	5190	Allow

MSN Messenger and Windows Messenger

Microsoft Network (MSN) Messenger and Windows Messenger allow messages to be sent immediately to online contacts in your address list. For authentication, both versions of Messenger use Passport authentication. Passport authentication is also used for other Microsoft services.

Table 7-9 shows the firewall rules required to allow MSN and Windows Messenger clients to send instant messages to other MSN and Windows Messenger clients on the Internet.

Table 7-9		Firewall Rules to Allow MSN Messenger/ Windows Messenger				
Protocol	Transport Protocol	Source IP	Source Port	Target IP	Target Port	Action
IM	TCP	Any	Any	Any	1863	Allow
HTTP	TCP	Any	Any	Any	80	Allow

In addition to instant messages, MSN Messenger and Windows Messenger also enable users to transfer files and transmit voice calls between two computers on the Internet. Because dynamic ports are used for this purpose, the firewall must implement a gateway or application service that enables the files and voice transmissions to be rerouted to the correct client behind the firewall.

Table 7-10 shows the ports that are used by the MSN Messenger and Windows Messenger for file transfers.

Table 7-10	MSN and Windows Messenger File Transfer Firewall Rules				
Messenger Feature	**Source IP**	**Source Port**	**Target IP**	**Target Port**	**Action**
File Transfer (Incoming)	Any	Any	Recipient IP	6891-6900	Allow
File Transfer (Outgoing)*	172.16.1.0/24	Any	Recipient IP	6891-6900	Allow

*If the firewall is performing NAT, the outgoing file transfer will only work if the firewall implements an application gateway that replaces the source address with the IP address of the application gateway.

Voice communications between MSN and Windows Messenger clients is even more complex to configure. Voice communications require that several ports be opened at the firewall to allow the voice connection to take place. If your firewall implements NAT, the use of static ports for the voice transmission limits voice transmissions to a single host behind the firewall at a time. The firewall can only have a single instance at a time using UDP port 6901. The ports used by MSN and Windows Messenger are shown in Table 7-11.

Table 7-11	Messenger Voice Firewall Rules	
Messenger Feature	**Source Port**	**Target Port**
Session Establishment	Any	TCP port 6901
Voice Transmission	UDP 6901	UDP port 6901
Voice Conversation Establishment/Termination	TCP 2200-4700	TCP 2200-4700

NetMeeting

Microsoft offers an alternative to instant messaging that allows for online collaboration. Microsoft NetMeeting allows application sharing, whiteboard sharing, and video/voice conferencing to take place over a network.

Microsoft NetMeeting uses two separate technologies to allow collaboration over network links:

- ✔ **T.120:** The T.120 standard allows multipoint data conferencing. This feature allows multiple users to take part in application-sharing scenarios, such as multiple users editing a single document.
- ✔ **H.323:** The H.323 standard allows for video and voice conferencing over unreliable, switched networks, such as the Internet.

A NetMeeting session is established by initially connecting to an Internet Locator Server (ILS) that listens on TCP port 389. After you have established a connection with the ILS server, you can then start a NetMeeting session with any other users that are connected to the same ILS server. Alternatively, you can connect directly to the IP address of the computer on which the person whom you want to communicate with is sitting; or you can implement an H.323 Gatekeeper, which routes calls to multiple people in an organization, just like a telephone switchboard routes voice calls from a central office phone number.

ILS is not the only service that uses TCP port 389. Port 389 is actually reserved for use by the Lightweight Directory Access Protocol (LDAP). Although similar in function, ILS is not an LDAP service.

Table 7-12 shows the ports used by NetMeeting that must be opened at the firewall to allow a NetMeeting client to participate in NetMeetings.

Table 7-12	Microsoft NetMeeting Firewall Rules	
NetMeeting Service	*Source Port*	*Target Port*
Internet Locator Service (ILS)	Any	TCP 389
User Location Server	Any	TCP 522
T.120 Protocol	Any	TCP 1503
H.323 Call Setup	Any	TCP 1720
Audio Call Control	Any	TCP 1731
H.323 Call Control	Any	TCP 1025-65536*
H.323 Streaming	Any	UDP 1025-65536*

The use of random TCP and UDP ports is often considered a headache to firewall administrators. We recommend that you allow NetMeeting requests to Internet-based clients to use video and audio only if the firewall implements an application gateway service for the H.323 protocol. For example, Microsoft Internet Security and Acceleration (ISA) Server has a built-in H.323 filter that allows video and audio conferencing through the firewall. The H.323 filter allows secure connections through the ISA Server and also allows multiple simultaneous incoming connections.

Thin Client Solutions

Many companies look to thin client solutions to allow full network access to users who don't have full computers or less powerful computers. Rather than requiring high processing power at the client level, a thin client solution performs all processing at the terminal server.

Two standards have evolved for thin client solutions: Citrix Metaframe and Microsoft Windows Terminal Services. Although they use different protocols, both thin client solutions enable clients to connect to a central terminal server, allow administrators to take remote control of thin client sessions, and give administrators the tools to remotely manage servers.

Microsoft Windows Terminal Services is the same suite of protocols now referred to as Remote Desktop in Windows XP and Windows Server 2003.

Citrix Metaframe

Citrix Metaframe makes use of the Independent Computing Architecture (ICA) protocol to allow thin clients to connect to a Citrix terminal server and execute applications by using the processor power of the terminal server. Citrix allows connectivity by using either native ICA clients or Web-based embedded applications. Citrix supports Java, ActiveX, and Netscape plug-ins for embedded clients. Many companies are moving toward embedded clients to reduce the costs associated with distributing the client software to all client computers that require access to the Citrix Metaframe server.

Table 7-13 shows the firewall rules that must be included at the firewall to allow access to a Citrix Metaframe terminal server at IP address 172.16.1.205 on the internal network.

Table 7-13	Firewall Rules to Allow External Access to a Citrix Metaframe Server					
Protocol	Transport Protocol	Source IP	Source Port	Target IP	Target Port	Action
ICA	TCP	Any	Any	172.16.1.205	1494	Allow

This set of firewall rules allows only external access to an internal Citrix Metaframe server. If you require internal clients to connect to Citrix Metaframe servers on the Internet, you then need to apply the firewall rules shown in Table 7-14 at your external firewall.

Table 7-14		Firewall Rules to Allow Access to External Citrix Metaframe Servers				
Protocol	Transport Protocol	Source IP	Source Port	Target IP	Target Port	Action
ICA	TCP	172.16.1.0/24	Any	Any	1494	Allow

Windows Terminal Services

Starting with Windows NT 4.0, Microsoft released its own version of terminal services based on the Remote Desktop Protocol (RDP). With the release of Windows 2000, additional features, such as remote control of nonconsole clients, were included to create parity with the Citrix Metaframe offering.

The Internet Assigned Numbers Authority refers to RDP as the Windows-Based Terminal (WBT) Protocol. Both names reference the protocol discussed here.

Table 7-15 shows the firewall rules that are required to provide access to a Windows terminal server located at IP address 172.16.1.204 on the internal network.

Table 7-15		Firewall Rules to Allow Access to an Internal Windows Terminal Server				
Protocol	Transport Protocol	Source IP	Source Port	Target IP	Target Port	Action
RDP	TCP	Any	Any	172.16.1.204	3389	Allow

Likewise, if access is required to Internet-based Windows terminal servers, the firewall rules shown in Table 7-16 must be implemented to allow outbound connections to the terminal servers.

Table 7-16		Firewall Rules to Access External Windows Terminal Servers				
Protocol	Transport Protocol	Source IP	Source Port	Target IP	Target Port	Action
RDP	TCP	172.16.1.0/24	Any	Any	3389	Allow

If you connect to a Citrix Metaframe server or a Windows terminal server using a Web-based client, you must add a firewall rule that allows access to the Web server hosting the ActiveX, Java, or Netscape plug-in to be downloaded to a Web-based client. The firewall rule must provide either HTTP or HTTPS access (as defined earlier in this chapter) in addition to the Citrix Metaframe or Windows Terminal Services firewall rules.

In addition to the protocols already discussed, you might consider the use of other protocols across your firewall. These protocols are often used when accessing the Internet and must be included in your firewall rule listing to ensure that you can connect to the resources as required. This section looks at two commonly used protocols:

Internet Control Message Protocol (ICMP)

In addition to the protocols already discussed, you must also create firewall rules for the ICMP protocol. When you learn TCP/IP, one of the first commands that you are taught is the PING command. PING is a command that uses the ICMP protocol to determine whether a host is reachable on the network. When you send a PING packet to another computer, that computer responds with an ICMP response packet that indicates that it is reachable.

The problem with this protocol on the Internet is that many attacks start by identifying whether a host exists. If your Internet-accessible computers respond to PING packets, an attacker may create a complete map of your internal network and follow that with a port scan to determine what services are available on your server. This could then be followed by an attack against your computers.

To prevent this scenario from occurring, you can configure your firewall to allow only specific ICMP packets to pass through the firewall, while blocking the ICMP packets that can reveal the existence of your network on the Internet. Before we show you the firewall rule that needs to be deployed at your firewall, look at the various messages that can be transmitted in an ICMP packet. ICMP indicates the purpose of a packet by setting the packet type to one of the following:

- ✔ **Echo Request:** The host initiating the PING request uses this type.

- ✔ **Echo Reply:** This type is used for the response packets to a PING request.

- ✔ **Redirect:** A router uses this message type when the packet should be transmitted through a different router that is closer to the ultimate destination of the PING packet.

✔ **Time Exceeded:** A router uses this type when the Time to Live (TTL) for a packet reaches zero, causing the packet to be discarded.

✔ **Parameter Problem:** If a router finds errors in the format of a PING packet, the packet must be dropped and the parameter type is used to indicate why the packet was dropped.

✔ **Unreachable:** If a router can't route a PING ICMP packet to the destination, the unreachable type is used.

✔ **Source Quench:** If packets arrive too quickly for a router to forward the packets, the packets may be dropped. In this case, a PING ICMP packet is sent to the originating computer with Source Quench as the type.

ICMP is not just used for PING; it's also used for status messages between hosts. When configuring your firewall for ICMP messages, be sure to consider more than just the Echo Request and Echo Reply messages used by the PING command. For example, data is transmitted between two networks that use different network topologies, such as Ethernet and Token Ring, ICMP messages are used to determine the *path maximum transmission unit (MTU).* The path MTU identifies the largest packet size that can be transmitted between two hosts over the network.

Only through the careful configuration of which ICMP packets are allowed to pass through the firewall can you prevent external hosts from determining the existence of your Internet-accessible servers. Table 7-17 shows the rules that are required.

Table 7-17		Firewall Rules to Allow Outbound PINGs Only			
Protocol	**Transport Protocol**	**Source IP**	**Target IP**	**ICMP Type**	**Action**
ICMP Outbound	ICMP	172.16.1.0/24	Any	Echo Request	Allow
ICMP Inbound	ICMP	Any	172.16.1.0/24	Echo Reply, Time Exceeded, Unreachable, Source Quench	Allow
ICMP Block*	ICMP	Any	Any	All	Drop *

*The final firewall rule ensures that all other ICMP packets are dropped at the firewall, no matter in which direction the packet is sent. If the firewall uses a "Drop all that are not listed" strategy, this firewall rule can be omitted.

What if the protocol that I need is not in this chapter?

So what do you do if the protocol that needs to pass through your firewall is not included in the preceding sections? Have no fear! Additional protocols are covered in the next chapter. Also, we included an extensive listing of protocol definitions in the Appendix.

If, on the other hand, you don't find the protocol listed, you can still determine what ports are used by the application by reading the Request for Comment (RFC) associated with the application. Another alternative is to roll up your sleeves and use a packet sniffer, such as Ethereal or Microsoft Network Monitor. Packet sniffers allow you to analyze the protocols and ports used when two computers communicate. Alternatively, you can use a port scanner to determine what open ports exist on your server to determine what ports must be opened at the firewall.

Chapter 8

Designing Advanced Protocol Rules

*T*his chapter looks at common applications, services, and connectivity solutions that are used on the Internet and their related protocols. In most cases, more than one firewall rule is required to enable these applications to be used through a firewall.

More specifically, we cover the required rules and design issues to consider when implementing the following:

✔ **Mail services:** Internet e-mail requires rules for both sending and receiving e-mail to ensure that only authorized packets can reach the e-mail server.

✔ **Authentication services:** Authentication is used to identify specific users when they connect to resources hosted on your network from the Internet. A user is authenticated against an account database. The section "Knock, Knock: Who Goes There?", located later in this chapter, looks at the most common authentication protocols used on the Internet today.

✔ **Internet Protocol Security (IPSec) encryption:** Not all protocols can take advantage of application layer security. For example, although a Web server is able to use Secure Sockets Layer (SSL) to protect HyperText Transfer Protocol (HTTP), another application may not know how to use SSL. In these cases, IPSec can be implemented to encrypt and decrypt data at the IP layer without the application being aware of the encryption process.

✔ **Tunneling solutions:** With the advent of broadband technologies and work-at-home policies, more employees are connecting to corporate networks by using tunneling solutions that send traffic in encrypted form across the Internet between the employee's computer and the corporate network. Depending on the tunnel solution implemented, different rules must be applied at the firewall.

Rain, Sleet, Snow, and Firewalls: Getting the E-Mail Through

Most of us can't live without e-mail services. Internet e-mail allows us to communicate with friends, colleagues, and business associates to exchange information. When a firewall is placed between you and the Internet, the firewall must be opened to allow e-mail to pass both to and from you. Before you go any further, look at the protocols related to e-mail services:

✔ **Post Office Protocol version 3 (POP3):** POP3 is the most common version of e-mail access protocol used today. POP3 is used to retrieve e-mail messages from a mail server. The most common misconception is that POP3 is also used to send e-mail; you can only retrieve e-mail by using POP3. By default, connections to a mail server using POP3 connect to TCP port 110. In many ways, the process is the same thing that you do every day when you check your mailbox for new mail (you know, snail mail). You don't camp out at the mailbox, but go at regular intervals (once a day) and see if you have received any new mail.

✔ **Internet E-mail Access Protocol version 4 (IMAP4):** IMAP4 is a newer protocol that provides access to a user's mailbox on a mail server. The advantage of IMAP4 over POP3 is that more folders are available to the user than just the Inbox. By using IMAP4, a user can access all e-mail-related folders on the mail server, such as the Outbox and Sent Items and Deleted Items folders. In addition, if the e-mail server supports public folders, IMAP4 also provides access to these folders. By default, connections to an e-mail server using IMAP4 connect to TCP port 143.

✔ **Simple Mail Transfer Protocol (SMTP):** SMTP provides outbound mail transport. Anytime that you send an e-mail message to another Internet e-mail user, SMTP is used to send the message to your mail server. Then your mail server transports the message to the target mail server, again by using SMTP. By default, connections to a mail server using SMTP connect to TCP port 25. You have no control over the actual routing used by the mail server to send the e-mail message. This is similar to what happens when you drop a letter off at the mailbox. All you know is that the letter will end up at the recipient's mail box (hopefully!).

✔ **Lightweight Directory Access Protocol (LDAP):** Have you ever tried to find a person's e-mail address? By sending a query to a mail server or directory server that uses LDAP, you can determine the e-mail alias for your intended recipient. By default, connections to a server using LDAP connect to TCP port 389.

Using Secure Sockets Layer (SSL) encryption

All of the listed mail protocols use cleartext authentication when transmitting a user's authentication credentials. Also, these protocols transmit the e-mail itself in unencrypted form. Cleartext authentication and cleartext messages can be read by a packet sniffer as the authentication packets are transmitted on the network. Although the risk of someone intercepting cleartext authentication or messages may not be a concern to some people, others may find it to be a security risk. To provide encryption between a mail client and the mail server, most mail services provide Secure Sockets Layer (SSL) encryption. To provide SSL encryption, you must perform the following two processes:

1. The mail server must acquire a Server certificate. The public/private key pair associated with the certificate is used to encrypt the data transmitted between the client and the mail server.

2. When SSL is implemented, the listening port at the mail server is changed to reflect the use of SSL as outlined in the following list:

Protocol	Transport Protocol	Standard Port	SSL Port
POP3	TCP	110	995
IMAP	TCP	143	993

Protocol	Transport Protocol	Standard Port	SSL Port
SMTP	TCP	25	25/465
LDAP	TCP	389	636
HTTP	TCP	80	443

Note: Some implementations of SMTP still use TCP port 25 for SSL-protected SMTP rather than using a different port, typically TCP port 465, like other SSL-protected protocols.

The SSL methods previously listed encrypt data as it's transmitted between the e-mail client and the e-mail server. The message remains in an unencrypted state at the sender's computer and the recipient's computer, where anyone can access the message. If you want to encrypt the contents of an e-mail message so that only the recipient can decrypt the message, you must use Pretty Good Privacy (PGP) or Secure Multipurpose Internet Mail Extensions (S/MIME). Although both PGP and S/MIME serve the same purpose, they are not interoperable. For more information on PGP and S/MIME, read *MCSE Designing Microsoft Windows 2000 Network Security Training Kit,* by Microsoft and Brian Komar, published by Microsoft Press.

Do not equate LDAP with your e-mail software's address book. An address book is simply a flat file of people's names and associated e-mail addresses used by your e-mail software. LDAP lets you query a centralized LDAP service so that you don't have to create entries manually for all people within your company.

✔ **HyperText Transfer Protocol (HTTP):** Many mail services, such as Hotmail and Yahoo! e-mail, make use of HTTP to allow access to mail resources. Users connect to a Web site by using standard Web traffic, and then the Web server either performs the necessary commands to view e-mail stored on the mail server or performs the SMTP commands to send outgoing mail. By default, clients that connect to a mail server with HTTP connections, connect to TCP port 80.

Several products are available that allow you to use HTTP to connect to your company's mail server. Microsoft Exchange Server's Outlook Web Access (OWA) and EmuMail, a freeware program, allow Web access to mail services.

Answering the right questions

Before you configure a firewall to support mail services, you must first determine exactly what type of e-mail-related network traffic will be allowed to pass through the firewall. To profile the allowed traffic, start by answering the following questions:

✔ **Does your company need to accept e-mail messages from the Internet?**

If your company receives e-mail from the Internet, you have to allow incoming e-mail to pass through your firewall. Allowing incoming e-mail requires that your e-mail server be protected so that it doesn't end up acting as a relay host for spam.

✔ **What mail clients are supported when accessing mail services for your company?**

Not every e-mail client supports the same features. Identifying which e-mail clients are supported assists you in providing the maximum level of security without blocking access to e-mail resources.

✔ **Will external e-mail clients connect from behind another company's firewalls?**

Not every organization allows access to external mail services. If the other company doesn't allow your clients to connect to your mail services through its firewall using mail protocols, sometimes solutions can be developed that make use of protocols commonly allowed through another company's firewalls, such as HTTP or HTTPS.

Spam, spam, spam, spam

One of the annoying drawbacks of e-mail is receiving unsolicited e-mail for services, products, or offers. This form of e-mail is commonly referred to as *spam*.

Although some people may like the Spam that you can get at a grocery store, most people don't appreciate receiving spam in their e-mail.

Spam e-mail is rarely sent from a person's actual mail server. Typically, a spammer will find a mail host on the Internet that allows *SMTP relaying*. SMTP relaying allows a mail client to bounce e-mail off a server that does not host mailboxes for the sender or for any of the recipients. After the e-mail is bounced off a legitimate SMTP server, the e-mail can be delivered using traditional SMTP mail transfer.

SMTP relay attacks are prevented by using the following solutions:

✔ Disable SMTP relaying entirely: Although this solution sounds good in theory, it doesn't work if you are using POP3 or IMAP4 clients. These mail clients must use SMTP relay to send e-mail messages to other organizations.

✔ Limit SMTP relaying to specific ranges of IP addresses: An SMTP server can be configured to allow only specific pools of IP addresses to relay SMTP mail messages. This configuration works only if the POP3/IMAP4 clients connect from a known range of IP addresses. If you travel for work and connect from a variety of locations, this configuration won't work for you.

✔ Enforce authenticated SMTP for outgoing mail: Forcing all clients to authenticate with the SMTP server ensures that the connecting user has a valid account on the SMTP server. Only if users authenticate can they send SMTP mail to a mailbox not stored on the SMTP server. Unauthenticated SMTP is only allowed when the mail is destined to a mailbox stored on your SMTP server.

The method that you choose depends on your business needs and mail clients used. For example, authenticated SMTP is supported only by newer versions of Eudora, Outlook Express, and Netscape Mail. If you have older versions of the client software, you can't implement this option.

The answers to these questions help you to design the necessary inbound and outbound firewall rules to ensure that only approved network traffic related to mail services is allowed to pass through the firewall.

Allowing access to external mail services

Table 8-1 shows the firewall rules that are required to provide external mail service access to computers on your internal network (IP subnet 172.16.1.0/24). These rules allow users behind your firewall to connect to other mail services on the Internet.

Table 8-1		Firewall Rules to Access an External Mail Server				
Protocol	*Transport Protocol*	*Source IP*	*Source Port*	*Target IP*	*Target Port*	*Action*
POP3	TCP	172.16.1.0/24	Any	Any	110	Allow
POP3/S	TCP	172.16.1.0/24	Any	Any	995	Allow
IMAP	TCP	172.16.1.0/24	Any	Any	143	Allow
IMAP/S	TCP	172.16.1.0/24	Any	Any	993	Allow
SMTP	TCP	172.16.1.0/24	Any	Any	25	Allow
SMTP/S	TCP	172.16.1.0/24	Any	Any	465	Allow
HTTP	TCP	172.16.1.0/24	Any	Any	80	Allow
HTTPS	TCP	172.16.1.0/24	Any	Any	443	Allow
LDAP	TCP	172.16.1.0/24	Any	Any	389	Allow
LDAPS	TCP	172.16.1.0/24	Any	Any	636	Allow

Note: Table 8-1 assumes that you will allow connections to any mail server on the Internet. If you want to restrict access to only specific mail servers, replace the Any entry in the Target IP with the IP address of the specific mail server.

Allowing access to internal mail services

Table 8-2 shows the firewall rules that are required to allow external clients to use internal mail services. In this example, the mail server (IP Address 172.16.1.210) is located behind a firewall that performs a static mapping from the externally advertised address to 172.16.1.210.

Table 8-2		Firewall Rules to Access an Internal Mail Server				
Protocol	*Transport Protocol*	*Source IP*	*Source Port*	*Target IP*	*Target Port*	*Action*
POP3	TCP	Any	Any	172.16.1.210	110	Allow
POP3/S	TCP	Any	Any	172.16.1.210	995	Allow
IMAP	TCP	Any	Any	172.16.1.210	143	Allow
IMAP/S	TCP	Any	Any	172.16.1.210	993	Allow

Protocol	Transport Protocol	Source IP	Source Port	Target IP	Target Port	Action
SMTP	TCP	Any	Any	172.16.1.210	25	Allow
SMTP	TCP	Any	Any	172.16.1.210	465	Allow
LDAP	TCP	Any	Any	172.16.1.210	389	Allow
LDAPS	TCP	Any	Any	172.16.1.210	636	Allow
HTTP	TCP	Any	Any	172.16.1.210	80	Allow*
HTTPS	TCP	Any	Any	172.16.1.210	443	Allow*

The HTTP and HTTPS rules assume that the mail server is hosting a Web-accessible mail client for checking e-mail. This service can reside on a different server on the internal network.

In addition to configuring the firewall, you must ensure that your Internet-accessible DNS server has a Mail Exchanger (MX) resource record that points to the externally advertised IP address of the mail server. Without an MX record, external clients can't direct e-mail messages to your mail server.

Knock, Knock: Who Goes There?

To allow remote connectivity to an organization's network, remote users must authenticate with the organization's directory service. The most common method used to provide remote authentication to a network is Remote Authentication Dial-In User Service (RADIUS) authentication.

RADIUS provides the ability to authenticate dial-in, virtual private network (VPN), and wireless network connection attempts. In all of these cases, RADIUS allows centralized authentication for the network, removing the need for separate directories for each remote connectivity service. Many remote access servers and wireless access points can be configured to forward authentication requests to a RADIUS server, rather than having to perform the dial-in authentication themselves. Figure 8-1 gives you an idea of how such a forwarded authentication takes place.

In this figure, the remote access client can dial in to any of the three dial-in servers, 23.222.15.8, 23.100.24.5, or 23.10.10.10, and use the same credentials. These credentials can be used even if the three dial-in servers are owned and operated by different Internet Service Providers (ISPs). Each dial-in server must be configured as a RADIUS client to the RADIUS server located at IP address 39.200.1.2.

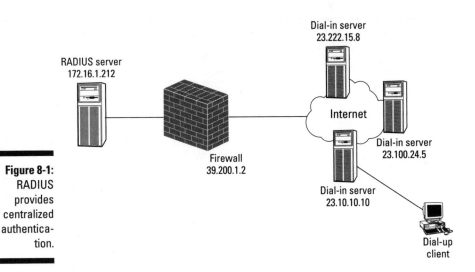

Figure 8-1:
RADIUS
provides
centralized
authentica-
tion.

The dial-in servers use the externally advertised IP address for the RADIUS server, which may not be the true internal IP address of the RADIUS server. The RADIUS server is advertised at the external IP address of the firewall, 39.200.1.2, and then a static address mapping at the firewall redirects the packets to the RADIUS server located at IP address 172.16.1.212 on the private network.

RADIUS functionality

RADIUS is used to provide the following functionality to dial-in network solutions:

- ✔ **Centralize authentication:** All authentication requests are passed to a single account database for an organization, which eliminates account and password synchronization issues.

- ✔ **Centralize accounting:** Dial-in servers that are configured as RADIUS clients can be configured to forward all logging and accounting information to a RADIUS server. This forwarding ensures that logging takes place at a centralized location.

- ✔ **Centralize security settings:** RADIUS servers distribute centralized security settings to configured RADIUS clients by implementing remote access policies. This centralized distribution of the remote access policies ensures that consistent security is applied at all dial-in servers, thus eliminating security breaches due to nonstandard security settings.

When a RADIUS server is deployed on your network, you must determine whether you want to use authentication services, accounting services, or both. The RADIUS server listens to different ports, depending on whether it is listening for authentication or accounting requests. RADIUS authentication requests are sent to UDP port 1812 at the RADIUS server, and RADIUS accounting information is sent to UDP port 1813.

Some RADIUS implementations use UDP port 1645 for RADIUS authentication and UDP port 1646 for RADIUS accounting. The new standard is UDP ports 1812 and 1813, but you should be aware of earlier implementations.

Configuring inbound RADIUS firewall rules

If you use RADIUS authentication or accounting, your firewall must be configured to allow RADIUS packets to be passed to the RADIUS server behind your firewall. As shown in Figure 8-1, only three dial-in servers are configured as RADIUS clients. To restrict RADIUS access to only those three dial-in servers, the rules in Table 8-3 can be configured at your firewall.

Table 8-3	Firewall Rules to Access an Internal RADIUS Server					
Protocol	*Transport Protocol*	*Source IP*	*Source Port*	*Target IP*	*Target Port*	*Action*
RADIUS Authentication	UDP	23.222.15.8	Any	172.16.1.212	1812	Allow
RADIUS Accounting	UDP	23.222.15.8	Any	172.16.1.212	1813	Allow
RADIUS Authentication	UDP	23.100.24.5	Any	172.16.1.212	1812	Allow
RADIUS Accounting	UDP	23.100.24.5	Any	172.16.1.212	1813	Allow
RADIUS Authentication	UDP	23.10.10.10	Any	172.16.1.212	1812	Allow
RADIUS Accounting	UDP	23.10.10.10	Any	172.16.1.212	1813	Allow

Some RADIUS implementations use UDP port 1645 for RADIUS authentication and UDP port 1646 for RADIUS accounting. The new standard is UDP ports 1812 and 1813, but you should be aware of earlier implementations.

Remote access clients never communicate with the RADIUS server. Only the dial-in servers communicate directly with the RADIUS servers. The only thing required of the remote access clients is the configuration of either a RADIUS prefix or suffix. For example, suppose that your company, BigCo, wants to implement a prefix to identify its clients. Thus, a user named Bob Jones would submit his name in the format BigCo\BJones. Likewise, if your company wants to implement a RADIUS suffix instead, Bob's name would be formatted as BJones@bigco.com.

IPSec Encryption

Many protocols in use today transmit data in cleartext. Using cleartext leaves your network open to packet-sniffer attacks, in which data packets are captured and viewed as they are transmitted across the network. Although some protocols, such as HTTP, provide the ability to use application-level security through SSL, many other protocols don't have built-in security mechanisms.

The solution to this problem is to implement Internet Protocol Security (IPSec). IPSec allows data to be encrypted as it is transmitted across the network.

The following two protocols that are part of IPSec can be used to protect transmitted data:

- **Authentication Header (AH):** AH provides authenticity protection to transmitted data by digitally signing each packet to ensure two things: that the packet is not modified in transit and that the originator of the packet is who she says she is.

- **Encapsulating Security Payload (ESP):** ESP provides encryption services by encrypting the payload of each packet so that the contents of the packet can't be observed.

In addition to the two protocols used by IPSec, you can use two modes to transmit the IPSec-protected data (see Figure 8-2). *Transport Mode* is used to encrypt data as it is exchanged between two endpoints. The data encrypted at one computer or network host is decrypted only when it arrives at the target computer or network host. *Tunnel Mode* encrypts the data for only a portion of the distance between the source and target hosts. Generally, Mode is used to encrypt data between network segments as it is transmitted over an unsecured portion of the network — such as the Internet.

The configuration that determines what — and over what path — data is encrypted is known as a *security association (SA)*. SAs are negotiated between computers/hosts; not between users. You can't configure an IPSec SA between two users on the network; it can be configured only between the computers that they use. Figure 8-3 shows how an IPSec SA is negotiated between a client and a server where IPSec is configured to encrypt Telnet sessions.

The steps shown in Figure 8-3 take place as follows:

1. A Telnet client sends an initial packet destined to the Telnet server.

2. The client computer's IPSec driver intercepts the packet before it is transmitted and compares protocol information with a list of IPSec filters. In this example, the client computer is configured to negotiate an SA between the client computer and the Telnet server. The negotiated SA defines the IPSec protocol, the algorithms used for protecting the transmitted data, and the authentication protocol.

To negotiate the SA, the two computers involved in the transmission of data must mutually authenticate each other. IPSec supports three methods of authentication: shared secret, Kerberos, and certificates. The method that you choose may require additional firewall rules at the firewall to allow authentication packets to be exchanged.

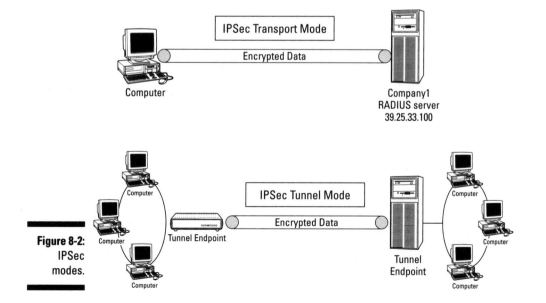

Figure 8-2: IPSec modes.

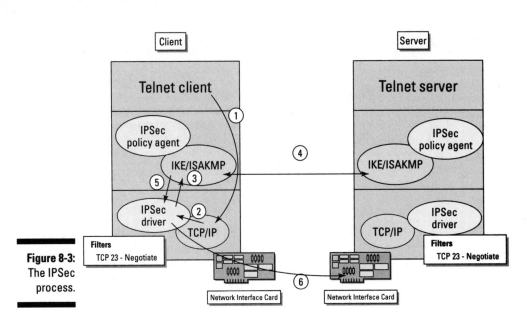

Figure 8-3:
The IPSec
process.

3. The IPSec driver stalls the packets and instructs the Internet Key Exchange (IKE) to negotiate an SA between the client and server.

4. The IKE protocol is used to negotiate the necessary SAs between the client and the server. Both the client and the server use UDP port 500 for the IKE negotiation.

5. The IPSec driver is informed about the resultant SA so that it can encrypt/sign the data by using the negotiated algorithms before it is transmitted.

6. The IPSec driver applies the required encryption and/or integrity algorithm to the data and then transmits the data to the server.

When does IPSec fail?

Because of the security applied to data when IPSec protection is applied, IPSec can't pass through a firewall that performs Network Address Translation (NAT). NAT replaces the original source IP address and port information in an outgoing packet with external address information. When IPSec is applied to a data packet, the source IP address and source port address fields are protected fields. For AH (Authentication Header), the modification of the source data invalidates the signature applied to the packet, and for ESP (Encapsulating Security Payload), the source data can't be read because it is encrypted.

What will the future bring?

Currently, two draft documents are before the Internet Engineering Task Force (IETF) that propose a method for the negotiation and passing of IPSec packets through NAT devices.

When a new standard is proposed to the IETF, this pre-Request for Comment (RFC) document is known as an Internet Draft.

The first draft, `draft-ietf-ipsec-nat-t-ike-05.txt`, proposes a method for two hosts to negotiate IPSec NAT traversal. The draft outlines a modification to the Internet Key Exchange (IKE) protocol that would allow the two endpoints to identify whether NAT traversal is supported by these endpoints and would also identify if one or more NAT devices exist between the two hosts. This modified IKE packet is sometimes referred to as a NAT-D, or NAT detection packet. NAT devices are detected by determining whether the IP addresses or port addresses in a packet are changed as the packet is sent between the source and destination hosts. This is accomplished by both sides calculating a hash that is based on the source and destination IP addresses and ports, and then comparing the results. If the results are the same, no NAT device exists between the two hosts.

The current version of the draft *Negotiation of NAT-Traversal in the IKE* (`draft-ietf-ipsec-nat-t-ike-05.txt`) is available at the time of this writing at `www.ietf.org/internet-drafts/ draft-ietf-ipsec-nat-t-ike-05.txt`. By the time you read this book, the draft may be updated with a newer draft or may have been released as a Request for Comment (RFC).

The second draft, `draft-ietf-ipsec-udp-encaps-06.txt`, proposes encapsulating the IPSec payload in a UDP header, which would allow the NAT device to translate the IPSec packets as they traverse the NAT device. This UDP encapsulation doesn't require firewalls or other NAT devices to do anything different when they perform NAT on outbound or inbound IPSec packets. This method is referred to as NAT-T or NAT traversal.

The current version of the draft *UDP Encapsulation of IPSec Packets* (`draft-ietf-ipsec-udp-encaps-06.txt`) is available at the time of this writing at `www.ietf.org/internet-drafts/draft-ietf-ipsec-udp-encaps-06.txt`. By the time you read this book, the draft may be updated with a newer draft or have been released as a Request for Comment (RFC).

Transport Mode ESP Encapsulation

The *UDP Encapsulation of IPSec Packets* draft proposes the addition of a new UDP header between the original IP header and the ESP header — the one added by the IPSec process — as shown in Figure 8-4.

The UDP header is initially configured with both source and destination ports of UDP port 4500. The use of this port indicates that the packet is a UDP encapsulated IPSec packet.

The *UDP Encapsulation of IPSec Packets* draft only supports ESP encryption. This draft includes no support for AH IPSec protection.

When the IPSec packet passes through a NAT, the NAT device can now translate the original IP header and the newly inserted UDP header without changing the hash value created by signing the ESP Header, TCP/UDP Header, Data, and ESP Trailer, as shown in Figure 8-4.

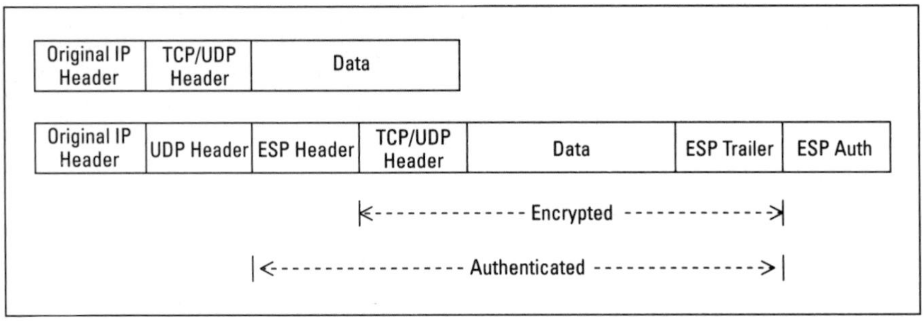

Figure 8-4:
UDP Encapsulation of an IPSec packet.

Original IP Header	TCP/UDP Header	Data			

Original IP Header	UDP Header	ESP Header	TCP/UDP Header	Data	ESP Trailer	ESP Auth

|<------------- Encrypted -------------->|

|<------------------ Authenticated ---------------->|

Tunnel Mode ESP Encapsulation

The *UDP Encapsulation of IPSec Packets* draft also includes documentation on how to pass IPSec Transport Mode packets through a NAT device. For Tunnel Mode, the original IP packet is encapsulated, as shown in Figure 8-5. The proposed tunnel packet construct differs from a typical ESP Tunnel Mode packet through the addition of the UDP header between the new IP header and the ESP header.

As with Transport Mode, the UDP header is initially configured with both source and destination ports of UDP port 4500, allowing for the translation of the source and destination IP and port information by a NAT device.

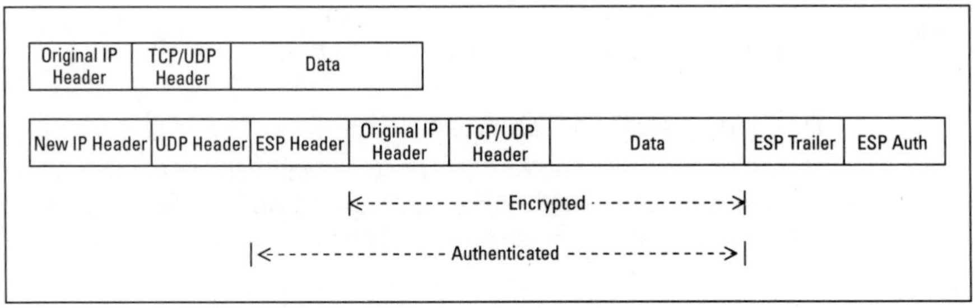

Figure 8-5:
UDP Encapsulation of an IPSec Tunnel Mode packet.

Original IP Header	TCP/UDP Header	Data					

New IP Header	UDP Header	ESP Header	Original IP Header	TCP/UDP Header	Data	ESP Trailer	ESP Auth

|<----------- Encrypted ----------->|

|<-------------- Authenticated -------------->|

Configuring a firewall to pass IPSec data

After you have determined whether your firewall supports IPSec (in other words, that your firewall is not performing NAT) or whether it supports IPSec NAT-T, you are ready to configure the necessary firewall rules.

ESP and AH are protocols that are similar to TCP or UDP. When you define a firewall rule for ESP, you define that the protocol ID is protocol ID 50. Likewise, for AH, you define the protocol ID to be protocol ID 51. You don't define ports as you would for a TCP- or UDP-based protocol.

Assuming that IPSec is used to protect all Telnet traffic sent to the Telnet Server located at the IP address 192.168.22.44, the firewall rules shown in Table 8-4 must be configured. Notice that you don't have to create firewall rules for the Telnet protocol (TCP port 23) because the data passing through the firewall is encrypted.

Table 8-4		Firewall Rules to Pass IPSec Traffic				
Protocol	*Transport Protocol*	*Source IP*	*Source Port*	*Target IP*	*Target Port*	*Action*
IKE	UDP	Any	500	192.168.22.44	500	Allow
ESP	ID 50	192.168.1.55		192.168.22.44		Allow
AH	ID 51	192.168.1.55		192.168.22.44		Allow

Note: These packets only allow the IPSec security association to be initiated by the Telnet Client.

If the Telnet client and Telnet server support NAT-T traversal, then different rules are required to allow for the translation of the UDP source ports, as shown in Table 8-5.

Table 8-5		Firewall Rules to Pass IPSec NAT Traversal Traffic				
Protocol	*Transport Protocol*	*Source IP*	*Source Port*	*Target IP*	*Target Port*	*Action*
NAT-D	UDP	Any	Any	192.168.22.44	500	Allow
NAT-T	UDP	Any	Any	192.168.22.44	4500	Allow

Let Me In: Tunneling through the Internet

As people acquire faster connections to the Internet from their homes by using Digital Subscriber Line (DSL) or cable modem connections, the methods that people use to connect to their offices from home change. Why use a slow modem connection when you can connect directly over the Internet by using your fast Internet connection? For users with a fast connection, a tunneling, or *Virtual Private Network (VPN),* solution fits the bill. Tunneling works like a dial-up connection, except that you gain the speed of your fast Internet connection. Rather than send packets over a slow phone line, data is encapsulated in a tunnel as it traverses the public network. Only when it reaches the tunnel endpoint is the data unencapsulated and transmitted in its regular format on the network.

Selecting a tunneling protocol

Two protocols are commonly used by tunnels when connecting to an office: *Point-to-Point Tunneling Protocol (PPTP)* and *Layer Two Tunneling Protocol (L2TP).* Both solutions allow secure connectivity over a public network to a tunnel server, but have differences in their implementations.

For example, PPTP uses Microsoft Point-to-Point Encryption (MPPE) to provide encryption of transmitted data. On the other hand, L2TP has no built-in encryption algorithm. Instead, IPSec is used to encrypt the transmitted data. Table 8-6 shows the common decision factors considered when deciding between implementing PPTP or L2TP tunnel solutions.

Table 8-6	Choosing a Tunneling Protocol	
Decision Factor	*PPTP*	*L2TP/IPSec*
Support older clients	x	
Pass through NAT	x	x*
Requires a public key infrastructure		x
Strongest form of encryption		x
Computer authentication		x

* As with the IPSec traffic, L2TP tunnels implemented by client operating systems that support NAT-D and NAT-T can implement a tunnel through a firewall that performs NAT.

Figure 8-6 shows a remote client that can connect to two different tunnel servers.

VPN Server 1 has an IP address of 23.23.2.35, whereas VPN Server 2 has an IP address of 172.16.1.211. Because PPTP can pass through any firewall solution that supports filters for protocol ID 47, the remote client can use PPTP to establish a tunnel to either VPN server. Likewise, if the remote access client and both VPN servers support NAT-D and NAT-T, L2TP/IPSec may be used to connect to both VPN servers. If the remote access clients or VPN Server 2 don't support NAT-D and NAT-T, L2TP can only be used to connect to VPN Server 1. L2TP access to VPN Server 2 is not possible in this case because the firewall at 39.200.1.2 is performing NAT on incoming traffic.

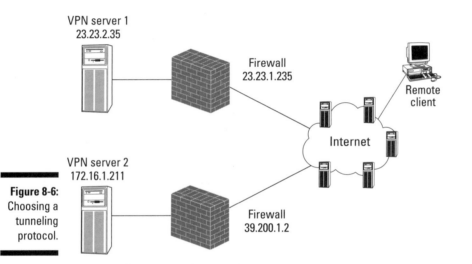

Figure 8-6:
Choosing a
tunneling
protocol.

Using PPTP firewall rules

As outlined in Table 8-6, the two most common reasons for selecting PPTP as a tunneling protocol are for supporting older Microsoft clients that require tunneling connectivity or for situations in which a tunnel must pass through a firewall that performs NAT.

A tunnel server receiving PPTP connections listens for the connection on TCP port 1723. In addition, PPTP packets are encapsulated using a protocol named Generic Routing Encapsulation (GRE). A GRE packet is identified by its protocol identification number, protocol ID 47. As with ESP and AH packets, no port numbers are associated with the GRE protocol. If you were configuring your firewall to allow PPTP connections to VPN Server 1, as shown in Figure 8-6, the firewall rules in Table 8-7 must be implemented at the firewall.

Table 8-7		Firewall Filters to Access a PPTP Tunnel Server				
Protocol	**Transport Protocol**	**Source IP**	**Source Port**	**Target IP**	**Target Port**	**Action**
PPTP	TCP	Any	Any	172.16.1.211	1723	Allow
GRE	ID 47	Any		172.16.1.211		Allow

Using L2TP/IPSec firewall rules

The tough part about configuring L2TP firewall rules is that you have to ignore the fact that L2TP is being used. Why, you ask? Because the L2TP protocol is encrypted using IPSec when it passes through your firewall. The firewall is unable to determine what protocol is actually encrypted in the IPSec packets.

The L2TP client and the L2TP server establish an IPSec security association (SA) that uses the ESP protocol to encrypt all data transmitted from the client to the L2TP server's UDP port 1701. The packets are only decrypted after they are received by the L2TP tunnel server.

So what do you do at the firewall to allow the L2TP/IPSec packets to pass? You simply define the same firewall rules that you use for IPSec. The difference is that you know the endpoint of the tunnel. Table 8-8 shows the rules required to allow L2TP/IPSec tunnel connections only to the tunnel server located at IP address 23.23.2.35.

Table 8-8		Firewall Rules to Access an L2TP Tunnel Server				
Protocol	**Transport Protocol**	**Source IP**	**Source Port**	**Target IP**	**Target Port**	**Action**
IKE	UDP	Any	500	23.23.2.35	500	Allow
ESP	ID 50	Any		23.23.2.35		Allow
AH	ID 51	Any		23.23.2.35		Allow

If the remote access clients and remote access servers support NAT-D and NAT-T, then the firewall can allow IPSec connections to both VPN Server 1 and VPN Server 2. In this case, the IPSec protocols are encapsulated in UDP packets, thus removing the need for the ESP and AH filters shown in Table 8-8.

Table 8-9 shows the firewall rules required to allow L2TP/IPSec tunnel connections only to the two internal tunnel servers.

**Table 8-9   Firewall Rules to Access an L2TP Tunnel Server
with IPSec NAT Traversal**

Protocol	Transport Protocol	Source IP	Source Port	Target IP	Target Port	Action
NAT-D	UDP	Any	Any	23.23.2.35	500	Allow
NAT-T	UDP	Any	4500	23.23.2.35	4500	Allow
NAT-D	UDP	Any	Any	172.16.1.211	500	Allow
NAT-T	UDP	Any	Any	172.16.1.211	4500	Allow

Note: The remote-access client will connect to VPN Server 2; it will connect to the external IP address of 39.200.1.2. As with all firewall rules, the actual rule will list the true IP address of the VPN server.

At this point, your head is probably spinning from all of these rules, rules, rules that you must implement at a firewall for the complex protocols. The bad news is that still more rules exist that you can implement at your firewall. The good news is that the rules are much more logical and definitely easier to digest (at least we think they are tasty). Rather than discussing protocols, the next chapter looks at how a firewall can implement a Security policy that restricts who can access the Internet and what they can do on the Internet, and even limits what hours they can access the Internet.

Chapter 9

Configuring "Employees Only" and Other Specific Rules

*A*s an administrator, you can place restrictions on which particular users are allowed to access the Internet by using specific protocols. Additionally, you can place restrictions on access during certain times of the day and to specific Web sites or content. The sections in this chapter walk you through the decisions of implementing these specific rules.

Limiting Access by Users: Not All Are Chosen

Sometimes, network administrators want to restrict access to the Internet to specific users on the network. In a perfect world, all the users that require access to the Internet sit in the same part of the office and are on a dedicated subnet. In this scenario, you could configure firewall rules at the firewall to allow only users on that specific subnet to access the Internet.

In the real world, however, people who require identical Internet access don't sit in the same section in the office. In fact, in larger organizations, they often don't even work in the same city.

To restrict access to only specific users or groups of users, many of today's firewalls interact with your network operating system to restrict access to specific protocols or Internet sites based on user identities or group memberships. Of course, in order for this interaction to happen, authentication must take place on the network so that the individual users can be identified. After users have been authenticated, the firewall uses their network identities to determine whether they have access to a requested protocol or site. If the user (or groups to which the user belongs) is allowed access, then the access will succeed. If the user (or any groups to which the user belongs) is explicitly denied access to a protocol or site, then the access will fail.

Restricting access to protocols to specific users or groups enables a firewall administrator to further refine firewall rules by restricting who can use a protocol that is allowed to pass through the firewall. Adding authentication helps a firewall administrator to better implement firewall filters that reflect the true Security policy of an organization.

Figure 9-1 shows an example of how a Microsoft Internet Security and Acceleration (ISA) server protocol rule that we created (named *Web for engineering*) is applied only to the engineering group. This is not just an ISA server feature! Most firewalls interact with the network operating system to authenticate access to Internet protocols.

In this chapter, all examples use the Microsoft ISA server.

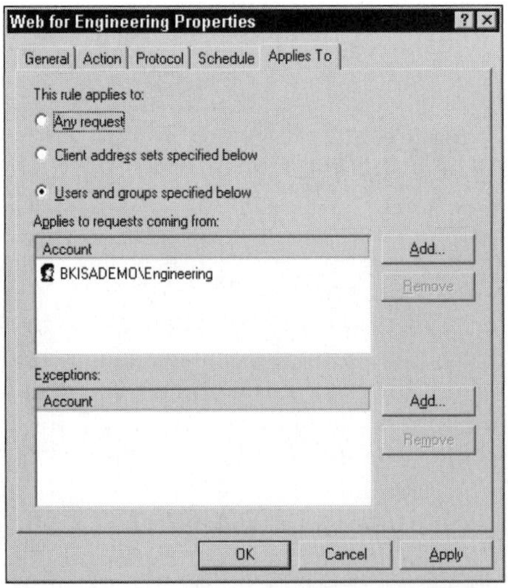

Figure 9-1:
Restricting an ISA Server Protocol Rule to the engineering group.

Web for Engineering Properties

General | Action | Protocol | Schedule | Applies To

This rule applies to:
- ○ Any request
- ○ Client address sets specified below
- ● Users and groups specified below

Applies to requests coming from:

Account	
BKISADEMO\Engineering	Add...
	Remove

Exceptions:

Account	
	Add...
	Remove

OK   Cancel   Apply

Many firewalls provide authentication by using protocols such as Remote Authentication Dial-In User Service (RADIUS) or Terminal Access Controller

Access Control System Plus (TACACS+). Both protocols allow a firewall to forward authentication requests to a central directory, thus allowing user- or group-based authentication.

Filtering Types of Content

For cases in which an office may have low bandwidth availability, a company may want to restrict the types of content that can be downloaded from the Internet. For example, if 50 people share a 64 Kbps Integrated Services Digital Network (ISDN) connection, you may want to prevent users from downloading video content from the Internet.

Another possibility is to prevent questionable content from being downloaded. For example, a company may prevent the downloading of MP3 files to prevent the storage and distribution of illegally copied music on the corporate network.

In this respect, filtering forms of content is not related to the actual information that is shown on a Web page or in an Internet application. Filtering content refers to the actual format of data that can be downloaded from the Internet. For example, Figure 9-2 shows an ISA Server Site and Content Rule setting that prevents the downloading of Audio, Video, and Virtual Reality Modeling Language (VRML). This filter prevents users from downloading bandwidth-intensive content in order to preserve the limited available bandwidth on the connection to the Internet.

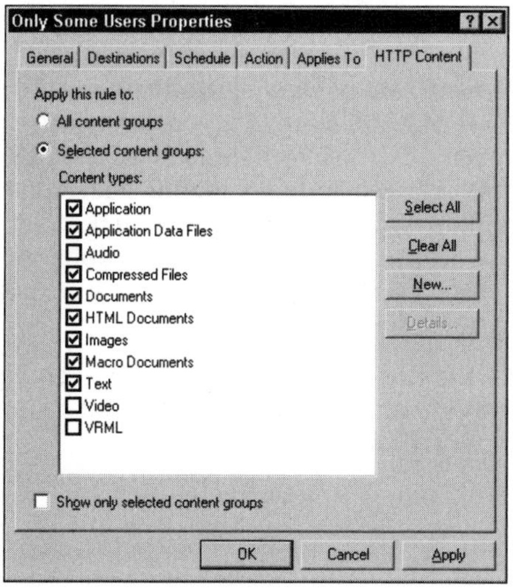

Figure 9-2:
Restricting content in an ISA Server Site and Content Rule.

Filtering Other Content

Okay, but what about the stuff that actually appears on the page? Up to this point in the chapter, we have talked about filtering based on the format of the content. In some cases, a company doesn't want its employees surfing for pornography, reading hate-group Web sites, or using the Internet for other content-related reasons. What can you do to prevent access to these types of resources on the Internet?

You have two solutions:

✔ Prevent the use of Uniform Resource Locators (URLs) that are known to be undesirable Web links.

✔ Implement content rating to prevent access to specific Web content.

A third possibility is to use a firewall that performs *content inspection*. Content inspection looks at the HTML content and searches for configured keywords and suppresses the display of such content.

Generally, a mix of the first two solutions is used to prevent access to undesired content.

Preventing access to known "bad" sites

Many Web sites are known to contain questionable content. For example, if you have children, you may want to prevent access to pornographic sites. You can use a couple of different strategies:

✔ **URL blocking at the firewall:** Many firewall products enable you to configure firewalls so that specific URLs are blocked. If any form of the URL is requested by a user, access to the Internet resource is blocked. Because creating your own list of bad sites and maintaining such a list can be an unmanageable chore, take advantage of the software that automatically blocks certain types of Web sites and corresponding subscriptions to lists of such Web sites. Such content-filtering solutions are often implemented as add-on programs to existing firewalls.

✔ **URL blocking at the client:** Most browsers allow you to configure a list of sites that are blocked. Any attempts to connect to a URL included in the listing are prevented by the browser.

Implementing Content Rating

What happens if you don't have the time, patience, or resolve to find all of the "bad" URLs on the Internet? Have no fear, content rating is here! Content rating applies content ratings defined by the Internet Content Rating Association (ICRA), formerly known as the Recreational Software Advisory Council on the Internet (RSACi), to all Web sites visited by a browser.

As shown in Figure 9-3, the RSACi settings allow access to Web sites to be defined based on four categories of content: language, nudity, sex, and violence. If the Web site is rated above the level defined in your browser, access is prevented. Likewise, you can also configure how your browser handles unrated sites. The configuration is pretty simple: You decide either to allow or block access to unrated sites.

Content Advisor

Ratings | Approved Sites | General | Advanced |

Select a category to view the rating levels:

- RSACi
  - Language
  - Nudity
  - Sex
  - Violence

Adjust the slider to specify what users are allowed to see:

Level 0: No violence

Description
No aggressive violence; no natural or accidental violence.

To view the Internet page for this rating service, click More Info. More Info...

OK   Cancel   Apply

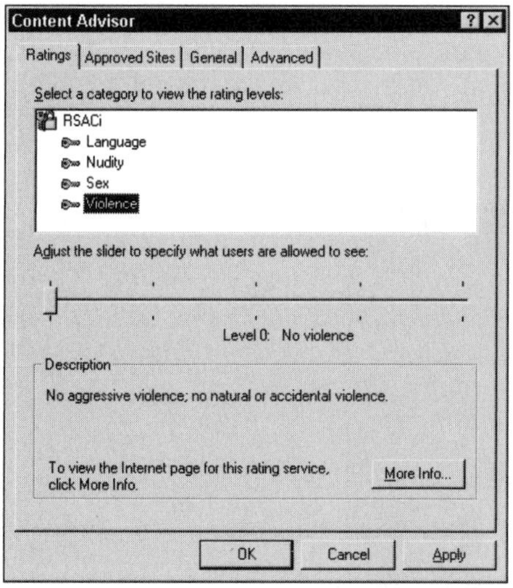

Figure 9-3:
Implementing RSACi ratings.

The RSACi ratings are applied by having the browser inspect *meta tags* embedded in a HyperText Markup Language (HTML) page. If these meta tags don't appear in the HTML page, the site is considered an unrated site. Blocking access to unrated sites is a tough decision. It can be a bad idea, because it can prevent access to useful Web sites that have not implemented the necessary meta tags. On the other hand, a pornography site can input meta tags that don't accurately describe the content of the Web site.

You can also try several third-party software applications, such as Net Nanny, on your home computer in order to prevent children from accessing adult-oriented Web sites. Although you can do the same thing through most browser settings, these third-party software applications make it easier for a parent because they are preconfigured with recommended settings. Be warned, however, that these applications are not perfect. You still may be able to access pornographic sites and also be blocked from accessing legitimate sites.

Setting the Clock: Filtering on Date/Time

The final configuration that you may want to use at your firewall is to limit access during specific times of day. For example, you may want to prevent the playing of Internet audio during the day due to bandwidth limitations, but allow access to the night shift.

This configuration is accomplished by defining time frames for a specific packet filter. For example, Figure 9-4 shows an ISA Server Site and Content rule that is scheduled to be only active on weekdays outside of regular work hours.

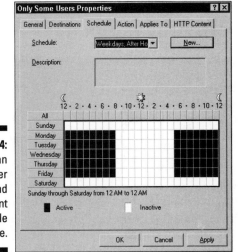

Figure 9-4:
Defining an
ISA Server
Site and
Content
Rule
schedule.

If someone attempts to use the protocol defined in the Site and Content Rule during the inactive hours, access is prevented. On the other hand, if access is attempted during the active hours, it is granted. Using time-based rules allows a company to lessen Internet restrictions after business hours, while ensuring that only approved Internet usage takes place during business hours.

Part III
Designing Network Configurations

The 5th Wave   By Rich Tennant

"Remember – I want the firewall surrounded by flaming workstations with the word 'Motherboard' scrolling underneath."

In this part . . .

Boot camp time! Defining rules on what your firewall
should do is not the complete picture. You have to
set up a working solution, too. In this part, you see how
you can place your firewall into your network to ensure
that the network gets the protection that it needs.

This part tells you everything you need to know to set up
a firewall for your home office or small office network. You
corporate types will hear about specially protected areas of
a network, called Demilitarized Zones (DMZs), and how you
can use multiple firewalls to create even stronger DMZs.

You can use several common firewall configurations to
protect your network. This part shows you how to put it
all together.

Now go put your boots on.

Chapter 10

Setting Up Firewalls for SOHO or Personal Use

A trade-off exists between how secure you want your firewall architecture to be and how much cost and effort is associated with realizing this goal. This trade-off is different for different companies. A small office or home office has different security needs from larger offices or enterprise-style businesses.

You can secure your connection to the Internet in many ways. All these solutions rank from not secure, when you use no firewall at all, to very secure, when you use several firewalls in sequence. Invariably, the most secure solutions take the longest to design and deploy, the most effort to administer, and generally are the most expensive. On the other hand, the most simple solution may be cheap, the easiest to set up and administer, but may not provide enough security for your network.

In this chapter, we look at deploying firewalls for small offices, home offices, or even for personal use.

No-Box Solution: ISP Firewall Service

Offices that don't want to spend the money to set up their own network firewall can rely on the ISP that they use to connect to the Internet to provide the firewall function. Although not all ISPs want to provide this service, it has the obvious benefit of being a low-cost solution.

However, for the following reasons, using an ISP to provide firewall function isn't necessarily an effective technique:

- ✔ ISPs may not want to assume the responsibility of guaranteeing your security on the Internet. Protecting against every possible attack is a complex undertaking and requires cooperation from your users, for example, when opening e-mail attachments.

- ✔ The ISP solution is not customized to your needs but provides protection to many other customers as well. This means that firewall rules will generally be more lax than you may want them to be.

- ✔ The ISP firewall rules may be too restrictive. If you want to use a protocol that isn't allowed through the ISP firewall, you may not be able to change that configuration.

- ✔ Generally, firewall solutions that don't fully meet the Internet access needs of your users may tempt them into secretly installing dial-up lines or port redirection software to circumvent the restrictive firewall rules, and thereby lower the security of your internal network. This is especially true for an ISP firewall service that can't be tailored to your specific needs.

Single-Box Solution: Dual-Homed Firewall

The simplest solution for a firewall architecture that you can deploy yourself is to use a single dual-homed computer as a firewall. A *dual-homed* computer is simultaneously connected to two networks — for example, the internal network and the Internet. For home users, this computer may be the only computer that they have. Personal firewalls, such as BlackICE or ZoneAlarm, are well suited for this scenario. For small offices or home offices, the single firewall machine can be a desktop computer used to dial in to the ISP or a dedicated machine. All other computers in the office are connected in a peer-to-peer style and use that single machine to access the Internet.

The following are the advantages of using a single firewall to secure your connection to the Internet:

- ✔ **Cost:** Obviously, deploying a single firewall is less expensive than solutions that require two or more dedicated firewall machines. This includes the cost of the firewall software and the hardware.

- ✔ **Simplicity:** The single firewall is the one place that needs to be configured to protect the connection to the Internet. You can concentrate on this single machine. More complex designs are harder to understand and have more room for configuration errors.

The single dual-homed firewall solution has some distinct disadvantages as well:

- ✔ **Single point of protection:** All network traffic going to and from the Internet is going through this single firewall. This makes it a simple solution, but also introduces a big risk. If the firewall is compromised, a hacker can access your entire network.

- ✔ **Long single rule list:** Although it may seem an advantage that all firewall rules are in one list, this single list may be quite long and complex. This complexity makes it harder to understand the current rule base of the firewall.

- ✔ **No dedicated network segment:** A dual-homed firewall only connects to two networks. One connection is to the Internet, and the other connection is to the internal network. This may be enough to provide security to a small business, but many businesses want a third dedicated network segment for protecting servers that are accessible from the Internet. We discuss these screened subnets, or demilitarized zones (DMZs), in Chapter 11.

A dual-homed host is capable of routing packets between the two network interfaces. You should make sure that these packets can't directly route from one network to the other network without being inspected by the firewall software on the computer. If the firewall software doesn't automatically prevent this, you should disable this routing function manually. Directly routing from one network interface to another network interface is also called *IP forwarding.*

Screened Host

If you want to provide services to the Internet, such as a Web site, FTP servers, or a VPN dial-in service for traveling users of your organization, you have to decide on which computer you want to run those services. You have a choice: You can either run those services on the dual-homed firewall itself, or you can designate a server on your internal network to run those services.

A designated server on your internal network that provides services to the Internet is called a *screened host.* We take this concept one step further in Chapter 11, where we explain that such designated servers are not on the internal network but on a separate network segment. This is a screened subnet or DMZ.

A screened host on the internal network can also be used to forward or proxy requests to other computers on the internal network. Or, if you want to provide outbound Internet access, it can forward packets from computers on the internal network to the firewall. Note that the screened host doesn't need to have two network adapters to do this task. The screened host can provide this forward or proxy service by using only one adapter connected to the internal network.

The advantage of this approach is that the firewall rules on the dual-homed firewall can restrict the network traffic to only go to and from the screened host. Because of this special role, the screened host should be secured more than other computers on the internal network. Such a highly secured computer that has relative direct contact with the Internet is called a *bastion host.* Computers on the Internet can't directly connect to other internal computers. All connections should go through the secured screened-host system.

Compare a screened host with a press officer for a large company. All contacts from the "hostile" press reporters should go through the press officer, who is probably extra-alert and media-trained to handle the press questions. The press can't directly contact other employees in the company. A press officer will probably see herself as a bastion host. To get into the press room, the press reporters have to show a press ID to the doorman. The doorman acts as the firewall in this scenario.

A screened host combined with a dual-homed firewall still has the same disadvantages of a single dual-homed firewall solution. Both the dual-homed firewall providing the packet filtering and the screened host providing the service to the Internet are each a single point of protection. If an attacker manages to break in and compromise either the dual-home firewall or the screened host, the entire internal network may be at risk.

Bypassing the screened host

In reality, a screened host may not be able to proxy or forward all protocols that users on the internal network are allowed to use to access the Internet. The screened host can only provide certain functions. This means that, for outbound network traffic, the firewall rules on the dual-homed firewall may allow direct connections from the computers on the internal network for some protocols, and only allow connections from a screened host for other protocols.

Table 10-1 shows the firewall rules for a dual-homed firewall that allows SMTP and POP3 e-mail network traffic from all computers on the internal network (subnet 192.168.222.0/24), and allows HTTP and HTTPS Web traffic only from the screened host (IP address 192.168.222.15).

Table 10-1   Outbound Firewall Rules (Direct and Screened Host)

Protocol	Transport Protocol	Source IP	Source Port	Target IP	Target Port	Action
SMTP	TCP	192.168.222.0/24	Any	Any	25	Allow
POP3	TCP	192.168.222.0/24	Any	Any	110	Allow
HTTP	TCP	192.168.222.15	Any	Any	80	Allow
HTTPS	TCP	192.168.222.15	Any	Any	443	Allow

The packet filter listing reads as if just one computer on the internal network can browse the Web. In effect, that is indeed what the configuration looks like for the dual-homed firewall. The screened host itself can be configured to proxy the HTTP and HTTPS requests from the other computers on the internal network.

Note that the computers on the internal network need to know this setup. They should send Web requests to the screened host, and send e-mail traffic directly to the internal network adapter of the dual-homed firewall.

Deployment Scenario

In order to understand the firewall solution for small offices, we will look at an example to allow the DNS and Web (HTTP and HTTPS) protocols for outbound Internet access.

Allowing internal network users to access the Internet

When users on the internal network want to "surf the Web," they typically type the Web site name in the address bar of the Web browser. This name is resolved to the IP address of the Web site with the help of DNS servers. After the Web browser obtains the IP address, it can connect to the IP address on the Internet by using the HTTP or HTTPS protocol.

DNS queries

You have good security reasons to not let the computers on the internal network connect directly to the firewall to resolve the DNS name by DNS servers on the Internet. The internal network may use DNS to locate internal resources as well. If the computers on the internal network connect directly (through the firewall) to DNS servers on the Internet, they may be tricked into resolving internal names to external IP addresses. The consequence could be that instead of sending files to what they think is their home folder on an internal server, they actually send their files to a rogue external server.

The method to "resolve" this problem, so to speak, is to send all DNS queries from all the computers on the internal network to an internal DNS server. This server is able to answer all queries that relate to internal resources directly. The internal DNS server should forward any DNS queries that it can't resolve to an external DNS server. To implement this solution, the only computer on the internal network that is allowed to send DNS queries out to the Internet is the internal DNS server.

HTTP/HTTPS requests

After the DNS name is resolved to an IP address, the computer on the internal network uses the IP address to connect to the external Web site, as shown in Figure 10-1. You may want to restrict outbound HTTP and HTTPS network traffic to only one server on the internal network, as well. All Web queries must then run through that server. This allows you to filter for hours of operation, suitable content, inappropriate Web sites and, if the Internet access is allowed, cache the Web responses.

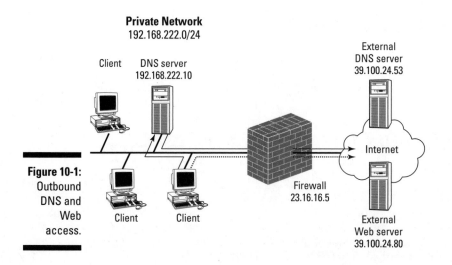

Figure 10-1:
Outbound
DNS and
Web
access.

We assume here for the sake of our example that you don't want to limit the access to external Web sites and that you also don't want to cache the results. This means that all computers on the internal network are allowed to contact the firewall directly for Web requests.

Table 10-2 shows the firewall rules needed on the dual-homed firewall.

Table 10-2		Outbound Internet Access					
Protocol	*Transport Protocol*	*Source IP*	*Source Port*	*Target IP*	*Target Port*	*Action*	
DNS	UDP	192.168.222.10	Any	39.100.24.53	53	Allow	
DNS	TCP	192.168.222.10	Any	39.100.24.53	53	Allow	
HTTP	TCP	192.168.222.0/24	Any	Any	80	Allow	
HTTPS	TCP	192.168.222.0/24	Any	Any	443	Allow	

In this example, the DNS queries can only be sent to the DNS server of the ISP (IP address 39.100.24.53). The DNS firewall rules can be changed to allow the internal DNS server to access any DNS server on the Internet.

Note that the firewall rules on the firewall don't allow DNS zone transfers that are initiated on the Internet, or even DNS queries from the Internet. This hides the internal DNS information, so that users on the Internet can't obtain it.

Chapter 11

Creating Demilitarized Zones with a Single Firewall

*T*he hosting of services on the Internet requires that you expose a portion of your network to the Internet while preventing access to your private network. Although a single firewall between the Internet and a private network provides security for smaller businesses, many larger businesses require that a dedicated segment of the network be established for protecting Internet-accessible resources. The common term for this segment of the network is a *demilitarized zone,* or DMZ.

This chapter examines the basics of configuring a DMZ using a single firewall. Topics include how a DMZ protects your network, typical DMZ configuration, and how to define firewall rules when using a DMZ.

Looking at the Demilitarized Zone: No-Man's Land

A network DMZ is similar to an actual DMZ found in war-torn countries. The DMZ in the military sense represents land near the borders of two warring countries, which, by mutual agreement, can't be entered by either side's military. A network DMZ resides between a public network, typically the Internet, and a company's private network.

Other similarities between a military DMZ and a network DMZ include

- ✔ **All traffic that enters and exits is inspected.**

  In a network, the DMZ is probably the most secured segment of the network because all data that enters or exits the DMZ is inspected against a firewall's rule listing to determine whether the traffic is approved to enter or exit the DMZ.

- ✔ **Resources in the DMZs are inspected to ensure that security is not compromised.**

  Many companies use intrusion detection software in the DMZ, both on the network itself and at each network device located in the DMZ, to identify attacks launched against the resources. The intrusion detection software immediately informs the firewall administrator that a suspected attack is taking place.

- ✔ **DMZs act as a protective boundary to the private network.**

  By placing Internet-accessible resources in the DMZ, a firewall can be configured to prevent all access attempts to the private network from the Internet. Only access attempts directed to the DMZ are permitted by the firewall, as long as the attempts use only approved protocols.

Examining Typical DMZ Configurations

Network administrators deploy two common configurations when deploying a DMZ to protect Internet-accessible resources:

- ✔ **Three-pronged firewalls:** The three prongs refer to the use of three network cards in the firewall. Each network interface card represents one of the "prongs" of the firewall and is assigned to a zone of the network: the private network zone, the Internet zone, and the DMZ.

- ✔ **Multiple firewall DMZs:** The deployment of a DMZ using multiple firewalls is discussed in Chapter 13. This chapter focuses on single firewall DMZ configurations.

As shown in Figure 11-1, a three-pronged firewall uses a single firewall to protect both the private network and the DMZ. This configuration saves money because the company has to purchase only a single firewall. This configuration can also be considered a security risk, however, because if the firewall is breached, the attacker can gain access to the private network as well as the DMZ.

Not every firewall product supports three or more interfaces. If your firewall product supports only two network interfaces, you won't be able to deploy a single firewall DMZ configuration.

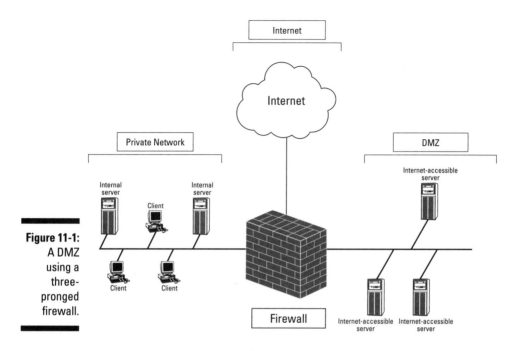

Figure 11-1:
A DMZ
using a
three-
pronged
firewall.

Figure 11-2 shows a typical multiple firewall DMZ configuration. In this scenario, two firewalls are used to separate the DMZ from both the private network and the Internet. Although additional costs are associated with the additional firewall, this configuration is believed to be more secure because an attacker has to breach two firewalls in order to access resources on the private network.

Other terms for DMZs

Although many network administrators approve of the term *DMZ* to describe the secured portion of a company's network, others find the term offensive due to the nature of the atrocities that historically occur in a military DMZ.

Due to the connotations of the term, other terms have evolved to describe a network DMZ, including *screened subnet* and *perimeter network*.

The term *screened subnet* helps to identify the function of a DMZ. All traffic that enters or exits the DMZ is screened against a list of firewall rules to determine whether the firewall should allow, drop, or log the data as it crosses the firewall.

The term *perimeter network* describes the location of a DMZ. Typically, the DMZ resides on the perimeter of a company's network, between the Internet and the private network.

Although both terms define the purpose of a DMZ, neither term catches the full definition of a DMZ because each definition focuses either on function or location.

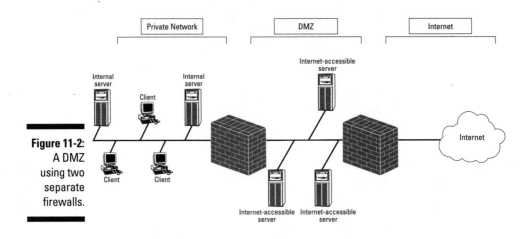

Figure 11-2:
A DMZ
using two
separate
firewalls.

Designing Three-Pronged Firewalls

You must make many decisions when implementing a three-pronged firewall. These decisions include weighing the pros and cons of deploying a single firewall DMZ and deciding how to handle IP addressing assignments based on the protocols that must pass through the firewall.

Pros and cons

After you decide to create a DMZ to protect Internet-accessible resources, you need to decide how to use it to provide the best security. A single firewall with three or more interfaces offers many advantages:

- ✔ **Lower cost:** By only using a single firewall for your DMZ solution, you reduce the costs associated with buying two or more firewall licenses and the hardware required to host the firewalls.

- ✔ **Simplification of zone definitions:** Each network interface card in the firewall represents a zone that must be protected. A three-pronged firewall has separate zones defined for the Internet, the DMZ, and the private network. By deploying zones, you can define the Security policy for each zone. The Security policy assists in defining the necessary firewall rules to provide the required level of security for each zone.

Each zone is physically represented by a network interface card in the firewall, and each zone must have a unique TCP/IP subnet network address to ensure that the firewall can make routing decisions when packets arrive at any of its network interfaces.

✔ **Fewer firewall rules listings to maintain:** With only a single firewall, only a single rules listing must be maintained for incoming packets to the network. This reduces the complexity for firewall rules when a protocol must be passed from the Internet to the private network through two or more firewalls.

As you can guess, deploying a DMZ with only a single firewall has some disadvantages, including

✔ **Your network has a single point of protection.** If an attacker compromises the firewall, he has access to all segments of the network connected to the firewall. This includes both the DMZ and the private network.

✔ **The length of the inbound and outbound lists of firewall rules creates complexities.** All firewall rules are included in a single listing for the firewall. The number of firewall rules that are created can make it difficult to determine why a firewall rule exists in the listing in the first place. Be sure to create detailed documentation on why a firewall rule exists — and what purpose it plays — in order to reduce the effect of this disadvantage.

The number of firewall rules in the listing varies based on the firewall product that you implement. Some firewalls define rules based only on direction (inbound or outbound), whereas other firewalls define rules based on network interface cards.

✔ **The firewall can become a bottleneck.** All network traffic that passes between the Internet and the DMZ, the DMZ and the private network, and potentially, the Internet and the private network, must be inspected by the firewall. This can result in the firewall becoming a bottleneck and reducing the performance between the network and the Internet.

Addressing decisions

After you implement a three-pronged firewall, the next decision you must make is what addressing schemes to use for each zone attached to the firewall. Typically, your organization will want to take advantage of Network Address Translation (NAT) in order to protect the private network-addressing scheme from the Internet.

For the DMZ, the decision on which addressing scheme to use is based on the protocols that must access resources in the DMZ. Two protocols that may not be able to pass through a NAT service are

✔ **Internet Protocol Security (IPSec):** IPSec protects data by either signing the data or encrypting the data, preventing NAT from translating the IP and TCP or UDP headers. Because the NAT process has to be able to read these fields in order to work, NAT services don't mix too well with IPSec (kind of like oil and water).

The Internet Engineering Task Force (IETF) is currently investigating a modification to IPSec that will allow NAT traversal. The combination of NAT detection (NAT-D) and NAT traversal (NAT-T) allows IPSec clients that implement the new IPSec drafts to pass traffic through a NAT device

✔ **Kerberos authentication:** If a Kerberos implementation uses the client address (CADDR) field, Kerberos authentication fails if the NAT process replaces the source IP address information in a Kerberos authentication exchange. The authentication fails because the contents of the CADDR field must match the source IP address in the IP header of the packet. If the two fields don't match, authentication fails.

Implementing private network addressing in the DMZ

If you're not using protocols that can't cross a NAT device, consider using RFC 1918 private network addressing in your DMZ, as shown in Figure 11-3.

As Figure 11-3 shows, the DMZ uses an RFC 1918 range of addresses, 192.168.1.0/24.

All servers located in the DMZ in this example are assigned IP addresses in the 192.168.1.0/24 network range.

The private network, in this case, uses addresses in the 192.168.2.0/24 address range. Although this is a private network address range, the firewall doesn't need to perform NAT on packets that are transmitted between the private network and the DMZ. NAT is performed only when a packet arrives with a public network address that is destined to a private network address.

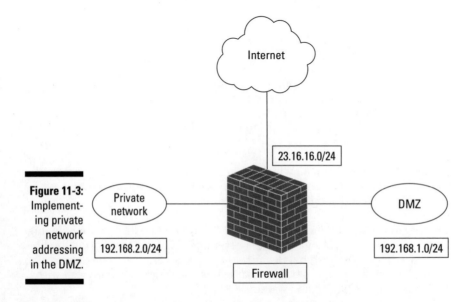

Figure 11-3: Implementing private network addressing in the DMZ.

Finally, the external network must use an IP address assigned by your Internet Service Provider (ISP). In Figure 11-3, the public network-addressing scheme used is 23.16.16.0/24. Because the firewall is performing NAT, the firewall must also be configured to perform static address mapping for all services located in the DMZ. The static address mappings map specific IP addresses and ports advertised on the Internet to IP addresses and ports located on the DMZ. For example, if the Internet-advertised address for a Web server on the Internet is 23.16.16.20, but its true IP address in the DMZ is 192.168.1.25, a static address mapping must be defined, as shown in Table 11-1.

Table 11-1	Static Address Mappings			
External IP Address	*Transport Protocol*	*External Port*	*Internal IP Address*	*Internal Port*
23.16.16.20	TCP	80	192.168.1.25	80
23.16.16.20	TCP	443	192.168.1.25	443

Implementing public network addressing in the DMZ

If you require Internet connectivity to resources that implement protocols that can't pass through a NAT device, you must use public network addressing in the DMZ, as shown in Figure 11-4.

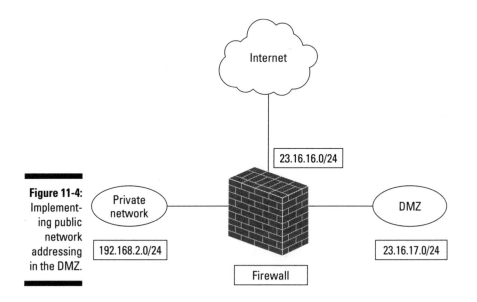

Figure 11-4: Implementing public network addressing in the DMZ.

In this scenario, the public network address range 23.16.17.0/24 is used in the DMZ. Remember that you can't just grab any public network address; you must acquire it from your ISP to ensure that the Internet routing tables know how to route data to and from your network. You must own both the externally accessible address range and the address range used in the DMZ.

Most commonly, companies simply subnet their assigned range of IP addresses so that the required number of IP addresses is available at both the external network and in the DMZ.

NAT is still performed by the firewall, but only on traffic that enters or exits the private network. No NAT is performed on the traffic that enters or exits the DMZ from the Internet.

Deploying a Three-Pronged Firewall

Now that we've discussed some of the design issues with three-pronged firewalls, take a look at three actual deployment scenarios so that you can see how firewall rules are affected by a three-pronged firewall.

The three examples that we look at are:

- ✔ A Point-to-Point Tunneling Protocol (PPTP) Server using RADIUS authentication
- ✔ A Layer Two Tunneling Protocol (L2TP) Server using RADIUS authentication
- ✔ A Web Server that connects to a SQL back-end server for storage of data

Deploying a tunnel solution using PPTP

Deploying a tunneling solution in which your network uses a three-pronged firewall allows you to perform the actual remote access authentication at the private network, rather than in the DMZ. Figure 11-5 shows the network configuration that we use for this example.

In this scenario, the key servers that are protected by the firewall are the tunnel server located in the DMZ at IP address 192.168.223.22 and the RADIUS server located in the private network at IP address 192.168.222.3. In addition, only connected tunnel clients are allowed to access resources on the 192.168.222.0/24 network. All other private network access will be blocked at the firewall.

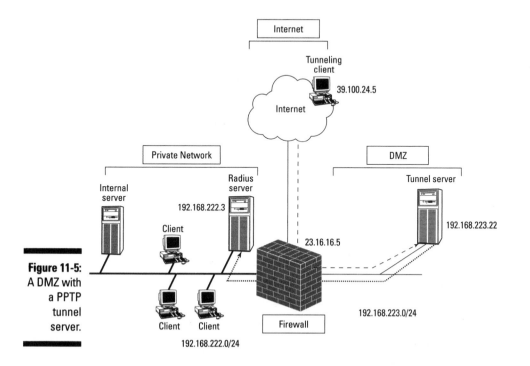

Figure 11-5:
A DMZ with
a PPTP
tunnel
server.

The first step in this deployment is to define a static address mapping for the tunnel server located in the DMZ. As Figure 11-5 shows, the firewall is assigned IP address 23.16.16.5. A static address mapping must be defined to allow only PPTP connections to be redirected to the tunnel server located in the DMZ, as shown in Table 11-2.

Table 11-2		Static Address Mappings		
External IP Address	*Transport Protocol*	*External Port*	*Internal IP Address*	*Internal Port*
23.16.16.5	TCP	1723	192.168.223.22	1723
23.16.16.5	ID 47		192.168.223.22	

The static address mapping ensures that all data sent to TCP port 1723 on the external interface of the firewall is redirected to the tunnel server's TCP port 1723 and that all Generic Routing Encapsulation (GRE) packets (protocol ID 47) are also routed to the tunnel server at IP address 192.168.223.22.

Table 11-3 shows the firewall rules that must be implemented at the firewall to ensure that only tunnel-related traffic is allowed to enter and exit the DMZ. These firewall rules assume that all tunnel clients will be assigned IP addresses in the range 192.168.223.128 to 192.168.223.255 (192.168.223.128/25).

Table 11-3					PPTP Firewall Rules	
Protocol	**Transport Protocol**	**Source IP**	**Source Port**	**Target IP**	**Target Port**	**Action**
PPTP	TCP	Any	Any	23.16.18.17	500	Allow
GRE	ID 47	Any		23.16.18.17		Allow
RADIUS Authenti cation	UDP	192.168.223.22	Any	192.168.222.3	1812	Allow
RADIUS Accounting	UDP	192.168.223.22	Any	192.168.222.3	1813	Allow
Internal Access	Any	192.168.223.128/25	Any	192.168.222.0/24		Allow

The packet filter listings in this chapter assume that stateful inspection is enabled at the firewall to allow return packets to be returned to the original source of the packet.

In this listing of firewall rules, the first two rules allow any tunnel clients to connect to the tunnel server using PPTP. PPTP encrypted packets are encapsulated in GRE packets, which are defined in the second packet filter.

To authenticate the tunnel clients and to record their connection information, the third and fourth firewall rules allow the tunnel server to use the RADIUS protocol to communicate with the RADIUS server located on the private network.

If the RADIUS authentication is successful, the tunnel client is assigned an IP address in the 192.168.223.128/25 address range. The final packet filter allows addresses in that range to use any protocol to connect to resources found in the private network.

If you want to restrict access to only specific servers or services on the private network, more specific firewall rules can be implemented in place of the last rule. Although more secure, implementing specific firewall rules may result in more configuration work for the firewall administrator as new protocols are introduced into the mix.

Deploying a tunnel solution using L2TP

L2TP tunneling doesn't have a built-in encryption algorithm. The IPSec ESP protocol is used to encrypt the L2TP packets as they are transmitted from the tunnel client to the tunnel server. The firewall rules that you implement will depend on whether the tunnel clients and tunnel server support the NAT-T draft.

Firewall Rules when NAT-T is not supported

If the tunnel client and server don't support NAT-T, then public network addressing must be used, as shown in Figure 11-6.

As Figure 11-6 shows, the DMZ uses public network addressing rather than private network addressing. In this example, the L2TP tunnel server is located at IP address 23.16.18.17. Because public network addressing is used in the DMZ, the firewall doesn't have to define any static address mappings for accessing the DMZ. In this case, the firewall must ensure only that its routing table knows that access to the DMZ must pass through the network interface connected to the DMZ.

Table 11-4 shows the firewall rules that must be implemented to allow an L2TP tunnel client to connect to the tunnel server located in the DMZ. The table assumes that once authenticated, the tunnel clients will be assigned an IP address in the 23.16.18.128/25 address range.

In this listing of firewall rules, the first two rules allow any tunnel clients to connect to the tunnel server using L2TP. You may be wondering, how do these rules allow L2TP when they are all related to IPSec and not to L2TP? An L2TP tunnel server accepts connections by listening on UDP port 1701. (For more information on the specific ports used by applications, see the Appendix.) IPSec firewall rules are used at the firewall because when the tunnel passes through the firewall, the data is encrypted with IPSec. You must be careful when you use IPSec because with these firewall rules, any protocol can be used to connect to the tunnel server, as long as it is encrypted using IPSec

The first firewall rule is used by the two IPSec endpoints to negotiate a security association using the Internet Key Exchange (IKE) protocol. After the initial negotiation is completed, the security association uses either ESP, AH, or some combination to encrypt all L2TP packets as they are transmitted through the firewall. The second and third firewall rules ensure that the AH and ESP packets can be sent only to the tunnel server located in the DMZ.

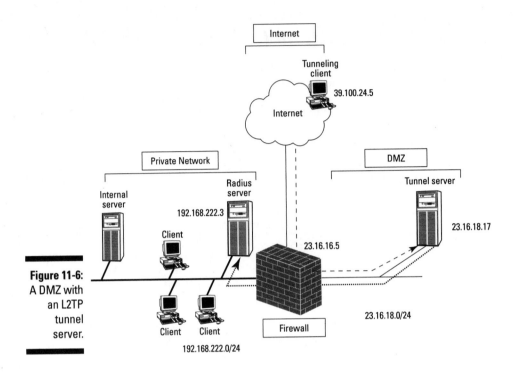

Figure 11-6:
A DMZ with an L2TP tunnel server.

Table 11-4		Firewall Rules to Access an L2TP Tunnel Server				
Protocol	*Transport Protocol*	*Source IP*	*Source Port*	*Target IP*	*Target Port*	*Action*
IKE	UDP	Any	500	23.16.18.17	500	Allow
AH	ID 51	Any		23.16.18.17		Allow
ESP	ID 50	Any		23.16.18.17		Allow
RADIUS Authenti-cation	UDP	23.16.18.17	Any	192.168.222.3	1812	Allow
RADIUS Accounting	UDP	23.16.18.17	Any	192.168.222.3	1813	Allow
Internal Access	Any	23.16.18.128/25	Any	192.168.222.0/24	Any	Allow

As with the PPTP example earlier, the third and fourth firewall rules allow RADIUS to be used for both authentication and accounting functions. These rules allow only the tunnel server to use RADIUS to communicate with the RADIUS server on the private network. External computers are not allowed to communicate with the RADIUS server directly.

The last rule allows only the tunnel clients to connect to resources on the 192.168.222.0/24 network. If connections are attempted to resources anywhere else on the private network, the firewall blocks the connection attempts. As with the PPTP example earlier, the final rule can be replaced with a series of rules that uniquely identify each protocol and resource that's accessible to tunnel clients connecting to the L2TP tunnel server in the DMZ.

Firewall rules when NAT-T is supported

If both the tunnel clients and tunnel server support NAT-T, then the addressing scheme shown in Figure 11-7 may be implemented in the DMZ. This configuration further protects the DMZ by using NAT to hide the addressing scheme implemented in the DMZ.

Because NAT is performed on all traffic that enters or exits the DMZ, a static address mapping must be defined to allow only L2TP/IPSec connections to be redirected to the tunnel server located in the DMZ, as shown in Table 11-5.

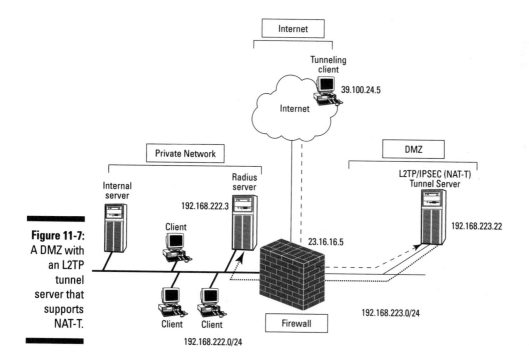

Figure 11-7: A DMZ with an L2TP tunnel server that supports NAT-T.

Table 11-5	Static Address Mappings			
External IP Address	*Transport Protocol*	*External Port*	*Internal IP Address*	*Internal Port*
23.16.16.5	UDP	Any	192.168.223.22	500
23.16.16.5	UDP	Any	192.168.223.22	4500

Note: The source port can't be determined for both NAT-D and NAT-T traffic because it is unknown whether additional NAT devices, other than the firewall protecting your network, lie between the tunnel client and the tunnel server.

The static address mappings ensure that all data sent to UDP port 500 (NAT-D) on the external interface of the firewall is redirected to the tunnel server's UDP port 500. Likewise, NAT-D traffic (traffic destined to UDP port 4500) is also redirected to the tunnel server. Static address mappings for ESP (Protocol ID 50) are not required because the original ESP data is encapsulated in the NAT-T packets.

The NAT-T draft only supports encapsulation of ESP traffic; therefore, AH is not supported in NAT-T implementations.

Table 11-6 shows the firewall rules that must be implemented at the firewall to ensure that only tunnel-related traffic is allowed to enter and exit the DMZ. These firewall rules assume that all tunnel clients will be assigned IP addresses in the range 192.168.223.128 to 192.168.223.255 (192.168.223.128/25).

Table 11-6	L2TP/IPSec with NAT-T Firewall Rules					
Protocol	*Transport Protocol*	*Source IP*	*Source Port*	*Target IP*	*Target Port*	*Action*
NAT-D	UDP	Any	Any	192.168.223.22	500	Allow
NAT-T	UDP	Any	Any	192.168.223.22	4500	Allow
RADIUS Authentication	UDP	192.168.223.22	Any	192.168.222.3	1812	Allow
RADIUS Accounting	UDP	192.168.223.22	Any	192.168.222.3	1813	Allow
Internal Access	Any	192.168.223.128/25	Any	192.168.222.0/24	Any	Allow

Deploying a Web server with a SQL back end

Our final example shows you how to configure access to a Web server that acts as a front end to a database application. The SQL Server that acts as the back end for the database application is located in the private network, as shown in Figure 11-8.

In Figure 11-8, the Web server located in the DMZ at IP address 192.168.223.13 must access a SQL back-end server located in the private network at IP address 192.168.222.5. To access the Web server, the firewall must allow both HyperText Transfer Protocol (HTTP) and SSL-secure HTTP (HTTPS) to access the Web server. In addition, the firewall must allow the Web server to communicate with the Oracle server using TCP/IP sockets. This requires connections to the Oracle server listening on TCP port 1521.

This example assumes that an Oracle SQL Server is acting as the database back-end server accepting SQL*Net connections. If you use a different SQL server, such as Microsoft SQL Server, read the documentation to determine the correct ports to open in order to allow access to the database server. For example, Microsoft SQL Server listens on TCP port 1433 for SQL connections.

The first step is to define the static address mapping that redirects HTTP and HTTPS packets received at the firewall to the Web server in the DMZ. Table 11-7 shows the static address mappings that must be deployed at the firewall to allow HTTP and HTTPS redirects to the Web server.

Table 11-7		Static Address Mappings		
External IP Address	**Transport Protocol**	**External Port**	**Internal IP Address**	**Internal Port**
23.16.16.5	TCP	80	192.168.223.23	80
23.16.16.5	TCP	443	192.168.223.23	443

After the static address mappings are defined, the firewall rules can be configured at the firewall. Table 11-8 shows the rules that must be implemented in order to allow connections to the Web server and to allow the Web server to communicate with the Oracle back-end database in the private network.

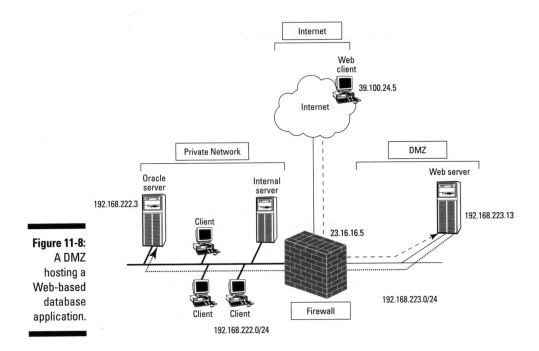

Figure 11-8:
A DMZ
hosting a
Web-based
database
application.

Table 11-8   Firewall Rules to Access an Internal Web Server

Protocol	Transport Protocol	Source IP	Source Port	Target IP	Target Port	Action
HTTP	TCP	Any	Any	192.168.223.33	80	Allow
HTTPS	TCP	Any	Any	192.168.223.33	443	Allow
Oracle SQL *Net	TCP	192.168.223.33	Any	192.168.222.5	1521	Allow

The first two firewall rules allow both HTTP and HTTPS connections to the
Web server located in the DMZ. The last rule allows the Web server to connect to the Oracle server located in the private network. This example differs
from the tunneling examples because the rule actually refers to the Web
server making the connection. In this case, the Web server is executing the
SQL query or update requested by the Web client. The Web client doesn't
have any direct access to the Oracle SQL database server, which increases
security because the Web pages can be coded to restrict the type of access
allowed to the Oracle SQL Server.

Why you may want more than four zones

At times, you may need more than four zones. For example, a training center where I used to work offered technical computer training to the public and wanted to provide Internet access to the classroom. The network had four zones, defined as follows:

✔ **Corporate Network:** This zone represented the private network of the company. All access to the corporate network from the DMZ, Internet, or the partner network was prevented by the firewall unless the traffic originated from the corporate network and was a response packet.

✔ **Partner Network:** This zone represented a VPN connection to a partner organization. The partner organization was restricted to a database server and application server located on this network segment.

✔ **DMZ:** All Internet-accessible resources were stored in a DMZ that used private network addressing. All tunneling to the network used PPTP so they experienced no issues with IPSec encryption that required public network addressing.

✔ **Internet:** The firewall was connected to the Internet through a fractional T1 line. No services were located in the Internet zone.

Creating an additional zone for the classrooms at the training center posed no problems. By creating a separate zone for the computers, the center ensured that no student could access financial or proprietary information stored on the corporate network. In addition, the center was able to restrict the classroom zone to using only preapproved protocols, such as HTTP, HTTPS, SMTP, and POP3 e-mail. The only difficulty in the setup was getting the firewall to recognize five network interface cards. Thank God for Plug and Play — nobody would have wanted to attempt a manual configuration of the interrupts and ports with non–Plug and Play network cards.

Because of the complexity involved, be sure that your design definitely requires four or more zones before purchasing your firewall. Be sure that you have a working design, because troubleshooting problems is more difficult in this type of environment. The most common business driver for such an approach is the requirement for both public addresses and private addresses in the DMZ.

Building a Case for Multi-Pronged Firewalls

In some cases, you may require more than three zones for a firewall. Based on the examples discussed already, you can make a case for maintaining both a public address DMZ and a private address DMZ to allow IPSec encryption into the DMZ. Firewalls with four or more prongs may cause difficulties, such as

- ✔ **Hardware-related confusion:** Questions from new firewall administrators such as "How do I get the computer to work with four network cards?" are a definite symptom of a multi-pronged solution.

- ✔ **Slower performance:** Look for statements from the users of your network such as "My access speed stinks!" and "The firewall just doesn't seem to be performing like it used to."

- ✔ **Firewall rules complexity:** Defining firewall rules for four or more zones can become quite confusing. In fact, what used to be a simple modification when only three zones existed becomes quite complex when additional zones must be configured.

- ✔ **Support problems:** Some firewalls can't support more than two interfaces. With four or more interfaces, you must research the firewall in order to ensure that it will support that many interfaces.

Be sure to read Chapter 18 to find out what other factors must be considered when purchasing a firewall.

Chapter 12

Designing Demilitarized Zones with Multiple Firewalls

Some organizations are apprehensive about implementing a single firewall between their private network and the Internet. Although you can add more network interfaces to the firewall, a single firewall solution has one big drawback: Only one point of failure exists between a hacker on the Internet and your private network resources.

This chapter examines some demilitarized zone (DMZ) designs that use two or more firewalls to protect the private network from the Internet, thus allowing secured access to Internet-accessible resources while still providing maximum security to the private network.

When Two Firewalls Are Better than One

Some organizations' Security policies dictate that a single firewall protecting the private network from the Internet is unacceptable. In Chapter 11, we stated that a single firewall can be used to deploy a DMZ that directs Internet-based traffic to a protected area of the network. However, some security personnel are uncomfortable with this design because the firewall becomes a single point of protection. If an attacker were to compromise the firewall, he or she would not only gain access to the DMZ but would also have access to the private network; therefore, security administrators generally prefer DMZ solutions with two firewalls, as shown in Figure 12-1.

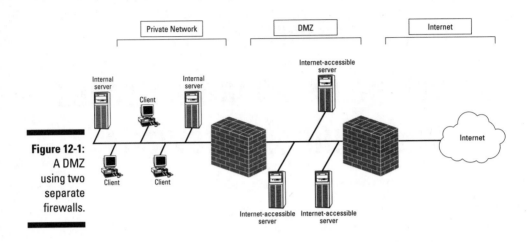

Figure 12-1:
A DMZ
using two
separate
firewalls.

In this scenario, the two firewalls separate the DMZ from both the private network and the Internet. Although additional costs are associated with the additional firewall, this configuration is considered more secure because an attacker must breach two firewalls in order to access resources on the private network.

Typically, the business factors that result in an organization's deploying two or more firewalls in its DMZ design include:

- **Clear definition of the DMZ:** When two firewalls are used, the DMZ physically resides between the private network and the Internet.

- **Increased security:** By deploying two separate firewalls, an attacker must circumvent or break through two separate firewalls to compromise resources that are located on the private network.

  You can further increase security by implementing two different manu-facturers' firewalls. When two different manufacturers' firewalls are used, an attacker must compromise each firewall by using different methods and strategies.

- **Reduced network loads on the two firewalls:** In a single firewall DMZ solution, the firewall may have to inspect the same data twice — once going from the Internet to the DMZ and again going from the DMZ to the private network. When a double-firewall DMZ is used, this inspection load is divided between two firewalls.

Deploying two separate firewalls doesn't necessarily solve all your problems instantly. Some of the disadvantages related to deploying a two-firewall solution — if the best practice of implementing two different manufacturers' firewalls is used, that is — include:

- ✔ **Increased costs:** This one is simple. Two firewalls generally cost more than a single firewall. The cost is even higher if your organization's Security policy requires multiple firewall brands.

- ✔ **Extra training required:** Although the configuration of each manufacturer's firewall is different, administrators must master the nuances of each firewall and be proficient in more than one firewall in order to be effective when deploying security.

- ✔ **Multiple firewall rule listings must be maintained:** A firewall administrator may have to modify two separate firewall rule listings to define the necessary firewall rules for allowing network traffic to securely pass between the zones. This results in more time spent administering the firewalls.

- ✔ **Multiple tools must be used:** Typically, each firewall product has its own custom interface for managing the firewall. These tools require additional ports to be opened at the firewall to allow management of the firewalls by computers not located in the DMZ — which increases the number of entry points into the network.

Some firewalls are moving toward standard protocols for firewall management (for example, GnatBox, or the text-based Cisco PIX firewall), and require nothing more than a HyperText Transmission Protocol (HTTP) or Telnet connection for management. By using industry standard protocols for management, external management configuration is simplified.

- ✔ **Configuration complexity when more than two firewalls are deployed:** If you require multiple DMZs to support protocols that can't pass through a Network Address Translation (NAT) service, the additional configuration to allow traffic to pass securely through the various zones can be quite complex. The complexity involves not only firewall rule configuration, but also DNS and routing table configuration.

NAT issues and two firewalls

If you're wondering whether using two firewalls eliminates NAT issues, the answer is a resounding "No!" The number of firewalls doesn't matter; it's the placement of services in the DMZs that you configure that matters.

The basic rule is that non-NATable services must be placed behind a firewall that doesn't perform NAT services. If the firewall is translating public network addresses to private network addresses as defined in RFC 1918, the firewall is performing NAT.

DMZs with Two Firewalls

When you use a two-firewall DMZ, the biggest difference with DMZ configuration is that you must configure the two separate firewalls in tandem to control what traffic can pass between the private network, DMZ, and the Internet.

This chapter refers to the firewall between the Internet and the DMZ as the *external firewall* and the firewall between the DMZ and the private network as the *internal firewall.*

The external firewall is typically configured to allow only specific traffic into the DMZ from the Internet. Typically, only protocols that are used in the DMZ are allowed to enter the DMZ. The internal firewall restricts which data is allowed to traverse between the private network and the DMZ.

The best way to describe two-firewall DMZ configurations is by using examples. The following examples describe two-firewall DMZ configurations:

- ✔ A Point-to-Point Tunneling Protocol (PPTP) server using RADIUS authentication
- ✔ A Layer Two Tunneling Protocol (L2TP) server using RADIUS authentication
- ✔ A Web server that connects to a SQL Back- End server for storage of data

If you need a refresher on how these configurations are implemented in a multi-pronged firewall scenario, flip back to Chapter 11.

Deploying a tunnel solution using PPTP

Figure 12-2 shows a common configuration used to provide PPTP access to the private network.

In the configuration shown in Figure 12-2, the DMZ can use either private network addressing or public network addressing. In this configuration, because the tunnel server is located at IP address 192.168.223.22 — an address in the RFC 1918–defined pools of IP addresses — private network addressing is used in the DMZ.

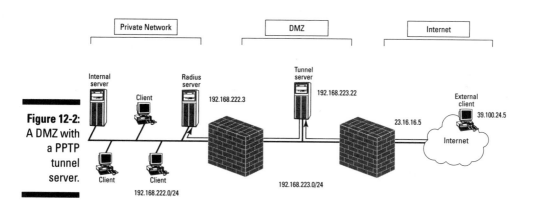

Figure 12-2:
A DMZ with
a PPTP
tunnel
server.

In addition, the DMZ restricts access to the private network so that

- Tunnel servers are allowed to access only the RADIUS server in the private network located at 192.168.222.3.

- Tunnel clients are assigned an IP address in the 192.168.223.128 to 192.168.223.255 range (192.168.223.128/25) and are allowed to access resources only on the 192.168.222.0/24 network.

As in a three-pronged firewall configuration, the first step in designing a DMZ with two firewalls is to define a static address mapping for the tunnel server located in the DMZ. The firewall is assigned IP address 23.16.16.5. (refer to Figure 12-2). A static address mapping must be defined to allow only PPTP connections to be redirected to the tunnel server located in the DMZ, as shown in Table 12-1.

Table 12-1	PPTP Static Address Mapping			
External IP Address	**Transport Protocol**	**External Port**	**Internal IP Address**	**Internal Port**
23.16.16.5	TCP	1723	192.168.223.22	1723
23.16.16.5	ID 47		192.168.223.22	

These static address mappings ensure that all data sent to TCP port 1723 on the firewall is redirected to the tunnel server's TCP port 1723 and that all Generic Routing Encapsulation (GRE) packets are also rerouted to the tunnel server.

Table 12-2 shows the firewall rules that must be implemented at the external firewall to ensure that only PPTP traffic is allowed to enter and exit the DMZ. In addition, the PPTP traffic is allowed to connect only to the tunnel server and not to any other servers in the DMZ.

Table 12-2		External PPTP Firewall Rules					
Protocol	*Transport Protocol*	*Source IP*	*Source Port*	*Target IP*	*Target Port*	*Action*
PPTP	TCP	Any	Any	192.168.223.22	1723	Allow
GRE	ID 47	Any		192.168.223.22		Allow

The firewall rule listings in this chapter assume that stateful inspection is enabled at the firewall to allow return packets to be returned to the original source of the packet.

At this point in the configuration, your process changes from the process used for a single firewall solution. The firewall rules used to allow RADIUS authentication and tunnel client access are configured at the internal firewall because the traffic originates in the DMZ — not on the Internet. Table 12-3 shows the firewall rules that must be configured at the internal firewall, based on the sample configuration.

Table 12-3		Internal PPTP Firewall Rules					
Protocol	*Transport Protocol*	*Source IP*	*Source Port*	*Target IP*	*Target Port*	*Action*
RADIUS Authentication	UDP	192.168.223.22	Any	192.168.222.3	1812	Allow
RADIUS Accounting	UDP	192.168.223.22	Any	192.168.222.3	1813	Allow
Internal Access	Any	192.168.223.128/25	Any	192.168.222.0/24	Any	Allow

As with a three-pronged firewall, you can replace the last firewall rule in Table 12-3 with more specific rules that restrict the tunnel clients to using either specific protocols or accessing only specific resources on the private network. For example, one of our clients doesn't allow tunnel clients to access servers containing customer data. Access to these servers is restricted to users logged on locally to the network.

Deploying a tunnel solution using L2TP

As with a three-pronged firewall, the firewall rules that you implement in a two-firewall scenario will differ, depending on whether the L2TP server and L2TP clients support NAT traversal (NAT-T).

Deploying firewall rules for clients that don't support NAT-T

L2TP uses Internet Protocol Security (IPSec) to encrypt data transmissions between the tunnel client and the tunnel server. Remember that IPSec can't pass through a firewall that has a Network Address Translation (NAT) service if the tunnel client and tunnel server don't support NAT-T. Therefore, the DMZ must use public network addressing to allow the use of an L2TP tunnel server, as shown in Figure 12-3.

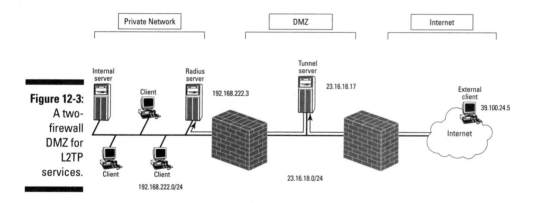

Figure 12-3: A two-firewall DMZ for L2TP services.

The use of public network addressing eliminates the need to define static address mappings. The external firewall allows direct access to the L2TP server using IPSec without having to readdress incoming packets.

Table 12-4 shows the firewall rules that are required at the external firewall in order to allow the L2TP tunnel client to connect to the L2TP Tunnel Server using IPSec. Remember that IPSec requires three firewall rules — rules to deal with Internet Key Exchange (IKE), Authentication Header (AH), and Encapsulating Security Payloads (ESP) packets.

Table 12-4	External Firewall Filters to Access an L2TP Tunnel Server					
Protocol	Transport Protocol	Source IP	Source Port	Target IP	Target Port	Action
IKE	UDP	Any	500	23.16.18.17	500	Allow
AH	ID 51	Any		23.16.18.17		Allow*
ESP	ID 50	Any		23.16.18.17		Allow

*AH is required only if the IPSec SA for the L2TP tunnel requires AH protection.

After the L2TP tunnel clients connect to the L2TP server, the RADIUS server (located on the private network at IP address 192.168.222.3) authenticates the client. After the tunnel client is successfully authenticated, the tunnel client is assigned an IP address in the 23.16.18.128/25 address range. To allow this access, the firewall rules shown in Table 12-5 must be configured at the internal firewall.

Table 12-5	Internal Firewall Rules to Access an L2TP Tunnel Server					
Protocol	Transport Protocol	Source IP	Source Port	Target IP	Target Port	Action
RADIUS Authentication	UDP	23.16.18.17	Any	192.168.222.3	1812	Allow
RADIUS Accounting	UDP	23.16.18.17	Any	192.168.222.3	1813	Allow
Internal Access	Any	23.16.18.128/25	Any	192.168.222.0/24	Any	Allow

Deploying firewall rules for clients that support NAT-T

If the tunnel clients and tunnel server support NAT traversal (NAT-T), you can deploy private network addressing in the DMZ, as shown in Figure 12-4.

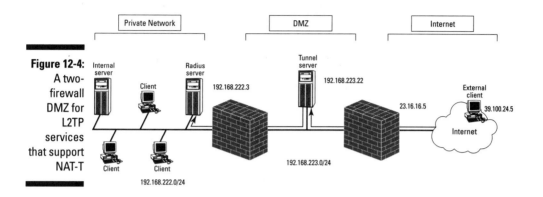

Figure 12-4:
A two-firewall DMZ for L2TP services that support NAT-T

As with a PPTP tunnel server, you must first define static address mappings at the external firewall to ensure that the NAT discovery (NAT-D) and NAT-T traffic are redirected to the tunnel server in the DMZ. These static address mappings are shown in Table 12-6.

Table 12-6		L2TP with NAT-T Static Address Mapping		
External IP Address	*Transport Protocol*	*External Port*	*Internal IP Address*	*Internal Port*
23.16.16.5	UDP	500	192.168.223.22	500
23.16.16.5	UDP	4500	192.168.223.22	4500

After the static address mappings are defined, you must define what protocols are allowed to pass through the external firewall to the DMZ. These firewall rules are defined in Table 12-7.

Table 12-7	External L2TP/IPSec Firewall Rules for NAT-T Clients					
Protocol	*Transport Protocol*	*Source IP*	*Source Port*	*Target IP*	*Target Port*	*Action*
NAT-D	UDP	Any	Any	192.168.223.22	500	Allow
NAT-T	UDP	Any	Any	192.168.223.22	4500	Allow

After the L2TP NAT-T tunnel clients connect to the L2TP server, the RADIUS server (located on the private network at IP address 192.168.222.3) authenticates the client. After the tunnel client is successfully authenticated, the tunnel client is assigned an IP address in the 23.16.18.128/25 address range. To allow this access, the firewall rules shown in Table 12-8 must be configured at the internal firewall.

Table 12-8		Internal L2TP/IPSec Firewall Rules for NAT-T Clients					
Protocol	Transport Protocol	Source IP	Source Port	Target IP	Target Port	Action
RADIUS Authentication	UDP	23.16.18.17	Any	192.168.222.3	1812	Allow
RADIUS Accounting	UDP	23.16.18.17	Any	192.168.222.3	1813	Allow
Internal Access	Any	23.16.18.128/25	Any	192.168.222.0/24	Any	Allow

Deploying a Web server with a SQL back end

Many Web sites collect information for registrations, newsletters, or purchasing information. Typically, this information is stored in a database. Figure 12-5 shows a typical DMZ configuration for a Web server with a back-end Oracle database located on the private network.

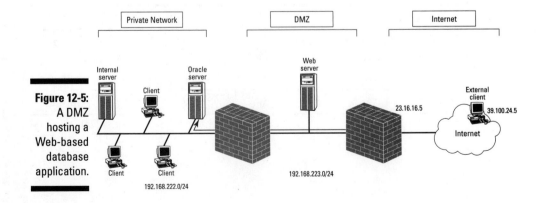

Figure 12-5: A DMZ hosting a Web-based database application.

In Figure 12-5, the Web server located in the DMZ at IP address 192.168.223.13 must access an Oracle SQL back-end server using a SQL*Net connection. The Oracle server is located in the private network at IP address 192.168.222.5. To access the Web server, the firewall must allow both HyperText Transfer Protocol (HTTP) and SSL-secure HTTP (HTTPS) to access the Web server. In addition, the firewall must allow the Web server to communicate with the Oracle Server using a SQL*Net connection. This requires connections to the Oracle server listening on TCP port 1521.

The first step is to define the static address mapping that will redirect HTTP and HTTPS packets received at the firewall to the Web server in the DMZ. Table 12-9 shows the static address mappings that must be deployed at the firewall in order to allow HTTP and HTTPS redirects to the Web server.

Table 12-9	Static Address Mappings			
External IP Address	Transport Protocol	External Port	Internal IP Address	Internal Port
23.16.16.5	TCP	80	192.168.223.13	80
23.16.16.5	TCP	443	192.168.223.13	443

After the static address mappings are defined, the external firewall rules must be configured. Table 12-10 shows the firewall rules that must be implemented in order to allow connections to the Web server.

Table 12-10	External Firewall Rules to Access an Internal Web Server					
Protocol	Transport Protocol	Source IP	Source Port	Target IP	Target Port	Action
HTTP	TCP	Any	Any	192.168.223.13	80	Allow
HTTPS	TCP	Any	Any	192.168.223.13	443	Allow

The last step is to configure the internal firewall to allow the Web server to connect to the Oracle back-end database in the private network. Table 12-11 shows the firewall rule that must be configured at the internal firewall.

Table 12-11		Internal Firewall Rule to Access a Back-End SQL Server					
Protocol	Transport Protocol	Source IP	Source Port	Target IP	Target Port	Action
Oracle SQL*Net	TCP	192.168.223.13	Any	192.168.222.5	1521	Allow

This firewall rule allows only the Web server to connect to the Oracle database — not the external Web clients themselves. By using forms on HTML pages, the types of queries performed by the external clients are restricted to specific types of queries.

Allowing private network users to access the Internet

In many ways, the more difficult configurations with a two-firewall DMZ involve outbound traffic rather than inbound traffic. This is because the original source address information is typically translated at either the internal or external firewall. Figure 12-6 shows a typical configuration in which internal clients on the 192.168.222.0/24 network will be allowed to access the Internet through the two firewalls between the private network and the Internet.

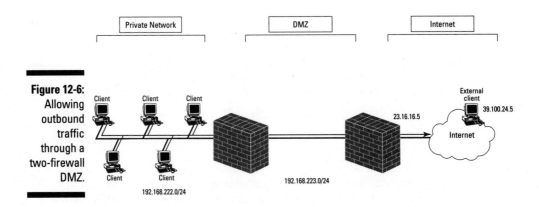

Figure 12-6:
Allowing outbound traffic through a two-firewall DMZ.

In this scenario, the best strategy is to configure the firewalls starting at the innermost firewall and work your way out to the firewall between the DMZ and the Internet.

If you assume that the DMZ in Figure 12-6 uses 192.168.223.0/24 private network addressing, the internal firewall requires the firewall rule shown in Table 12-12 to allow outbound network traffic to the Internet from the private network.

Table 12-12		Internal Firewall Outbound Firewall Rule					
Protocol	*Transport Protocol*	*Source IP*	*Source Port*	*Target IP*	*Target Port*	*Action*
Any	Any	129.168.222.0/24	Any	Any	Any	Allow

Because both the private network and the DMZ use private network addressing, the packets have the same source IP and port information when they reach the external firewall (but before the packets are transmitted on the Internet). To allow this traffic, the external firewall must be configured with the same outbound firewall rule as the internal rule shown in Table 12-12.

The only catch is that the external firewall must be configured to perform network address translation (NAT) on the outbound packets. All outbound packets that arrive at the external firewall that originated from either the private network or the DMZ must be translated to the external browsing address configured at the firewall. Table 12-13 shows the network address translation that must be performed at the external firewall.

Table 12-13	External Firewall NAT Configuration			
Source IP	*Source Port*	*Translated IP*	*Translated Port*	*Action*
192.168.222.0/24	Any	23.16.16.5	Any	Allow
192.168.223.0/24	Any	23.16.16.5	Any	Allow

The scenario changes if the DMZ is configured to use public network addressing. When public network addressing is used in the DMZ, the internal firewall — not the external firewall — must be configured to perform network address translation. Assuming that the internal firewall's network interface connected to the DMZ uses the IP address 23.16.18.5, the translation must be configured at the internal firewall, as shown in Table 12-14, so that the outbound packets have public network addresses after they enter the DMZ.

Table 12-14		Internal Firewall NAT Configuration		
Source IP	*Source Port*	*Translated IP*	*Translated Port*	*Action*
192.168.222.0/24	Any	23.16.18.5	Any	Allow

The internal firewall must be configured to allow the original source addresses to pass into the DMZ. You use the true IP addresses, as shown in Table 12-15, rather than the translated addresses because the firewall rules are applied at one firewall while the NAT takes place at the other firewall.

Table 12-15		Internal Firewall Outbound Firewall Rule				
Protocol	*Transport Protocol*	*Source IP*	*Source Port*	*Target IP*	*Target Port*	*Action*
Any	Any	192.168.222.0/24	Any	Any	Any	Allow

The external firewall requires different address information in its outbound firewall rules because the original source address information has now been translated to the common IP address of 23.16.18.5. Table 12-16 shows the outbound firewall rule required to allow private network users to access the Internet.

Table 12-16		External Firewall Outbound Firewall Rule				
Protocol	*Transport Protocol*	*Source IP*	*Source Port*	*Target IP*	*Target Port*	*Action*
Any	Any	23.16.18.5	Any	Any	Any	Allow

Part IV

Deploying Solutions Using Firewall Products

The 5th Wave   By Rich Tennant

"So far it's saved us from Denial of Service attacks, as well as attacks from locust swarms, frogs, and zombies."

In this part . . .

Wat firewall product should you use to protect your network? Several options are available. This part shows you the steps to securing your network using Windows or Linux. We also describe how to use a personal firewall, such as ZoneAlarm or Norton Personal Firewall, or two popular enterprise firewalls: Microsoft Internet Security and Acceleration (ISA) Server and Check Point FireWall-1.

Vendors are all too happy to tell you to buy their firewall product, which is no surprise. The last chapter in this part helps you decide what features you need and what firewall product to use. This part also gives you criteria for choosing a firewall solution.

Chapter 13

Using Windows as a Firewall

*O*ver the years, the Windows operating system has grown by leaps and bounds. It now does much more than provide just the core functionality, or — as operating system buffs like to call it — the *kernel functionality*. Entire applications are part of Windows now. The inseparable inclusion of Internet Explorer in the Windows operating system was even the reason for a major lawsuit against the software giant.

However, one thing that can be considered a core functionality of an operating system is the provision of a solid security infrastructure. It is considered much better to let one dedicated party, such as the operating system itself, handle all the details of implementing security protocols and object access enforcement, than it is to make each separate application responsible for handling this complex task.

For secure Internet access, this concept is taken one step further. Often a truly dedicated application, such as the firewall software, handles all the packet inspection and housekeeping that comes with providing Internet access.

Yet, the increased functionality in more recent versions of Windows has also added many features that can be used to provide secure Internet access. Windows XP, the latest version of the Microsoft Windows desktop operating system, even includes a built-in Internet Connection Firewall.

In this chapter, we look at how you can use the functionality of various Windows operating systems, from Windows 98 to Windows Server 2003, to secure your connection to the Internet.

Go to `http://windowsupdate.microsoft.com` to stay up-to-date with the latest Service Packs and security patches for the Windows operating systems.

Firewall Functions in Windows

Do you still need to buy a separate firewall product if you already have Windows running on your machines connecting to the Internet? The answer — as always when you want a straight answer — is "It depends." Besides, the publisher wants you to read the other chapters in this book too, so we're not allowed to say "no" here.

An application that's dedicated to performing a specific task almost always does a better job than an operating system that's responsible for performing many tasks. For example, Windows comes with a built-in word processor named *WordPad,* yet anyone who wants to do serious word processing installs another word processor, such as Microsoft Word, because a specialized program offers added functionality. The same principle also applies to the built-in firewall functionality.

The newer versions of Windows have several features that are used in firewall products, such as:

- ✔ **Packet filtering:** Each subsequent Windows version provides more configurable packet-filtering capabilities. Windows 98 had none. Windows 98 Second Edition (SE) and Windows Me, however, both block NetBIOS ports on the external interface. Windows NT 4.0 allows incoming traffic destined for the computer per individual port. Windows 2000 allows or blocks routed incoming and outgoing traffic based on port, source address, and destination address. You can configure Windows XP to block all incoming traffic on an Internet connection. Finally, Windows Server 2003 extends this capability to blocking all incoming traffic when the computer is still initializing its network software at startup.

- ✔ **Network Address Translation (NAT/ICS):** The Windows 2000 server versions contain a flexible implementation of NAT, which is part of the Routing and Remote Access Service. Windows 2000 also contains a simplified and much less configurable service, *Internet Connection Sharing (ICS),* which is already present in Windows 98 SE and Windows Me.

- ✔ **Encrypted tunnel:** All Windows computers can create a Virtual Private Network (VPN) connection using PPTP or L2TP. The Windows server versions can be endpoints for these VPN tunnels.

Using these techniques, you can connect your Windows computers to the Internet and be reasonably secure. Note, however, that many of the basic required functions of a true firewall as discussed in Chapter 3 are not present. Here are some shortcomings of using Windows as a complete firewall solution:

- ✔ **(Almost) No stateful packet filters:** Some of the packet filters options in the Windows versions use stateless packet filters. This means that return ports greater than 1023 have to remain open constantly. Stateful packet filters are much more secure than stateless packet filters. The Internet Connection Firewall function uses stateful packet filters.

- ✔ **No application proxies:** Although packet filters inspect traffic arriving at the external interface, packet filters can inspect only the packet header. Application proxies can inspect the entire data portion of the packet. Filtering based on more than the packet header is not possible.

- ✔ **No (or less-than-ideal) monitoring or logging:** Because Windows doesn't have a dedicated firewall function, the monitoring and logging of packets arriving at the interfaces is rudimentary at best. Windows 98 computers can't log anything that may help detect problems, except for creating dump logs when an application crashes. Windows NT and Windows 2000 computers can report events in the Event Logs, but this capability doesn't compare to a true firewall log. Windows XP and Windows Server 2003 do feature a log file to report on the Internet Connection Firewall.

- ✔ **No data caching:** This is not strictly a security aspect, but data caching can be a function that a firewall product performs. Internet access for users on the internal network can be sped up considerably when the Web proxy software can cache frequently requested Web pages. Using Windows for Internet access provides no option to perform any caching on returned Web page data.

- ✔ **No firewall mindset:** Windows isn't designed to function as a firewall. This means that the IP implementation of the older Windows versions may contain flaws that render it unsuitable to be directly connected to a hostile environment, such as the Internet. Many of those weaknesses have since been addressed in hot fixes of Service Packs, but not until Windows NT 4.0 — with the latest Service Packs — and beyond does Windows have a strong enough IP stack to withstand common attacks from the Internet. Even so, it's possible that a crash in the packet-filtering software or the NAT process can leave the computer in a vulnerable state, in which it will route every packet from the external network to the internal network unfiltered.

With so many shortcomings in using Windows as a firewall, is it still safe to dial in or otherwise directly connect to the Internet with a Windows computer? Here's the short answer: In our opinion, if you don't have a true firewall or if you don't have Internet Connection Firewall enabled, you're asking for trouble.

A few years ago, the answer was different. At that time, you could find some safety in numbers. Because many people connect to the Internet, you could gain some protection just from the sheer total numbers of computers connected at any one time. Fish swimming in schools essentially use the same technique. Too many computers were dialed in to the Internet relatively unprotected to focus specific hacker attention on your single computer.

The landscape is changing, though. When people use techniques that keep them connected to the Internet constantly, such as cable Internet access or DSL, the likelihood of a successful attack increases. Not only will your computer be exposed to the Internet for a longer period of time, but the computer will most likely be using the same IP address for an extended time, too. Furthermore, automated attacks that scan the entire IP range of an ISP for vulnerable targets are commonplace as well, and you can clearly see that the odds are changing in favor of the bad guys. The protection provided by the "safety in numbers" approach has essentially disappeared.

With this warning out of the way, it is still worthwhile to look at how you can protect your connection to the Internet by using only built-in Windows functionality. This chapter provides you with enough information to decide whether using Windows as a firewall will provide enough security in your situation.

Windows 98 and Windows Me

When you use the original version of Windows 98 to dial in to the Internet, you can't do much in the operating system to protect that connection. You essentially establish an open connection to the Internet. Granted, Windows 98 doesn't have a lot of services loaded that can be (mis)used for remote administration, either.

File and printer sharing

However, if your Windows 98 computer is used for local network file sharing or printer sharing, the computer can easily be misused for remote administration. The File and Printer Sharing network component binds to all adapters in the Windows 98 computer. This includes any dialup adapters used to connect to the Internet. External users on the Internet may have access to all files on your computer.

TIP

To avoid the situation in which file and printer sharing can be misused from the Internet, disable the File and Printer Sharing component for the dialup adapter. This process is called *unbinding.* In the Network Control Panel console, choose TCP/IP⇨Dial-up Adapter. Clear the File and Printer Sharing for Microsoft Networks check box on the Bindings tab, as shown in Figure 13-1.

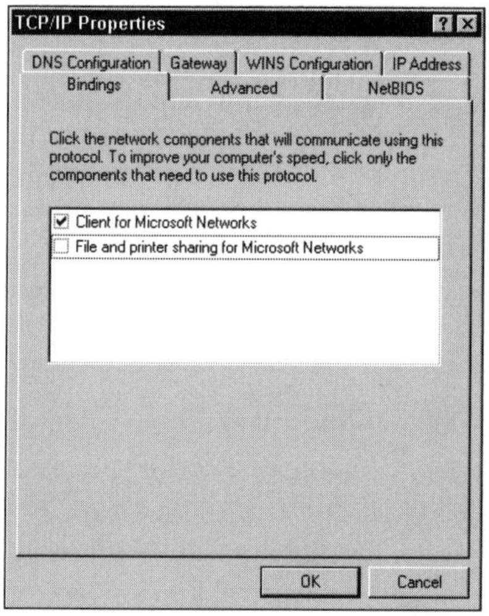

Figure 13-1:
Unbind file
and printer
sharing.

Microsoft agrees that enabling the File and Printer Sharing component on the dialup adapter is not a preferable configuration, and that disabling the component makes your connection to the Internet more secure. When you connect to the Internet using dialup networking, you may even be prompted with this: `Would you like Windows to disable file and printer sharing on the TCP/IP connection to the Internet?`

PPTP client

You can use all recent Windows versions, including Windows 95, to create a Virtual Private Network (VPN) connection to another network. The tunneling protocol used is Point-to-Point Tunneling Protocol (PPTP).

The support of the PPTP protocol doesn't mean that the Windows 98 or Windows Me computer suddenly acts as a firewall just because it can initiate a VPN connection. But at least the computer is able to establish a secure connection to another network, such as the company network, after it is connected to the Internet.

Note that the presence of a VPN connection from the Windows 98 or Windows Me computer to the company network makes it even more important to think about whether those computers are adequately protected on their initial non-VPN connection to the ISP. You are essentially creating an additional entry point into your company network. Direct attacks from the Internet to your company network may be blocked by the company firewall, but the attack path through the Windows 98 or Windows Me VPN clients are only protected by the strength of those computers.

PPTP is considered less secure than the L2TP tunneling protocol. Some weaknesses in the PPTP protocol are related to the way passwords are used to generate encryption keys. These vulnerabilities are not present in L2TP, which is a built-in feature in Windows 2000 or later. You can download the L2TP software for Windows 98, Windows Me, or Windows NT 4.0 from Microsoft's Web site at www.microsoft.com.

Internet Connection Sharing: NAT for Dummies

Starting with Windows 98 Second Edition (SE), Microsoft added Network Address Translation (NAT) functionality to Windows. Windows versions from then on contain a network component called Internet Connection Sharing (ICS). ICS provides networked computers the capability to share a single connection to the Internet. This is typically used for home networks with a few computers that share a single dialup connection from one computer to an ISP.

Note that Windows 2000 and Windows Server 2003 include both the simplified ICS functionality and a full-fledged implementation of NAT.

The address translation done by ICS provides a security benefit called *IP hiding*. IP hiding was originally introduced to conserve the number of public IP addresses on the Internet. However, ICS or NAT hides the true IP numbers on the internal network, as well. This means that one public IP address obtained from the ISP can be used to allow multiple computers on the internal network access to the Internet, while nobody on the outside will know the internal IP addresses.

Strictly speaking, ICS uses Network Address Port Translation (NAPT), but everybody simply calls it NAT. If you don't want to look like a geek, you better not correct somebody at a party who proudly declares that he is using NAT to connect his home network to the Internet. *Firewalls For Dummies* readers know better, but it's our secret. You may, of course, quietly suggest this book to Mr. Loudmouth.

ICS installation

Before you enable ICS on your computer that's connected to the Internet, be advised that many ISPs don't allow you to share that connection with multiple computers on the internal network. Although they may not be able to detect that you are using NAT technology, their usage agreement may not allow it.

To install ICS on a Windows 98 SE or Windows Me computer, you need to have two adapters in the computer: a network adapter that connects to the internal network and either a dialup adapter or another network adapter (for use with cable Internet access or DSL) to connect to the Internet. The same is true for the other ICS-capable Windows versions. Then proceed with these steps:

1. **Choose Control Panel⇨Add/Remove Programs.**

2. **Select Windows Setup and then select Internet Tools.**

3. **Check the Internet Connection Sharing check box to start the ICS Wizard.**

   The ICS Wizard helps you to enable ICS on the computer.

ICS should be installed only on the computer connected to the Internet. All other computers on the internal network use the ICS computer as their default gateway.

The ICS computer does more than just provide the NAT function. ICS also has a DHCP Allocator component. It acts as a mini DHCP service and provides computers on the internal network with a dynamically assigned IP address when they are configured as DHCP clients. By default, the ICS computer uses the IP address 192.168.0.1 on its internal network adapter and offers IP addresses in the range 192.168.0.2 through 192.168.0.253 to computers on the internal network. The ISP assigns the IP address that's used on the external adapter of the ICS computer.

To enable computers on the internal network to resolve DNS queries, such as www.dummies.com, to the correct external IP address, the ICS computer acts as a DNS Proxy and forwards DNS queries from the internal network to the DNS server of the ISP. The DHCP Allocator will tell the internal computers to use the ICS computer for DNS queries.

The IP configuration of a computer on the internal network will look like this:

```
C:\>ipconfig.exe /all

    DHCP Enabled. . . . . . . . . : Yes
    IP Address. . . . . . . . . . : 192.168.0.5
    Subnet Mask . . . . . . . . . : 255.255.255.0
    Default Gateway . . . . . . . : 192.168.0.1
    DNS Servers . . . . . . . . . : 192.168.0.1
```

On Windows 98 SE and Windows Me systems, you can configure the ICS computer to use different IP addresses than 192.168.0.0/24. Search the Microsoft support Web site for Microsoft Knowledge Base article Q230148 for details. In later versions of Windows, you can no longer change the default range of IP addresses for ICS.

After ICS has been installed, a Windows Me ICS computer will feel important and can no longer be put in standby or hibernation mode.

ICS and ports used

When a computer on the internal network sends an IP packet to a computer on the Internet, the ICS computer substitutes its own external IP address as the source IP address and forwards the packet on its way to the Internet computer. The ICS computer keeps a list of current translations on hand in order to successfully forward any response that may arrive back from the Internet that is destined for a computer on the internal network.

A translation entry consists of two pairings: the internal computer's IP address and ports and the Internet computer's IP address and ports. Only packets that match one of the entries in the translation table are forwarded to the computer on the internal network. Packets that are sent unsolicited by computers on the Internet don't have an associated entry in the translation table and therefore, can't reach computers on the internal network.

If a translation entry is not used for ten minutes, ICS removes the entry automatically. ICS can dial up to the ISP automatically when a computer on the internal network wants to access the Internet. If the dialup connection is not used for five minutes, ICS automatically disconnects the line again.

You have the option of creating a static port mapping, in which case ICS is configured to always forward incoming traffic by using a particular port (for example, port 80), thus linking the external IP address of the ICS computer to one of the computers on the internal network.

By default, ICS blocks two ports on the external adapter: TCP port 135 and UDP port 139.

These ports are used for file- and printer-sharing requests. ICS automatically blocks those requests at the external adapter. We discussed earlier in this chapter that Windows may offer to disable the File and Printer Sharing component when you connect to the Internet. This only applies to dialup adapters. ICS blocks ports 135 and 139 on an external network adapter (cable Internet access or DSL) as well.

ICS and application support

Not all applications work when they are connected through an ICS computer. The protocols used by the applications may embed IP or port information in the data portion of the IP packets. The ICS software must know how to replace the information in those locations of the IP packet. To do this, the software uses so-called NAT editors to do the substitution.

Windows 98 SE comes with NAT editors for ICMP (PING), FTP, PPTP, CuSeeMe, DirectPlay, NetMeeting (H.323) and the popular productivity tool Quake. Windows Me has a longer list of NAT editors. A NAT editor isn't needed for the HTTP (Web) protocol because it doesn't embed IP or port information in the data portion of the IP packets.

The presence of a PPTP NAT editor in ICS is important. When you enable ICS on a computer, be careful when you create a PPTP VPN tunnel from the ICS computer to another network because this changes the default gateway on the ICS computer. Network traffic from all the computers on the internal network will be sent into the VPN tunnel, which may not be what you want. You can prevent this happening in two ways: You can disable the default gateway for the VPN connection, or you can create a PPTP VPN tunnel from a computer on the internal network through the ICS computer (and PPTP NAT editor) to the other network.

Windows NT 4.0

The design of Windows NT 4.0 allows for a more secure connection to the Internet than the desktop operating systems in Windows 98 and Windows Me. Windows NT 4.0 has local file system security and more support for packet filtering.

However, when a Windows NT 4.0 computer is connected to the Internet, you can't use it to provide Internet access to other computers on the internal network that use private IP addresses because Windows NT 4.0 doesn't have the NAT (ICS) functionality found in post–98 SE versions of Windows.

Computers on the internal network that use a public IP address can route through a Windows NT 4.0 computer connected to an ISP. In this situation, no address translation is needed.

Of course, the advice we gave earlier to not bind the File and Printer Sharing component to external adapters applies to other Windows versions, such as Windows NT 4.0, as well. Windows NT doesn't use the term *File and Printer Sharing* for the component that provides access to files over the network; it uses the term *Server service*. You can disable the binding of the Server service to the external adapters or dialup adapters in the Network Control Panel console.

Be sure to use the latest Service Pack for Windows NT 4.0 computers. Many security patches have been included in the Service Packs to address discovered vulnerabilities in the Windows NT 4.0 implementation of the IP protocol. This is especially important for computers that are connected to the Internet. The best example is perhaps the vulnerability to attack of malformed IP packets. Without a Service Pack, Windows NT 4.0 computers may crash if hackers send special malformed IP packets to the computers' external interfaces.

Packet filtering

Windows NT 4.0 provides some packet filtering possibilities. By default, packet filtering is not enabled, but you can configure it in the Network Control Panel console. Click the Advanced button for the TCP/IP protocol properties and click the Enable Security check box. The Configure button lets you specify which packets are allowed. Figure 13-2 shows an example in which only network traffic on TCP port 21 and TCP port 80 are allowed.

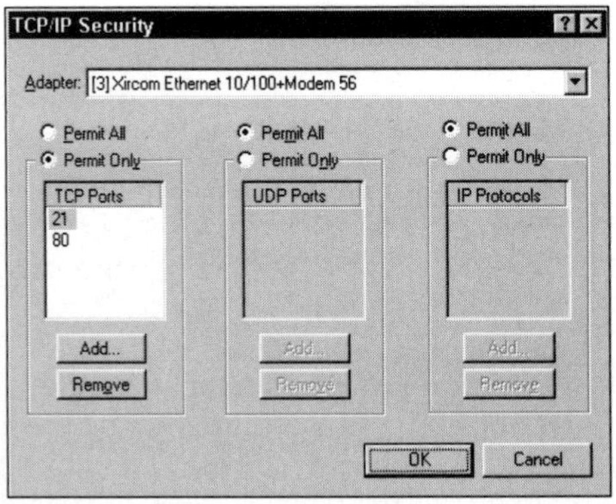

Figure 13-2: Windows NT 4.0 packet filtering.

The packet filtering in Windows NT 4.0 can be specified per network interface. Some limitations on the filtering you can specify are

- ✔ Filtering applies only to inbound packets. Outbound packets are not filtered.

- ✔ Filtering applies only to packets destined for the Windows NT 4.0 computer. Packets that are routed or forwarded between the external interface and the internal interfaces are not affected by the packet filtering.

✔ Filtering can be specified to permit only specific TCP ports, UDP ports, and IP protocols. It can't be used to block specific ports or protocols.

Because the packet filtering found in Windows NT 4.0 doesn't apply to outbound packets, this is considered stateless packet filtering.

Be sure that you haven't inadvertently enabled IP Forwarding on the Routing tab of the TCP/IP protocol properties. If IP Forwarding is enabled on a computer connected to the Internet, packets can enter the internal network without being affected by the packet filtering.

PPTP server

If you want to support VPN connections from the Internet to your internal network, you can use a Windows NT 4.0 Server as a PPTP server. All Windows versions that support the PPTP protocol can create a VPN connection to your Windows NT 4.0 PPTP server.

To enable Windows NT 4.0 as a PPTP server, you need to install the Remote Access Service (RAS) and the Point-To-Point Tunneling Protocol in the Network Control Panel console.

Users who want to create a VPN connection to the server must have dial-in permission. By default, no user can dial in. Use the User Manager for Domains tool or the Remote Access Admin tool in the Administrative Tools folder to grant dial-in permission to users.

On the Advanced dialog box of the TCP/IP protocol properties, you can check the Enable PPTP Filtering check box. When you use this option, all inbound network packets are blocked on the network interface except for PPTP packets. This is equivalent to allowing only TCP port 1723 (PPTP control channel) and IP protocol ID 47 (GRE).

To further restrict Internet access to the Windows NT 4.0 PPTP server, you can limit which computers on the Internet can create a PPTP connection to the server. The PeerClientIPAddresses entry in the Registry can list the IP addresses from which the Windows NT 4.0 server will accept PPTP calls. Search the Microsoft support Web site for Microsoft Knowledge Base article Q154674 for details.

Note that Microsoft offers a free download that can be used to enhance the remote access and filtering capabilities of Windows NT 4.0. This Routing And Remote Access Service Update for Window NT 4.0 can be downloaded from windowsupdate.microsoft.com.

Windows 2000

Windows 2000 is far more secure than its predecessor Windows NT 4.0. Many enhancements and newly added technologies enable you to better protect your connection to the Internet. Enhancements and new technologies in Windows 2000 that relate to Internet connection security are

- ✔ **Better packet-filtering capabilities:** Windows 2000 can specify both incoming and outgoing packet filters based on port, source address, and destination address.

- ✔ **More flexible NAT implementation:** Windows 2000 provides a highly configurable NAT implementation. This is more flexible than the ICS service in Windows 98 SE and Windows Me. Windows NT 4.0 doesn't have any NAT functionality.

- ✔ **Support for incoming L2TP VPN protocol:** Windows NT 4.0 only supports the PPTP VPN protocol. Windows 2000 computers can use the more secure L2TP VPN protocol for incoming VPN tunnels.

- ✔ **Support for IPSec encrypted traffic:** Network traffic can be authenticated or encrypted without using a VPN connection. The industry standard is IPSec. Windows 2000 supports IPSec policies to configure protected network traffic to and from Windows 2000 computers.

Windows 2000 provides many more security improvements, such as the use of the Kerberos authentication protocol, but those are not directly related to the use of Windows 2000 as a firewall.

Packet filtering

Windows 2000 allows you to specify packet filters at four different locations.

- ✔ **TCP/IP filtering in the Network Control Panel console:** This is a slightly changed implementation of the packet filtering that was provided by Windows NT 4.0.

- ✔ **Input filters and Output filters per network interface:** These packet filters can be specified in the Routing and Remote Access console. The Allow or Block filters can be specified for different ports, source addresses, and destination addresses.

- ✔ **Input filters and Output filters per remote access policy:** These are essentially the same filters that can be applied per network interface, but they now apply to the active dial-in connections that are governed by a specific remote access policy.

✔ **Block and Permit filters in an IPSec policy:** IPSec filters are typically used to define how network traffic should be encrypted, but each IPSec filter can be used to block or allow matching IP packets as well.

Packet filters in Network Control Panel

You should probably never use the TCP/IP Filtering option in the Network Control Panel console. The packet filters that can be specified here have the same limitations as the packet filters in Windows NT 4.0. They only apply to inbound traffic that is destined for the computer itself, and can list only TCP ports, UDP ports, and IP protocols that are allowed in. They can't be used to block specific ports or protocols. Routed network traffic from one network interface to another network interface will be unaffected by these filters.

In Windows 2000, Microsoft further limited the usefulness of these packet filters. Unlike in Windows NT 4.0, you can no longer specify to which network adapter the filters should apply. They will automatically apply to all external and internal adapters. The option to enable PPTP filtering is also no longer present in the Network Control Panel console.

The Windows 2000 packet filters that you can specify per network interface in the Routing and Remote Access console are much more powerful.

Packet filters per network interface

The new Routing and Remote Access Service in Windows 2000 allows you to configure separate filters per network interface. You can define filters for incoming network traffic and filters for outgoing network traffic. The filters are defined at a much lower level in the IP network stack; thus, these filters also affect network traffic that's routed from one network interface to another network interface.

You can either specify filters that describe the traffic that should be blocked (Receive All Except the Matching filters), or you can specify filters that describe the traffic that should be allowed in or out (Drop All Except the Matching filters).

To define the packets filters, use the following steps:

1. **Click Start and then select Programs and Administrative Tools to open the Routing and Remote Access console.**

2. **Select the IP Routing⇨General node to open the Properties dialog box of the network interface for which the filters should be defined.**

3. **Click the Input Filters button to display (and define) the list of packet filters for incoming traffic.**

4. **When done, click the Output Filters button to examine (and define) the filters for outgoing traffic.**

Figure 13-3 shows a list of input filters.

Windows 2000 packet filters are stateless. This means that you should explicitly define the needed Input filters and explicitly define the related Output filters for the response packets.

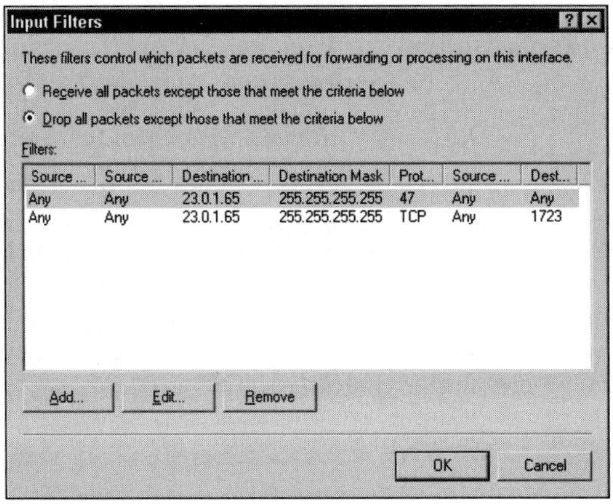

Figure 13-3:
Windows
2000 input
filters
(PPTP).

To further restrict the packets that can enter the internal network, you may want to check the Enable Fragmentation Checking check box on the Properties dialog box of the network interface. This option configures the Windows 2000 computer to discard all incoming fragmented IP packets at this network interface.

Packet filters per remote access policy

All dial-in connections to a Windows 2000 remote access server are represented by the network interface labeled Internal in the Routing and Remote Access console. However, you can't specify packet filters on this network interface in the same manner as on the other network interfaces. Instead, if you want to filter packets that travel to and from dialed-in computers, you have to create the filters in the remote access policy that is used to define the properties of the dialed-in connections.

To define packet filters for remote access clients, open the Routing and Remote Access console. Select the Remote Access Policies node and click the Edit Profile button on the Properties dialog box of the remote access policy for which the filters should be defined. The From Client button (Input filters) and the To Client button (Output filters) on the IP tab display the list of packet filters. If you use a Windows 2000 Radius server to authenticate remote access clients, you should edit the profiles of the remote access policies on the Radius server instead.

IP filters in an IPSec policy

IPSec filters allow you to define different encryption methods for network traffic that matches specific IPSec filters. You can also configure the filter action of an IPSec filter to block or permit network traffic, without regard to encryption settings. These Block and Permit filters can be used to implement packet filters on Windows 2000 computers.

The only time you would use IPSec to implement packet filters in Windows 2000 is when you want to use Group Policy Objects (GPOs) to apply the same packet filters to multiple computers.

Network Address Translation (NAT)

Windows 2000 contains two versions of NAT: the simplified version (ICS) that was introduced in Windows 98 SE and a much more configurable version that can be installed in the Routing and Remote Access console.

Due to the specific translation function that NAT provides (replacing source or destination IP addresses), you should never install two or more NAT services on the same computer. This means that on a Windows 2000 server connected to the Internet, if you need NAT functionality, you should either enable ICS or install the NAT protocol in Routing and Remote Access but never use both at the same time.

ICS

The ICS service in Windows 2000 is actually very similar to the ICS service in Windows 98 SE and Windows Me. You don't have to install the service using the Control Panel; you just check a single check box on the Sharing tab of the external network adapter or the dialup connection to the Internet. If you don't have another network adapter connected to the internal network, the Sharing tab is not present.

After you enable ICS on the external interface, the IP address of the internal network adapter changes to 192.168.0.1. The Windows 2000 ICS computer is automatically configured to assign IP addresses in the 192.168.0.2 through 192.168.0.255 range to DHCP clients on the internal network, and DNS queries from the internal network are forwarded to the DNS server of the ISP.

You should not enable ICS on a Windows 2000 server that runs the DHCP service or the DNS service. The ICS DHCP Allocator or the ICS DNS Proxy use the same ports and interfere with those services. Use the NAT protocol in Routing and Remote Access instead, because it can be configured to not provide the DHCP Allocator or DNS Proxy functionality.

NAT protocol

Windows 2000 can also provide the network address translation function — as long as you install the NAT routing protocol. To do so, right-click the IP Routing⇨General node in the Routing and Remote Access console and choose New Routing Protocol to add the NAT protocol.

This version of NAT is much more configurable than ICS. For example, you can configure whether NAT should include the DNS Proxy function or the DHCP Allocator function and which IP address range that the DHCP Allocator should use. You can even specify that NAT should only translate IP addresses (true NAT) and not translate ports as well (NAPT). If you don't enable port translation, the number of computers that can share the Internet connection is limited by the number of IP addresses that your ISP has assigned to your external interface. This is called an *address pool*.

You can configure the NAT protocol to forward all incoming network traffic on a specific port on the external IP address to a computer on the internal network. Windows 2000 calls this a *special port mapping*. If your ISP has assigned you multiple public IP addresses, you can also map traffic on all ports on a specific external IP address to a computer on the internal network. Windows 2000 calls this particular kind of static address mapping a *reservation*. Figure 13-4 shows the dialog box to add a reservation.

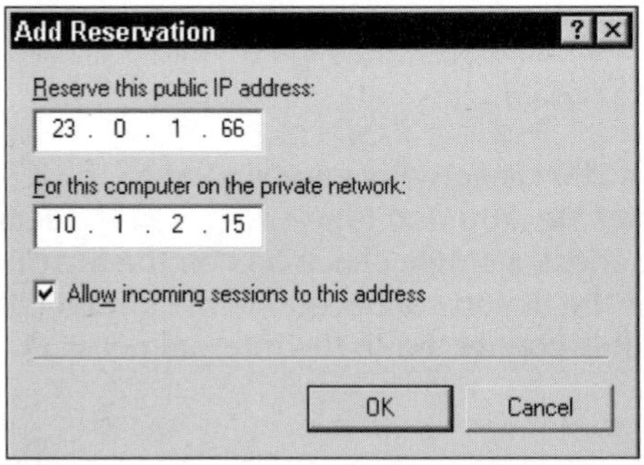

Figure 13-4:
Windows
2000 NAT
static
address
mapping.

Add Reservation ? X

Reserve this public IP address:

    23 . 0 . 1 . 66

For this computer on the private network:

    10 . 1 . 2 . 15

☑ Allow incoming sessions to this address

    OK   Cancel

For applications that embed IP or port information in the data portion of the IP packets, NAT requires specific NAT editors to substitute that information correctly. Windows 2000 includes fewer NAT editors than what is provided in Windows 98 SE and Windows Me. NAT editors are included for ICMP (PING), FTP, PPTP, and DirectPlay.

Note that the PPTP NAT editor allows you to create a PPTP VPN tunnel from a computer on the internal network through the Windows 2000 NAT computer to a PPTP server on the Internet, but doesn't allow you to establish a PPTP VPN tunnel from a computer on the Internet to a PPTP server on the internal network.

L2TP and IPSec

L2TP and IPSec are two new technologies in Windows 2000. Layer Two Tunneling Protocol (L2TP) is a standards-based protocol used to create a VPN tunnel. IP Security (IPSec) is a standards-based protocol used to authenticate or encrypt data transmitted between two computers.

L2TP uses IPSec to encrypt the data in the VPN tunnel, but IPSec can be used without a VPN tunnel as well.

L2TP server

Windows 2000 supports two tunneling protocols: PPTP and L2TP. The L2TP protocol is considered to be more secure than the PPTP protocol.

The Windows 2000 computer that is connected to the Internet can be the endpoint of a L2TP VPN tunnel. If you want to restrict the network traffic to this Windows 2000 L2TP VPN server, you have to create the packet filters that are shown in Table 13-1. In this example, the Windows 2000 L2TP server has external IP address 23.0.1.65.

Table 13-1   Windows 2000 L2TP Firewall Rules (Tunnel Endpoint)

Filter	Source	Destination	Transport Protocol	Source Port	Destination Port	Description
Input	Any	23.0.1.65	UDP	500	500	IKE
Input	Any	23.0.1.65	UDP	1701	1701	L2TP
Output	23.0.1.65	Any	UDP	500	500	IKE
Output	23.0.1.65	Any	UDP	1701	1701	L2TP

In this situation, no specific firewall rules are required to allow IPSec ESP traffic because the Routing and Remote Access filters are applied after the IPSec module of Windows 2000 TCP/IP has removed the ESP header.

IPSec

Windows 2000 can also use IPSec without bothering to establish an L2TP VPN tunnel. How, you may ask? Remember that IPSec is mainly used to authenticate or encrypt network packets between computers on the internal network itself. However, you can also deploy IPSec to authenticate or encrypt data packets traveling between two Windows 2000 computers that are connected to the Internet. An example is using an IPSec ESP tunnel to connect two branch offices.

If you want to filter the network traffic to include only IPSec packets, you have to create the packet filters that are shown in Table 13-2.

Table 13-2			IPSec Firewall Rules in Branch Office			
Filter	**Source**	**Destination**	**Transport Protocol**	**Source Port**	**Destination Port**	**Description**
Input	23.0.2.12	23.0.1.65	UDP	500	500	IKE
Input	23.0.2.12	23.0.1.65	ID 50	Any	Any	IPSec ESP
Input	23.0.2.12	23.0.1.65	ID 51	Any	Any	IPSec AH
Output	23.0.1.65	23.0.2.12	UDP	500	500	IKE
Output	23.0.1.65	23.0.2.12	ID 50	Any	Any	IPSec ESP
Output	23.0.1.65	23.0.2.12	ID 51	Any	Any	IPSec AH

On the other Windows 2000 server with IP address 23.0.2.12, you have to create similar filters.

The IPSec ESP protocol provides integrity for the entire packet except for the IP header. If you want to provide integrity for the entire packet including the IP header, you have to implement an IPSec tunnel that uses both the ESP and AH protocol. For an IPSec tunnel that doesn't use the IPSec AH protocol, you don't have to create the two IPSec AH packet filters from Table 13-2.

Windows XP

Windows XP is Microsoft's latest desktop operating system. It contains many security enhancements over earlier Windows desktop versions, such as Windows Me and Windows NT Workstation 4.0.

Some of the security enhancements in Windows XP are related to protecting the connection to the Internet. For example, Windows XP won't allow any local users to connect to the Windows XP computer as themselves. All incoming connections are done as Guest, even if you know the password of the Administrator account of the computer. This technique is called Simple File Sharing. By default, this option is enabled for Windows XP computers that are used at home. Open Explorer and use the Folder Options command from the Tools menu. The View tab in the Folder Options dialog box contains the Use Simple File Sharing option.

Internet Connection Firewall (ICF)

By far the most important improvement related to protecting the connection to the Internet is the new Internet Connection Firewall (ICF) in Windows XP.

ICF is a stateful firewall built into Windows XP and Windows Server 2003. The firewall can be enabled per network adapter or dialup adapter. Enabling the firewall consists of enabling a single check box.

1. **Choose Control Panel⇨Network Connections.**

2. **Right-click on the dialup adapter or the network adapter that is connected to the Internet and select Properties.**

3. **On the Advanced tab, enable the check box in the Internet Connection Firewall box and then click OK.**

After the firewall is enabled, the icon for the network connection is displayed with a little padlock to indicate that it is firewalled. Figure 13-5 shows ICF enabled on the dialup adapter.

ICF allows any outgoing traffic and will normally only allow inbound traffic to the Windows XP computer if it is a response to an earlier packet sent out.

When you click the Settings button on the Advanced tab where you enabled ICF, you can configure ICF to allow more incoming network packets by specifying the services that this computer uses. Examples are FTP Server, Web Server (HTTP), and Remote Desktop.

Figure 13-5:
ICF on
dialup
adapter.

In the Advanced Settings dialog box, you can also configure the logging of dropped packets or successful connections to a log file — called `pfirewall.log` — in the Windows folder. The log file can be used to analyze the kinds of packets dropped by ICF.

ICF doesn't have features that you usually find in personal firewalls, such as those that prompt the user to include additional rules when a packet is about to be dropped. ICF doesn't bother to ask you anything during its operation — which can be considered a good thing!

Windows Server 2003

Windows Server 2003 is the successor of Windows 2000 Server. This new server operating system from Microsoft has been available since April 2003.

The features of Windows Server 2003 that are related to protecting the connection to the Internet are a combination of the functions described for Windows 2000 and the Internet Connection Firewall of Windows XP. The same functionality with regard to packet filtering, Routing and Remote Access support, and IPSec encryption is included in Windows Server 2003.

Internet Connection Firewall (ICF) in Windows Server 2003 is basically the same as the one in Windows XP, with one minor improvement — one of the shortcomings of ICF in Windows XP is that it doesn't work during startup or shutdown of the computer. This possible window where the server could be contacted without the protection from the firewall is closed by a new feature of IPSec in Windows Server 2003. Whenever a Windows Server 2003 computer starts, the IPSec driver blocks all connections from the network to the computer. This includes the internal network and a possible connection from the Internet. During startup, the IPSec driver only allows outgoing network packets and their answer. The only exception to this is that incoming network traffic on port 68 is allowed, to support DHCP configuration of the server.

Note that you can only enable ICF on a Windows Server 2003 computer if Routing and Remote Access is not configured. If Routing and Remote Access is enabled, then you must use a special version of ICF — known as Basic Firewall — built into Routing and Remote Access. Its functions are exactly the same as ICF.

This is similar to the way in which Internet Connection Sharing (ICS) in Windows 2000 is the simple version of the much more configurable NAT, found in the Routing and Remote Access console of Windows 2000.

Chapter 14

Configuring Linux as a Firewall

● ●

In This Chapter

▶ Making installation choices

▶ Introducing iptables

▶ Using iptables commands

▶ Simplifying things with firewall GUIs

▶ Adding proxy functionality

● ●

*A*s Linux gains increasing acceptance in corporate datacenters and other places, more and more people are discovering something that Linux enthusiasts have known for a long time: Linux has built-in firewall features that allow an administrator to build a firewall. Recent versions of Linux generally ship with at least basic firewall capabilities, and several Linux versions include even more advanced features. Because Linux is open source software, and because it has only minimal hardware requirements, you can build a Linux-based firewall relatively inexpensively. Be forewarned, though — doing so does require some knowledge of Linux and how it fits into the networking scheme of things.

Making Installation Choices

To use the firewall built into Linux, you should make sure that the operating system you install includes iptables functionality. *Iptables* is the most popular Linux firewall, and this chapter covers it in detail. Fortunately, most Linux distributions do this by default, so you probably don't have to worry about this.

Which Linux?

If you go to the store to buy yourself some Linux, you can easily get confused by the different versions (called *distributions*) that are available. Because Linux is open source software, it's pretty darn easy to enhance Linux, as long as core components remain unchanged. Many vendors have taken advantage of this by creating distributions that add more features and capabilities.

One consequence of having different distributions is that the installation procedures for each may be different — meaning that things may look a little different with your Linux flavor from what we describe in this chapter. Although most current distributions do include the *iptables* capabilities that we describe in this chapter, some do not. Some distributions also require that you download and install firewall components separately. Finally, some distributions may include proprietary firewall programs. Just so you can keep score, know that most of this chapter is based on one of the most popular distributions, Red Hat Linux 8. To keep you on your toes, we also cover some features that are available in SuSE Linux 8.1, just for the heck of it. If you use a different distribution, don't worry! You can transfer what you learn in this chapter to most other distributions.

Before you install Linux, make sure that all your network cards and any modem that you may use are installed in your computer. Generally, it's much easier to have all your hardware in place before installing your Linux software than it is to install Linux first and then try to get Linux to recognize all the hardware stuff after the fact.

Red Hat Linux, in its ongoing effort to be top dog in the Linux field, goes one step further along the customer satisfaction road by giving you a choice of configuring the firewall during installation. One of the screens that you see during the installation procedure is shown in Figure 14-1. The choices you see on this screen are good starting points, whether you are just setting up a personal computer, or whether you are planning to configure a corporate firewall. Of course, when you are indeed configuring a dedicated firewall, you will have to perform some additional configuration after the installation is complete.

If you are using another distribution, just skip this section and go on to the section on iptables. The process of configuring the firewall after installation is virtually identical in all Linux distributions.

Let's look at each of the available choices:

   ✔ **Off:** This option does just what its name implies: It configures Linux to allow all network traffic to enter or leave the computer. Obviously, this is not an appropriate setting for a firewall unless you want to do all your configuring at some later point. (No, deciding just to skip this whole firewall business is not an option. Need to reread Chapter 1?)

✔ **Medium:** This is an appropriate choice if you want to use Linux as a personal firewall or if you are installing a server that performs limited functions, such as a Web server. When you select this option, Linux configures iptables to allow certain types of traffic into your computer. You can specify which types of traffic are allowed; for example, you can disable HTTP traffic or allow SMTP traffic. One of the limitations of the Red Hat setup program is that it can only perform very simple firewall configuration tasks for you. Keep in mind that you can add or remove rules later, but if you already know which traffic you want to allow and which traffic you want to block, you can easily configure this during setup.

✔ **High:** When you select this option, you enable and configure the iptables firewall to block all traffic. This is the configuration that you should choose when you install a dedicated firewall. Best practices dictate that you configure your firewall to drop all network traffic unless you specifically allow it. Choosing this option gives you this starting configuration; you get to do all the other configuration steps after the operating system installation is complete.

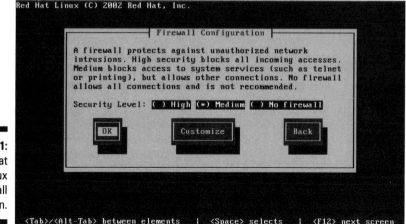

Figure 14-1:
Red Hat
Linux
firewall
installation.

Introducing iptables

Although we already mentioned iptables a few times in this chapter, this is the section where we actually get down to brass tacks about the whole iptables business. Iptables is the command that you use to tell the Linux kernel — the core part of the operating system — how to treat network traffic. For example, you can use the iptables command to drop IP packets, forward them, or perform network address translation (NAT).

What about the ipchains command?

If you have configured firewall rules using older versions of Linux, you may have encountered the `ipchains` command. The ipchains facility was used to configure firewall capability in Linux kernels up to version 2.3. The iptables facility is the preferred method for configuring firewalls using version 2.4 of the Linux kernel, which all current versions of Linux are based on. The `iptables` command allows for improved control over firewall rules and adds more flexibility in configuring firewall rules.

Before you can configure rules with the `iptables` command, you have to understand a few concepts and Linux-specific terms:

- ✔ **Tables:** Locations where a Linux firewall stores and maintains sets of rules. The main table is the *filter table,* where you define most rules that apply to incoming and outgoing traffic. This is also the default table that commands apply to when you don't specify a specific table. The *nat table* contains rules that define how Linux performs NAT. The *mangle table* is used for advanced packet routing, but isn't used frequently. (Don't worry; despite its name, this table won't mutilate all your important data.)

- ✔ **Chains:** At the core of a Linux firewall. Using a chain to lock your computer to a desk may be a good idea, but in this case, we're talking about a different kind of chain. Linux uses this term to refer to a set of rules that Linux applies when filtering network traffic. Here are the three main chains, each of which is part of the filter table:

  - **Input chain:** This chain applies to all traffic destined for the firewall computer. For example, if you want to enable remote administration of your firewall, you have to configure a rule for the input chain to allow whatever network traffic your remote administration tools use.

  - **Output chain:** The output chain applies to all traffic that leaves the firewall computer. For example, if your firewall needs to contact a DNS server for name lookups, you have to configure the output chain to allow this traffic.

  - **Forward chain:** This chain applies to all traffic that your Linux firewall handles for other computers. For example, if your firewall allows network traffic from client computers to the Internet, you have to configure the forward chain to allow this traffic.

The nat table and mangle table also contain separate chains, but most firewall rules that you define are contained in the chains just described.

✔ **SNAT, DNAT, and Masquerading:** These terms refer to different forms of network address translation. SNAT changes a packet's source address before sending it on; this is most often used to hide the real IP address of a client computer in outgoing traffic. DNAT changes the destination address of packets, which is commonly used for transparent proxies — proxy servers that handle network traffic for clients without the client knowing. Masquerading is a specialized form of NAT because it doesn't require a static IP address. Masquerading also hides internal clients from the outside world and is used when your external IP address changes dynamically — for example, when you use a dialup connection to connect to the Internet. Just like dressing up in a costume changes someone's appearance, masquerading changes a packet's appearance to the outside world.

Using iptables Commands

Linux includes a number of different `iptables` commands. All of them start with `iptables` and add a number of command-line options. The best way to start using the `iptables` commands is to look at the basic syntax for simple firewall rules.

To instruct Linux to add a rule to one of the chains or to remove one of its rules, the syntax is as follows (optional parameters are shown in square brackets):

```
iptables [-t table] CMD [chain] [filter_match] [target]
```

`Iptables` commands must specify the table where the command will be applied, the command itself, the chain to which the command will belong, an expression that defines what type of traffic the filter will apply to, and what Linux should do with the packet. For example, to add a simple rule to the input chain of the filter table that would drop all ICMP traffic, your code would look something like this:

```
iptables -t filter -A INPUT -p icmp DROP
```

As you can see, this command starts with the required *iptables*. It then specifies which table and chain it refers to, goes on to include a match expression, and then finally defines a target. This particular command tells Linux: When the Filter table's Input chain receives a packet that uses the ICMP protocol, send the packet to the Drop target. In other words: Dump all ICMP traffic.

iptables commands

Before you can build your own rules, you have to familiarize yourself with the basic commands, filter match expressions, and targets. Table 14-1 describes the most commonly used `iptables` commands.

Table 14-1		Common iptables Commands
Command	*Name*	*Description*
-A	Append	This command appends a rule to the end of a chain.
-I	Insert	This command inserts a rule to the beginning of a chain.
-D <chain> <rule number>	Delete Rule	This command deletes a rule.
-L [<chain>]	List	This command lists all rules in a chain. If you don't specify a chain, the command lists the rules in all chains.
-N <chain>	New	This command creates a new user-defined chain. You can create new chains with separate processing rules that can process packets before they are returned to normal processing
-X <chain>	Delete Chain	This command deletes a user-defined chain.
-F [<chain>]	Flush	This command deletes all rules in a chain. If you don't specify a chain, the command deletes all rules in all chains.
-h	Help	This command lists all `iptables` commands and options. If you add -h to another command, iptables lists all available options for that command.

iptables targets

Before using `iptables` commands, you also must understand the concept of a target. A target is the destination where the chain will send a packet, but you can also think of a target as an action that Linux will perform with the packet. Table 14-2 lists the most common targets.

Table 14-2	Common iptables Targets
Target	**Description**
DROP	When a rule sends a packet to the DROP target, it is silently discarded and never heard from again. Don't feel bad for the packet, though. If you didn't want it to get through your firewall in the first place, then you don't need to get all teary-eyed for getting rid of it.
REJECT	When a rule sends a packet to the REJECT target, it is discarded. However, instead of doing so silently, Linux sends an ICMP packet to the source, informing it that the packet was dropped. Although this is a polite response to dropping a packet, in most cases, it isn't recommended because it can give an attacker an indication that some thing is responding at the other end. Most of the time the safer choice is the DROP target.
ACCEPT	Use rules to specify this target for packets that you want to pass through your firewall. Choosing this target means that the packet is accepted and sent on its merry way, either into your network or out of your network, depending on its destination.
LOG	This target simply means that the packet is logged. No further action is taken. A common place for the LOG target is a user-defined chain to which you send packets to be logged and dropped while the regular chain keeps processing other packets.
SNAT	This target can only be used in the POSTROUTING chain of the nat table. Using SNAT changes the source address of a packet to an address that you specify. Keep in mind that you use this option with firewalls that have a static IP address. SNAT is normally used with outgoing packets.
DNAT	This target can only be used in the PREROUTING chain of the nat table. Using DNAT changes the destination address of a packet to an address that you specify. DNAT is normally used with incoming packets.
MASQUERADE	This target performs NAT for a packet when your firewall has a dynamic IP address — when you connect to the Internet using a dialup connection, for example. This target can only be used in the POSTROUTING chain of the nat table.

(continued)

Table 14-2 *(continued)*

Target	Description
user chain	The italics here mean that you have to replace the words "user chain" with the name you gave your user-defined chain. You can choose whatever name you want. You can send a packet to such a chain for further processing. For example, a user-defined chain can perform further processing — such as logging packets that match certain conditions and then dropping them — without interrupting the order of processing for other packets.

Order matters

The order in which the rules are processed matters with `iptables` commands. Because of this, iptables has the convenient `-A` command that appends commands to the end of the processing chain and the equally convenient `-I` command that adds commands to the beginning of the processing chain or a user-specified location. Of course, an even better strategy is to plan for the order of processing of commands before you define your rules.

Unlike some other firewalls, iptables applies each filter command and stops processing commands once a match takes place. For example, if you create a rule that allows all network traffic and then you create other rules that deny specific types of traffic, you should make sure that the Drop All rule is at the end of the chain. That way, Linux stops processing the rules as soon as it recognizes that the packet should be allowed. The Drop All rule won't be processed. If you reversed the order and applied the Drop All rule first, Linux would examine the packet and drop it when the Drop All rule is encountered. The rule that allows the packet would never be processed.

It's a good practice in designing firewalls to place the rules that allow network traffic first and then apply rules that deny traffic later. To create more involved rules, you can create additional user-defined chains, which are chains that perform further processing, or add conditional statements, or create rules that contain more than one condition that the packet must match in order for a rule to apply.

Finally, rule processing doesn't end when a packet is logged. You can make a decision to allow or drop a packet even after a rule has been applied to log the packet.

iptables options and conditions

Options are the last component of iptables commands that you need to have under your belt in order to build firewall rules. Options determine how a command is processed. Most often, these options are conditions that are checked before a command is applied. These conditional expressions are evaluated by Linux to decide whether a command should be applied or ignored for a given packet. Table 14-3 lists the most commonly used options, including conditional expressions.

Table 14-3	Common iptables Options
Option	*Description*
-p *protocol*	Specifies to what protocol the rule applies. The parameter *protocol* can be tcp, udp, or icmp. You can also use the name of the protocol — if it is listed in /etc/protocols — or the protocol number. You can apply the rule to all protocols by using the number 0 or the word *all*. Finally, you can combine several protocols in a command by separating them with commas. For example, -p 47 refers to all packets that use protocol 47 (the Generic Routing Protocol, GRE); -p tcp,udp matches all packets that use the TCP or the UDP protocols.
-s *source_ address[/mask]*	Specifies the source address of a packet. The optional *mask* parameter specifies a subnet mask, expressed in classless IP addressing. This addressing scheme uses a single number — one that specifies the number of bits in a subnet mask — for the subnet mask. For example, -s 192.168.1.1 indicates a packet from the IP address 192.168.1.1. -s 192.168.1.0/24 indicates a packet from any address between 192.168.1.0 and 192.168.1.255. The number 24 indicates that the range of addresses includes all IP addresses where the first 24 bits — corresponding to the first 3 octets — are the same.
-d *destination_ address[/mask]*	Specifies the destination address of a packet. As in the source address, you can specify a subnet mask to refer to an address range. -s 23.2.4.7, for example, indicates a packet addressed to the IP address 23.2.4.7. -s 23.0.0.0/8 indicates a packet to any address between 23.0.0.0 and 23.255.255.255.

(continued)

Table 14-3 *(continued)*

Option	Description
--source-port *port*	Specifies the source port of a TCP or UDP packet. Because only these protocols use ports, this condition can only be used in conjunction with the `-p udp` or `-p tcp` options. You can refer to a range of ports by using a colon between two port numbers. For example, `-p udp —source-port 53` refers to all UDP packets with a source port of 53; `-p tcp —source-port 0:1023` refers to all TCP packets with a source port lower than 1024. Finally, if a service is listed in the `/etc/services` file, you can refer to the name of the service instead of the port number.
--destination-port *port*	This option is analogous to the source-port option, but it refers to the destination port of a TCP or UDP packet. For example, `-p tcp —destination-port 80` refers to all TCP packets with a source port of 80; `-p udp —source-port 1024-1100` refers to all UDP packets with a source port between 1024 and 1100.
-i *interface*	Specifies the network interface on which an incoming packet is received. For example, you can refer to all packets that arrived on the interface eth0 by specifying `-i eth0`. If you want to refer to all interfaces of a specific type, you can use a plus sign (+) as a wildcard character. For example, `-i eth+` matches all packets that arrive on an interface with a name that begins with eth, such as eth0 and eth1.
-o *interface*	This option is analogous to the `-i` option, but it refers to the output interface on which a packet is to be sent. For example, you can refer to all packets that are about to be sent on the interface eth1 by specifying `-o eth1`. You can also use the plus sign (+) as a wildcard character with this option.
--syn	This option specifies TCP packets that establish a new connection. The first packet of a three-way handshake operation when a new TCP connection is established carries a SYN flag, but not an ACK or FIN flag. The —syn option tests packets that look like they might be trying to start a new TCP connection — they have the telltale "SYN flag, but no ACK or FIN flag" signature. Packets that follow later during the three-way handshake or during a data connection don't meet these conditions, they also don't meet the criteria of the —syn option. Because of this behavior, you can use the —syn option to check whether a packet is the first packet that is part of a new connection. For example, *-p tcp —syn* tests whether a packet is part of a new TCP connection. This test is most often used in rules that disallow the establishing of new TCP connections.

Option	Description
--icmp-type *type*	This option tests for specific ICMP types and can only be used if the ICMP protocol is specified. ICMP packets have an option field that specifies the purpose of the packet. You can either use the name of an ICMP type or the corresponding number to filter specific ICMP packets. For example, `-p icmp -icmp-type source-quench` applies to all source quench messages; `-p icmp -icmp-type 0` refers to all ICMP echo reply packets — the number 0 corresponds to the type `echo reply`.
!	The exclamation point is not a condition by itself, but it applies to all the optional expressions listed here. The ! reverses the logic of the expression. For example, where `-p 47` means Protocol 47, `-p ! 47` means "not protocol 47," or all protocols except for protocol 47.
-j target	This is not an optional expression, but rather specifies that a packet should be sent to a specific target. For example, `-j DROP` means that a packet should be sent to the DROP target, and thus discarded.

Putting it all together: Building a simple Linux firewall

Now that you have all the building blocks at hand, you're ready to build a simple Linux firewall. How simple? The firewall that we have in mind is designed to allow all outgoing traffic and block all incoming traffic, with two exceptions: It allows incoming TCP traffic that is part of an established connection, and it allows incoming UDP traffic on port 53. The reason why we allow this UDP traffic is because we assume that our firewall has to make DNS lookup requests and also has to accept replies to these queries.

Although you can type each command in the following list manually each time you start Linux, it makes much more sense to add the commands to a script so you don't have to type each command separately. Using a script also makes it less likely that you make typing mistakes. After you've created and tested the script, go ahead and have the script run each time you start your computer. If you need more information on how to create scripts, we recommend the book *Linux For Dummies,* by Dee-Ann LeBlanc, Melanie Hoag, and Evan Bloomquist, published by Wiley Publishing, Inc.

```
# Lines starting with this character are comments
# and are not executed.
# When you end a line with a backslash, \
    Linux treats the next line as a continuation of \
    the current line.
# Let's start by clearing all chains that may have
# something in them.
iptables -F
# Just in case there are user-defined chains,
# let's delete those too.
iptables -X
# Next, let's allow all packets that arrive on the
# eth0 interface. If your internal interface has a different
# name, you have to use that name instead.
iptables -A INPUT -i eth0 -j ACCEPT
# Most likely your computer has to perform DNS lookups
# and will need to receive replies to these lookup requests.
# The following rule allows this. Replace xxx.xxx.xxx.xxx
# with your firewall's external IP address.
iptables -A INPUT -p udp -s xxx.xxx.xxx.xxx -sport 53 \
    -j ACCEPT
# Before you drop packets that do not meet the above
# criteria, let's log those packets.
iptables -A INPUT -I eth0 -j LOG
# Finally you drop all packets that have not been
# allowed above.
iptables -A INPUT -I eth0 -DROP
```

After you have entered all the rules for the input chain, you can list them by using the `iptables -v -L INPUT` command. By using the `-v` option with this command, you get more verbose — another word for *more detailed* — information.

Masquerading and NAT

Linux provides two versions of NAT. Masquerading is designed for dynamic IP addresses; for example, an IP address assigned by an ISP to dialup connection. If you have a static external IP address, then you normally use a combination of SNAT and DNAT.

Enabling Masquerading

In most cases, you enable Masquerading — NAT for dynamic addresses — for all outgoing traffic from your network. This is a form of *source NAT,* which means that your firewall changes the *source* address of packets.

To enable Masquerading, you need to enter the following `iptables` command.

```
iptables -t nat -A POSTROUTING -o ppp0 -j MASQUERADE
```

Notice that you are using iptables to modify the POSTROUTING chain of the NAT table. This means that the command is applied after the packet's address is modified — after Linux has applied routing rules — but before it leaves the computer. The command also assumes that your outgoing interface is called `ppp0` and your internal interface is called `eth1`. If either has a different name, you need to change the command accordingly.

You can find out all the gory details about the `iptables` command, as well as all other commands by reading the *man* page — short for manual — for it. To do this, simply type `man iptables` in a Linux command shell.

Masquerading means that NAT will be applied to all traffic that is forwarded, or routed. However, you still need to specify which traffic you allow to be forwarded. The following commands allow all TCP traffic from your internal network to be forwarded to the Internet, as well as all TCP traffic belonging to an established session to be returned. The example assumes that your internal interface is called `eth1` and your external interface is called `ppp0`.

```
iptables -A FORWARD -i eth1 -o ppp0 -m state \
    --state NEW,ESTABLISHED -j ACCEPT
iptables -A FORWARD -i ppp0-o eth1 -m state \
    --state ESTABLISHED -j ACCEPT
```

If you have other network traffic that you want to allow from your internal network, then you need to configure additional rules for this traffic.

Using SNAT

Configuring source NAT, or SNAT, is similar to configuring Masquerading. The difference is that for SNAT, your external interface must have a static IP address. The following command enables SNAT. The command also assumes that your firewall's external interface is called `eth0`. If it has a different name, you need to change the command accordingly. You also need to replace xxx.xxx.xxx.xxx with the external IP address of your firewall.

```
iptables -t nat -A POSTROUTING -o eth0 -j \
    SNAT -to-source xxx.xxx.xxx.xxx
```

Using DNAT

Destination NAT, or DNAT, is used to allow incoming traffic into a network that uses NAT. For example, to make a public Web server at the IP address 192.168.1.80 available to your customers, you need to use the following series of commands. The first command enables DNAT. The second command creates the required forwarding rule to allow the traffic to be processed. The commands assume that your firewall's external interface is called eth0, and the internal interface is called eth1. If either has a different name, you need to change the command accordingly. You also need to replace xxx.xxx.xxx.xxx with the external IP address of your firewall.

```
iptables -t nat -A PREROUTING -i eth0 -p tcp \
    -sport 1024:65635 -d xxx.xxx.xxx.xxx -dport 80 \
    -j DNAT -to-destination 192.168.1.80
iptables -A FORWARD -i eth0 -o eth1 -p tcp \
    -sport 1024:65635 -d 192.168.1.80 -dport 80 \
    -m state --state NEW -j ACCEPT
```

By using SNAT or DNAT, you can apply very flexible rules to incoming traffic. You can change the port of the traffic as you perform NAT, for example, or you can configure outgoing traffic from one internal host to be sent out with one external IP address as its source and all other traffic with a different IP address. No matter which kind of NAT you use, remember that SNAT, DNAT and Masquerading only control how NAT is performed. You also need to configure corresponding FORWARD rules to allow the traffic to be sent.

Simplifying Things: Firewall GUIs

Depending on which version of Linux you are using, you may have a graphical user interface, or GUI-based utility to do much of the work for you. Generally, such utilities allow you to configure basic personal firewall functionality. This may be all you need, but even if you are configuring a full-fledged firewall for your network, it's a good idea to do the initial setup using a GUI and then add more rules later on.

One Linux distribution that has such an interface is Red Hat Linux. With the GUI interface, you get the same configuration choices that Red Hat Linux presented during setup. You start by configuring general security settings and then you specify the particular services to which you want to grant access. To start configuring the firewall using this utility, simply run the lokkit command. You'll see a screen like the one shown in Figure 14-1 Then simply follow the on-screen instructions to configure firewall functionality.

Another distribution with a GUI-based firewall setup is the SuSEfirewall2 package included with SuSE Linux 8. You start the configuration program by selecting it on the YaST2 (Yet another Setup Tool) menu. This starts a wizard, shown in Figure 14-2, that guides you through the firewall configuration.

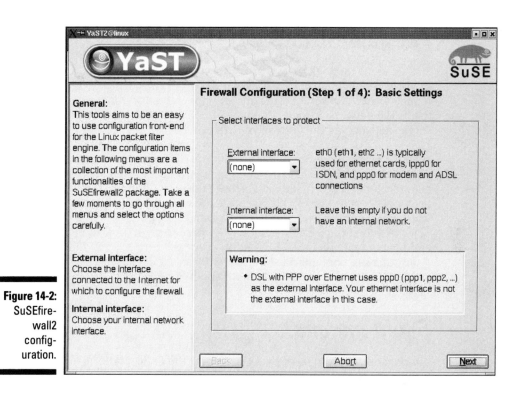

Figure 14-2:
SuSEfire-
wall2
config-
uration.

Adding Proxy Functionality

You can enhance your firewall functionality by adding proxy support. Adding
a proxy server to your network design enhances the packet filtering and
stateful inspection capabilities of your iptables firewall by allowing the firewall to inspect network traffic at the application layer. A proxy server can
also perform user-based authentication of network traffic.

Applications that are aware of the proxy server can send network requests to
it instead of sending packets directly to the target. Unfortunately, not all
applications are capable of doing this neat trick. To support applications that
can't use a proxy server, you have to install a piece of client software that
intercepts regular network requests from an application and forwards it to
the proxy server. This is often referred to as *transparent proxy.* Proxy capabilities for Linux are available by using two different types of proxy servers,
SOCKS and Squid.

Put your SOCKS on

SOCKS, short for Sockets, is a proxy server — currently in version 5 — that can process all types of network requests. After the client forwards network requests, a SOCKS server performs an Application layer inspection and then fulfills the network request. The type of processing that occurs at the SOCKS server depends on the version you are using.

SOCKS specifications are defined in several RFCs (requests for comments) and several versions of SOCKS servers are available. Even Microsoft Security and Acceleration (ISA) Server, which we cover in Chapter 16, supports this protocol. Most of these SOCKS servers are commercial products, but you can use a version that's available for non-commercial purposes, free of charge. You can find out more about SOCKS — where to get it, how to implement it, and how to wash dirty SOCKS — at www.socks.permeo.com. Among other items, this site contains a list of frequently asked questions (FAQs) that is a good starting point for learning more about SOCKS.

Squid anyone?

A more specialized type of proxy server for the Linux platform is the free bit of software known affectionately as Squid. Squid is a caching server, which means that it can accelerate Internet access by keeping local copies of frequently accessed Web pages and other Web objects, such as graphics. Most Web browsers allow you to configure a Squid-based caching server as a proxy server. Squid servers generally only support Web requests, which include HTTP and FTP requests that are issued by a proxy-aware client, such as a Web browser. However, Squid servers can't handle other network requests, such as connections to mail servers. Several versions of Squid servers are available, some of which are free and some of which are commercial software. You can find out more about Squid and how to implement it at www.squid-cache.org. As was the case with the SOCKS Web site, the best starting point to learn more is the FAQ section.

Chapter 15

Configuring Personal Firewalls: ZoneAlarm, BlackICE, and Norton Personal Firewall

*J*ust a few years ago, only companies and organizations had to worry about hackers attempting to break into their computer network. Terms like "security control," "access policies," "intrusion detection," and "audit rules" only seemed appropriate in corporate lingo; they weren't something home users needed to worry about. Hackers pretty much ignored home users and small offices.

The landscape is changing rapidly, though.

Home computers are no longer safe when they connect to the Internet: Hackers are getting more and more interested in getting to your home computer. In this chapter, we look at how you can use personal firewalls to protect your home computers when they're connected to the Internet. We specifically look at three personal firewalls: Zone Labs' ZoneAlarm (www.zonelabs.com), Network ICE's BlackICE Defender (www.networkice.com), and Symantec's Norton Personal Firewall (www.norton.com).

Before you're tempted to skip this chapter, it may be good to mention that some of the best personal firewalls are totally free and downloadable from the Internet. Some free personal firewalls, such as ZoneAlarm, come with the provision that the free license is only for personal use, and not for business use.

Home Computers at Risk

Not too long ago, when an uncle at a birthday party would ask you how to be safe on the Internet, suggesting a decent anti-virus program was a good answer. Depending on how much you like your uncle, it can still be a sufficient answer, but the truth is that viruses are no longer the only threat to home computers.

Hackers have gained interest in your home computer for several reasons. We cover said reasons in the following sections.

Home computers have changed

First of all, your computer has become more powerful over time. Don't be surprised if your new multimedia home computer that's just sitting on your desk has more processing power than all the computers aboard the first space shuttle, combined. Granted, heat-resistance, boost absorbance, and not being affected by weightlessness are not features you look for when you shop for a new computer, but you get the picture.

Here are some other things that make your current home computer attractive to bad elements on the Internet:

- ✔ **Always connected:** This is perhaps the number one reason why home computers can be broken into in the first place. If you just dial in to your ISP to get your e-mail, and then disconnect a couple of minutes later, an outsider doesn't have much time to stage an attack. However, if you use new broadband techniques, such as a cable connection or DSL, your computer is connected to the Internet 24 hours a day. And not only is the connection on all the time, but those broadband techniques let you use the same IP address for a long period of time, too. If a single hacker ever finds out that you have interesting files on your computer, such as the complete collection of Mozart's symphonies orchestrated for two flutes in MP3 format, just a simple message in one of the underground "Mozart rul3z" newsgroups will mobilize lots of other flute-loving hackers to flock to your computer for weeks.

✔ **Powerful operating system:** Every new version of Windows has added features and more powerful networking capabilities. This also increases the options for hackers to utilize your computer. Current versions of Windows think nothing of scheduling tasks automatically, checking for online activity, or even managing and routing between several types of dialup and VPN network connections at the same time. Although these features are great aids to getting a lot of work done or starting a chat session the second your friends get online, they also enable the hacker to do all kinds of tricks with your computer that weren't possible before.

✔ **Inadequate protection:** Businesses are starting to understand that they should install firewalls and think about security (not in that order). This shifts attention to less-protected computers automatically. Especially for Sunday-afternoon hackers, breaking into a neighbor's computer two blocks down on the same cable segment is easier than trying to penetrate a well-implemented corporate firewall. (In much the same way, your home is at risk when you're the only one on the street who doesn't lock his back door at night.)

Hackers have changed

The hacker community has changed at least as much as your home computer has. The interests and capabilities of hackers have shifted. Here are some reasons why hackers have an interest in your home computer:

✔ **Hazard by numbers:** A common misconception is that you're safe because of the sheer number of home computers that are connected to the Internet. Well, the argument works the other way around, too. The Internet has also increased the number of people who use the relative shelter of being anonymous to hack other computers. Hackers' Web sites offer easy-to-follow "how to hack" tutorials that can give anyone the skills needed to start hacking.

✔ **Bots and scripts:** Although this sounds like an '80s sitcom about two characters who get in constant trouble with the police, we're actually talking about automation tools that hackers can use. *Bots* (an abbreviation for robots) are software programs that automatically monitor entire ISP IP ranges for computers that come online and immediately do a scan for well-known vulnerabilities. When a hacker comes home from school, or whatever he does when he's not hacking, he finds a neatly printed bot report that lists all the computers vulnerable for certain attacks. An even more helpful bot may have planted malicious back door programs on those home computers already. *Scripts* are programs that hackers use to utilize an earlier planted back door, or do whatever tasks need to be done to find and get access to a vulnerable computer. Don't make the mistake of thinking that hacking is hard work.

✔ **Staging DDOS attacks:** A relative new phenomenon is staging attacks on well-known public Web sites, such as eBay and Amazon.com, by overwhelming those sites with data. A distributed denial-of-service (DDOS) attack like this only has an effect if enough data can be sent to the same Web site during the same time frame. One way to achieve the needed amount of data is to plant a DDOS agent at various home computers and let them all send data at a preset time. The hacker wouldn't be interested in the content of the files on your hard drive, per se, but only in using your home computer as one of his soldiers.

✔ **Stealing CPU cycles:** This is also a fairly new concept. Current home computers are so powerful that you probably wouldn't even notice if some other process were running, too. Hackers want to use the combined CPU power of many home computers to do CPU-intensive processing. Why would they need that processing power, you ask? Well, they're certainly not crunching away to find a new medicine for some disease, although that would be a very noble thing to do. (Maybe we'll post a suggestion about this on the friendly "Mozart rul3z" board.) And they aren't doing nuclear explosion research, either. Instead, some groups use this to earn higher marks at the various combined-CPU contests on the Internet. Some of these are just harmless secret message-cracking contests that can earn you $1,200 if you are the first to decode the secret message "You won!"

✔ **Personal information:** Don't think you have nothing of value on your computer. Of course, hackers may be interested in your credit card details and use them for fraudulent charges. However, a scam was recently discovered in which hackers were only interested in obtaining your ISP dial-in account and password. This group, or *legion* as they like to call themselves, used a different dial-in account every day to minimize the risk of being traced. Part of their daily task was to scan home computers to stock their supply of dial-in accounts to use for a day.

✔ **Anti-hacking laws:** In some countries, anti-hacking laws have toughened dramatically in the last few years. Maybe those new tough laws work, as legislators want you to believe. If they do, hackers wouldn't dare touch businesses that are more likely to press charges against them, but instead practice their skills on lower-profile objects, such as home computers.

You have changed

Don't blame everything on the hackers. You have a personal interest in protecting your home computer, as well. Just as you're careful with your new car, a home computer is getting more and more important, too. Here are some reasons you have to protect your home computer:

✔ **Use of interactive tools:** Many current applications are used to connect to other users or computers on the Internet. This ranges from chat and ICQ-style communication programs to interactive Internet games to programs that automate peer-to-peer exchange of files such as Italian recipes — just to name some of the less controversial uses. While you are happily "fragging" your game opponent at the other side of the world, your computer may get fragged by using the same interactive applications, too.

✔ **Use of Internet-aware applications:** Software vendors realize the potential of the Internet. Some applications may even contain special spy modules that call home every now and then to report on you. You may not like this, and you may not even be aware of this. A personal firewall can alert you that a particular application is attempting to access the Internet. Such a warning may at least make you realize which programs on your computer initiate a connection. The same approach can be used to detect a Trojan horse or back door programs, as well.

✔ **Financial transactions:** Your credit card isn't the only thing that needs to be protected. When you use your computer to handle your finances, do online shopping, or even use Internet banking, the local files on your hard drive need to be protected against access from the outside.

✔ **Corporate connection:** You can use your home computer to dial in to the office through a Virtual Private Network (VPN) connection. Although the data may travel securely encrypted over the Internet to the company computers, the open end-point of such a VPN tunnel is your home computer. If hackers can break into your computer from the Internet, they may use it as a way to get right into the company network.

We know that this long list of reasons for using a personal firewall makes us sound like anti-virus program sales folk. But the fact of the matter is that people aren't paranoid enough about their connection to the Internet. The chance of suffering from some type of Internet hack is rising, especially when you connect to the Internet using cable or DSL.

Most people are genuinely surprised when they discover that their newly installed personal firewall reports that their home computer is getting scanned or probed from the Internet multiple times per day.

Features of Personal Firewalls

Personal firewalls are not comparable to enterprise firewalls. Both firewall categories have different purposes and therefore support different features. Unlike applications such as Microsoft Word, where business users and home users alike use the same program, firewalls come in two distinct classes. In this section, we look at why you can't use an enterprise firewall at home, and what the ideal personal firewall looks like.

Enterprise firewalls versus personal firewalls

Cost is a big issue when it comes to using an enterprise firewall at home. A normal enterprise-class firewall can easily cost several thousands of dollars. Some even use a license model that charges thousands of dollars per individual CPU that you may have in the firewall computer.

If the price isn't enough to dissuade you, enterprise firewalls have a lot of features that are very unlikely to be used in a home environment:

- Automatic synchronization of the configuration of several firewalls

- Automatic load sharing on the Internet connection among multiple firewalls

- Division of the administrative burden between central administrators who define the overall security policy settings and branch office administrators who can adjust only a smaller subset of the policy settings

- Support for various techniques for user authentication to validate access for users on the internal network from a list on another computer

Unless you want to host the next all-week Quake-a-thon, it's unlikely that you need these features at home.

On the other hand, personal firewalls require features that most enterprise firewalls lack.

- The configuration model of a personal firewall concentrates on the fact that the person who uses the firewall is also the person who configures the firewall. When a new protocol is used for the first time, a personal firewall may ask the user to confirm that the traffic is allowed. It really is a "personal" firewall.

- It's very likely that an enterprise firewall can't be installed on a desktop operating system that you use at home. For example, the firewall may require Windows NT 4.0 Server or Windows 2000 Server; it just won't run on a Windows 98, Windows Me, or Windows XP computer.

✔ You aren't supposed to work on the computer that has the enterprise firewall installed on it. However, in a home situation, it is very common to work on the computer that is connected to the Internet. Some packet filter rules that you define on an enterprise firewall may not work unless you access the Internet from another computer behind the firewall. The enterprise firewall is truly a dedicated computer.

✔ If you aren't sure which application uses which protocol to access the Internet, personal firewalls may help you with a special learning mode. In this mode, the firewall automatically adds the correct rules to the rule set when you attempt to use the specific application. This is a feature that you won't find on an enterprise firewall, because all the rules are supposed to be described in some sort of firewall policy document.

To be honest, not all personal firewalls are all that secure, to put it mildly. Some are even outright insecure and only give you a false sense of security, which may even be worse than no firewall at all! Some only start when you log onto your computer. This means that, depending on the kind of Internet connection you have, you may be exposed to the Internet before you log on.

The ideal personal firewall would have the following features:

✔ **Inexpensive:** Of course, the cheaper the better. Several personal firewalls are free for personal use, and charge something like $40 for business use. Although downloading the free personal firewalls and using them for a test-run is easy, be sure to look at the ones that aren't free as well.

✔ **Easy to install and use:** The installation of the firewall software and the use of the firewall shouldn't be overly complicated. The personal firewall should definitely contain good documentation on how to use it. We used to say that it's also important that the documentation not only tell you what the various firewall settings are, but also explain some of the concepts behind firewall security. This makes it much easier to understand the alerts you may receive or the severity of detected scans. But of course, because you already bought this fine *For Dummies* book we won't have to say that again.

✔ **Easy to configure:** Nobody wants to read through an 800-page manual before the Web browser can be configured to access the Internet. And you shouldn't have to draft several pages of firewall policy either before you can distill what network traffic should be allowed in and what should be allowed out. If, after three days of continuous work in the attic, you finally come down to the living room to ask your husband what he thinks about the firewall security policy you created, he will definitely think that you lost your mind. Many personal firewalls have some sort of learning mode in which they offer to add rules for the application that was just blocked at the firewall.

Learning mode

Some personal firewalls make it really easy to configure the packet filter rules on your firewall. Whenever you use an application or a protocol that isn't allowed by the current rules at the firewall, the program offers to add those rules to the rule set. This intelligent rule learning may look like a godsend if you don't know which applications access the Internet or which ports are used by those applications (Hint: Look in the Appendix for a long list).

In reality, these autogenerated rules can work against you, too. It's all too easy to just say yes if the firewall complains about yet another application that needs to access the Internet. How are you supposed to know that `Regprog.exe` says it should be allowed access to the Internet in order to play this hot new Internet game, while `Regapp.exe` is really a Trojan horse program attempting to touch base with its creators? These file names are very similar.

One cool learning trick is that you can drag an unwanted Web advertisement to the firewall's trashcan, and the firewall will get the hint and block the ad the next time.

Some personal firewalls even come with a preapproved list of hundreds of applications that are granted access to the Internet already. That's probably a little bit too much self-learning on behalf of the firewall. The whole point of installing a personal firewall is that you can decide what network traffic travels to and from your computer.

- ✔ **Monitor incoming traffic:** The firewall should look at all network packets coming from the Internet and allow only

    - Those network packets received in response to requests you sent out to the Internet.

    - Those packets for which you have configured rules at the firewall.

- ✔ **Monitor outgoing traffic:** Personal firewalls have their own special version of scanning for outgoing traffic. Whereas enterprise firewalls define allowed outgoing traffic in terms of protocol, user, time of day, or addressed Web site, personal firewalls are often application-aware. They only allow outgoing traffic from applications that are on a trusted application list. This is an important measure if you want to prevent Trojan horse programs from communicating with the Internet. It also stops so-called *adware* or *spyware* programs that connect to their home server on the Internet to relay the list of sites you have visited or something similarly inappropriate. (If you don't put them on the trusted applications list, that is!) Anti-virus programs usually don't scan for these adware programs.

If you like this feature, you may even use a personal firewall as a second line of defense on your office computer, behind your corporate enterprise firewall.

WARNING!

Some adware or spyware programs are getting smarter and know that certain personal firewalls look only at the filename of the application to decide whether outgoing traffic is allowed. They can easily rename themselves to something innocuous-looking like `iexplore.exe`, the filename of Microsoft's Internet Explorer. If you think that detecting outgoing traffic is an important feature of a personal firewall, be sure to get one that decides about outgoing access based on a checksum of the entire application executable file, instead of just the filename.

✔ **Detection intrusion attempts:** Besides monitoring incoming network packets and deciding which should be allowed in and which should be blocked, a personal firewall may also go one step further and scan for patterns of network traffic that indicate a known attack method or intrusion attempt. The personal firewall may even have an updateable list of intrusion-detection signatures to respond to newly discovered attack methods.

✔ **Alert the user:** When something suspicious is detected during the monitoring of the incoming and outgoing network traffic or while scanning for known attack patterns, the firewall usually alerts the user. It can do this either by displaying a dialog box or by flashing an icon on the Windows system tray in the lower-right corner of the screen. Whereas enterprise firewalls tend to concentrate on creating extensive log files, personal firewalls like to get the user into the live action. Initially, it may scare you how often the firewall deems things important enough to warn you about. Those are usually automated scripts or bots scanning your ports. In fact, this "knob rattling" may happen so often that you don't pay attention to it anymore. Steve Gibson of grc.com, a well-known firewall test Web site, calls it *IBR — Internet Background Radiation.*

What should you do when your firewall alerts you that something is up? Basically, not much. You may temporarily disconnect the computer from the Internet, if it makes you feel better, but the idea is that the firewall will prevent anything bad from happening. Some firewalls offer to backtrack the alleged intruder to find his IP address, computer name, and perhaps user name. This information may help if you want to contact the intruder's ISP to report the excessive intrusion attempts.

✔ **Performance:** Of course you want performance — who doesn't? — but this is usually not a problem for personal firewalls. With enterprise firewalls, many users use the same firewall to access the Internet, but in the case of a personal firewall, you are the only user. The firewall can easily handle that.

How to Be Safe on the Internet

You can be safe when you connect to the Internet. Here are a few precautions you should take:

✔ Install the latest patches and updates for your operating system (especially if those updates are security-related, and they usually are). If you use Windows, go to `windowsupdate.microsoft.com` to make sure you have the latest updates.

✔ Disable or unbind the File and Printer Sharing component (or Server Service in Windows NT 4.0) if you don't use that function. See Chapter 13 for instructions on how to do that.

✔ Select and install a good personal firewall. And if you are still reading the chapter at this point, I suspect you will do that.

✔ Select and install a good anti-virus program. Some personal firewalls have this function built-in, but we prefer to keep the firewall function and the anti-virus functions separate.

✔ Be careful with files that you download and with attachments in e-mail messages. These could be stealth Trojan horse programs to trick you into opening up access to your computer, or they could be plain malicious viruses.

✔ Never reveal your computer password or ISP password to anything or anyone. Never use the same password for two different purposes. Ideally, you should use different passwords for every program or Web site that needs it. If that's too much to remember, write down your passwords somewhere on a piece of paper that you keep hidden. If that's still too much work, use at least four totally different passwords:

  • Password to log on to your computer

  • Password to log on to your ISP

  • Password to use in applications that want a password to encrypt stuff, such as Word to encrypt a document or WinZip to encrypt the files in the Zip file

  • Password to use on Web sites that ask for a password

If that's still too much to ask, why are you reading this book?

✔ Even if you use a personal firewall and have an always-connected subscription for a cable connection or DSL line to the Internet, consider switching off the computer when you're away for a longer period of time.

✔ Make a backup of important data files. That's another good answer to give to your uncle at that birthday party.

Personal Firewall: ZoneAlarm

Zone Labs' ZoneAlarm is one of the most widely used free personal firewalls. It has a friendly user interface, a few easy-to-understand security settings, and prompts you when applications attempt to access the Internet.

For personal use, you can use ZoneAlarm free of charge, although the license agreement states that this is limited to one computer only. For business use, you have to pay a small fee.

ZoneAlarm actually comes in three editions. The free edition is described here. You can also choose from a ZoneAlarm Plus edition and a ZoneAlarm Pro edition, which aren't free and add a couple of features, as well as technical support.

This section describes the free ZoneAlarm version 3.7, which you can download from www.zonelabs.com.

ZoneAlarm features

The key to understanding how ZoneAlarm works is to get familiar with the three predefined security levels that you can set for two different network zones. Combine that with the program alerts and firewall alerts that you may receive and you've got pretty much the whole picture.

ZoneAlarm maintains a list of applications that are allowed to access the Internet. Initially, this list is empty. The first time that each application attempts to get out to the Internet, ZoneAlarm asks the user whether the application should be added to the list.

Internet Zone and Trusted Zone

ZoneAlarm distinguishes two network zones.

- ✔ **Internet Zone:** This network zone contains all computers out there in the big bad world that are not in your trusted zone.

- ✔ **Trusted Zone:** This network zone should contain all computers on your local network.

Each zone has its own security level. The default security level is High for the Internet Zone and Medium for the Trusted Zone.

The Zones tab on the Firewall panel allows you to define which computers are in the Trusted Zone, as shown in Figure 15-1.

Security levels

ZoneAlarm uses three predefined security levels that can be set for the Internet Zone and the same three predefined security levels for the Trusted Zone. The definition of the security levels is as follows:

- **High:** ZoneAlarm enforces the application list. It blocks all access to Windows services (NetBIOS) and file and printer shares. It also doesn't reply to PING (ICMP Echo) requests from the Internet.

- **Medium:** ZoneAlarm enforces the application list, blocks all access to Windows services (NetBIOS) and file and printer shares, but allows replies to PING (ICMP Echo) requests from the Internet. If you are connected from a computer in the Trusted Zone, access to Windows services and shares is allowed.

- **Low:** ZoneAlarm enforces the application list, but allows access to Windows services (NetBIOS) and file and printer shares, and allows replies to PING (ICMP Echo) requests from the Internet.

The security level can be set in ZoneAlarm's Security panel.

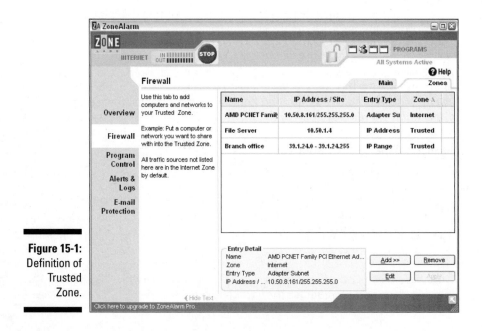

Figure 15-1:
Definition of
Trusted
Zone.

Program alerts and firewall alerts

ZoneAlarm learns which applications are allowed to access the Internet by presenting the user with a dialog box the first time the application attempts to get out. The dialog box asks the user whether the application should be added to the application list. This is called a *program alert* (see Figure 15-2).

A program alert offers the user the following options:

- ✔ **Yes:** Add this program to the application list and allow access now.

- ✔ **No:** Add this program to the application list, but block access now.

- ✔ **Remember This Answer:** If selected, ZoneAlarm will use the same answer the next time the application attempts to access the Internet. It won't show the program alert for this application again.

If you only select Yes or No, without selecting the Remember This Answer option, then ZoneAlarm will still ask you what to do the next time the application accesses the network, even though it is listed in the application list.

You can always remove an application from the list — or change your answer later on — with the help of ZoneAlarm's Program Control panel.

The first couple of days after you have installed ZoneAlarm, you'll receive a lot of program alerts, depending on which Internet applications and games you use. If you picked the Remember this answer option in the Program Alerts dialog box, the number of program alerts that pop up quickly diminishes.

When someone on the Internet attempts to make a connection to your computer, ZoneAlarm presents you with a dialog box specifying the source IP address and port that was attempted to access, as shown in Figure 15-3. This is called a *firewall alert*.

Initially, the Trusted Zone definition is empty. This means that even network traffic from the local network is seen as coming from the Internet. If you have already defined the Trusted Zone, keep in mind that you may still receive firewall alerts coming from the local network, depending on the security level of the Trusted Zone.

When a lot of port scanning from the Internet occurs (and it always does), you can disable the Firewall Alert dialog boxes in ZoneAlarm's Alerts & Logs panel and only log the alerts to a text file.

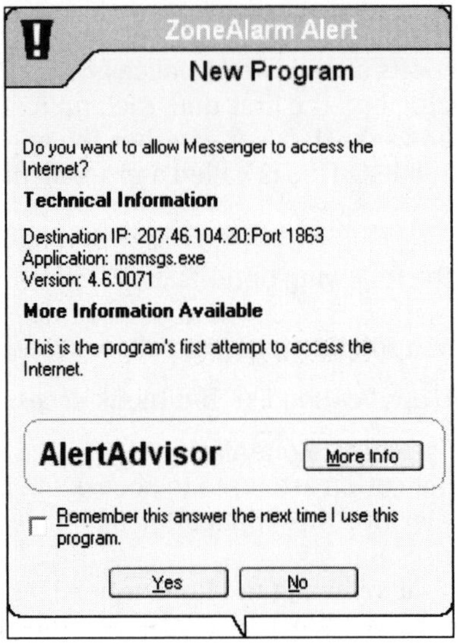

Figure 15-2:
Program
alert for
MSN
Messenger.

Figure 15-3:
Firewall
alert from
the Internet.

Lock option and Stop button

ZoneAlarm allows you to set a Lock option, which automatically blocks all network activity after a specified period of inactivity. If needed, you can enable the Pass Lock option for specific applications in the application list to allow them to use the network even after the Lock has engaged.

The ZoneAlarm user interface provides a big Stop button that you can use to immediately block all network activity, even from applications that have the Pass Lock option enabled.

ZoneAlarm user interface

The configuration of ZoneAlarm is done in the ZoneAlarm Control Center. This is one large dialog box, consisting of five configuration panels, each one decked out with its own set of tabs. By default, a ZoneAlarm icon shows up in the Windows system tray in the lower-right corner of the screen.

Overview panel

The Overview panel, shown in Figure 15-4, contains three tabs. This panel gives you a quick view of the status of ZoneAlarm and allows you to change general preferences.

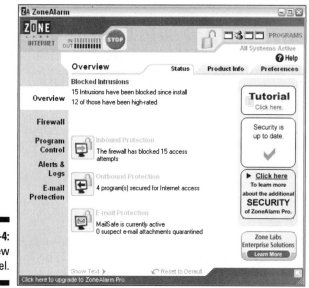

Figure 15-4: Overview panel.

Firewall panel

The Firewall panel, shown in Figure 15-5, contains two sliders to configure the security level for the Internet Zone and the Trusted Zone.

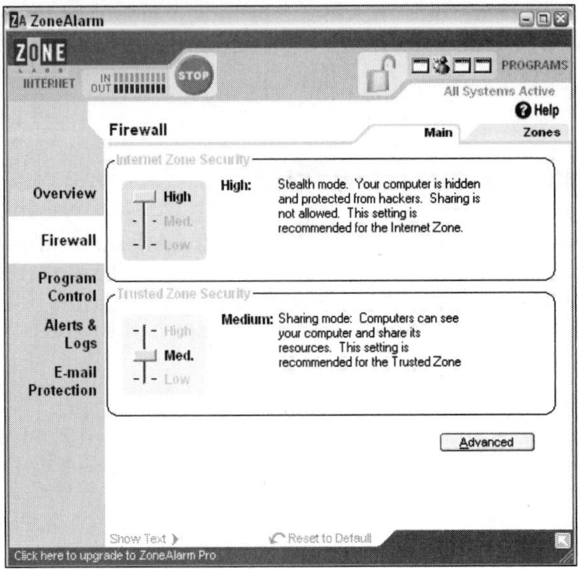

Figure 15-5:
Firewall
panel.

The Zones tab lets you define which computers or subnets are in the Trusted Zone. Make sure that you don't select the network cards that provide the connection to the Internet. Those subnets should not be in the Trusted Zone. If you leave the definition of the Trusted Zone empty, ZoneAlarm will effectively only know one zone, the Internet Zone.

The Advanced button allows you to configure additional settings to prevent any application from acting as server and accepting Internet connections.

The default security level is High for the Internet Zone and Medium for the Trusted Zone.

Program Control panel

The Program Control panel, shown in Figure 15-6, lets you configure applications that are on the application list. You can specify per application whether the application

- ✔ Is allowed to access the network either in the Trusted Zone or the Internet Zone.
- ✔ Can be a server for access from the Trusted Zone or the Internet Zone.

Figure 15-6:
Program
Control
panel.

The settings are Allow, Block, or "Ask next time?". You can also specify per application whether it should have the Pass Lock option set. Click on the icons to change the settings. You set the Pass Lock option in the column sporting the padlock icon.

Right-click on an application to remove the application from the list.

Alerts & Logs panel

The Alerts & Logs panel, shown in Figure 15-7, enables you to view recent firewall or program alerts. You can also control how you want to be notified if a firewall alert occurs.

The default is to both log the alert to a text file and show an alert pop-up window.

E-mail Protection panel

The E-mail Protection panel, shown in Figure 15-8, lets you enable or disable the MailSafe option. When MailSafe is enabled, ZoneAlarm will rename e-mail attachments with the file extension .VBS (Visual Basic Script). This prevents any inadvertent execution of those attachments. ZoneAlarm calls this *quarantining* the attachment.

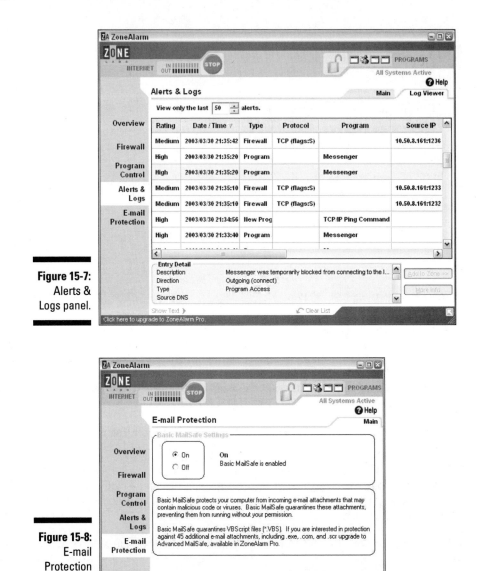

Figure 15-7:
Alerts &
Logs panel.

Figure 15-8:
E-mail
Protection
panel.

ZoneAlarm installation

The installation of ZoneAlarm is straightforward. If you download the free ZoneAlarm from www.zonelabs.com, you receive one 3.6 MB executable file named zaSetup_37_xxx.exe, where xxx is the minor version of ZoneAlarm 3.7. Running this program will install ZoneAlarm.

Note that the instructions in this section are based on ZoneAlarm version 3.7.143.

To install ZoneAlarm, follow these steps:

1. **Determine whether your computer meets the minimum system requirements described in Table 15-1.**

Table 15-1	Minimum System Requirements for ZoneAlarm
Component	*Minimum Requirement*
Operating system	Windows 98 (original or SE), Windows Me, Windows NT 4.0 (SP3 or higher), Windows 2000, or Windows XP.
Processor	486 or higher
Required disk space	3 MB
Memory	8 MB
Network interface	Ethernet, DSL, cable modem, or dialup

2. **Download the free ZoneAlarm version 3.7 from** `www.zonelabs.com`.

   You'll download one executable file named `zaSetup_37_143.exe`.

   The Web site also offers ZoneAlarm Pro and ZoneAlarm Plus, which are not free.

3. **Run** `zaSetup_37_143.exe` **from the folder where you downloaded the file.**

4. **On the ZoneAlarm Installation page, accept the default installation directory and then click Next.**

5. **On the User Information page, type your name, company or organization name, and e-mail address. Choose from the two registration options, and then click Next.**

6. **On the License Agreement page, read the license agreement. Enable the check box to accept the License Agreement, and then click Install.**

   The installation program installs the software in the destination directory.

7. **On the User survey page, answer the four survey questions, and click Finish to complete the installation process.**

   You can click No on the final dialog box that asks whether you want to start ZoneAlarm now.

When you want to start the ZoneAlarm Control Center, choose Start⇨ All Programs⇨Zone Labs⇨ZoneAlarm. The first time you start ZoneAlarm, a Welcome dialog box appears. Click Next to review your alert settings and click Finish to preconfigure your browser settings. Click Next to step through a nine-page tutorial to get a quick idea of the main features of the product. When you finish the tutorial, the ZoneAlarm Control Center starts up.

You'll quickly notice bunches of program alerts and firewall alerts popping up when you access the Internet. A good description of ZoneAlarm's behavior, found in an earlier ZoneAlarm manual, puts it quite nicely: "Talkative at first, then quiets down."

ZoneAlarm configuration tasks

The following section provides you with step-by-step configuration instructions for typical tasks you do when working with ZoneAlarm.

✔ To start the ZoneAlarm Control Center:

  1. Choose Start⇨All Programs⇨Zone Labs⇨ZoneAlarm.

✔ To hide the Firewall Alert pop-up windows:

  1. In the ZoneAlarm Control Center, click the Alerts & Logs panel.

  2. On the Main tab of the Alerts & Logs panel, select Off in the Alert Events Shown box.

✔ To add subnets to the Trusted Zone:

  1. In the ZoneAlarm Control Center, click the Firewall panel.

  2. On the Zones tab of the Firewall panel, click the Add button and then click Subnet.

  3. In the Add Subnet Zone Properties dialog box, type an IP Address, Subnet Mask, and Description, and then click OK.

✔ To configure applications on the Application List:

  1. In the ZoneAlarm Control Center, click the Program Control panel.

  2. In the Program Control panel, click the Access or Server setting that you want to configure.

  3. In the settings menu that appears, select Allow, Block, or Ask.

Personal Firewall: BlackICE

Internet Security Systems (ISS) BlackICE PC Protection is a personal firewall with strong intrusion detection capabilities. The firewall watches all network traffic arriving at your computer and compares the network traffic with a built-in database of hundreds of well-known intrusion patterns.

If a scan of your ports or any other intrusion is detected, BlackICE informs you of the attempts to hack your computer. You can then either tell BlackICE to ignore the intrusion, or block all network traffic coming from the IP address staging the attack.

BlackICE really enjoys working in the trenches. It can even automatically block the IP address by itself and present you with information it has collected about the intruder, such as his computer name and perhaps even his NetBIOS user name. BlackICE calls this feature *Intruder Back Trace.*

BlackICE is not a free personal firewall. You have to pay for a license key in order to use it. However, ISS also offers a free 30-day fully functional evaluation edition. Go to `www.blackice.iss.net` for more information.

Note that ISS has bought the company Network ICE, which created BlackICE. At that time, the product was called BlackICE Defender Workstation. It is now renamed to BlackICE PC Protection.

The documentation of BlackICE is a very good. One really outstanding aspect is the vast amount of security-related information and articles you can find at their Web site. The user interface even contains an Event Info button that brings you immediately to the ISS site. Very nICE. (Back in Network ICE's time, this button was cutely called advICE.)

This section describes BlackICE PC Protection v3.6.cbd.

BlackICE features

BlackICE is a totally different slant on the idea of a personal firewall than the one put forward by ZoneAlarm. BlackICE concentrates heavily on the intrusion detection side, but it also has facilities for blocking outgoing network traffic, which is ZoneAlarm's strong point.

To work with BlackICE, you have to understand that it uses four predefined protection levels and consists of three basic layers of traffic filtering: an

Intrusion Detection System (IDS) layer, a Firewall layer for incoming traffic, and an Application Protection layer for outgoing traffic.

Protection levels

BlackICE uses four predefined protection levels, as shown in Figure 15-9. The definition of the protection levels is as follows:

- ✔ **Paranoid:** This is the default security setting and is very restrictive. BlackICE blocks all inbound traffic not in response to packets you send.

- ✔ **Nervous:** BlackICE blocks most inbound traffic that is not in response to packets you send out. Some interactive content, such as streaming media, is allowed.

- ✔ **Cautious:** All unsolicited inbound traffic that accesses operating system or network services is blocked.

- ✔ **Trusting:** Not restrictive at all. BlackICE warns you about intrusion attempts, but will allow any inbound network traffic.

You can set the protection level in BlackICE's configuration program.

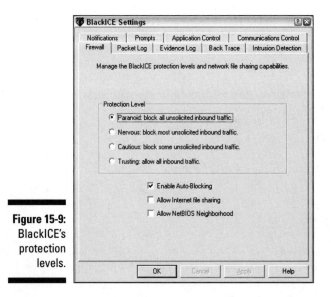

Figure 15-9: BlackICE's protection levels.

The difference among the four protection levels lies in which TCP and UDP ports are blocked. Table 15-2 shows the port settings per protection level.

Table 15-2		BlackICE Port Settings		
Protection Level	*Type*	*Inbound (1-1023)*	*Inbound (1024-65535)*	*Outbound (All)*
Paranoid	TCP/UDP	Blocked	Blocked	Open
Nervous	TCP	Blocked	Blocked	Open
Nervous	UDP	Blocked	Open	Open
Cautious	TCP/UDP	Blocked	Open	Open
Trusting	TCP/UDP	Open	Open	Open

You can use BlackICE's Advanced Firewall Settings to override these port settings, per individual port.

IDS layer and Firewall layer

BlackICE filters incoming packets at two different layers: the IDS layer and the Firewall layer. When an intrusion attempt is detected, the name of the matching attack signature and the IP address of the intruder are recorded.

If the intrusion type that is detected is severe enough, BlackICE automatically blocks any network traffic from the intruder IP address. However, you can manually configure what should happen to the detected intrusion event as well (see Figure 15-10).

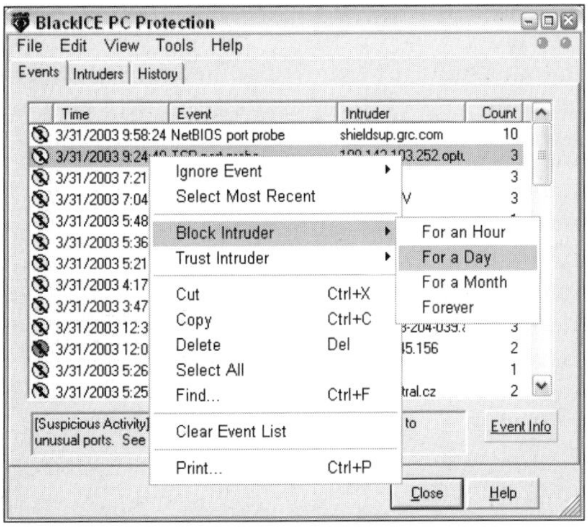

Figure 15-10: Manually block an intruder.

You can specify whether the detected intrusion should cause a change in filtering at the IDS layer or at the Firewall layer.

Possible filtering actions at the IDS layer are:

- **Ignore This Event:** The specific attack — a TCP SYN flood attack, for example — won't be reported anymore by BlackICE. When faced with recurring harmless "attacks," such as automated port scans, it may be best to just tell BlackICE to ignore it.

- **Ignore This Event by This Intruder IP:** BlackICE won't report the specific attack anymore if it comes from this particular intruder's IP address. Some Internet Service Providers (ISPs) carry out routing port scans that you may want to ignore.

- **Trust Intruder:** BlackICE won't report all attacks coming from this particular intruder's IP address anymore.

Possible filtering actions at the Firewall layer are:

- **Accept Intruder:** BlackICE explicitly allows any incoming network traffic from the IP address in the event.

- **Block Intruder:** All incoming network traffic from this IP address is rejected.

You need to understand the difference between trusting an intruder (do not filter as intrusion detection), and accepting an intruder (do not block traffic). In this case, the term *intruder* may be a bit misleading. It just means "sender of incoming IP packets."

When you right-click on a detected intrusion attempt, you can specify that you want to both Trust and Accept the intruder. In effect, this means that all network traffic coming from that intruder's IP address will be allowed to enter your computer without being scanned by either the IDS layer or the Firewall layer.

The BlackICE strikes back

BlackICE constantly monitors the incoming network packets. When it finds a network pattern that matches one of its built-in intrusion signatures, it records the event as well as the intruder's IP address.

All detected events are categorized with a severity level:

- **Critical (red !-icon), severity 7-10:** Deliberate attacks on the computer. These attacks may damage data or crash the computer.

- **Serious (orange !-icon), severity 4-6:** Deliberate attacks on the computer in order to access information.

> ✔ **Suspicious (yellow ?-icon), severity 1-3:** Network activity that may indicate that a hacker is attempting to locate security vulnerabilities.
>
> ✔ **Informational (green !-icon), severity 0:** Non-threatening network activity, but worthy of note.

When an intrusion event occurs, BlackICE can trigger several actions:

> ✔ **Flash Icon:** When a Critical (red), Serious (orange), or Suspicious (yellow) event occurs, BlackICE notifies you by flashing the BlackICE shield icon in the Windows system tray.
>
> ✔ **Back Trace:** When BlackICE detects an intrusion attempt, it attempts to collect information about the intruder automatically, such as his IP address, DNS host name, and, if possible, his NetBIOS user name. You can specify the minimum severity level needed to start the Back Trace process. The default severity level to start the collecting is 3.
>
> ✔ **Evidence File:** When an intrusion attempt is detected, BlackICE saves incoming network packets in so-called Evidence Files. These files are actually network capture files, and can be inspected by programs like Windows 2000's Network Monitor tool. You can use these files to see what happened, or even send them to your ISP for further action.
>
> ✔ **Auto-Block:** Detected events categorized as Critical (red) or Serious (orange) may trigger protective measures from BlackICE. The intruder's IP address will automatically be blocked.

Although obtaining information about a possible hacker may feel like the right thing to do, be very careful in doing so. ISS recommends that you don't attempt to retaliate or otherwise try to get even. Here are several good reasons that you should not "hack back," no matter how tempting and interesting this may be:

> ✔ Hacking back is most likely against your ISP's usage policy. Whether you like it or not, you are bound by that agreement. You will quickly lose your Internet account if they detect your retaliatory activity. Or, how ironic, the original intruder may run BlackICE and just report you to your ISP, complete with Evidence File and all. How embarrassing would that be?
>
> ✔ You don't want to start a war with an intruder that you don't know — or even one you do know, for that matter. It is relatively easy for somebody "in-the-know" to post your IP address on one of the hacker's forums. Before you know it, BlackICE will be working overtime to defend your system from countless attacks.
>
> ✔ It's doubtful that hacking back even makes a difference. What do you expect? That the intruder would suddenly think: "Gee, being hacked is really not nice. I better clean up my act. Thanks for the eye-opener, buddy."

- ✔ The attacker may have used a spoofed source IP address or launched the attack from a computer that he has hacked earlier. In both cases, you would counterattack an innocent user.

- ✔ Most states and countries have laws against hacking, even against unsuccessful, poorly executed, wouldn't-make-a-dent hacking attempts. You can get into serious trouble.

Of course, if you find out that your computer is constantly under siege from the same intruder, you can report him to his ISP. See Chapter 19 for tools that you can use to back trace an intruder's IP address to his ISP.

By the way, don't be surprised to see BlackICE report intrusion events very often. Web sites you visit, bots by script kiddies that are targeting your ISP's IP address range, or even your ISP itself may probe your computer regularly.

Don't panic: That's why you have BlackICE, isn't it?

Application Protection layer

BlackICE has two methods for controlling what specific applications on your computer are allowed to do. The Application Protection layer handles this.

The two methods are:

- ✔ **Application Control:** When an application is started, BlackICE checks whether the application is allowed to launch. New or unknown applications are not allowed to start. Strictly speaking, this function is unrelated to being a firewall.

- ✔ **Communication Control:** If the application is allowed to start, then BlackICE checks whether the application is allowed to communicate out to the Internet. New or unknown applications are not allowed to create a connection to the Internet.

When BlackICE is installed, a list of all applications on your computer is created. All these initial applications are allowed to start and are allowed to communicate out to the Internet.

However, when a new application is installed, or suddenly appears in the case of a virus or Trojan horse application, BlackICE will detect that the application is not on the initial list and prevent the start of the application or the connection to the Internet.

Figure 15-11 shows the dialog box that appears when an unknown application is started.

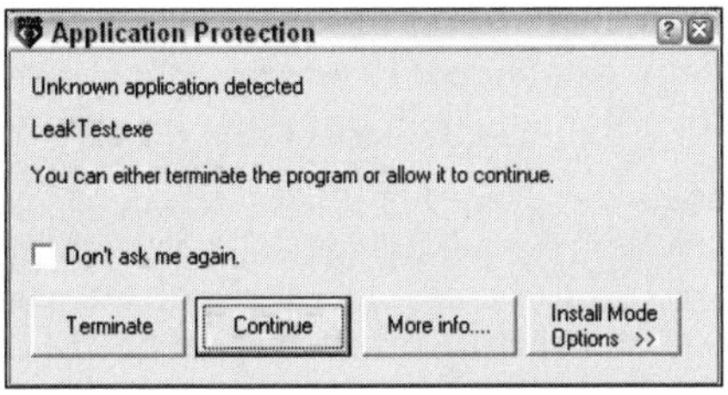

Figure 15-11:
Application
Control.

Figure 15-12 shows the dialog box when the unknown application is indeed allowed to start and attempts to create a connection to the Internet.

You can change the Application Control or Communication Control setting for each application, initial or new, by using the Advanced Application Protection Settings choice on the Tools menu in the BlackICE Utility.

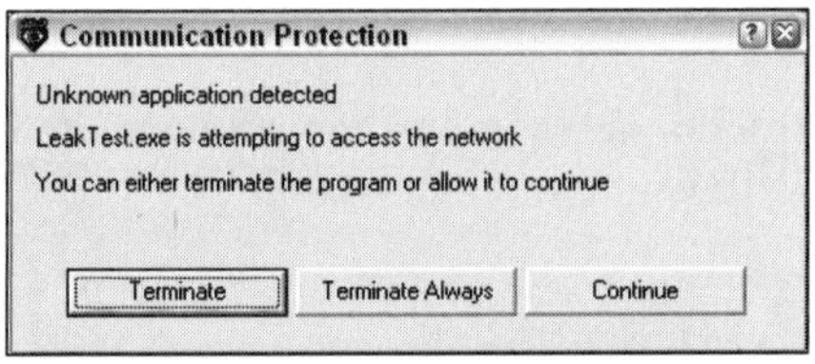

Figure 15-12:
Communica-
tion Control.

BlackICE user interface

The configuration of BlackICE is done in the BlackICE Utility. It consists of three tabs that report information about the intrusions that BlackICE has detected. The BlackICE Utility is also used to access three additional configuration dialog boxes: the BlackICE Settings dialog box, the Advanced Firewall Settings dialog box, and the Advanced Application Protections Settings dialog box.

When BlackICE starts up, a shield icon shows up in the Windows system tray. Simply click on the shield icon to open the BlackICE Utility.

BlackICE Utility

The BlackICE Utility is the program that you use to configure BlackICE's options and to handle detected intrusions. The main screen consists of three tabs that summarize the intrusion information.

The two activity lights in the top-right corner indicate the currently detected intrusion. Green lights indicate normal network traffic. Yellow, orange, and red are used to indicate the severity level if an intrusion is underway.

Events tab

The Events tab, shown in Figure 15-13, shows a list of all the intrusion attempts that BlackICE has detected. You can sort the event list on any of the columns by clicking the column header.

By default, only the Severity (icon), Time, Event, Intruder, and Count columns are displayed. However, if you right-click on any of the column headers and select Columns, you can add optional columns that give additional information about the intrusion events. The Destination Port column and the Response Level column may be especially interesting to add.

Right-clicking on an Attack line allows you to specify whether you want to ignore the attack, block the intruder's address, or trust the intruder's address.

A click on the Event Info button connects you to the ISS Web site for the latest information about that attack, including possible remedies.

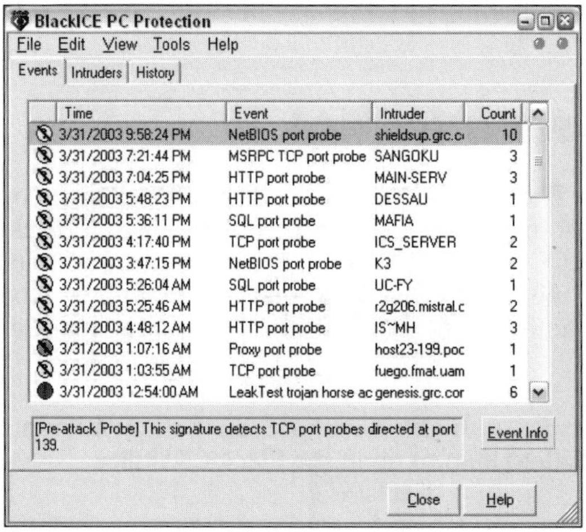

Figure 15-13:
Events tab.

Intruders tab

The Intruders tab, shown in Figure 15-14, lists all intruders that have initiated attacks against your computer. You can right-click an intruder to block the intruder's address, or to trust the intruder's address.

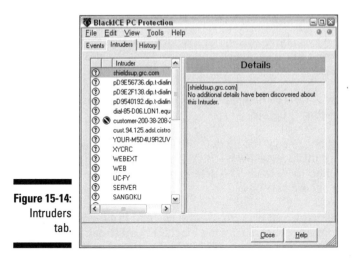

Figure 15-14:
Intruders
tab.

The icon in the second column indicates whether the intruder's IP address is blocked.

History tab

The History tab, shown in Figure 15-15, shows a timeline of the intrusion activity and general network activity over the last 90 minutes, 90 hours, or 90 days. The most recent data is on the right side of the two graphs.

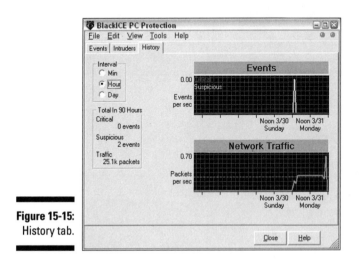

Figure 15-15:
History tab.

BlackICE Settings dialog box

To customize BlackICE, you have to use the BlackICE Settings dialog box. In the BlackICE Utility, click the Tools menu and select Edit BlackICE Settings to display the Settings dialog box.

You can use the Firewall tab to change BlackICE's protection level. The default protection level is Paranoid.

The option Auto-Blocking is enabled by default. The options Allow Internet File Sharing (TCP port 139) and Allow NetBIOS Neighborhood (UDP ports 137 and 138) are not enabled by default. The default settings of these three options are the most secure settings.

If you have a home network and want to use the File and Printer Sharing component on the computer that is running BlackICE, you should enable the Allow Internet File Sharing and Allow NetBIOS Neighborhood options. You should also add the IP addresses of all the computers on the home network to the Addresses to Trust list on the Detection tab.

You can use the Notifications tab, shown in Figure 15-16, to limit for which severity level of detected intrusions the BlackICE shield icon in the system tray flashes. The default is to trigger a visual indication for critical intrusions (red), serious intrusions (orange), and suspicious events (yellow).

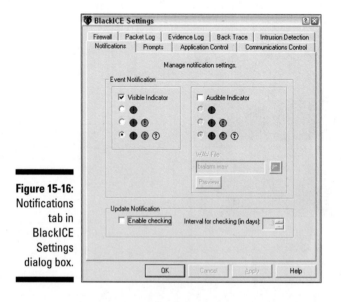

Figure 15-16:
Notifications
tab in
BlackICE
Settings
dialog box.

Changing this setting doesn't limit the number of intrusions that BlackICE will detect; it only limits for which intrusions you will be notified.

If you want to limit the number of intrusions that BlackICE records, either add an Exclude from Reporting entry on the Intrusion Detection tab, or right-click on any attack in the Events tab of the BlackICE Utility and select Ignore Event.

Advanced Firewall Settings dialog box

The Advanced Firewall Settings dialog box is used to manage Accept and Block entries for the Firewall filter function. To access this dialog box, go to the BlackICE Utility, click the Tools menu and select Advanced Firewall Settings.

Advanced Application Protection Settings dialog box

The Advanced Application Protection Settings dialog box allows you to specify application control and communication control settings for each application on the computer.

After installation, all applications on the computer are listed in the dialog box.

BlackICE installation

The installation of BlackICE starts with running the 5.9MB executable file named `BIPCPSetup.exe`.

Note that the instructions in this section are for BlackICE PC Protection version 3.6.cbd.

To install BlackICE, follow these steps:

1. **Determine whether your computer meets the minimum system requirements described in Table 15-3.**

Table 15-3	Minimum System Requirements for BlackICE
Component	*Minimum Requirement*
Operating system	Windows 98 (original or SE), Windows Me, Windows NT 4.0 (SP5 or higher), Windows 2000 (SP2 or higher), or Windows XP
Processor	Pentium or higher
Required disk space	10MB
Memory	16MB
Network interface	Ethernet, DSL, cable modem, or dial-up

2. **If you have purchased a license for BlackICE, you can use your license key to download a copy of BlackICE from** www.blackice.iss.net.

   The file that you download is an executable file named BIPCPSetup.exe. (A free 30-day fully functional evaluation version is named BIPCPEvalSetup.exe.)

3. **From the folder where you downloaded the file, run** BIPCPSetup.exe.

   Setup unpacks the file and starts the Installation Wizard.

4. **On the Welcome page, click Next to continue the installation.**

5. **On the License Agreement page, read the license agreement and then click the I Accept button.**

6. **On the License Key page, type your license key and then click Next.**

   The license key is in the form 123456-RS-12345. (No, this particular one does not work.)

7. **On the Choose Destination Location page, accept the default destination folder and click Next.**

8. **On the Select Program Folder page, accept the default Start menu program folder named ISS and click Next.**

9. **On the BlackICE PC Protection Configuration page, accept the default AP On option, and then click Next.**

   AP On means that Application Protection is enabled. This does require an initial scan of all your executable files at the end of the installation.

10. **On the Start Copying Files page, review the installation parameters and click Next.**

    The installation program will now install the software in the destination folder.

11. **On the Wizard Complete page, select whether you want to view the** README **file now, and then click Finish to complete the installation process.**

    If you enabled Application Protection, BlackICE will scan all executable files. This may take a few minutes.

The BlackICE shield icon now appears in the Windows system tray in the lower-right corner of the screen.

When you want to start the BlackICE Utility, just click the BlackICE icon in the system tray.

BlackICE configuration tasks

The following section provides you with step-by-step configuration instructions for typical tasks that you do when working with BlackICE.

✔ To start the BlackICE Utility:

1. **Choose Start➪All Programs➪ISS➪BlackICE PC Protection or click the BlackICE shield icon in the Windows system tray.**

✔ To set the Protection Level:

1. **In the BlackICE Utility, click the Tools menu and select Edit BlackICE Settings.**

2. **In the BlackICE Settings dialog box, select the Firewall tab.**

3. **On the Firewall tab, select either Paranoid, Nervous, Cautious, or Trusting as your protection level.**

4. **Click OK to close the BlackICE Settings dialog box.**

✔ To block an Intruder's address:

1. **In the BlackICE Utility, select the Intruders tab.**

2. **In the Intruders list, right-click on the intruder you want to block and select Block Intruder. In the submenu, select For an Hour, For a Day, For a Month, or Forever.**

3. **In the Please Confirm dialog box, click Yes to confirm this change.**

✔ To unblock an Intruder's address:

1. **In the BlackICE Utility, click the Tools menu and select Advanced Firewall Settings.**

2. **In the Advanced Firewall Settings dialog box, right-click on the intruder, and select Unblock Only.**

3. **In the Please Confirm dialog box, click Yes to confirm this change.**

✔ To open a port to play Quake II:

1. **In the Appendix, find out which TCP or UDP port is needed to play Quake II. (Answer: UDP port 27910.)**

2. **In the BlackICE Utility, click the Tools menu and select Advanced Firewall Settings.**

3. **In the Advanced Firewall Settings dialog box, click the Add button to add a new firewall entry.**

4. **In the Add Firewall Entry dialog box, fill in the information, as shown in Figure 15-17.**

5. **Click Add to close the Add Firewall Entry dialog box.**

6. **Click OK to close the Advanced Firewall Settings dialog box.**

   If a particular application or game requires several open ports on your computer, you have to create separate port rules for each of those ports.

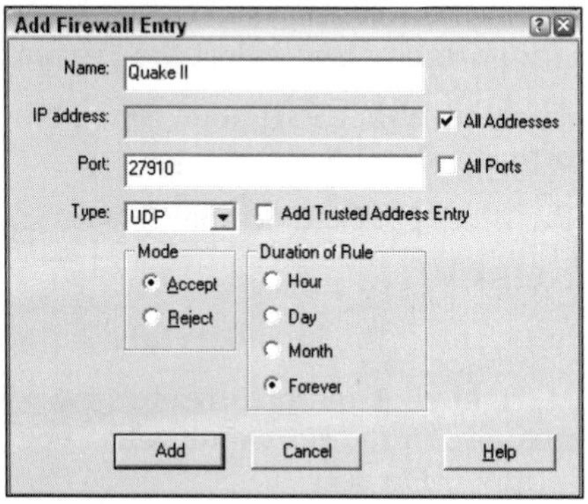

Figure 15-17: Quake II port rule.

To trust and accept computers from your home network:

If you have a home network, you probably want to add all the IP addresses of the computers on your home network to the Trust list (don't scan for intrusions from those computers) and the Accept list (all network traffic allowed). Be honest, you're not going to hack yourself, are you?

1. **In the BlackICE Utility, click the Tools menu and select Edit BlackICE Settings.**

2. **In the BlackICE Settings dialog box, select the Detection tab.**

3. **On the Intrusion Detection tab, click the Add button to add an Exclude from Reporting entry.**

4. **In the Exclude from Reporting dialog box, fill in the appropriate information, as shown in Figure 15-18.**

5. **Click the Add button to close the Exclude from Reporting dialog box.**

6. **Click OK to close the BlackICE Settings dialog box.**

If you have more than one other computer on your home network, you will have to create Exclude from Reporting entries for the IP addresses of each of those computers.

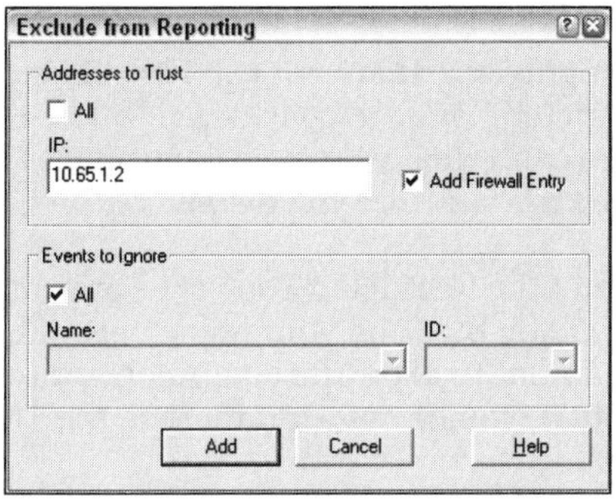

Figure 15-18:
Trust and
accept
computers
from home
network.

Norton Personal Firewall

Norton Personal Firewall is a well-rounded personal firewall. It contains features that are related to intrusion detection, firewall rules that specify allowed incoming and outgoing network traffic, program control, and even has an option to block unwanted ads on Web pages.

You don't get all this for free. However, Symantec offers a free 15-day trial version of the software. Go to www.norton.com for more information.

This section describes Norton Personal Firewall 2003, version 6.0.2.25.

Norton Personal Firewall features

Admittedly, most of the features found in Norton Personal Firewall can be found in ZoneAlarm or other personal firewalls as well. However, the Norton Personal firewall does have a few unique features, such as privacy control and ad blocking. Read on to find out more.

Home Networking zone

Like ZoneAlarm, Norton Personal Firewall divides all IP address into zones. These are the three zones available:

✔ **Trusted Zone:** All computers that need to have full access to your computer must be listed in the Trusted Zone. This means, in effect, that the firewall rules don't apply to computers in the Trusted Zone.

✔ **Restricted Zone:** All computers that are explicitly not allowed to connect to your computer must be listed in the Restricted Zone.

✔ **Other computers:** All computers that are not explicitly listed in the Trusted Zone or the Restricted Zone are considered "other computers." Whether these computers can actually create a connection to your computer depends on the firewall rules that you define.

By default, the Trusted Zone and the Restricted Zone are both empty. This means that all computers, including those on your home network, are in the "other computers" zone. If you want to allow the computers on your home network access to your computer, you have to add them to the Trusted Zone.

To add computers to the Trusted Zone or the Restricted Zone, select the Personal Firewall feature on the main screen of the Security Center and then click Configure. In the next dialog box, select the Home Networking tab, as shown in Figure 15-19.

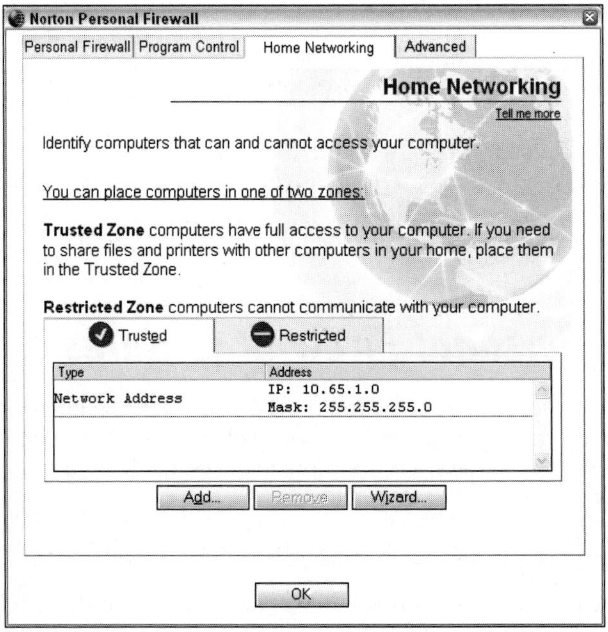

Figure 15-19: Configure zones on Home Networking tab.

Click the Wizard button on the Home Networking tab to add the IP address connected to the local network adapter to the Trusted Zone. Select the Restricted tab to add addresses to the Restricted Zone.

Intrusion Detection and AutoBlock

Norton Personal Firewall has a database of known intrusion detection traffic patterns. Such traffic patterns are known as *attack signatures*.

Network attacks often consist of several network packets in a row. When the firewall detects a known sequence of packets, it will block access to the computer sending the packets for 30 minutes. This is called AutoBlock.

The intrusion detection scan is not done for network traffic from computers in the Trusted Zone.

Program Control

Program Control determines which applications are allowed to connect to the Internet from your computer. The firewall keeps a list of programs that are allowed to access the Internet.

When an unknown program attempts to connect out, Norton Personal Firewall warns the user and asks to Block or Allow the connection, as shown in Figure 15-20.

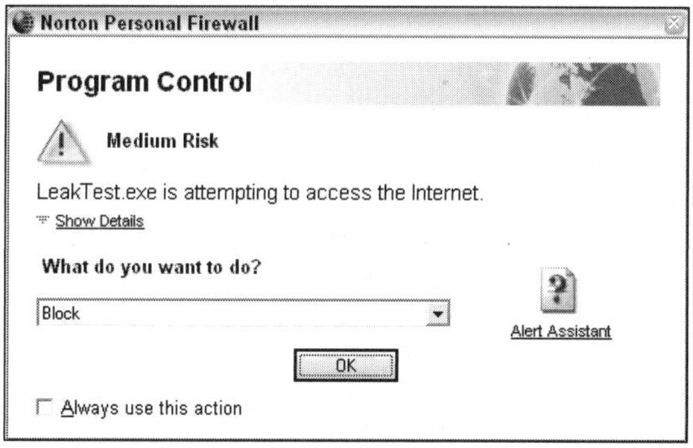

Figure 15-20: Program Control alert.

The Alert Assistant link provides access to more information about the program.

You can answer Block or Allow for this particular instance of the connection, or specify that this action must always be used for this program.

You have the option in Norton Personal Firewall to scan your entire hard drive and add all programs currently installed on your computer to the list of known programs allowed to access the Internet.

Besides keeping a list of known programs, Norton Personal Firewall also has a list of more than 60 Trojan horse applications that are known to roam the Internet. The Trojan horse rules are shown in Figure 15-21.

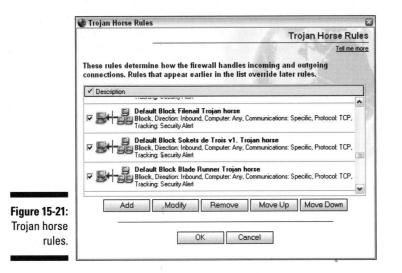

Figure 15-21:
Trojan horse
rules.

Privacy Control

Norton Personal Firewall has an interesting method to ensure that no private information is sent to the Internet without your knowledge.

For all outgoing Web, instant messaging, and e-mail traffic, the firewall scans for private information about you. If it finds out that private information is being sent out, it displays a privacy alert asking you to approve the sending of the data, as shown in Figure 15-22.

How does the firewall know what constitutes private information? You must specify all the private information that you want to protect in the configuration of the firewall. For credit card numbers, it is sufficient to only specify the last few digits, of course.

Note that the firewall can't scan traffic that is protected by SSL or is encrypted by other means. This feature only works for cleartext transmission of the private information that you explicitly listed first.

Norton Personal Firewall

Private Information Alert

High Risk

Your computer is attempting to send Private Information over the Internet.

Hide Details

Sending To	: 39.1.1.5
Category	: Home Address
Information Blocked	: 14 Parkstreet

What do you want to do?

Block (Recommended)

Alert Assistant

OK

Figure 15-22: Private information alert.

Ad blocking

Although disabled by default, Norton Personal Firewall allows you to block ads from well-known sources when browsing the Internet. The firewall keeps a list of known URLs for advertisements and blocks them when the Web browser attempts to download those ads.

You can, er . . . add more ads to the list as well.

Norton Personal Firewall is really into ad blocking. Besides specifying text strings to identify ads, you can also use a true Ad Trashcan. You can drag unwanted ads from an opened Web site to the Ad Trashcan to indicate future blocking.

LiveUpdate

To keep your software up-to-date, Norton Personal Firewall has an option to connect to Symantec's Web site and download program updates, intrusion detection database updates, and blocked ad list updates.

You can run LiveUpdate by clicking the large LiveUpdate button at the toolbar in the Security Center. This is shown in Figure 15-23.

You can indicate in the Options section that Norton Personal Firewall must automatically check for updates every four hours. This option is enabled by default.

Figure 15-23:
LiveUpdate
dialog box.

Norton Personal Firewall interface

Like any other personal firewall, you only need to bother with the user interface of the software if you want to change any of its settings.

Security Center dialog box

All configuration is done in the Security Center dialog box. You open this dialog box by double-clicking on the globe icon in the system tray or by starting Norton Personal Firewall by choosing Start⇨All Programs⇨Norton Personal Firewall⇨Norton Personal Firewall.

The Security Center is shown in Figure 15-24.

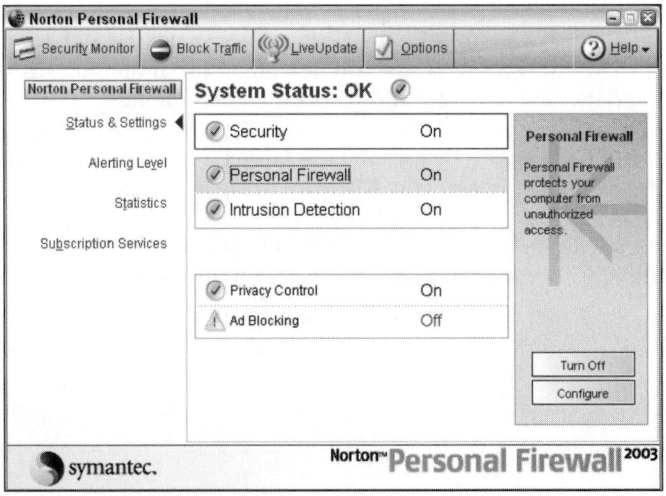

Figure 15-24:
Security
Center
dialog box.

On the main screen of the Security Center dialog box, you can select a feature and then click the Configure button to configure settings for this topic.

The Personal Firewall configuration settings allow you to manually specify programs on the Program Control list, computers in the Trusted Zone and Restricted Zone, and the firewall rules.

The firewall rules consist of general rules and Trojan horse rules. An example of a general rule is shown in Figure 15-25.

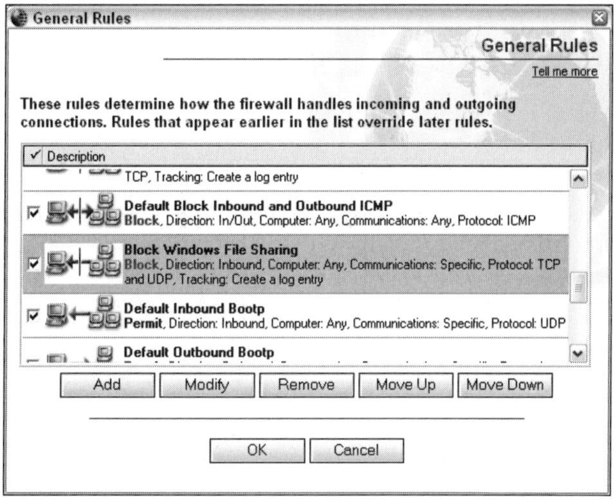

Figure 15-25:
General rule
to block
Windows
file sharing.

In the Security Center dialog box, you can choose from four categories on the left side. These categories are:

- ✔ **Status & Settings:** Configure Personal Firewall settings, Intrusion Detection settings, and Privacy Control settings.

- ✔ **Alerting Level:** Specify the security events for which users receive alerts. You can choose from Low (default), Medium, and High.

- ✔ **Statistics:** Displays statistics on the number of intrusion attempts that were detected and the number of Blocked and Permitted actions. This category also provides access to the detailed log files.

- ✔ **Subscription Services:** The last category lets you manage your subscription to updated information from Symantec's Web site.

The Security Center dialog box also has a toolbar containing five large buttons:

- ✔ **Security Monitor:** Switches to the Security Monitor dialog box.
- ✔ **Block Traffic/Allow Traffic:** This is an emergency button that lets you block all traffic to and from the Internet instantly. Note that the Stop icon on the button doesn't change when you click the button. The globe in the system tray will change its appearance when the emergency button is clicked.
- ✔ **LiveUpdate:** Opens the LiveUpdate dialog box to update components of Norton Personal Firewall from Symantec's Web site.
- ✔ **Options:** Opens the Options dialog box that lets you configure the firewall and manage things like the blocked ads list.
- ✔ **Help:** Help is help.

Security Monitor dialog box

When you click the Security Monitor button in the Security Center, the dialog box switches to the Security Monitor dialog box. This is a small window that you can leave on the screen while browsing the Internet. It displays the last event alert, and also provides the Block Traffic/Alert Traffic emergency button.

The Security Monitor dialog box is shown in Figure 15-26.

Figure 15-26:
Security
Monitor
dialog box.

Click the Security Center button to switch back to the Security Center dialog box.

Alert Tracker

After the installation of Norton Personal Firewall, you'll discover half a globe at the edge of the right or left side of the screen. At first, you may think that this is an icon that mistakenly has moved partly off the screen. (See Figure 15-27.) Not so.

This is the Alert Tracker, a neat feature that gives you quick access to all the recent alerts and the Ad Trashcan. Just double-click the half-globe to slide it open. And double-click again to slide it back to its screen-edge position.

Figure 15-27:
Alert
Tracker or
misplaced
icon?

You can move the Alert Tracker up and down the side of the screen, and of course, you can opt not to display it. Just right-click the half-globe and select Hide the Alert Tracker.

Norton Personal Firewall installation

You can start the installation of Norton Personal Firewall from the product CD-ROM, or you can download a free 15-day trial version from www.norton.com.

Note that the instructions in this section are for Norton Personal Firewall version 2003.

To install Norton Personal Firewall, follow these steps:

1. **Determine whether your computer meets the minimum system requirements described in Table 15-4.**

Table 15-4	Minimum System Requirements for Norton Personal Firewall	
Component	*Minimum Requirement*
Operating system	Windows 98 (original or SE), Windows Me, Windows 2000 Professional, or Windows XP
Processor	Pentium or higher
Required disk space	25MB
Memory	48MB
Network interface	Ethernet, DSL, cable modem, or dial-up

Norton Personal Firewall doesn't support Windows NT 4.0.

2. **If you have purchased a license for Norton Personal Firewall, then start the installation by running** CDSTART.exe **from the product CD-ROM, and continue with Step 4.**

3. **If you have downloaded a 15-day trial version of Norton Personal Firewall, then start the downloaded 750KB application named** NPF15Try.exe.

   A Delivering Norton Personal Firewall 2003 window appears. The application will download and unpack a 25MB file. After this is done, click the Launch button to start the downloaded CDSTART.exe application.

4. **In the Welcome to Norton Personal Firewall window, click Install Norton Personal Firewall.**

   Windows Installer will prepare the installation and start the Setup program.

5. **On the Welcome to Norton Personal Firewall Setup page, click Next.**

6. **On the License Agreement page, read the license agreement and then select the I Accept the License Agreement option and click Next.**

7. **On the Run LiveUpdate After Installation page, select whether you want to update the software after installation, and click Next.**

8. **On the Set the Destination Folder page, accept the default destination folder and click Next.**

9. **On the Ready to Install page, click Next to start the installation.**

   Setup will now install the software on your computer. This will take a few minutes.

10. **On the Please Register Norton Personal Firewall page, click Next if you want to register the software, or click Skip.**

    If you register the software, you have to fill out a few additional pages.

11. **On the Readme page, read the installation notes and click Next.**

12. **On the Installation Successful page, click Finish to complete the installation.**

    After the installation, you have to restart the computer.

13. **On the Installer Information page, click Yes to restart the computer.**

    The computer will now restart.

14. **After the restart and logon, the Security Assistant window appears. You can click Next to configure Norton Personal Firewall now, or click Close to configure the software later.**

    You can configure all the settings in the Security Assistant from the Security Center dialog box later.

15. **If you selected to enable LiveUpdate during installation, the LiveUpdate window appears. Click Next to see the updates found.**

   For a security product, it is always a good idea to use the latest version of the software.

16. **If updates are found, click Next to download and install the updates.**

   LiveUpdate downloads and installs the updates from the Symantec Web site.

17. **After all updates are installed, click Finish to complete the update of the software.**

   It is possible that some of the updates require you to restart the computer again. Click OK to confirm the restart.

The Norton Personal Firewall globe icon now appears in the Windows system tray in the lower-right corner of the screen.

When you want to start the Security Center, just double-click the globe icon in the system tray.

Norton Personal Firewall configuration tasks

The following section provides you with step-by-step configuration instructions for typical tasks that you do when working with Norton Personal Firewall.

✔ To start the Security Center:

   1. **Choose Start⇨All Programs⇨Norton Personal Firewall⇨Norton Personal Firewall or double-click the globe icon in the Windows system tray.**

✔ To block all traffic instantly:

   1. **Open the Security Center (or the Security Monitor).**

   2. **In the Security Center or Security Monitor dialog box, click the Block Traffic button.**

   or

   1. **Right-click the globe icon in the Windows system tray, and click Block Traffic.**

✔ To change Trusted Zone (Home Networking) settings:

   1. **Open the Security Center.**

   2. **In the Security Center main screen, select Personal Firewall and then click Configure.**

3. In the configuration dialog box, select the Home Networking tab.

4. On the Home Networking tab, click Add or Remove to configure the Trusted Zone.

✔ To enable ad blocking:

1. Open the Security Center.

2. In the Security Center main screen, select Ad Blocking and then click Configure.

3. In the Ad Blocking dialog box, select the Turn on Ad Blocking check box.

✔ To disable or enable the Alert Tracker (half-globe icon) on screen:

1. Open the Security Center.

2. In the Security Center window, click the Options button.

3. On the General tab of the Options dialog box, disable or enable the Show the Alert Tracker check box.

✔ To inspect log files:

1. Open the Security Center.

2. In the Security Center window, select Statistics.

3. In the Statistics screen, click the View Logs button.

4. In the Log Viewer window, select one of the nine logging categories, as shown in Figure 15-28.

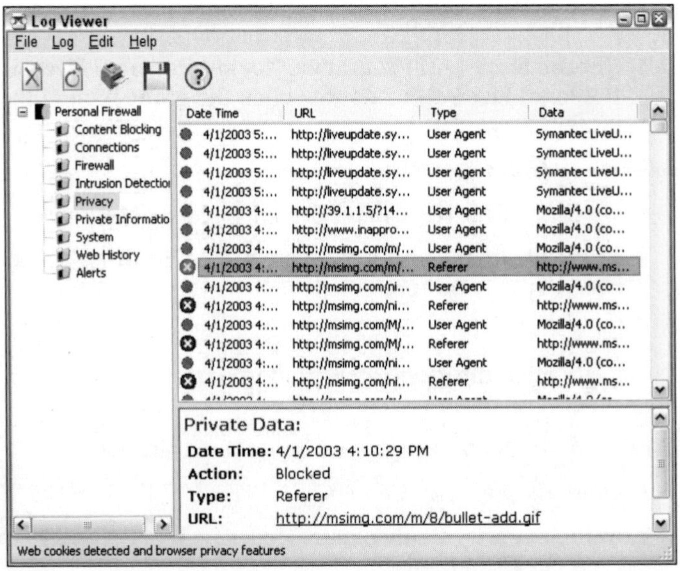

Figure 15-28:
Log Viewer
window.

Chapter 16

Microsoft's Firewall: Internet Security and Acceleration Server

- -

- -

*M*icrosoft Internet Security and Acceleration Server 2000 — quite a mouthful, but the name is an apt description of what Microsoft's entry in the firewall market does. In this chapter, we explore what ISA Server (as it is commonly known) can do for you and how it performs its two functions: providing Internet security and accelerating Internet access by caching Web content.

How do you pronounce it?

Nobody likes to use the long, cumbersome name "Microsoft Internet Security and Acceleration Server," so everyone just uses the abbreviated form, ISA Server. But how do you pronounce it? Is it "eye-sah" or "I-S-A?" Even the developers at Microsoft who wrote this software don't agree. Half the developers pronounce it one way, the other half, the other way. And if *they* can't agree on a pronunciation, *you* are certainly allowed to use the pronunciation that sounds best to you.

Making Internet Access Faster and More Secure

Microsoft created a solution that addresses two problems that many organizations face when connecting their network to the Internet: making the best possible use of network bandwidth to the Internet, and screening all network traffic to and from the Internet to ensure that traffic is allowed by your Security policies. In other words, ISA Server caches Web content in addition to being a firewall. Here's how ISA Server performs these tasks:

- **Accelerating Internet Access:** No matter how much Internet bandwidth you have, as more people in your company or organization use the Internet for more purposes, everyone is bound to see a slowdown before too long because of increasing usage of your link to the Internet. Your link to the outside world is becoming congested. Much of the network traffic of many organizations consists of employees viewing Web pages that co-workers accessed just minutes or hours ago. Because of this duplication, ISA Server — which screens all network traffic to and from the Internet — keeps a copy of most Web pages in a cache, and when the same Web page is accessed again soon, ISA Server retrieves the page from its cache rather than from the Internet. The most noticeable effect is that the Web browser receives the requested page faster and can display it with almost no delay. The other effect is that little or no network bandwidth to the Internet is used when someone requests a Web page that is already in ISA Server's cache. Everyone benefits: Web surfers often see the requested Web pages faster, and you save money because you don't have to buy more bandwidth to the Internet.

- **Securing Internet Access:** ISA Server can inspect both outgoing and incoming Internet traffic and decide whether this traffic is allowed according to the rules that you defined. For example, if Fred tries to download a file from the Internet, ISA Server checks whether Fred is allowed to download files, whether Fred is allowed to do this during this time of the day, whether access to the specific Web location is allowed, and whether files of this type can be downloaded. ISA Server is very flexible when it comes to enforcing rules for Internet access. Also, like every good firewall, ISA Server allows inbound network traffic only when it is part of a data transfer that was initiated from someone in your organization — such as a Web page that a server returns after a user requested the page — or if you specifically allow the incoming traffic, such as allowing requests from people on the Internet who access your public Web server.

Running the numbers

When evaluating ISA Server, calculate how much money the reduction of Internet traffic can save you and how this cost compares to the cost of ISA Server. For example, suppose that you are paying $200 per month to your ISP to access the Internet. The bandwidth that the ISP provides for this amount is not enough for your needs, and doubling the capacity will cost you another $200 a month. Buying a new server and installing Windows 2000 and ISA Server may cost you as much as $5,000, but the resulting reduction in bandwidth usage means that you won't have to buy the additional bandwidth at $200 a month. In this example, you'll need 25 months to break even, but with ISA Server you also get a first-rate firewall, and ISA Server allows you to monitor all Internet usage. Buying separate products for these functions could cost you thousands of dollars. By running the numbers for your own company or organization, you may find that ISA Server can more than pay for itself and even save you money in the long run.

Looking under the Hood: How ISA Works

How does ISA Server do it? First, like any good firewall, ISA Server can perform packet filtering and stateful inspection. Second, ISA Server works as a *proxy server.* A proxy server intercepts Internet requests, examines them, and then issues the request to the Internet, making them look as if they originated from the proxy server. This means that no direct connection ever exists between an internal computer and an external computer. Essentially, a proxy server acts as an agent that sends IP traffic, receives IP traffic, and fetches Web pages on a client's behalf.

Take a look at two examples of how this process works. In the first example, a user's browser issues a request for a Web page. Because the browser is aware of the presence of a proxy server, it doesn't request the Web page directly. Instead, it contacts the proxy server and asks the proxy server to retrieve the Web page. The proxy server then requests the Web page from the Web server and sends the results to the browser. Just like a butler who performs the shopping for you and everyone in your household, the proxy server is the computer that issues all Internet requests and appears as the initiator of all requests to the outside world.

In the second example, a user downloads mail messages from a mail server on the Internet. Inside the computer, the request is translated into a series of IP packets. Depending on your configuration, these IP packets are then intercepted by a piece of client software and sent to the proxy server, or the proxy server may intercept them en route without the client computer's knowledge.

Again, the proxy server changes the outgoing information. In this case, it changes the header of each IP packet to disguise the packets so it looks as if the packets came from the proxy server. When return packets are received from the mail server on the Internet, ISA Server again changes the information in the packet headers before sending the packets on to the client. Because of this manipulation of header information, both the mail program on the client computer and the mail server on the Internet are unaware of the role that the proxy server plays. Depending on the type of network traffic involved, ISA Server can request *content* as a proxy for a client (in the case of Web traffic) or it can establish an IP connection on behalf of the client (in the case of non-Web traffic). In either case, the client computer and the server that it tries to contact never communicate directly with each other.

One thing to keep in mind about this process is that ISA Server always performs Network Address Translation (NAT) between internal and external computers. NAT is explained in detail in Chapter 3.

Using a proxy server offers a number of benefits:

- ✔ All Internet traffic passes through a single point where you can control it and apply the rules that enforce your Internet Acceptable Use policy and your Security policy. Unlike a packet-filtering firewall, a proxy server can examine entire communication sequences, such as the requesting and receiving of a Web page, and is not limited to checking single IP packets.

- ✔ Because servers on the Internet never see the actual IP addresses of the computers that establish a connection, a proxy server effectively hides your internal network structure. Furthermore, the proxy server can drop all network packets that are not valid before they ever reach the client.

- ✔ Your entire company or organization requires only a single IP address that is valid on the Internet, which is the IP address of the proxy server. For your internal IP addresses, you can use addresses from the private IP addressing ranges defined in RFC 1918. Using private IP addresses completely ensures that nobody from the Internet can initiate a direct connection with a computer on your network, and you won't have to pay your ISP to use a large number of IP addresses for Internet access.

ISA Server performs the roles of a proxy server and a caching server rather well, but it can do even more. Here's a list of some of the other features that make it a very capable firewall:

- ✔ **Dynamic Packet Filters:** Whenever a client issues an Internet request, ISA Server duly opens the ports that are required for this connection — but only for the time that the ports need to be open. When someone on the Internet tries to connect to the ISA Server computer using any port other than one of those that has been opened for a limited time to accommodate a client request, ISA Server doesn't respond in any way to the connection attempt. A curious hacker or malicious intruder gets no indication that the computer running ISA Server is even running at all.

✔ **Static Packet Filters:** Clients don't initiate all connections, nor are internal clients always involved in the network traffic that ISA Server handles. For example, ISA Server may route network traffic between the Internet and your perimeter network or DMZ (demilitarized zone). In order to accomplish such routing and other tasks, you have to configure ISA Server with static packet filters. These static packet filters allow or deny traffic through your ISA Server firewall based on the protocol used and the source and destination IP addresses and ports. For more information on DMZs, see Chapters 11 and 12.

✔ **Application Filters:** Packet filters determine what network traffic ISA Server forwards, based on the characteristics of each IP packet — the protocol used and the source and destination IP addresses and ports. However, packet filters can't determine whether ISA Server forwards network traffic based on patterns that span more than one IP packet. For example, to make a decision about whether to forward the packets that comprise an e-mail message, ISA Server must be able to assemble the incoming IP packets that comprise an e-mail message, assemble the message, and then examine the contents of the message. In other words, ISA Server can apply rules based on *Application layer* protocols, such as SMTP and HTTP. For ISA Server to apply rules at the application level, it must have application filters that are designed with knowledge about the characteristics of the Application layer protocol. ISA Server contains several built-in application filters — for example, an SMTP filter for applying rules to incoming e-mail. ISA Server is particularly strong when it comes to examining HTTP traffic. Developers can also create more application filters in addition to the ones that are included with ISA Server.

✔ **Server Publishing and Web Publishing:** Sometimes you want external users to have access to servers that are located on your internal network. For example, you may have a public Web server that you want to make available to users on the Internet. Or, your screened subnet may contain your company's public DNS server or mail server. Server publishing rules allow you to make these servers available to the Internet. Web publishing gives you similar functionality for Web servers. In addition, because ISA Server can cache published Web content, Web publishing provides performance benefits for users who access your Web server from the Internet through the ISA Server-based firewall.

Adding new features

If you are publishing a Web or mail server with ISA Server, you should take a look at Feature Pack 1, which is a collection of useful tools and additions that simplify publishing of these types of servers. Feature Pack 1 offers other features, too, but most of the added value comes in the area of publishing. The best part is that you can download this add-on for free from `www.microsoft.com/isaserver`.

✔ **Monitoring and Reporting:** ISA Server provides multiple levels of monitoring. You can choose to have ISA Server log several types of information, including Internet access by internal users, incoming network packets from the Internet that ISA Server blocks, or even every single network packet that ISA Server processes. You can — and *should* — regularly review these logs and a few of the more readable reports that ISA Server creates from the logs. Because the logs can be very detailed, they are a powerful tool for keeping track of all aspects of your organization's Internet access. ISA Server also includes tools that allow you to monitor ISA Server's operations and your company's Internet traffic. You can even configure ISA Server to contact you when a predefined condition, such as a security breach, has occurred.

✔ **Support for Remote Access:** Many companies allow remote access into their internal network by employees. These users may be working from home or traveling. Virtual private networks, or VPNs, have become increasingly popular for providing this access. A VPN is a secure connection that is accomplished over an insecure connection by using an encryption mechanism. In most cases, a user establishes a connection to the Internet via an Internet Service Provider. The user then establishes a secure connection to his or her company's remote access server over the Internet. After this connection has been established, all further traffic between the user's computer and the company's internal network is encrypted. This connection is completely transparent to all applications that access the company's internal network from the remote computer. These applications access the internal servers as if the user's computer were directly connected to the internal network. Configuring a VPN often turns into a lot of work because the firewall and the VPN server need to be configured. ISA Server simplifies this process by making it very easy to configure both ISA Server settings and the Windows 2000 RRAS (Routing and Remote Access) service in one procedure. You can configure ISA Server to allow VPN clients to connect to your network in as little as three mouse clicks after you have done your planning. More importantly, using ISA Server's wizards ensure that you don't accidentally end up with an insecure configuration.

✔ **Extensibility:** This may be the most impressive aspect of ISA Server. Anything that you wish ISA Server did for you, but Microsoft hasn't thought of, can be acquired by using the ISA Server SDK (Software Development Kit). Programmers can use this SDK to extend the functionality of ISA Server. Anyone familiar with a scripting language, such as Microsoft Visual Basic, can create scripts that automate common administrative tasks. With knowledge of a programming language, such as C++, you can create an ISA Server extension that handles network packets or streams of network packets according to the rules that are built into this extension. Third-party vendors have also developed a number of extensions that perform tasks, such as virus checking or blocking user access to Web sites based on categories into which these Web sites fit.

Choosing between the Two Editions

Now that you know about what ISA Server can do for you, you may decide to evaluate it further. Pretty soon you will discover that ISA Server comes in two editions, the Standard Edition and the Enterprise Edition, and you begin to wonder, "Which of these editions is right for me?" Because the Enterprise Edition is considerably more expensive than the Standard Edition, examine what you may gain by using the Enterprise Edition. The Enterprise Edition can do everything that the Standard Edition does — and more. You should consider the Enterprise Edition only if you need any of the added functionality that it provides over the Standard Edition. The Enterprise Edition can help you

✔ **Build big servers:** You can install ISA Server Standard Edition on a computer that has up to four processors. This hardware configuration covers most servers in existence today. However, some large organizations use servers that have eight or more processors. Microsoft requires that you use the Enterprise Edition on servers with more than four processors.

✔ **Distribute the load:** By using ISA Server Enterprise Edition you can create an array of multiple ISA Server computers that automatically distribute the load of client requests among themselves. Although you may be tempted to add more processors to the ISA Server computer as the load on your firewall grows, you can often achieve the same increase in performance more efficiently and effectively by creating an array of multiple computers running ISA Server. All computers in an array must run ISA Server Enterprise Edition.

✔ **Manage the work:** Arrays give you another benefit besides distributing the workload among multiple computers. When you create an ISA Server array, all computers in an array work together to perform largely identical tasks. You can also manage all the servers in such an array as a single unit. Doing so saves you a lot of administrative work. Remember that you need the Enterprise Edition to create an array.

Some servers cost more

Purchasing a large server with multiple processors results not only in a higher cost for the hardware, but if you use that server to run ISA Server, remember that Microsoft licensing rules require you to buy an ISA Server license for each processor that is installed in the ISA Server computer. However, after you have taken care of the per-processor licenses, you can allow as many client computers as you want to access the Internet through the ISA Server computer. Other firewall products, in contrast, are priced based on the number of clients.

✔ **Administer an enterprise:** ISA Server allows an organization to adopt enterprise policies. An enterprise administrator can use these rules to enforce corporate security policies enterprise-wide and to ensure that all ISA Server arrays in the enterprise use these rules. An enterprise administrator can also decide how much leeway an array administrator has in augmenting enterprise policies. Enterprise policies apply only to arrays, so to implement enterprise-wide policies, you must use ISA Server Enterprise Edition for all ISA Server computers in your organization.

Preparing for Installation

Installing ISA Server is easy. You can insert the CD in your computer's CD-ROM drive, complete the installation wizard within five minutes, and the ISA Server installation is finished. However, if you haven't planned adequately for your ISA Server installation, or if you make incorrect decisions during the installation, you may create a huge security risk for your network. So, to help you avoid these situations, take a look at what you should consider before installing ISA Server.

First, carefully examine your network infrastructure. Will it require arrays, or do you just need a single ISA Server computer? If you do need arrays, you need to implement Active Directory in your company. Active Directory is Microsoft's directory service. Committing your organization to Active Directory is an issue that you have to assess based on many factors, only some of which are related to ISA Server. The implications of implementing Active Directory go beyond the scope of this book, but fortunately, even if you're not ready to move to Active Directory entirely, you can create an Active Directory-based domain that contains only your ISA Server computers. This allows you to create an ISA Server array even before you are ready for an all-out implementation of Active Directory.

After you begin using Active Directory in your network, you have to do one more thing: You need to modify the Active Directory schema so that Active Directory can store ISA Server data. Although modifying the Active Directory schema for ISA Server can be done easily enough, it can have some major implications on your Active Directory and thus your network. Before installing ISA Server as an array, make sure that you understand all the implications. For more information on this topic, see *Active Directory For Dummies,* by Marcia R. Loughry (published by Wiley Publishing, Inc.).

This chapter covers installing ISA Server as a standalone, or non-array, server, which doesn't require Active Directory. Don't worry, though — you can later upgrade to the Enterprise Edition and then promote an ISA Server standalone server to an array, and ISA Server even preserves most of your settings.

You should definitely do a few basic tasks before installing ISA Server:

✔ **Map your network:** Make sure that you have a list of all IP addresses that are used in your network, including those that you will use for future expansion. If your ISP assigned you static IP addresses, create a list that includes the IP address or addresses that the ISA Server computer uses to connect to the Internet. If you use a dialup connection to connect to the Internet, you can skip this step. Finally, if you are planning to use a demilitarized zone (DMZ), create another list of the IP addresses in the DMZ.

✔ **Install all hardware:** Add all the required hardware to the ISA Server computer. ISA Server requires at least one NIC (network information center) that's connected to your internal network. The connection to the Internet can be another NIC or a modem. You can't use the same NIC to connect to the Internet and your internal network if you want to use the firewall functionality of ISA Server.

✔ **Install Windows 2000 Server:** Install Windows 2000 Server and include only the components that are required. In particular, don't install any of the optional network components or Internet Information Services (IIS). Also, check to make sure that Windows 2000 detected all hardware (NICs, modems, and so forth) during installation. After you're done installing Windows 2000 Server, also install the latest Service Pack and any critical hot fixes. Your computer should be as secure as possible before you install a firewall on it.

You can also run ISA Server on Microsoft Windows Server 2003. To install it in this configuration, you need Service Pack 1 for ISA Server or later. The Release Notes for Service Pack contain important information on how to proceed with this type of installation. You can download the latest Service Pack from `www.microsoft.com/isaserver`.

✔ **Configure TCP/IP:** Use the Networking applet in the Control Panel to configure the TCP/IP settings for all network adapters. Configure the internal adapter with an IP address that is valid on your internal network. If you are connecting to the Internet via a NIC, configure that adapter with an IP address that your ISP provided.

✔ **Configure the default gateway:** While using the Networking applet in the Control Panel, also configure a default gateway. The default gateway is the destination to which a computer sends all IP packets for which it doesn't have a specific route. Because your computer doesn't have routes for any destinations on the Internet, you have to ensure that ISA Server can forward all packets for external destinations to the Internet. Therefore, you should configure a default gateway only for the NIC that you will connect to the Internet. Don't configure a default gateway for your internal network adapter. Yes, we know, it looks strange to leave this prominent box in the TCP/IP Properties dialog box empty, but doing so is required in order for ISA Server to route packets correctly.

✔ **Configure the routing table:** By defining the default gateway, you have told Windows 2000 how to route packets to the Internet. Next, you have to tell Windows 2000 how to route any packets that go to computers on your internal network. If your network contains only one range of network addresses, such as 192.168.1.0 to 192.168.1.255, then this indicates that Windows 2000 built the required entries when you configured the network adapter that is connected to your internal network. If your internal network contains more than one range of network addresses, you have to add those to the routing table by using the route add command. You can find more information about this command in Windows 2000 Server online help. Similarly, if you are using a DMZ, make sure that the routing table contains the entries that are required in order for Windows 2000 to send all packets to the DMZ through the network adapter that is attached to it. You can easily confirm that Windows 2000 Server has the correct routing table entries by opening a command prompt window and typing **route print.** Figure 16-1 shows what the output of the route print command looks like with an internal network of 192.168.1.0 and a DMZ of 23.10.10.0. Notice that the default gateway is on the same network as the network adapter with the IP address 23.10.10.200. This is the NIC that connects this computer to the Internet.

Figure 16-1:
The output
of the
route
print
command.

✔ **Configure the dialup connection:** If you are connecting to the Internet via a phone line, you have to configure a dialup connection. To do this, open the Network and Dial-Up Connections item in the Control Panel, and then double-click New Connection. Follow the instructions in the Network Connection Wizard to configure the dialup connection with the telephone number and logon information for your Internet Service Provider.

Installing ISA Server

Installing ISA Server is easy. A setup wizard asks you for a few pieces of information, and when you are finished providing this information, ISA Server starts. Be careful during the setup, however, because it's very easy to enter incorrect information, and doing so may compromise your network's security. In this section, you learn what to watch out for and how to configure ISA Server so that it protects your network the way it's intended.

Gathering information

During the installation, ISA Server requires several pieces of information. Collect this information before you start the installation. Here is a checklist:

- ✔ **CD Key:** Like many Microsoft products, ISA Server requires that you provide the CD Key. You can find this ten-digit number on an orange sticker on the back of the ISA Server CD case.

- ✔ **Cache size and location:** ISA Server uses a portion of your computer's hard drive for caching Web objects that client computers request. Before installing ISA Server, make a note of which hard drive has enough space for this cache. The recommended size is 100 MB and another 0.5 MB for each user. You can change the amount of disk space and location after installation, but you should start out with a configuration that works. Make a note of the drive that you will use for caching and how much space you will allocate. You can also spread out the cache over multiple hard drives. To allow for efficient cache access and to ensure security, any drive that you use for caching has to be formatted with the NTFS file system.

- ✔ **The Local Address Table (LAT):** ISA Server uses a table to keep track of all IP addresses that are on the internal network. This table is referred to as the Local Address Table, or LAT. Initially, ISA Server builds the LAT based on information that you provide during setup. Misconfiguring the LAT is the worst mistake that you can make. The LAT should contain only the addresses on your internal network. If you add any external addresses to your LAT, you will be opening serious security holes. If the LAT doesn't contain all internal IP addresses, some client computers may not be able to communicate with the Internet. Make sure that you have a list of all internal IP addresses when you start the installation of ISA Server.

Getting the best performance

One of the best things that you can do to improve the performance of your server is to optimize how the hardware is used. In the case of ISA Server, you should place the cache file on a hard drive by itself. So, if you have a hard drive that is not used for other heavy data access or to hold the operating system, place the cache file on that hard drive. You can also place the cache file on the same hard drive as Windows, but performance won't be as good as it would be with a dedicated hard drive for caching.

When you have gathered all required information, you can start the installation of ISA Server:

1. **Log on to Windows with an account that is a member of the Administrators group.**

2. **Insert the ISA Server CD-ROM.**

   The screen in Figure 16-2 appears. If it doesn't, start the Setup program manually from the CD.

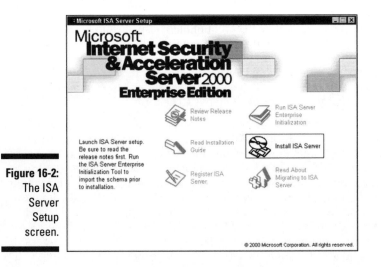

Figure 16-2:
The ISA
Server
Setup
screen.

3. **In the Microsoft ISA Server Setup screen, click Install ISA Server.**

4. **Click Continue.**

5. **Type the CD key, and then click OK twice.**

   Good thing you made sure you had the CD key before you started! You wouldn't want to start searching for it now while you are in the middle of the installation.

6. **Read the license agreement and click I Agree.**

7. **Click the button for the installation type that you want to perform: Typical Installation, Custom Installation, or Full Installation.**

   The Typical Installation works best in most environments. You have to choose another installation type only if you are setting up an H.323 infrastructure to allow users on the Internet to connect to users in your network for teleconferencing or voice over IP (VOIP) phone calls, or if you need to install the Message Screener, which is an ISA Server component that performs filtering of incoming e-mail. You can also use the Custom Installation if you want to install only the administration tools on a computer that isn't running ISA Server.

8. **If a dialog box appears that informs you that ISA Server Setup can't join an array, click OK.**

   If you are installing ISA Server Enterprise Edition, you have to prepare Active Directory before creating an array. Because you are installing a standalone server, you can ignore this warning if it appears.

9. **In the next dialog box, click Yes to install ISA Server as a Standalone Server. You don't want to join an ISA Server array at this point.**

10. **When ISA Server Setup prompts you for the installation mode, ensure that Integrated Mode is selected, and then click Continue.**

    Integrated Mode gives you both caching of Web objects and firewall protection. Integrated Mode is the best choice for connecting your network to the Internet. Generally, you select a different mode only if you use another firewall or caching server in conjunction with ISA Server.

    If your computer is running Internet Information Services (IIS) and IIS uses TCP port 80 or 8080, ISA Server Setup displays the warning message shown in Figure 16-3. The Setup program warns you that it is stopping IIS because ISA Server uses the same ports as IIS, and services running under Windows can't share the same port. The ISA Server Setup program only temporarily stops IIS, but IIS will run again the next time you restart your computer. After the ISA Server installation is complete, you should change the ports that IIS is using or, better yet, remove IIS.

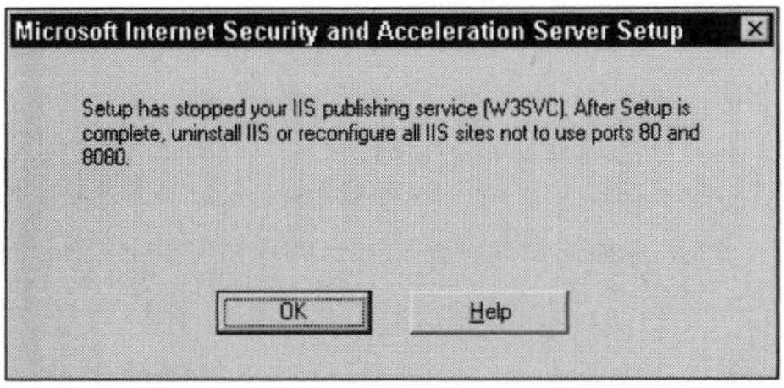

Figure 16-3:
The IIS
warning.

11. **Click OK to acknowledge that ISA Server Setup has stopped your Web sites.**

    Next, ISA Server displays a dialog box with choices for the cache configuration. You can use multiple cache files, one on each hard drive. To do so, specify the size for each drive. To prevent ISA Server from placing a cache file on one of your drives, simply enter 0 as the size of the cache file on that drive.

12. **To configure caching in this dialog box, select the drive that you want ISA Server to place the cache file on, type the size of the cache file, and then click Set. When you're done, click OK.**

    ISA Server displays a dialog box that prompts you for your internal IP addresses. You can enter these addresses manually or let ISA Server create them automatically.

13. **When ISA Server prompts you to enter your network's internal IP address ranges, click Construct Table to display the dialog box shown in Figure 16-4.**

    When you enter the internal address ranges, ISA Server creates the LAT. This is what you prepared for by configuring your routing table and noting all internal address ranges. It is important to configure your routing table correctly because ISA Server uses this information to create the LAT for you.

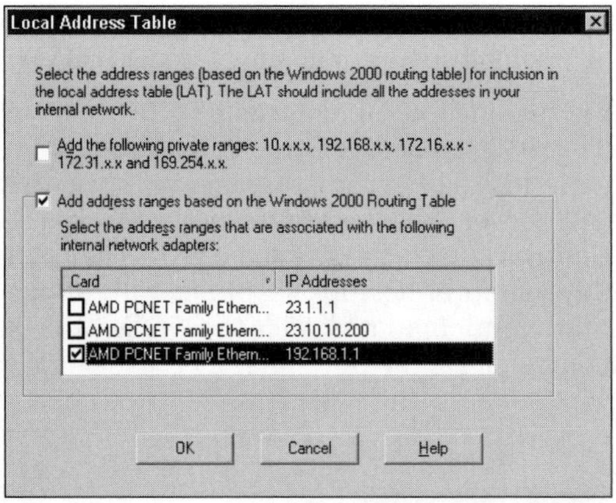

Figure 16-4:
The Local
Address
Table
construction
dialog box.

14. **In the Local Address Table dialog box, check the check box to indicate that you want to add addresses from the Windows routing table, and then check the check box for the network adapter that is connected to your local network.**

    Don't select any network cards connected to the Internet or the DMZ. If you are using the private address ranges that ISA Server Setup refers to for your internal network, you can also check the check box that will add these ranges to the LAT.

15. Click OK.

A warning message appears, prompting you to ensure that the LAT contains the correct addresses. Remember that your LAT should contain all the IP addresses on your local network and not any other IP addresses.

16. Click OK to acknowledge the warning message about the dangers of a misconfigured LAT.

ISA Server displays the results of the automatic creation of the LAT contents. (See Figure 16-5.)

17. In the listing of internal IP addresses confirm that all internal IP addresses are listed and that none of the IP addresses listed are external to your network or in the DMZ.

If your routing table was configured before you started the installation, the list of internal IP addresses should be complete. If the list doesn't have the correct entries, you can add or remove entries here.

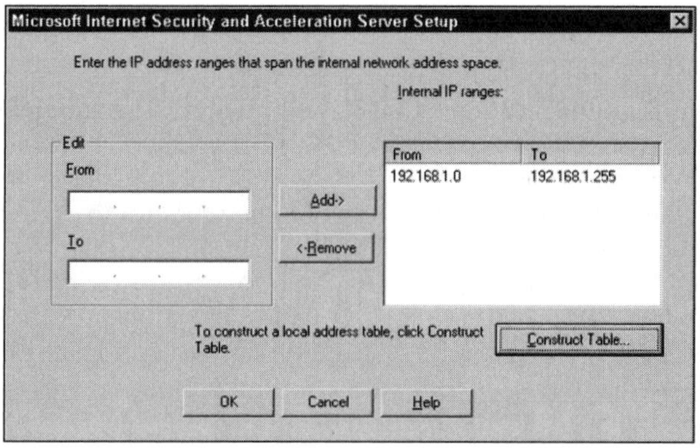

Figure 16-5:
The Local
Address
Table
confirmation
dialog box.

Microsoft Internet Security and Acceleration Server Setup

Enter the IP address ranges that span the internal network address space.

Internal IP ranges:

From	To
192.168.1.0	192.168.1.255

Edit

From

Add->

To

<-Remove

To construct a local address table, click Construct Table.

Construct Table...

OK   Cancel   Help

Making a mistake when configuring the LAT can cause ISA Server to treat the Internet as a trusted network, thus rendering ISA Server completely ineffective. During the installation, always double-check that your LAT only contains internal addresses. Better yet, triple-check this setting before you continue.

18. Click OK in the Microsoft Internet Security and Acceleration Server Setup dialog box.

After ISA Server Setup finishes, you are prompted to run the Getting Started Wizard.

Help! I can no longer get to the Internet

"How come I can no longer access the Internet?" This is probably the most frequently asked question after an administrator has installed ISA Server. The answer is — nothing is wrong. ISA Server is just doing its job — protecting your network and not allowing any network traffic to pass through ISA Server. It simply means that ISA Server is functioning correctly. To allow yourself or other users to access the Internet, you have to create access rules that allow outgoing traffic. This chapter shows you how to configure these rules. And don't forget that ISA Server also blocks incoming traffic from the Internet. After all, that's what a firewall is supposed to do. If anybody on the Internet is trying to connect to your ISA Server computer, he or she won't even be able to tell that the computer exists.

19. Deselect the check box to run the wizard, and then click OK.

You can start the wizard at any time from the ISA Server console. This wizard is rather helpful in guiding you through the most important configuration steps, and you should explore it later, but right now you won't use it.

Before continuing, you should ensure that ISA Server has been updated with the most recent fixes for problems that have appeared since the program was created. Fortunately, ISA Server is one of the most secure firewalls on the market, but Microsoft has released a few fixes for problems. First, install the latest Service Pack, and then install any recommended hot fixes. In most cases, you will also benefit from Feature Pack 1, a free set of ISA Server enhancements. You can download all of these from www.microsoft.com/isaserver.

Now that your ISA Server is running, you are ready to configure client computers to access the Internet through ISA Server. After your client computers are configured and you set up rules to allow these clients to access the Internet, setup is complete.

Connecting by telephone

If you use ISA Server to connect to an ISP via a modem, you have to perform a few additional steps. Before you begin configuring ISA Server, though, make sure that you have already configured a *dialup connection* in Windows that contains the telephone number and other required settings to connect to your ISP. When you create the dialup connection, make sure that you select to allow all users to access this dialup connection. Next, you have to configure ISA Server to use this dialup connection. To do this, you first have to configure an ISA Server *dialup entry,* which is a link that ISA Server uses to refer to the connection settings that you defined. You then have to tell ISA Server to use this dialup entry to connect to the Internet. To do all these things, perform the following steps:

1. **Open ISA Management from the Microsoft ISA Server menu.**

   The ISA Management window opens.

2. **In the Console Tree (the left pane), expand Server and Arrays, your server, and Policy Elements, and then click Dial-up Entries.**

3. **In the Details pane (the right pane), click Create a Dial-Up Entry.**

   The New Dial-up Entry dialog box appears.

4. **Type a name for your dialup entry, type an optional description, and then click Select to link the dialup entry to the dialup connection that you have defined in Windows.**

   The Select Network Dial-up Connection dialog box appears.

5. **Select the dialup connection that you want to use and then click OK.**

6. **To tell ISA Server which credentials to use when connecting to your ISP, click Set Account.**

   The Set Account dialog box appears.

7. **Enter the user name and password that your ISP has assigned to you and then click OK.**

   The dialog box should look similar to the one shown in Figure 16-6.

8. **Click OK to save your settings.**

Figure 16-6:
The New
Dial-up
Entry dialog
box.

9. **In the Console Tree, expand Network Configuration, and then click Routing.**

   The Default Rule appears in the Details pane.

10. **Right-click the default rule, and on the shortcut menu click Properties.**

    The Default Rule Properties dialog box appears.

11. **On the Action tab of the Default Rule Properties dialog box, check the Use Dial-Up Entry for Primary Route check box, and then click OK.**

    You have configured ISA Server to send all requests from clients for HTTP requests to the Internet via the dialup entry. Next, you have to configure ISA Server to use this entry, as well as for requests that use other protocols.

12. **In the Console Tree, right-click Network Configuration and choose Properties from the context menu that appears.**

13. **In the Network Configuration Properties dialog box, check the Use Dial-Up Entry check box and then click OK.**

Now ISA Server uses the dialup entry for all Internet requests. The dialup entry, in turn, dials the dialup connection with the user settings that you configured in the dialup entry. And if you are not at all confused about dialup issues by this point, you have already turned into a firewall nerd.

Examining the Three Clients

ISA Server supports three different client types. Before you configure the client computers to use ISA Server, you have to understand what each of these client types does and which one — or which combination of these — will work best for your needs. Take a look at each of the clients.

SecureNAT client

Configuring your computer as a SecureNAT client ensures that any IP packet from the client computer goes straight to the ISA Server computer. ISA Server then performs NAT (Network Address Translation) — converting between addresses that you use inside your network and ISA Server's address on the Internet. While ISA Server is doing this, it also applies all security rules that you configured, thus the name SecureNAT.

Any computer or other device that uses the TCP/IP protocol suite can be a SecureNAT client. All you have to do is configure the computer's default gateway to the internal IP address of the ISA Server computer. For example, if the internal IP address of the ISA Server computer is 192.168.1.1 and you are configuring a client computer running Windows 2000, just do the following steps:

1. **Right-click the My Network Places icon on the desktop, and then choose Properties from the context menu that appears.**

   The Network and Dial-up Connections window appears.

2. **Right-click the network adapter that you are configuring, and then choose Properties from the context menu.**

   The Properties dialog box for your network connection appears.

3. **Scroll down until you find the entry for Internet Protocol (TCP/IP). Select the entry without clearing the check box next to it, and then click the Properties button.**

   The Internet Protocol (TCP/IP) Properties dialog box appears, shown in Figure 16-7.

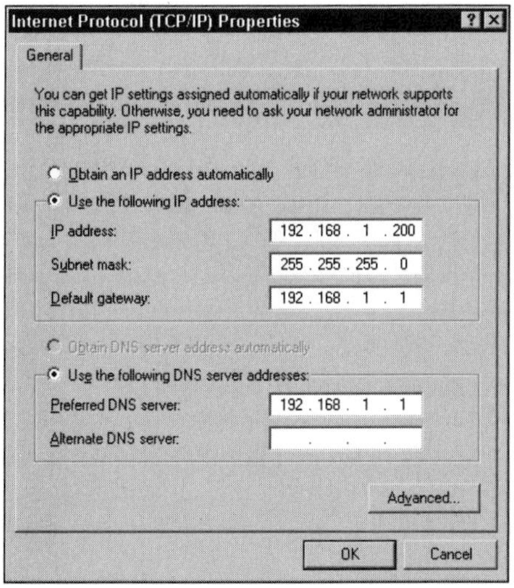

Figure 16-7:
The Internet
Protocol
(TCP/IP)
Properties
dialog box.

4. **Enter the internal IP address of your ISA Server computer in the Default Gateway field of the Internet Protocol (TCP/IP) Properties dialog box.**

5. **Click OK twice and then close the Network and Dial-Up Connections window.**

Configuring the default gateway on computers using other operating systems is similar to the configuration of a Windows 2000 computer. Generally, you can find information on how to do this in an online help system that is included with your computer.

After a computer is configured as a SecureNAT client, ISA Server intercepts all IP traffic from the client to the Internet as it arrives at ISA Server. The client is not even aware of the presence of a firewall.

Firewall Client

If your computer is running at least a moderately recent version of Windows (Windows 95 OSR2, 98, Me, NT, 2000, XP, or Windows Server 2003), you can install Firewall Client software on your computer. The Firewall Client intercepts all Winsock (Windows Sockets) requests from applications that use TCP/IP and forwards them to ISA Server over a connection that it previously established with the ISA Server computer. This includes all network traffic that uses the TCP and UDP protocols and that is not addressed to the local network, which comprises the vast majority of Internet traffic. Installing the Firewall Client gives you several advantages over configuring your computer as a SecureNAT client:

- **User authentication:** Before the Firewall Client sends any data, it establishes a session with ISA Server. Part of this session involves authentication, which means that ISA Server knows which user is sending the data that follows. Therefore, you can then use user-based rules, confident in the knowledge that ISA Server knows how to apply them. For example, you can set up a rule that allows only the CEO of your company to access a sports site. ISA Server and the Firewall Client work together to determine whether a request for this site is indeed coming from the CEO.

- **Support for complex protocols:** Some network protocols require more than one connection to perform an action. ISA Server supports some of these multiconnection protocols for all clients. However, because the Firewall Client can communicate with ISA Server about how different connections fit together, Firewall Clients can use almost any protocol that uses more than one connection.

Before you can use the Firewall Client on a computer, you have to install it from a shared directory that ISA Server creates. You can't install the Firewall Client directly from the CD because the installation uses configuration information from your ISA Server computer. To install the Firewall Client, perform the following steps:

1. **On the client computer's desktop, click the Start button, and then choose Run from the menu that appears.**

   The Run dialog box appears.

2. **In the Open box, type** _server_\mspclnt\setup.exe **(where _server_ is the name of the ISA Server computer), and then click OK.**

   The Microsoft Firewall Client Install Wizard appears.

3. **In the Install Wizard, click Next twice, and then click Install.**

   The Firewall Client software is installed.

4. **Click Finish.**

   That's it. Don't you wish every software installation were that easy?

Now that the Firewall Client is installed, you can access the Internet through ISA Server. You may notice an icon in the system tray on your desktop. You can right-click this icon to disable the Firewall Client (if you ever need to) or to request updated configuration information from ISA Server.

Don't install the Firewall Client on the ISA Server computer itself. Doing so prevents ISA Server from functioning correctly. If you need to access the Internet from the ISA Server computer, use the Web Proxy Client or configure packet filters.

Web proxy client

The remaining client type is the Web proxy client, which can retrieve only Web objects. These are objects that are accessed from your Web browser by using the HTTP or FTP protocols. You can configure most Web browsers, such as Netscape Navigator and Microsoft Internet Explorer, as Web proxy clients. Also, some other applications, such as MSN Messenger, can function as Web proxy clients. A Web proxy client gives you the best possible performance for retrieving objects from the Web, and it's smart enough to get configuration information from ISA Server so that it can always communicate with ISA Server most efficiently. The configuration of your Web proxy clients depends on the browser or other Web applications that you use. The following steps tell you how to configure Microsoft Internet Explorer as a Web proxy client:

1. **In Internet Explorer, choose Tools⇨Internet Options from the main menu.**

   The Internet Options dialog box appears.

2. **Click the Connections tab, and then click the LAN Settings button.**

   The Local Area Network (LAN) Settings dialog box appears, shown in Figure 16-8.

3. **In the Local Area Network (LAN) Settings dialog box, check the Use A Proxy Server check box, type the name of your ISA Server computer in the Address box, and then type** 8080 **in the Port box.**

4. **For the best performance when accessing Web sites on your internal network, check the Bypass Proxy Server for Local Addresses check box and then click OK twice.**

After you configure your Web browser to use ISA Server as a proxy server, it forwards all requests for Web objects to ISA Server instead of trying to retrieve them directly.

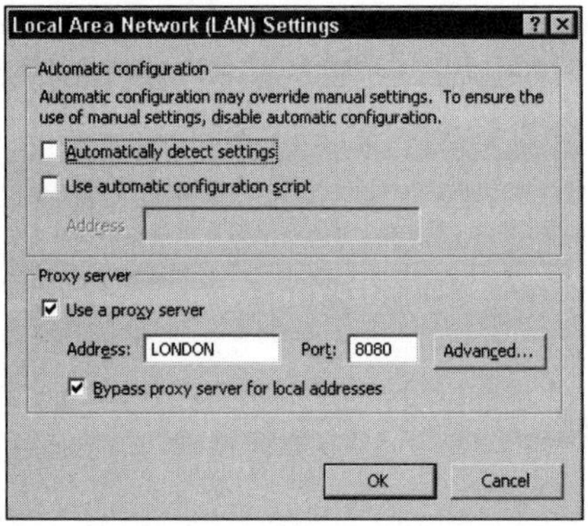

Figure 16-8:
The LAN
Settings
dialog box in
Internet
Explorer.

Local Area Network (LAN) Settings

Automatic configuration

Automatic configuration may override manual settings. To ensure the use of manual settings, disable automatic configuration.

☐ Automatically detect settings

☐ Use automatic configuration script

Address

Proxy server

☑ Use a proxy server

Address: LONDON   Port: 8080   Advanced...

☑ Bypass proxy server for local addresses

OK   Cancel

You can configure the Web browser on the computer running ISA Server as a Web proxy client, which enables the browser to access the Internet. If you do end up wanting to configure the browser on the ISA Server computer as a Web proxy client, make sure that you configure the proxy settings to point to the internal IP address of your ISA Server computer.

The best client for you

So far, you've had a chance to see what each client can do. Now you're probably wondering which one to use. The answer depends on your Internet access needs. And, for the best possible performance, you may want to use two or three of the clients on your computer at the same time. You can use Table 16-1 to make a decision about which clients to use:

Table 16-1	Client Installation Decisions
If . . .	**Then . . .**
You allow the use of protocols other than TCP and UDP between your network and the Internet.	Configure a SecureNAT client.
You are running an operating system that doesn't support the Firewall Client.	Configure a SecureNAT client or a Web proxy client.
You want to use TCP/IP-based applications in addition to a Web browser.	Configure a SecureNAT client or install the Firewall Client.
You want the best possible performance for Web access.	Configure a Web proxy client.
You want to control Internet access based on the identity of a user.	Configure a Web proxy client or install the Firewall Client.
You want the best of all worlds.	Configure a SecureNAT client as well as a Web proxy client, and then install the Firewall Client.

As you can see, the decision about which clients to use depends on a number of factors. Fortunately, if you use all the clients that your computer supports, you'll be sure to get the best possible performance and the widest support for applications. When you use your Web browser, the Web proxy client is used. When you use any other TCP/IP-based application, the Firewall Client is used, unless you use protocols other than TCP and UDP. In this case, the SecureNAT client takes over. So, if you're not sure, simply install the Firewall Client, and configure the computer to act as a Web proxy client and SecureNAT client, too.

Following the Rules: The Two Types

If you try accessing the Internet after you install ISA Server, you may discover that ISA Server blocks all requests. Before you can access the Internet, you need to configure rules that allow users Internet access. ISA Server uses two types of rules:

✔ **Protocol rules:** Protocol rules allow or deny Internet access for internal users based on the protocol they use. For example, you can set up a rule that allows Internet access using the HTTP protocol but doesn't allow access using any other protocol.

✔ **Site and content rules:** Site and content rules allow or deny Internet access for internal users based on the Internet site that they are accessing. For example, you can set up a rule that denies access to a Web site that users should not access during work hours. You can also create a site and content rule that prevents users from downloading program files.

Putting the two types together

To access anything on the Internet, a protocol rule and a site and content rule that allow access must exist. For example, if a user wants to access www. dummies.com, a protocol rule that allows access by using the HTTP protocol and a site and content rule that allows access to the www.dummies.com site must exist. Also, no protocol rule or site and content rule that denies access can apply. For example, if you configure a protocol rule that allows all users to use the HTTP protocol and another protocol rule that denies a particular user, such as the mail clerk, use of the same protocol, then he or she can't access Web sites.

Rules should implement the Security policy of your organization. Before you configure any rules, spend some time planning how this Security policy translates into specific rules. When you have the list of rules, make sure that all the decision-makers in your company agree with it. For example, you don't want the CEO to find out by surprise that she can no longer access her favorite Web site — and you certainly want her to back you up if other people in your company start complaining about being locked out of this or that.

The first step is to decide whether you want to allow all access unless denied, or whether you want to deny all access unless allowed. ISA Server assumes that most organizations want to allow access to all sites and then create exceptions to this rule, which is why ISA Server comes with a preconfigured site and content rule that allows access to all sites. However, ISA Server has no preconfigured protocol rule because most organizations want to allow only certain protocols and not allow any others.

To create a rule, you may need *policy elements*. Policy elements are the building blocks of rules. For example, if you want to create a rule that allows Internet access only during the lunch hour, you have to create a schedule policy element that defines your organization's lunch hour. Similarly, if you want to create a rule that denies access to a specific Web site, you have to create a destination set that defines the address of the Web site. ISA Server also contains some built-in policy elements. For the simple protocol rule that we are creating in this chapter, you don't need to configure additional policy elements, but remember that for more involved rules, you may have to create the required building blocks first. You can find out more about policy elements from ISA Server Help.

Creating a protocol rule

Suppose that you want to give all users access to all Web sites during all hours of the day. To do this, you have to create a protocol rule that allows Internet access using the HTTP protocol. The following steps show you how to do this:

1. **Open ISA Management from the Microsoft ISA Server menu.**

   The ISA Management window opens.

2. **In the Console Tree (the left pane), expand Server and Arrays, expand your server, expand Access policy, and click Protocol Rules.**

   The Details pane (the right pane) shows that no protocol rules are defined. Several buttons allow you to perform common actions.

3. **In the Details pane, click Create a Protocol Rule.**

   The New Protocol Rule Wizard appears.

4. **In the Protocol Rule name box, type the name of the protocol; for example, Allow all HTTP, and click Next.**

5. **On the Rule Action page, ensure that Allow is selected, and click Next.**

6. **On the Protocols page, check the Selected Protocols check box.**

   The wizard displays a list of all built-in protocol definitions.

7. **Scroll down until you find HTTP. Check the check box next to HTTP and then click Next three times to allow this type of access during all hours and for requests from all computers and all users.**

   The summary page appears, confirming your choices (see Figure 16-9).

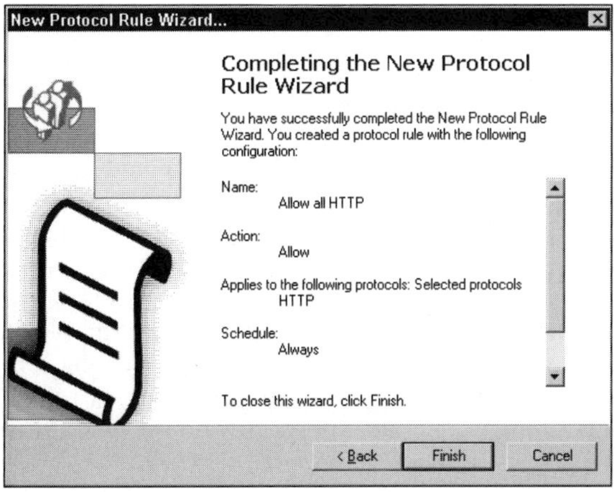

Figure 16-9:
The New
Protocol
Rule Wizard
summary
page.

New Protocol Rule Wizard...

Completing the New Protocol
Rule Wizard

You have successfully completed the New Protocol Rule
Wizard. You created a protocol rule with the following
configuration:

Name:
        Allow all HTTP

Action:
        Allow

Applies to the following protocols: Selected protocols
        HTTP

Schedule:
        Always

To close this wizard, click Finish.

< Back   Finish   Cancel

8. Review your selections and click Finish to create the rule.

The rule now appears in the list of protocol rules in the Details pane (see Figure 16-10). Because ISA Server by default includes a site and content rule that allows access to all sites, you can now test your rule by accessing any Web page from a browser on a client computer. This can be a Web proxy client, a firewall client, or a SecureNAT client.

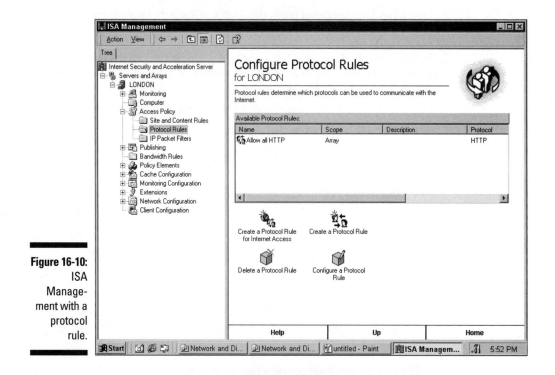

Figure 16-10:
ISA Management with a protocol rule.

Letting the Good Guys In

After you have created all your protocol rules and site and content rules, internal users can access the Internet. At the same time, ISA Server keeps the bad guys out. In fact, it prevents anyone from accessing your internal network from the Internet. ISA Server keeps the good guys as well as the bad guys out. However, you may have good reasons to grant some users access to selected servers on your internal network from the Internet. For example, you may want to allow customers to have access to an internal Web server. You can allow such access by using Web publishing rules and server publishing rules. You create Web publishing rules for requests to Web servers and server publishing rules to give access to all other types of servers.

Publishing a Web server

Web publishing rules redirect requests from external computers and users to servers on your internal network. Users on the Internet may think that they are connecting directly to your Web site, but what they're really doing is connecting to your ISA Server, which then responds to such user requests and reissues them to your internal Web server. This protects the Web server located in your internal network from possible attacks that could happen if it were directly connected to the Internet. For example, a properly configured ISA Server computer by default protects Web servers against common worms, such as Code Red and Nimda. In addition, ISA Server is the only firewall product that can inspect the content of incoming Secure Sockets Layer (SSL) connections. Finally, when you publish a Web server, ISA Server caches frequently requested Web objects so it can send them to users on the Internet more quickly.

Publishing a Web Server involves three steps:

- **Allow incoming Web requests:** Configure ISA Server to accept incoming Web requests. You only have to do this once and it will be in effect for all Web publishing rules.

- **Create a destination set:** A destination set is a policy element. Remember, policy elements are the building blocks of rules. For incoming Web requests, the destination set defines the address of the Web site that external users are connecting to, such as www.mybigcorporation.com. You don't have to create a destination set for your internal Web site that requests will be forwarded to.

- **Create the Web publishing rule:** In ISA Management, under Publishing, create a Web publishing rule. Specify that all requests to your Web site will be forwarded to an internal Web server.

Web publishing rules let you do a number of additional nifty things, such as redirecting parts of a Web site to different internal servers. Suppose that mybigcorporation.com gets a lot of traffic for its Web site. Web publishing rules allow the company to redirect requests for www.mybigcorporation. com/products to one internal Web server and requests for www.mybig corporation.com/services to another internal server.

Publishing a non-Web server

ISA Server also allows you to publish other types of servers, such as mail servers or DNS servers. Compared to Web publishing rules, you're going to have less flexibility with server publishing rules, but you'll soon discover that server publishing rules are easier to configure than their Web publishing counterparts.

To create a server publishing rule, go to the ISA Management window and choose Publishing⇨Create a Server Publishing Rule. In the New Server Publishing Rule Wizard that appears, specify that all requests to the ISA Server computer that arrive at a specific port are redirected to the same port on an internal server.

When you create a server publishing rule, you also have to make sure that the published server is configured as a SecureNAT client.

ISA Server contains the nifty Mail Server Security Wizard, a little helper that can save you literally hours of work compared to performing the same tasks with other firewalls (see Figure 16-11). You can find the button to start this wizard when you click Publishing in the ISA Server Console Tree. The wizard asks you a few questions about your mail server and — in about a minute — configures everything to either make an internal mail server available to the Internet in a secure manner or allow users limited access to the ISA Server computer if that computer is also configured as a mail server. Anyone who has spent hours configuring another firewall to accomplish the same task will agree that the Mail Server Security Wizard is one of the coolest timesavers that ISA Server has to offer.

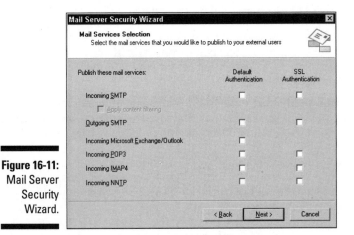

Figure 16-11:
Mail Server
Security
Wizard.

Creating Packet Filters

Like most other firewalls, ISA Server uses packet filters as a method of protecting a network. ISA Server uses the packet filters to make decisions about whether to forward IP packets or drop them. ISA Server uses two types of packet filters:

✔ **Dynamic packet filters:** These are the packet filters that ISA Server creates "on the fly" to implement the rules that you configured. You don't have to worry much about dynamic packet filters. ISA Server creates them whenever necessary to implement a rule and removes them when the network connection has been terminated. You actually never see these packet filters — they operate in the background.

✔ **Static packet filters:** These are the packet filters that you specifically define. Basically, you have to create static packet filters for everything that your ISA Server rules can't handle.

These are the situations that require you to define packet filters:

✔ **Applications and services running on the ISA Server computer:** ISA Server can't be a Firewall Client or a SecureNAT client to itself. You have to define packet filters to allow applications on the ISA Server computer access to the Internet or to allow users on the Internet access to the ISA Server computer. For example, ISA Server comes with a packet filter that allows ISA Server to send DNS queries to the Internet.

✔ **Protocols other than TCP and UDP:** Protocol rules only apply to network traffic that uses the TCP or UDP protocol. Everything else requires that you create a packet filter. For example, ISA Server includes a packet filter that allows you to use the `ping` command, which uses the ICMP protocol.

✔ **Servers in a DMZ:** ISA Server treats both the Internet and the DMZ in a three-pronged DMZ configuration as external networks. Because protocol rules and publishing rules move only network traffic between the internal network and an external network, ISA Server uses routing to move packets between two external networks, and packet filters control which packets are routed. For more information about DMZs, see Chapters 11 and 12.

✔ **Secondary line of defense:** Deny packet filters always override any Allow packet filters. This means that you can create a static packet filter that denies a specific type of network traffic and this filter will block all packets, even if it is allowed by a rule.

To allow ISA Server to forward packets that use protocols other than TCP or UDP, or to forward packets between the Internet and a DMZ, you have to configure ISA Server to perform routing. To do this, open the IP Packet Filters Properties dialog box in ISA Management and select the Enable IP routing check box.

Take a look at what is involved in creating a packet filter. Suppose that you have a Web server in your DMZ and you want to allow external users to access the Web server using the HTTP protocol. The Web server's IP address is 23.10.10.80. Suppose also that you have a mail server in your DMZ and you want to allow SMTP traffic to pass through. The mail server's IP address is 23.10.10.25. Remember to allow SMTP traffic in both directions because your SMTP server may send mail messages as well as receive them. However, you have to allow only incoming traffic to your Web server because the Web server never initiates connections with other servers. To configure these packet filters in ISA Server, the packet filters need to look like those shown in Table 16-2.

Table 16-2		Packet Filters for Servers in DMZ				
Protocol	*Transport Protocol*	*Source IP*	*Source Port*	*Target IP*	*Target Port*	*Action*
HTTP inbound	TCP	Any	Any	23.10.10.80	80	Allow
SMTP inbound	TCP	Any	Any	23.10.10.25	25	Allow
SMTP outbound	TCP	23.10.10.25	Any	Any	25	Allow

To configure these protocol rules, perform the following steps in ISA Management:

1. **In the Console Tree, expand Access Policy, and then click IP Packet Filters.**

   ISA Server displays any packet filters that you have displayed in the Details pane.

2. **In the Details pane, click Create a Packet Filter.**

   The New IP Packet Filter Wizard appears.

3. **Type a name for the packet filter, such as** Allow HTTP traffic to Web server, **and click Next.**

   The Filter Mode page appears.

4. **Ensure that Allow Packet Transmission is selected and then click Next.**

5. **On the Filter Type page, in the drop-down list, select HTTP server (port 80), and then click Next.**

   ISA Server contains predefined filter types for a number of popular protocols. Selecting these instead of creating your own can save you a lot of time.

   The Local Computer page appears.

6. **Click This Computer (on the perimeter network), type** 23.10.10.80, **and then click Next.**

   ISA Server refers to the DMZ as a perimeter network, but it's the same thing.

   The Remote Computers page appears.

7. **Ensure that All Remote Computers is selected, click Next, and then click Finish.**

   Your first packet filter has been created and appears in the Details pane.

8. **Now, create the packet filter for incoming SMTP traffic called Allow SMTP Traffic to Mail Server. Follow the same steps that you performed to create the first filter, but make sure that you specify SMTP as the protocol and that you include the correct IP address for your mail server.**

   After you finish creating the second packet filter, you can create the third one.

9. **In the Details pane, click Create a Packet Filter.**

   The New IP Packet Filter Wizard appears.

10. **Type a name for the packet filter, such as** Allow SMTP Traffic from Mail Server, **and then click Next.**

    The Filter Mode page appears.

11. **Ensure that Allow Packet Transmission is selected, and then click Next.**

12. **On the Filter Type page, click Custom, and then click Next.**

    ISA Server only has a built-in definition for incoming SMTP traffic. For outgoing SMTP traffic, you need to create a custom protocol definition. (Don't worry — this is very easy as long as you know how the protocol in question works.)

13. **In the IP protocol drop-down list, select TCP; under Direction, select Outbound; then change the setting for the Local Port to Dynamic (which includes ports 1024 and above). Under Remote Port, select Fixed Port; in the Port Number box, type** 25.

    After you're done configuring all these settings, click Next. The Local Computer page appears.

14. **Click This Computer (on the perimeter network), type** 23.10.10.25, **and click Next.**

    The Remote Computers page appears.

15. **Ensure that All Remote Computers is selected, click Next, and then click Finish.**

    Your third packet filter has been created and appears in the Details pane.

Congratulations! All packet filters to make your servers in the DMZ available are in place. Obviously, for a more complicated network, you have to create a number of additional packet filters, but ISA Server makes this about as easy as it gets.

Designing Your Network with ISA Server

Before finishing the overview of ISA Server, take a look at how ISA Server can fit into three different network designs. For each of these network designs, look at what's required to make ISA Server work in this environment

A simple network

A simple network is shown in Figure 16-12. ISA Server connects the internal network to the Internet. As you can see, there is no separate DMZ, but the internal network contains a Web server and a mail server.

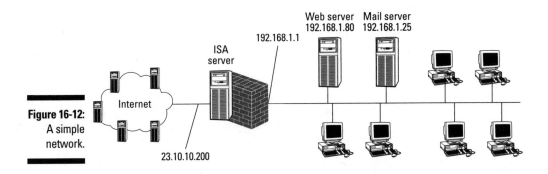

Figure 16-12: A simple network.

Take a look at what's required to configure ISA Server to support this network:

- ✔ **LAT:** The LAT has to contain all internal IP addresses; in this case, 192.168.1.0 through 192.168.1.255.

- ✔ **Protocol rules and site and content rules:** You have to configure these rules to allow client computers access to the Internet. Also, if your mail server needs to send e-mail to the Internet, you may have to configure a protocol rule and a site and content rule just for that.

- ✔ **Web publishing rules:** You have to configure a Web publishing rule to make the Web server available to users on the Internet.

✔ **Server publishing rules:** You have to configure a server publishing rule to make the mail server available to users on the Internet.

✔ **Packet filters:** You have to configure packet filters only if you want to allow programs or services on the ISA Server computer to communicate with the Internet or if you want protocols other than TCP and UDP to be forwarded by ISA Server.

A network with a three-pronged DMZ

To make the network a little more involved, we add a DMZ that is connected directly to the ISA Server computer. This design is shown in Figure 16-13. Notice that, unlike the internal network, the DMZ contains IP addresses that are valid on the Internet.

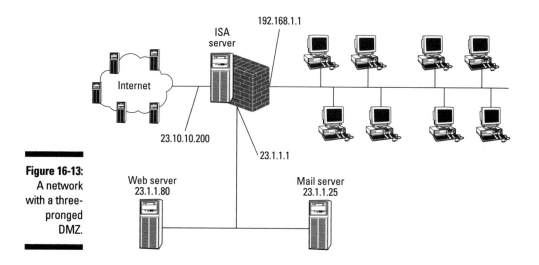

Figure 16-13:
A network with a three-pronged DMZ.

Take a look at what's required to configure ISA Server to support this network:

✔ **LAT:** The LAT has to contain all internal IP addresses, in this case 192.168.1.0 through 192.168.1.255. Make sure that the LAT does not contain any IP addresses in the DMZ.

✔ **Protocol rules and site and content rules:** You have to configure these rules to allow client computers access to the Internet.

✔ **Web publishing rules:** You don't configure any Web publishing rules because your internal network doesn't contain a Web server that you want to make available to users on the Internet.

✔ **Server publishing rules:** You don't configure any server publishing rules because your internal network doesn't contain a server that you want to make available to users on the Internet.

✔ **Packet filters:** First, you need packet filters that allow Web traffic to reach the mail server and the Web server in the DMZ. For the mail server, you have to configure packet filters both for incoming and outgoing SMTP traffic. For the Web server, you have to create a packet filter that allows incoming HTTP traffic. You also have to configure packet filters if you want to allow programs or services on the ISA Server computer to communicate with the Internet or if you want protocols other than TCP and UDP to be forwarded by ISA Server.

A network with a back-to-back DMZ

Configuring a network with a three-pronged DMZ design wasn't too bad, either, so we make this just a little more complex. To provide the best level of protection for your network, configure a back-to-back firewall design, which is shown in Figure 16-14. Notice that this design contains two separate ISA Server computers. ISA Server 1 connects the DMZ to the Internet, and ISA Server 2 connects that internal network to the DMZ. The DMZ is an internal network to ISA Server 1, but an external network to ISA Server 2. ISA Server 1 allows only traffic between the Internet and the DMZ. ISA Server 2 allows only traffic between the DMZ and your internal network.

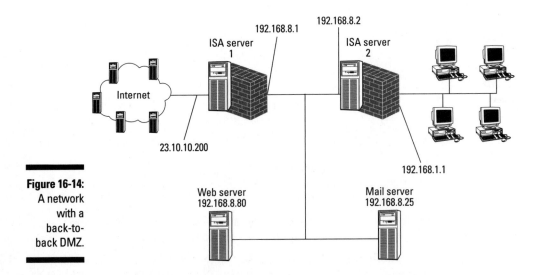

Figure 16-14:
A network with a back-to-back DMZ.

Take a look at what's required to configure ISA Server to support this network:

- ✔ **LAT:** The LAT of ISA Server 2 has to contain all internal IP addresses; in this case, 192.168.1.0 through 192.168.1.255. Make sure that the LAT doesn't contain any IP addresses in the DMZ. The LAT of ISA Server 1 has to contain all IP addresses in the DMZ; in this case, 192.168.8.1 to 192.168.8.255.

- ✔ **Protocol rules and site and content rules:** You have to configure these rules on ISA Server 2 to allow client computers access to the Internet. You also have to configure a rule on ISA Server 1 that allows requests that arrive from ISA Server 2 to be forwarded to the Internet.

- ✔ **Web publishing rules:** You have to configure a Web publishing rule on ISA Server 1 to make the Web server in the DMZ available to users on the Internet.

- ✔ **Server publishing rules:** You have to configure a server publishing rule on ISA Server 1 to make the mail server in the DMZ available to users on the Internet.

- ✔ **Packet filters:** You have to configure packet filters only if you want to allow programs or services on the ISA Server computer to communicate with the Internet or if you want protocols other than TCP and UDP to be forwarded by ISA Server.

- ✔ **Forwarding requests:** You have to configure ISA Server 2 to forward all requests for Internet access to ISA Server 1. You can do this by configuring settings within ISA Server, or you can set the default gateway of ISA Server 2 to the IP address of ISA Server 1 in the DMZ.

Taking the Next Step

If you decide that you will be betting your organization's Internet security on ISA Server, take the time to become more familiar with its features. And, along the way, check out some of the really cool things that it can do, such as the spectacular-looking reports that you can create with ISA Server. You can find more information about this in the online Help files. Even better, take a look at some of the excellent tutorials on the ISA Server Web site (www.isaserver.org). You can read more about this site in Chapter 20.

Chapter 17

The Champ: Check Point FireWall-1 Next Generation

Check Point FireWall-1 is the most widely implemented firewall today. With Check Point FireWall-1 Next Generation (NG), Check Point has developed more than just a firewall. Check Point NG is a suite of applications that provides a comprehensive network security solution to organizations. This chapter looks at the key features and components of FireWall-1 and guides you through installing and configuring FireWall-1 on a Windows 2000 Server.

 Check Point FireWall-1 can also be installed in a UNIX environment. For detailed information on how to install and configure FireWall-1 in a UNIX environment, see the *Check Point: Getting Started Guide* included with your Check Point software.

FireWall-1 Features

The FireWall-1 suite of applications provides an integrated security solution for your organization by providing the following forms of security:

- ✔ Access control
- ✔ Comprehensive logging
- ✔ Attack detection

  ✔ Network Address Translation (NAT)

  ✔ Virtual Private Networking (VPN)

  ✔ Performance enhancement

The following sections detail how the FireWall-1 suite provides these features to your network security solution.

FireWall-1 doesn't require any installation of client software to use all of the features of FireWall-1. The only client software that you may consider installing is the VPN-1 client software, which allows remote clients to use a VPN to connect to the corporate network.

Access control

The main feature of FireWall-1 is its access control features. FireWall-1 provides access control through a combination of stateful inspection and authentication mechanisms. Stateful inspection ensures that only desired protocols can enter and exit the network, and authentication allows restrictions based on the credentials provided by users and computers when connecting to the firewall.

Check Point Software Technologies invented stateful inspection.

Stateful inspection

FireWall-1 provides stateful inspection by placing its inspection module between the Data Link and Network layers of the protocol stack, as shown in Figure 17-1.

The location of the inspection module allows each packet that enters the firewall to be inspected before the packets are passed to the upper layers of the protocol stack. Stateful inspection allows Application layer filters to be applied before the packets reach the Application layer. For example, a filter can prevent the use of the FTP PUT command, which is used to upload data to an FTP server. The inspection module would discard the packet before it ever reached the FTP server application.

Do you have to define all protocols?

FireWall-1 includes definitions for more than 250 applications, services, and protocols that are commonly used by organizations that connect to the Internet. However, FireWall-1 does not forget about advances in technology. A firewall administrator can extend FireWall-1 to include definitions for newly implemented protocols and services so that the firewall can implement the protocols and services in a rules base in the Check Point SmartDashboard.

Stateful inspection also allows the firewall to provide security for stateless protocols — UDP-based applications such as Trivial FTP (TFTP), for example, because the firewall tracks the ports used by a TFTP client and server to ensure that a session has not been hijacked by an attacker.

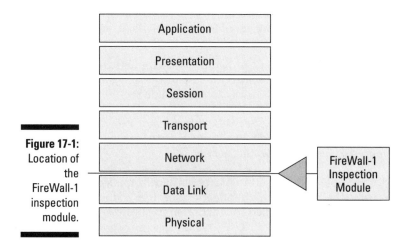

Figure 17-1:
Location of the FireWall-1 inspection module.

Application

Presentation

Session

Transport

Network

Data Link

Physical

FireWall-1 Inspection Module

Authentication

Many organizations require that some protocols be restricted to specific users or computers on the network. FireWall-1 provides this capability by supporting many industry-standard authentication protocols. FireWall-1 can either provide authentication services itself or forward the authentication requests to a back-end authentication service. The support authentication protocols include

- ✔ **Remote Authentication Dial-In User Service (RADIUS):** The FireWall-1 firewall module, which functions as a RADIUS client, forwards all authentication requests to the configured RADIUS server.

- ✔ **Terminal Access Controller Access Control System (TACACS, TACACS+):** Similar to RADIUS, TACACS and TACACS+ authentication forwards the inputted user logon name and password combination to the configured TACACS server. The TACACS server compares the logon name/password combination with its password file. Typically, you see TACACS authentication required only in environments that have older Cisco devices.

- ✔ **Single Key (S/Key):** This authentication scheme protects the firewall from replay attacks or network-sniffing attacks intended to intercept password information transmitted across the network. S/Key passwords consist of several words rather than a single word. The phrase encrypts the password a few times by using a random string and the resulting encrypted data is transmitted to the authentication server. This method ensures that the actual password is not transmitted on the network.

✔ **OS Password:** FireWall-1 integrates into the operating system and forwards all authentication requests to the operating system. Supported operating systems include Windows NT, Windows 2000 and Windows 2003 Active Directory, and Novell NetWare.

✔ **VPN-1 & FireWall-1:** If your network doesn't use a centralized authentication solution, you can use FireWall-1 as your user database. The account and password information configured in the Check Point SmartDashboard can be used to authenticate users.

✔ **SecurID:** The RSA SecurID token provides two-factor authentication by requiring a remote user to provide both a SecurID token and a PIN associated with the SecurID token. SecurID authentication requires that each user be supplied with a SecurID authenticator and a PIN associated with the SecurID authenticator. The SecurID authenticator generates a random numeric code every 60 seconds. This code, along with the associated PIN, is transmitted to the authenticating server.

The support of multiple authentication protocols allows applications to be implemented using their support authentication services, rather than requiring that the applications be modified to function in the firewall-protected environment.

FireWall-1 allows an administrator to monitor and track all authentication attempts in the Log Viewer.

Tracking access: advanced logging, reporting, and alerting

After you set up your firewall, you cannot simply leave it running unattended. You must monitor the firewall to ensure that it is securing the network as it should. FireWall-1 provides the following functionality to the firewall administrator:

✔ **Connection accounting:** FireWall-1 captures detailed log information into the FireWall-1 log. For each connection that is handled by the firewall, FireWall-1 logs information that includes the user, service, connection time, source IP, destination IP, connection duration, and action performed.

✔ **Reporting tools:** Using the Check Point SmartView Monitor, a firewall administrator can generate detailed reports using the collected log file information.

✔ **Active connection viewing:** At times, a firewall administrator must deal with the here and now, rather than what occurred in the past. Real-Time Viewing allows the firewall administrator to view all current connections and, on a connection by connection basis, kill a specific connection. For example, if the firewall administrator catches an employee connecting to a disallowed Web page on the Internet, the firewall administrator can immediately terminate the connection.

✔ **Security alerting:** FireWall-1 integrates into a network's Simple Network Management Protocol (SNMP) solution and uses SNMP traps to alert a network management system when events, such as the firewall being unable to connect to the Internet, are detected. Alternatively, FireWall-1 can be configured to alert a firewall administrator using e-mail notification, paging, or existing help desk systems.

Protection against commonly used attacks

Out of the box, FireWall-1 provides protection against two of the most common attacks performed against networks connected to the Internet: *IP spoofing,* where packets are sent with a rogue source IP address such as an internal network IP address, and *denial-of-service (DoS) attacks,* where hackers attempt to prevent a computer from responding to other valid requests.

FireWall-1 protects against an attacker using IP spoofing by allowing the firewall administrator to clearly define the address ranges used by the private network and any configured demilitarized zones (DMZs). By defining each network segment, the firewall detects if an external attacker is submitting packets that attempt to masquerade as a packet that originated on the trusted network segments. If a packet arrives at the external interface with a source address from the private network, FireWall-1 immediately discards the packet.

FireWall-1 protects against specific denial-of-service attacks by using its SYNDefender feature. This feature protects against DoS attacks by providing early detection of the attack and disconnecting incomplete connection attempts after a short period of time to ensure that system resources are freed to prevent a lockup of the firewall.

Content security

The ability to inspect content ensures that FireWall-1 provides more than just packet filter security. Content inspection enables FireWall-1 to inspect the actual commands that are used within an FTP session. Content inspection can also remove potentially dangerous Java content from a Web page so that it is not downloaded to the employee's Web browser.

In addition, third-party applications can be integrated into the FireWall-1 deployment to provide additional features, such as URL filtering and antivirus protection. URL filtering allows FireWall-1 to prevent access to specific Internet sites based on their URL address. Antivirus protection moves the responsibility for performing antivirus protection from the desktop to the actual point of entry to the network. Deploying antivirus protection at the firewall ensures that virus-infected content is discarded before it enters the network.

Check Point provides interoperability with third-party products that support the Open Platform for Security (OPSEC). OPSEC-compliant devices can be managed by having the FireWall-1-defined Security policy downloaded to the devices. This allows centralized and uniform management of your network's perimeter security solution.

Intrusion detection

The final form of protection against attackers that is provided by FireWall-1 is intrusion detection through Check Point SMARTDefense.

SMARTDefense provides protection against external attacks by tracking potential attacks and providing notification of the attack attempts. SmartDEFENSE provides the following features for detecting potential attacks:

- **Validation of stateless protocols.** Protocols such as User Datagram Protocol (UDP) and Remote Procedure Calls (RPC) do not maintain an active connection. SmartDEFENSE tracks source and destination ports to validate that a session was not hijacked and/or is not attempting an attack through these protocols.

- **Inspection of sequence numbers**. Transmission Control Protocol (TCP) packets use sequence numbers to re-order packets that arrive out of sequence at a destination host. Incorrect sequence numbers can indicate a replay attack taking place against a protected host. SmartDEFENSE can drop these incorrect sequence number packets, or even strip the data component from the packets.

- **Fragmentation inspection.** Many attacks send malformed packets that are incorrectly fragmented in an attempt to bypass or breach the firewall. SmartDEFENSE identifies these packets, logging the attempt and dropping the packets.

- **Malformed packet logs.** SmartDEFENSE performs application level inspection to identify File Transfer Protocol (FTP) and Domain Name System (DNS) malformed packets. Both forms of attack are logged as events in the VPN-1/FireWall-1 log database and the malformed packets are dropped at the external interface. For both protocols, allowed actions may be defined.

✔ **SYNDefender.** This module prevents denial-of-service attacks known as SYN (synchronization) flooding. If a large number of TCP connection initiation packets are received by the server without any further packets, SYNDefender terminates those connections.

✔ **Kernel-level pattern blocking**. This feature detects and blocks any and all attacks against the indexing server that attempt to take over the target server as a launch point for further attacks.

Code Red is an example of this form of attack. By compromising the indexing service, the Code Red attack made the target server a drone that carried out attacks against other servers on the network and the Internet.

Network Address Translation (NAT)

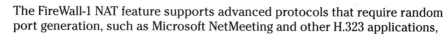

The NAT process replaces RFC 1918 private network addresses with public network IP addresses for outgoing packets and public network IP addresses with private network addresses for incoming packets in FireWall-1. Rather than implement separate NAT and static address mapping functions, FireWall-1 uses the same NAT editor for protecting both inbound and outbound traffic. This simplifies NAT design by using only a single tool to define all address mappings.

The FireWall-1 NAT feature supports advanced protocols that require random port generation, such as Microsoft NetMeeting and other H.323 applications,

For outgoing traffic, FireWall-1 uses dynamic mode to map all internal network addresses to a single external IP address. This hides the private network behind a single outbound address. You can configure this NAT option by editing the properties of an internal network object within the FireWall-1 object database.

Dynamic NAT can only be defined for outbound network traffic. This is, in fact, a security feature because limiting Dynamic NAT in this way protects the network from hacking attempts that attempt to spoof internal IP addresses. FireWall-1 drops any packets that have internal IP addresses as the source address that it receives on its external interface.

For inbound traffic, the firewall administrator defines static mode NAT definitions that will perform a 1:1 mapping between the Internet-accessible IP address and port and the true IP address and port of the Internet-accessible resource. When the firewall receives a connection to the externally accessible resource, the destination information is translated to the true IP address of the network resource.

VPN-1

Virtual Private Networks (VPNs) allow remote users to create a "tunnel" between their remote client computer and a tunnel server at the corporate network. The advantage of using tunneling solutions is that the tunnels leverage an existing public network, such as the Internet, instead of requiring the deployment of a network infrastructure to support high-speed remote access.

Check Point provides VPN access through its VPN-1 line of products. These products include

- ✔ **VPN-1 Gateway:** Provides secure connectivity between corporate networks, remote network partners, and mobile users. The VPN-1 Gateway supports industry standards, including Internet Protocol Security (IPSec) to encrypt the transmitted data.

- ✔ **VPN-1 SecuRemote:** Provides the client-side solution for remote users that require connectivity to the corporate network using dialup, Digital Subscriber Lines (DSL), or cable modem connections. In addition to providing external access to the network, SecuRemote can also support intranet tunneling to protect data that's transmitted on the private network.

- ✔ **VPN-1 SecureClient:** Allows the firewall administrator to enforce security on connecting client computers. SecureClient ensures that remote clients don't become access points to corporate resources by preventing session hijacking. SecureClient ensures that a remote client is properly configured to provide the required level of corporate security.

- ✔ **VPN-1 Accelerator Card:** Provides offloading — moving cryptographic functions from the VPN server's processor to the VPN-1 accelerator card — to increase the performance of a VPN-1 server.

Performance

All network traffic that enters and exits your corporate network will pass through the FireWall-1 server. To ensure that performance is optimal, FireWall-1 includes two products: FloodGate-1 and the ClusterXL module.

- ✔ **FloodGate-1:** Provides FireWall-1 with a Quality of Service (QoS) solution. QoS prioritizes specific network traffic and provides more bandwidth to these preferred data streams. An organization can first analyze the current incoming and outgoing traffic and then use FloodGate-1 to ensure that the mission-critical applications don't suffer performance losses due to non-critical applications overusing available bandwidth. QoS is like a reservation system. A specific percentage of available bandwidth is reserved for a specific application.

In Figure 17-2, two FireWall-1 servers are configured as a cluster with each node in the cluster sharing a common external IP address (represented by the letter *A* in Figure 17-2). Incoming connections can connect to either member of the cluster. If one of the FireWall-1 servers fails, all connections are automatically redirected to the other FireWall-1 server in the defined cluster.

✔ **ClusterXL module:** Allows FireWall-1 and VPN-1 to be deployed in a fault-tolerant configuration for high availability, as shown in Figure 17-2.

Not only must the external adapters share a common IP address, but the external adapters must also have the same MAC address so that routing is not affected if one FireWall-1 server fails and data is redirected to the other node in the cluster.

The firewalls participating in the ClusterXL cluster must also have internal network interfaces that share an IP address and MAC address. This allows outbound traffic to *failover* to another node in the cluster by using a common default gateway address. Failover is the process of automatically connecting to the other server in a cluster, without the connecting clients having to do anything. The firewalls should have unique IP addresses to ensure that management of the individual servers can take place.

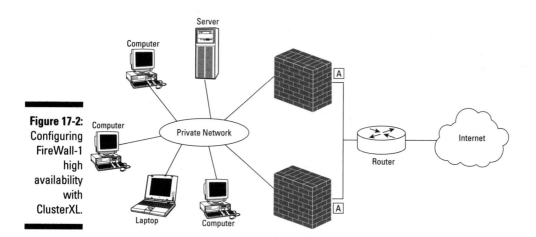

Figure 17-2: Configuring FireWall-1 high availability with ClusterXL.

FireWall-1 Components

FireWall-1 can be deployed in either a standalone or enterprise environment because it is composed of three separate components, which can be loaded on one server (a standalone environment) or on many servers (an enterprise environment):

- ✔ SMART client
- ✔ SmartCenter server
- ✔ VPN/FireWall module

The SMART client graphical user interface (GUI) enables the FireWall-1 administrator to define the Security policy that will be implemented by an organization. The SMART client can execute at the actual firewall or at a standalone administrative console.

The SMART client can be installed on a non-server class computer. The SMART client has been successfully deployed on Windows 2000 Professional or Windows XP Professional desktop computers to manage Check Point FireWall-1 deployments.

The SmartCenter server functions as the storage location for all defined Security policies. When a firewall administrator defines Security policy using the SMART client, the Security policies are saved to the defined SmartCenter server. The SmartCenter server also serves as the storage location for network object definitions, user object definitions, log files, and FireWall-1 database files.

Finally, the VPN/FireWall module can be deployed on numerous devices that are FireWall-1-aware. This includes UNIX servers, Windows 2000 Server, switches, routers, and network appliances. The Security policies defined at the SmartCenter server by the SMART client are downloaded to the network device hosting the FireWall module.

Standalone deployments

Smaller organizations or organizations with a single connection to the Internet may prefer to implement FireWall-1 in a standalone deployment. In a standalone environment, the SMART client, the SmartCenter server and the FireWall module all reside on the same physical device, as shown in Figure 17-3, rather than on separate computers in the network.

The advantage of using this configuration is that the cost of the firewall solution is minimized because only a single FireWall-1 license is required. The disadvantage is that if the firewall is compromised, an attacker will also have access to the SmartCenter server component. With the information stored on the SmartCenter server, especially the definition of network objects, an attacker will be able to fully determine the interior structure of the network protected by the firewall.

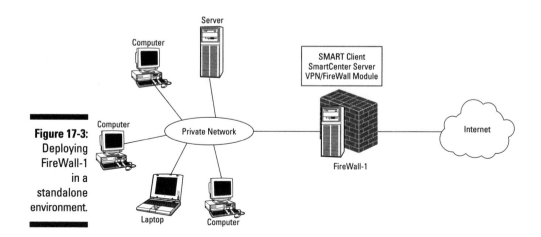

Figure 17-3:
Deploying
FireWall-1
in a
standalone
environment.

Client/Server deployment

A more secure deployment of FireWall-1 is to deploy FireWall-1 in a
client/server configuration, as shown in Figure 17-4.

In this figure, the SMART client connects to the SmartCenter server (Action
1) to define Security policy and network objects. The SmartCenter server can
then download the Security policy to the VPN/FireWall module installed on
the perimeter server (Action 2).

The advantage of this configuration is that the SmartCenter server can store
Security policy for multiple FireWall modules. Likewise, the SMART client can
be used to connect to multiple SmartCenter servers for configuration of
Security policies.

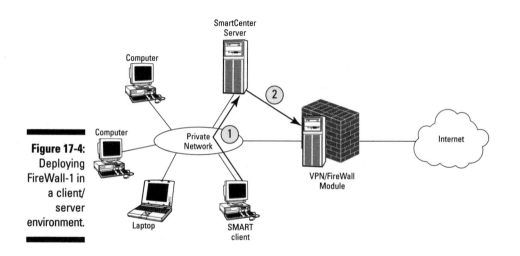

Figure 17-4:
Deploying
FireWall-1 in
a client/
server
environment.

FireWall-1 Next Generation Installation

The installation of FireWall-1 involves both the installation of the FireWall-1 software and the configuration of the FireWall-1 software after the necessary files are copied to the local computer's hard drive.

Installing and Configuring FireWall-1 NG

To install the FireWall-1 NG files, do the following:

1. **Determine whether your systems meet the minimum hardware requirements for the FireWall-1 SMART client, as shown in Table 17-1, and for the FireWall-1 SmartCenter server and FireWall module, as shown in Table 17-2.**

Table 17-1	Minimum Hardware for FireWall-1 SMART Client
Component	*Minimum Requirement*
Operating system	Windows 9x, Windows Me, Windows NT 4., Windows 2000, Sun Solaris SPARC
Required disk space	40MB
Memory	32MB
Network interface	Must be on Operating Systems Hardware Compatibility List (HCL)

Table 17-2	Minimum Hardware for FireWall-1 SmartCenter Server and FireWall Module
Component	*Minimum Requirement*
Operating system	Windows 2000 (SP1 and SP2), Windows NT 4.0 SP6a, Sun Solaris 7 (32-bit mode only), Sun Solaris 8 (32- or 64-bit mode), Redhat Linux 6.2, 7.0, and 7.2
Required disk space	40MB
Memory	128MB or higher
Network interface	An ATM, Ethernet, Fast Ethernet, Gigabit Ethernet, FDDI, or Token Ring adapter on the Operating System's Hardware Compatibility List (HCL)

2. Insert the Check Point Enterprise Suite CD-ROM in the CD-ROM drive of the computer.

3. On the Welcome to NG Feature Pack 3 screen, click Next.

4. On the License Agreement page, click Yes.

5. On the Product Menu page, click Server/Gateway Components, and then click Next.

6. On the Server/Gateway Components page (see Figure 17-5), check theVPN-1 & FireWall-1, SMART Clients, and Policy Server boxes on the left and then click Next.

7. On the Information page, ensure that you have selected the VPN-1& FireWall-1, SMART Clients, and Policy Server boxes, and then click Next.

8. On the VPN-1 & FireWall-1 Enterprise Product page, check the Enforcement Module and SmartCenter Server (including Log Server) boxes, and then click Next.

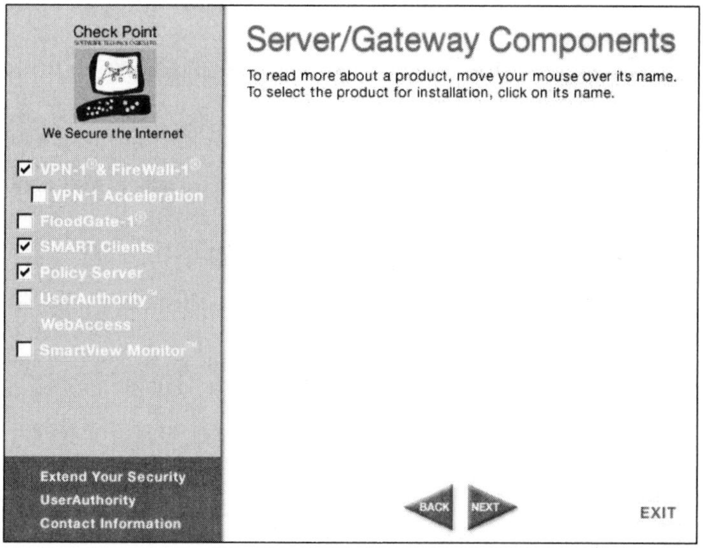

Figure 17-5:
Selecting the setup type.

9. On the VPN-1 & FireWall-1 Enterprise Management page, click Enterprise Primary Management, and then click Next.

10. On the Backward Compatibility page, click Install Without Backward Compatibility and then click Next.

Backward compatibility allows management of older versions of Firewall-1. If you plan to manage any VPN-1/Firewall 4.1 enforcement modules, make sure that you do install with backward compatibility; otherwise, who knows what security will be implemented on those stations?

11. **On the Choose Destination Location page, accept the default destination directory and then click Next.**

Selecting a directory other than the default directory will require you to modify the FWDIR environment variable. Failure to do so will reduce the ability to debug firewall issues with the FWInfo debugging tool included with FireWall-1 NG.

This starts the actual copying of the software to your computer's hard drive.

12. **In the Information dialog box, click OK.**

You now have a nicely installed FireWall-1.

At this point, the installation of the feature pack is complete. The firewall is not ready for use, however, until you install the necessary SMART clients, as described in the following step list:

1. **On the Choose Destination Location, accept the default destination folder, and then click Next.**

2. **On the Select Clients page, enable all options, and then click Next.**

3. **In the Information dialog box, click OK to confirm the completion of Setup.**

4. **On the Licenses page, click Fetch from File.**

You must obtain a license key from the User Center at the Check Point Web site (www.checkpoint.com/usercenter). You obtain the license key after you input the certificate key included with your FireWall-1 NG software. Failure to input a valid license key will result in your installation of FireWall-1 being unusable.

5. **In the Open dialog box, select the CPLicenseFile.lic file provided from Check Point, and then click Open.**

6. **In the cpconfig dialog box, click OK to confirm the installation of the license file.**

7. **On the Licenses page, click Next.**

8. **On the Administrators page, click Add.**

9. **In the Add Administrator dialog box (see Figure 17-6), enter an Administrator name and password, designate the permissions assigned to the Administrator, and then click OK.**

You can designate any number of administrators for FireWall-1, and even delegate specific customized permissions. But always make sure that your account can manage the other Administrators. It shows them who's the boss!

10. **On the Administrators page, click Next.**

11. **On the Management Clients page (see Figure 17-7), add any remote workstation names where remote management is approved for the firewall, and then click Next.**

12. **On the Key Hit Session page, type random characters until you hear a beep, and then click Next.**

    These random characters are used as the source for generating a private and public key pair for the firewall's digital certificate.

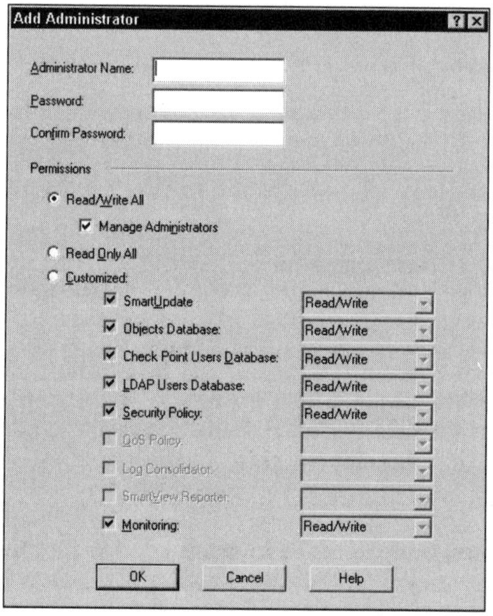

Figure 17-6:
Adding
Admini-
strators.

If your child aspires to be a computer hacker, this is his or her opportunity to aid in the installation of your firewall!

13. **On the Certificate Authority page, click Initialize and Start Certificate Authority.**

14. **In the cpconfig dialog box, click OK to confirm the initialization.**

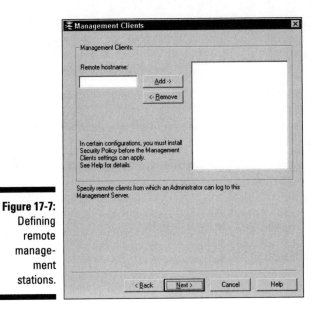

Figure 17-7:
Defining
remote
manage-
ment
stations.

15. **In the cpconfig dialog box, click OK again to confirm the trial period expiration date.**

16. **On the Certificate Authority page (see Figure 17-8), ensure that the Management FQDN is in the form of a DNS name, and then click Send to CA.**

Ensure that your Management station hostname is a fully qualified domain name (FQDN) — not just the NetBIOS computer name — before you click Send to CA. Using a NETBIOS name can result in name resolution problems in a multiple-segment network.

17. **In the cpconfig dialog box, click OK to validate the hostname.**

18. **In the cpconfig dialog box, click OK to acknowledge that the FQDN was successfully sent to the Certificate Authority.**

19. **On the Certificate Authority page, click Next.**

20. **On the Fingerprint page, click Export to File.**

Although the words in the fingerprint may seem meaningless, this fingerprint will help a remote user verify that the FireWall-1 SmartCenter server that the user connects to is not an imposter. By verifying that the fingerprint matches, an administrator is assured that the user is connecting to the actual SmartCenter server.

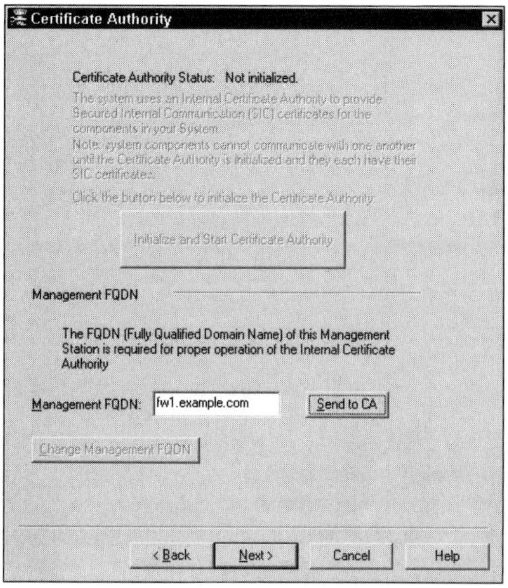

Figure 17-8:
Defining the management station FQDN.

21. **In the Save As dialog box, choose a file location and file name for the fingerprint file, and then click Save.**

22. **On the Fingerprint page, click Finish.**

23. **In the cpconfig message box, click OK to verify that the initial policy is applied to the firewall.**

24. **In the Information message box, click OK.**

25. **On the Setup Complete page, click Yes, I Want to Restart My Computer Now and then click Finish.**

26. **In the Information dialog box, click OK.**

    This completes the installation of the SMART Client, allowing you to start configuration of the Firewall-1 NG firewall.

FireWall-1 NG Configuration Tasks

The following section provides you with step-by-step configuration steps for typical tasks performed by a FireWall-1 administrator.

Starting the SmartDashboard client

The SmartDashboard client is used to define firewall rules and to load the rules to a FW-1 device.

1. **Choose Start⇨Programs⇨Check Point Smart Clients⇨SmartDashboard NG FP3.**

2. **In the Check Point SmartDashboard authentication screen (see Figure 17-9), enter the following information and then click OK.**

   User Name: An administrator user account

   Password: The password of the administrator account

   SmartCenter Server: The name of the FireWall-1 SmartCenter server

3. **In the Check Point SmartDashboard Fingerprint verification screen verify the displayed fingerprint against the fingerprint recorded during setup. If they match, then click Approve.**

4. **The Check Point SmartDashboard — Standard window opens with an empty rule base, as shown in Figure 17-10.**

Figure 17-9:
Starting the SmartDash-board client.

The SmartDashboard client window is divided into four panes. On the left-most pane is the object browser. This pane can be changed to view network objects, services, resources, OPSEC applications, servers, users, time objects, virtual links, and VPN communities. Whatever objects you view, the details will be shown in the middle pane on the right side of the window. The top pane displays the configured security rules and the bottom pane shows a Smartmap — a graphical representation of the Firewall-1 objects on the network.

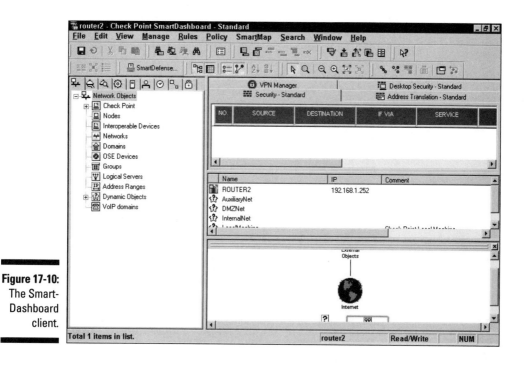

Figure 17-10:
The Smart-
Dashboard
client.

Defining a computer object

Each computer that requires either internal or external access definitions must be defined as a computer object in the FireWall-1 database of information. Typically, these are the computers located in the DMZ, a screened network typically located at the perimeter of your organization's network:

1. **In the Check Point SmartDashboard console, choose Manage⇨Network Objects.**

2. **In the Network Objects dialog box, click New, point to Node, and then click Host.**

3. **In the Host Node dialog box (see Figure 17-11), click General Properties in the navigational tree on the left and then enter the following information:**

    Name: The hostname of the network object

    IP address: The IP address of the network object

    Comment: A comment describing the role of the network object

    Color: Select a color for graphical representation

4. **In the Host Node dialog box, click OK.**

5. **In the Network Objects dialog box, click Close.**

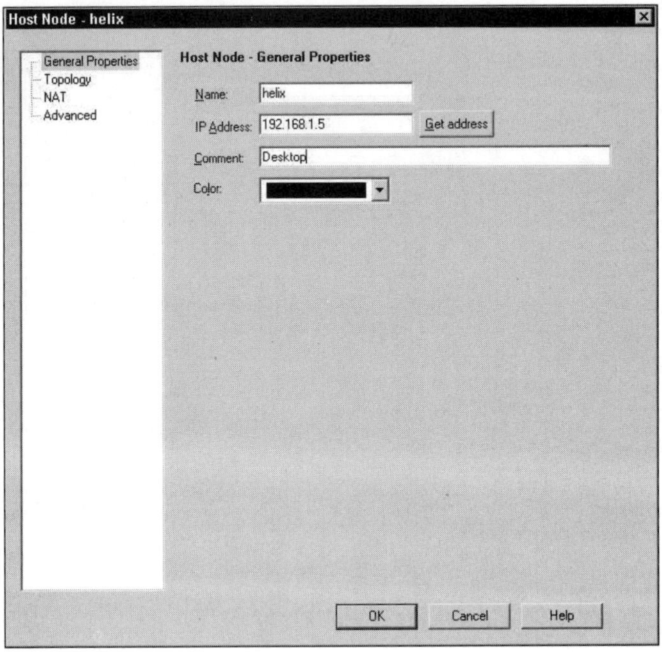

Figure 17-11:
Creating a
new host.

Defining a firewall object

A firewall object requires additional configuration over a standard workstation. As with a typical network host, the first step in defining a firewall is defining the general properties of the firewall.

1. **In the Check Point SmartDashboard console, choose Manage⇨Network Objects.**

2. **In the Network Objects dialog box, click New, point to Check Point, and then click Gateway.**

3. **In the Check Point Gateway dialog box, click General Properties in the navigational tree on the left and then enter the following information:**

    Name: The hostname of the network object

    IP address: The IP address of the firewall used on the demilitarized zone (DMZ) or private network

    Comment: A comment describing the role of the network object

Check Point products: FireWall-1, VPN-1 Pro, or VPN-1 Net, or other Check Point products

Version: NG Feature Pack 3

After the general properties are defined, the additional network interfaces of the firewall must be defined.

4. **In the Check Point Gateway dialog box, click Topology in the navigational tree on the left.**

5. **On the Topology page, click Add.**

6. **In the Interface Properties dialog box, enter the following information on the General tab:**

    Name: A logical name for the interface

    IP Address: The IP address for the network interface

    Net Mask: The subnet mask for the network interface

7. **In the Interface Properties dialog box, enter the following information on the Topology tab:**

    External or Internal: Defines whether the network interface is connected to the public network or the private network.

    IP Addresses Behind this Interface: Defines the expected IP addresses set to initiate traffic to this interface.

    For the external interface, you typically define valid addresses as Not Defined, whereas other interfaces use Network Defined by the Interface IP and Net Mask as the IP Addresses Behind This Interface setting.

    Anti-Spoofing: Select from None, Logs, or Alerts

8. **Click OK.**

9. **Repeat the process for all other network interfaces installed on the firewall.**

If authenticated access is required for specific firewall rules, complete the following procedure:

1. **In the Check Point Gateway dialog box, click Authentication.**

2. **On the Authentication page, indicate which authentication protocols are supported by the firewall.**

    You can select from S/Key, SecurID, OS Password, VPN-1 & FireWall-1 Password, RADIUS, or TACACS.

Defining a network segment

Each subnet that exists on the private network, and in the DMZ, must be defined as a network segment for firewall rules.

1. **In the Check Point SmartDashboard console, choose Manage➪Network Objects.**

2. **In the Network Objects dialog box, click New, point to Check Point, and then click Network.**

3. **In the Network Properties dialog box, click General Properties in the navigational tree on the left and then enter the following information:**

    Name: The logical name of the network

    Network Address: The IP subnet address used by the network segment

    Net Mask: The subnet mask used to identify the network segment

    Comment: A further description of the network

    Color: A color used in graphical representations of the network

    Broadcast address: Designates whether the broadcast address is considered part of the network segment

4. **In the Network Properties dialog box, select the NAT tab.**

5. **On the NAT tab, enable the Add Automatic Address Translation rules check box and then enter the following information:**

    Translation Method: Set the value to Hide so that all traffic within the network's source address is translated to the Hiding IP Address.

    Hiding IP Address: The IP address used to hide the true IP addresses of this network can be set to the Gateway interface's IP address or to a designated IP address.

    Install On Gateway: The FireWall-1 devices that the NAT configuration will be installed on.

6. **Click OK.**

Creating a user account

If you want to implement any security rules based on users, rather than computers, you'll have to create user accounts to identify individual users.

1. In the Check Point SmartDashboard console, choose Manage⇨Users and Administrators.

2. In the Users and Administrators dialog box, click New, point to User by Template, and then click Default.

3. In the User Properties window, enter the Login Name for the new user on the General tab.

4. In the User Properties window, define an Expiration date for the user account on the Personal tab.

5. In the User Properties window, enter the authentication method required for the user account on the Authentication tab.

6. Click OK.

Creating a group account

When user accounts are defined, it is more efficient to define security based on groups of users rather than on individual users. After you've defined all your user accounts, they can be collected into group accounts.

1. In the Check Point SmartDashboard console, choose Manage⇨Users and Administrators.

2. In the Users and Administrators dialog box, click New and then click Group.

3. In the Group Properties dialog box, enter the following information:

   Name: The name of the group account

   Comment: A comment describing the user account

   Color: Select the display color for the user account

4. In the Group Properties dialog box, click the user accounts in the Not in Group list that should be members of the new group and then click Add to add the user accounts to the In Group list.

5. Click OK.

Defining a rule base

After all objects are defined for the network, the individual packet filters — also known as *rules* — can be defined in a listing known as a *rule base*.

1. In the Check Point SmartDashboard console, choose Rules⇨Add Rule⇨Top.

2. In the Source column, right-click the Source cell and then click Add.

3. In the Add Object dialog box, select the appropriate network or workstation object that represents the source object and then click OK.

4. In the Destination column, right-click the Destination cell and then click Add.

5. In the Add Object dialog box, select the appropriate network or workstation object that represents the destination object and then click OK.

6. In the If Via column, right-click the If Via cell and then click Add.

7. In the Add Object dialog box, select the appropriate network or VPN community object that represents the destination object and then click OK.

    If you don't implement VPNs, then leave this value as Any.

8. In the Service column, right-click the Service cell, and then click Add.

9. In the Add Object dialog box, select the desired Service from the list of defined Services, and then click OK.

10. In the Action column, right-click the Action cell and then select the desired action for the packet filter.

    You can choose from Accept, Drop, Reject, or various authentication options.

11. In the Track column, right-click the Track cell and then select what tracking options to enable for the rule.

12. In the Install On column, right-click the Install On cell, click Add and then select the FireWall-1 devices that the packet filter are to be installed on.

13. In the Time column, right-click the Time cell and then click Add.

14. In the Add Object dialog box, add or create a *Time object* — an object that defines the time interval that the packet filter will be active — and then click OK.

15. In the Comment column, right-click the Comment cell and then click Edit.

16. In the Comment dialog box, enter a description of the packet filter and then click OK.

17. Repeat the process for each packet filter required.

Installing the Security policy

After the rules base is defined, it must be loaded to the firewall to be enforced.

1. **In the Check Point SmartDashboard console, ensure that you select the correct policy (Security — Standard, VPN Manager, Desktop Security — Standard, or Address Translation — Standard) before you proceed.**

2. **In the Check Point SmartDashboard console, choose Policy⇨Install.**

3. **In the SmartDashboard Warning dialog box, click OK to proceed.** This warning reminds you that you may be affected by implied rules as well as by explicit rules.

4. **In the Install Policy dialog box, select the target server or servers, and then click OK.**

   The Installation Process dialog box appears, showing the progress of the installation.

5. **In the Installation Process — Standard dialog box, click Close when the installation has completed.**

Chapter 18

Choosing a Firewall That Meets Your Needs

*A*fter you define your company's security requirements, you need to choose a brand of firewall. The most common question that we firewall experts hear is, "What firewall do you recommend?" This chapter discusses the criteria that we use for choosing firewall solutions for our customers. Trust us — it is not a simple decision.

How Do You Decide?

The decision on which firewall product to use should not be made by a single person unless the organization is so small that only a single person has any idea what a firewall does. Using a committee to make a group decision is the best solution because it ensures that a single person's preferences won't cloud the decision.

When making the decision, the committee should draft a set of criteria against which to evaluate the available firewall solutions. Furthermore, weights should be assigned to each criterion to make it easier to compare competing products. The committee should rank the products according to which one matches the criteria most important to the organization. For example, you wouldn't choose a product that is three times more expensive than a competing product when your most important criterion is to keep down the price of the firewall.

When drafting the criteria for firewall selection, you must ensure that the criteria support your organization's *Security policy*. A Security policy is a written document that details your organization's attitude toward security. The Security policy will assist you in identifying the features that your organization requires from its firewall solution.

What to Compare?

Several features must be included in your criteria for choosing among different firewalls. When drafting your criteria, consider the following:

- ✔ **ICSA Labs certification status:** ICSA Labs, a division of TruSecure Corporation, performs standards testing for commercially available security products. Testing is provided for firewalls, antivirus solutions, Internet Protocol Security (IPSec) products, and cryptography solutions. A firewall product with an ICSA Labs certification has undergone extensive tests performed by ICSA Labs to ensure that the firewall product meets a number of demanding security standards.

Just because a firewall is certified by ICSA Labs does not mean that it is secure in all cases. Any firewall can be configured so that it is susceptible to an attacker from the Internet. You must implement a secure configuration for an ICSA Labs–certified firewall in order to be truly secure.

- ✔ **Ease of use:** The firewall that you choose must be easy for the firewall administrators to configure. If the interface for the firewall is too complex or not intuitive, the firewall may not be secured to the level required by the organization because the firewall administrator is unable to find the necessary configuration settings. Ease-of-use can also be measured by considering the location from which the firewall can be administered. In some cases, a firewall administrator may be required to configure the firewall from the external network. You must decide whether your firewall must be remotely administered.

- ✔ **Current expertise of administrators:** When choosing a firewall, look at the expertise of your firewall administrators. Choose a product for which you have local expertise in configuration and management in order to reduce training and deployment costs. If you do so, deployment can take place in a far shorter time interval.

- ✔ **Supported platforms:** Some organizations are not comfortable with a firewall solution that runs on top of a full operating system. The firewall administrators feel that the firewall then inherits any security weaknesses of the underlying operating system. Although this is not true in most cases, this concern must be addressed. An organization must define which operating systems that it will support for the firewall.

If your organization wants a firewall that only runs on IBM AIX or on a dedicated firewall appliance, you can easily eliminate any firewalls that run on Windows or Linux.

✔ **Support for multiple zones:** When deciding on a firewall solution, make sure it can support all security zones you need. In addition to an internal network, many organizations use separate networks for resources that are accessible from the Internet — separate networks often referred to as demilitarized zones, or DMZs. DMZ configurations should be designed beforehand. Knowing how you want to deploy your DMZ helps you to eliminate firewall products that don't support your required configuration. For example, some firewall products support only two interfaces. If your DMZ requires three zones using a single firewall, you can easily remove these products from your list of selections.

✔ **Protection against common attacks:** Many different types of attacks are commonly used on the Internet, such as Denial of Service (DoS) attacks and buffer overflow attacks directed against Web servers. A firewall should detect all attacks that your network is susceptible to and implement measures to either block these attacks completely or reduce their effectiveness.

✔ **Intrusion detection:** The ability to detect intrusion attempts goes hand in hand with protection against common attacks. Intrusion detection means that a firewall detects when a hacking attempt occurs and alerts you about what's happening. Some firewalls have excellent intrusion detection capabilities. Others may block attacks but have no method to alert you when an attack takes place. If you are concerned about intrusion detection, make sure that you check which types of attack the firewall detects and what alert mechanism it uses.

Other security certifications

In addition to the ICSA Labs certification, another certification that is becoming more popular in the security world is Common Criteria, or more specifically, the Common Criteria for Information Technology Security Evaluation (CCITSE).

Common Criteria is a security certification supported by the governments of the United States, Canada, Australia, New Zealand, France, Finland, Germany, Greece, Israel, Italy, the Netherlands, Norway, Spain, and the United Kingdom. Common Criteria helps to standardize security definitions. In the United States, Common Criteria now replaces the previous C2 configuration supported in previous years.

The Common Criteria process involves an in-depth security evaluation of the product that tests all aspects of security for a specific hardware and software configuration. To find out more details on CCITSE, visit www.commoncriteria.org/ and csrc.ncsl.nist.gov/cc/.

✔ **Logging options:** The only place to find the details of an attack is in the firewall's logs. When researching firewalls, determine what log formats are supported by the firewall. For example, does the firewall support recording data to a database, or does it store the information in proprietary log file formats? The use of databases opens the door to more analysis products than proprietary log files allow. Another important aspect is the reporting capabilities of the firewall. Can the firewall give you an understandable report on your network traffic, or do you have to read through hundreds of pages of logs to analyze network activity?

✔ **Management options:** Not all firewall management is performed on the internal network or from the actual firewall console. If remote management is required, the tools required to manage the firewall may help you make a decision. For example, a firewall that can be managed by using either a Telnet client or a Web interface enables management from any client on the network without the installation of additional software. If additional software is required, your firewall rules may have to be configured to allow additional ports to be open for the management console.

On the other hand, some people may consider using Telnet or Web clients to manage a firewall a security weakness because anyone can do the management. If specific software is not required, anyone can modify your firewall's configuration if the passwords and security of the firewall don't protect against nonauthorized remote administration.

✔ **Product support options:** Don't fall into a trap of thinking that you simply install the firewall and it works exactly as expected. You may have to contact the software vendor for technical support. Be sure that you research what methods of support are available to you. Does the vendor provide e-mail support, telephone support, or only Web support? Even more importantly, how long will it take to respond to your queries?

An excellent Web site for researching software is groups.google.com. This Web site (formerly www.dejanews.com) enables you to search multiple newsgroups for other users' evaluations of software products. You can also search for solutions to configuration problems that you may be facing with your firewall. Also, some independent sites are dedicated to the support of specific firewall products, such as for Microsoft ISA Server and for Check Point FireWall-1. You can get a good idea of how current users of these products feel about them by perusing such sites.

✔ **Real-time monitoring:** A firewall that provides real-time monitoring allows a firewall administrator to see the exact use of a firewall at any given moment in time. Real-time monitoring also allows a firewall administrator to see exactly what resources are being accessed by each individual connection. It also allows the firewall administrator the ability to terminate a connection immediately, if required.

✔ **Application layer filtering:** A firewall should do more than provide packet filters. Application layer filtering allows the firewall to inspect the actual commands or actions that take place within a protocol. For example, Application layer filtering enables you to configure the firewall to allow only `FTP-GET` commands to an FTP server while preventing `FTP-PUT` commands, or to inspect incoming HTTP traffic for attacks, including the Nimda or Code Red worms. Almost all firewall vendors have begun offering some Application layer filtering. As you evaluate products, ensure that the firewall can inspect the Application layer protocols that your organization uses. For example, if you want to filter instant-messaging traffic, it won't help you if the firewall can inspect e-mail traffic only. Common types of Application layer filtering are for Web content, e-mail content, FTP file transfers, instant-message content, and viruses. Finally, make sure that adding Application layer filters to a firewall does not significantly reduce the firewall's performance.

✔ **Extensibility:** New protocols and services are introduced each year. Your firewall should allow you to define new services and protocols if they don't exist in your services listing. If you can't add new required protocols or services, you must plan for additional upgrade expenses or switch to a different firewall solution later.

✔ **Plug-in availability:** A plug-in integrates with your firewall to provide additional capabilities, such as virus scanning or methods for allocating available network capacity between different types of traffic. When purchasing a firewall, research what plug-ins are available and whether they provide services that your network requires.

✔ **Client software requirements:** Some firewalls, such as Microsoft ISA Server, require that client software be installed on all participating clients in order to provide the full benefits of the firewall. Your organization may not want to add the deployment of client software to its firewall deployment plan, or your company may not have clients for which client software is available. Investigate client software requirements. Be sure that you know the minimum hardware requirements. Also be sure to enumerate all supported platforms and compare them to your deployed platforms.

✔ **Network Address Translation (NAT) support:** Before you deploy a firewall, review the IP addressing scheme deployed at your office. If your office is using private IP addresses (as defined in RFC 1918) on your network, your firewall must provide NAT to allow internal clients to access the Internet. Likewise, if Internet-accessible resources use private addresses, the firewall should also support static mapping to map a public network IP address to an RFC 1918 address. For more information about NAT, see Chapter 3. For more information about private IP addressing, see Chapter 2.

✔ **Available licensing options:** Networks grow in size over time. Be sure to research what licensing options are available for your firewall, and how easy (and more importantly how expensive!) it is to upgrade to provide more licenses.

✔ **Virtual Private Network (VPN) support:** Do members of your organization require external access to your internal network? Some firewalls include VPN services within their base services. By deploying the VPN directly at the firewall, you only have to administer a single device for all incoming traffic and you don't have to deal with some obstacles, such as IPSec being unable to traverse a NAT service. If the firewall does provide a VPN service, be sure to investigate how interoperable the solution is with other VPN client software. You don't want to lock your organization into a single vendor because this may restrict future changes to your firewall product.

✔ **Track record:** Look at the track record of the firewall. Some firewalls have a long history of security bugs. Others have a clean record, while still others have only a few blots. Despite what they say in the world of investing, "past performance is not necessarily an indication of future results," a product that has a track record of few bugs and a fast response by vendors to bugs that have been discovered can indeed have an influence on your level of confidence in a firewall.

✔ **Cost:** Although we mention cost last, it is probably the most important factor in a firewall decision. Administrators often ask, "Why should I pay $25,000 for a firewall, when I can build one myself for $1,500?" In that case, you must ask yourself, "How much confidence do I have in a $1,500 home-brew solution?" At the same time, cost is not always an indication of quality. Excellent firewalls are available that are one-tenth the cost of competing products. If both products serve your purpose, you don't need to buy the more expensive one. And, as with any purchase, make sure that you can trust the advice of the person selling you the firewall. Finally, look at all the costs. Some firewalls charge extra for client licenses, yearly maintenance fees, support calls, additional processors in your computer, or the features that you use.

The amount that you spend on your firewall should be directly related to the value of the data that the firewall is protecting. That is not to say that the more you spend, the better the firewall will be. Just be sure to look at all criteria and how well each firewall meets the criteria. When you examine all criteria and find two or more firewalls that meet the criteria, by all means choose the cheaper solution. But don't just choose a firewall simply because it's the cheapest.

What Are Some of the Choices?

In many ways, the most important factor that should affect your firewall decision is whether the firewall has undergone extensive testing. ICSA Labs provides a certification service for firewalls. In its latest Firewall Product Certification Criteria, version 4.0, ICSA evaluates firewalls based on the type of network that the firewall protects. The evaluation includes separate criteria for residential, small/medium businesses, and corporate firewalls. In addition, baseline requirements must be met by all submitted firewalls. You can view a listing of all of the ICSA 4.0 Certified firewall products at www.icsalabs.com/html/communities/firewalls/newsite/cert.shtml. Also, make sure that you look at previous versions of the criteria. Some vendors may have been certified under a previous version of the criteria but don't want to spend the effort and money that is required to get certified for the latest version, especially if their firewall is about to be replaced with a newer version.

When reviewing the list of certified firewalls, always be sure to look at the versions of the firewall and the operating systems that were tested for certification. Many times, a firewall that is certified for the UNIX platform is not certified initially when the firewall is modified to run on Windows. Verifying the tested underlying operating system ensures that you are truly selecting a certified firewall.

You can download full descriptions of the ICSA 4.0 certification criteria from the following location: www.icsalabs.com/html/communities/firewalls/certification/criteria/Version4_FW_Criteria.zip.

Part V
The Part of Tens

The 5th Wave   By Rich Tennant

Now maybe these folks have a decent disaster recovery plan and maybe they don't...

DANGER WILD RHINOCEROS

In this part . . .

The title says it all: In this part, you find stuff in groups of ten. For example, you find ten tools that you can use to assess your network vulnerabilities and test your firewall configuration. The world doesn't stop, and the same goes for the Internet. New technologies and new hacker techniques are introduced constantly.

The last chapter lists ten Web sites that help you find out about security issues and answers questions about firewall protection. Too bad the *For Dummies* books don't have a Part of Twenties!

Chapter 19

Ten Tools You Can't Do Without

*I*f you already have a firewall installed, you should spend some time testing it. Just assuming that your firewall works is as bad as not having a firewall at all. After all, you can be pretty certain that hackers on the Internet are trying to hack into your system. Why not find out how your firewall appears to them? If your intrusion logs list attempted attacks by someone on the Internet, you should do some research to determine where the attack originated. If you discover the source of the attack, you may be able to contact a system administrator for the site from which the attack originated and have the attacker's account cancelled. Finally, when an attack happens, you may have to collect some evidence to be used in future legal proceedings. This chapter describes some tools that can help you to accomplish all of these tasks.

If you don't have a firewall installed, you should also assess your current vulnerabilities. Most likely, the results will convince you that your computers are more open to attack than you realized. Some of the tools described in this chapter can assist you in evaluating the security of your system.

Finally, this chapter includes some general-purpose tools that can tell you more about how programs on your computer use the network. You can use these tools to assess your firewall, or you can use them to investigate which protocols need to be allowed to pass through your firewall.

Whether you're checking your systems before or after you install a firewall, it's important that you have tools to accomplish this task. This chapter lists our favorite tools. Most of these tools are free downloads from the Internet; some must be purchased. Regardless of price, all of these are excellent tools, and anyone running a firewall should consider using at least some of them. However, remember that this list is not comprehensive. You should also investigate other tools, including alternatives to the tools that we mention here.

In addition to using the tools described in this chapter, make sure that your network is also protected by a good antivirus system. Such a system may include programs running on all computers in your network as well as some virus protection features of your firewall and mail server.

Several tools described in this chapter were originally developed as hacker tools. Some were designed to probe your network for vulnerabilities or to test how vulnerable your defenses are. Only use these tools on your own network or with the permission of the network's owner. Just like your employer would not appreciate your trying to open the office safe for educational purposes, most network owners would not appreciate the use of these tools on their networks by unauthorized people and may respond accordingly.

Sam Spade

Remember Sam Spade, the private eye played by Humphrey Bogart in the movie *The Maltese Falcon?* Sam Spade, the tool, was named after that character and is one of the most comprehensive network investigation tools in existence. It comes as both an online version and a downloadable version that you can install on your computer. Sam Spade acts as a sleuth that finds as much public information about an IP address or DNS address as you can imagine. Suppose that your logs show that someone tried to scan your network for open ports and the log lists the potential intruder's IP address. No problem — Sam Spade to the rescue!

You can use Sam Spade to find more information about the IP address, such as who the address is registered to and the route between your computer and the computer at the remote IP address. Then you can query the registration records for this IP address and find out the Internet Service Provider (ISP) who owns the IP address, including the contact information. This is just one example of the many tools included with Sam Spade that you can use to track down information. Check it out for yourself by using the online tool at www. samspade.org or by downloading the free standalone Windows version. However, be prepared to spend a little time becoming familiar with the features of this tool, which is not always very intuitive.

Nmap

Nmap is one of the most capable port scanners available. A port scanner checks your computers or firewalls to see which ports are open and then reports back the results. Hackers use port scanners to probe systems for TCP ports on which there is a reply. After an open TCP port has been located, the hacker can try to break into the computer by using this port. Like many tools that hackers may find useful, a port scanner is also of tremendous value to anyone who wants to secure a network. You can use a port scanner to check for open ports that may signal vulnerabilities.

The strength of Nmap is that it uses a number of different techniques to map a network — some of which are rather sneaky and are designed to bypass detection. Nmap can do a number of other things, too. It uses specially crafted IP packets to bypass some protection mechanisms and it uses the responses to these packets to make an educated guess about what hosts are running on your network, what operating system they are running, and how firewalls are configured. Nmap's Web site explains these methods in detail. Nmap is one of the best port scanners available; it runs on Windows and several Linux versions; and it's free. What else can you ask for?

To test your firewall, run a port scan against it and make sure that your firewall replies only on those ports that you have set up for authorized connections from the Internet into your network. You can configure Nmap to check any range of ports, and you can even tell it to scan an entire range of IP addresses, so you can check your entire network at once. You can download this program from www.insecure.org/nmap/index.html. Just make sure that you run a port scan against only computers on which the owner has given you permission to do so. Running this tool against other computers may result in you getting reported to your ISP — which may cancel your account.

Netstat

Netstat is a TCP/IP tool that is included with most versions of Windows and UNIX. It's the quickest way to check what TCP and UDP ports are in use on a computer. Best of all, because it's a built-in utility, it's available on most computers. You don't need to download anything. After you use Netstat to provide a list of ports in use, you can check to see whether all of them should indeed be in use. The output from the `netstat` command can also give you pointers to programs that are running on your computer and that may present vulnerability. In addition, you can use Netstat to list all current connections that your computer has established to other computers, as well as what incoming connections exist. You get results about both open connections and listening ports by using the –a option, as in **netstat –a**. Because Netstat is most likely included with your operating system, you can use it directly from a command line.

Sometimes the Netstat command takes some time to complete because it tries to resolve all IP addresses to DNS names. You can speed up the operations by using the –n option, as in **netstat –n**, which instructs Netstat to skip the time-consuming name lookups and just show IP addresses.

TCPView

TCPView is a Windows program that gives you information similar to that provided by the `netstat` command. Unlike Netstat, it presents this information in a much more usable format. Visit `www.sysinternals.com` for a free downloadable version of TCPView. TCPView Professional is a version of TCPView that features several enhancements, such as a more usable display and a view of which applications currently access the network. You can download an evaluation version of TCPView Professional and find out more about how to purchase it at `www.winternals.com`.

TDIMon

TDIMon is a Windows program that gives you detailed information about programs on your computer that access the network by using TCP/IP. TDIMon can show you in real time what programs are using the network and what port each program has opened. This can be very helpful when you need to have exact information about how a given program is accessing the network. You can download TDIMon from `www.sysinternals.com`. The functions of TDIMon are also included in TCPView Professional from `www.winternals.com`.

Tools that go without mentioning

In addition to the Netstat command, the TCP/IP software that comes with most operating systems also includes other tools that are important for testing and troubleshooting a firewall. Although you are probably already using these tools, we mention them here just to be sure that you know about them.

✔ Use the venerable `ping` command to diagnose a network connection.

✔ Use the `tracert` or `traceroute` command to trace the path that network packets take from your computer to a remote computer.

✔ Use the `nslookup` command to check entries on DNS servers for troubleshooting.

✔ Use the `ipconfig` command to confirm the TCP/IP configuration of your computer. Some versions of Microsoft Windows include a graphical version of `ipconfig` called `winipcfg`.

You can find more information about these commands in your operating system's help system or in a TCP/IP book, such as *TCP/IP For Dummies, 5th Edition,* by Candace Leiden and Marshall Wilensky, published by Wiley Publishing, Inc.

FPort

Netstat, TCPView, and TDIMon give you useful information about the ports that are used by applications running on your computer. FPort performs similar tasks from a slightly different angle. It shows you all the ports that are currently open on your computer and lists the programs that have opened each of these ports. You can use this tool to get a good idea of why certain ports are open, and whether you should use your firewall to close them. FPort is a free utility that you can download from `www.foundstone.com/rdlabs/tools.php`.

Snort

Despite its funny name, Snort is a capable intrusion detection system that works well on smaller networks. Snort performs real-time network traffic logging and analysis. For example, you can configure Snort to capture all packets on a network segment and scan them for the telltale signs of intrusion attempts. Although Snort is very capable, you should be prepared to spend some time learning how to use it. Also, if you want to customize Snort to look for newly discovered attacks, you may have to spend additional time configuring and customizing it. Snort is available for Windows and several UNIX platforms, and you can download it from `www.snort.org`.

Before you run Snort, make sure that you either own the network that you run it on or that you have permission from the network's owner or administrator. Snort captures all network traffic that could potentially be used for illegitimate purposes. Because of this, many organizations have strict policies on the use of such tools; usually, only network administrators are authorized to use them. Snort works well on smaller networks, but is not designed for larger networks. If you find that your intrusion detection needs go beyond the capabilities of this program, you should evaluate other intrusion detection systems, such as RealSecure by Internet Security Systems. You can find more information about RealSecure at www.iss.net.

Internet Scanner

Internet Scanner, a product from Internet Security Systems (ISS), is a network security scanner. It scans computers on your network for known vulnerabilities. This may include problems, such as misconfigured Web servers or user accounts with weak passwords. Unlike an intrusion detection system, which performs real-time analysis based on actual network traffic, Internet Scanner gives you an assessment for your current system configuration, either for a single computer or for an entire network. You can get more information about features and pricing and download an evaluation version of the software at www.iss.net.

Alternatives

You can find alternatives to many of the tools that are listed in this chapter. Although we prefer the tools we list here, you should also investigate some alternatives before implementing security software, such as a network security scanner. Also, you may find that it is worthwhile to invest in more than one system. Each intrusion detection system or network security scanner has some weaknesses, and using more than one at a time results in a more thorough check of your network's security. For example, eEye (www.eeye.com) sells Retina, a network security scanner, and Iris, a network traffic analyzer. Network Associates (www.cybercop. co.uk) sells CyberCop Monitor, an intrusion-detection system, and CyberCop Scanner, a network security scanner. You can find more information about both of these products at www.pgp.com. Also, don't forget other tools that can help you to secure your firewall's operating system, such as the Microsoft Baseline Security Analyzer, which you can download from www.microsoft.com/technet/Securit/tools/tools/MBSAHome.ASP.

Nessus

Nessus, like Internet Scanner, is a security scanner that scans your network to detect security vulnerabilities. Nessus consists of two parts: a server and a client. The server tries to run attacks against your computers and the front-end client is what you use to configure how the server does this. The server part of Nessus runs on Linux, while the client can run under Linux or Windows.

As with any security scanner that probes your network for vulnerabilities, Nessus performs the equivalent of trying to break into your computer and then reports back to you. Make sure you only run Nessus on your own network or with the permission of the network's owner. You can download Nessus for free from www.nessus.org.

Network Monitor

If you are using Windows NT Server or Windows 2000 Server, you have access to a powerful network protocol analyzer. Network Monitor is similar to Snort in its ability to capture network packets. You can then look at the packets — including all characters included in the network packet — to troubleshoot connection information. You can also see exactly which packets were sent across the network. Network Monitor breaks up the packets into individual components and gives you detailed information on packet headers and other components of the network traffic.

The version of Network Monitor that is included with Windows NT and Windows 2000 captures only network traffic that was sent or received by the computer on which it runs. To use the full-featured version that captures all network traffic, you have to buy Microsoft Systems Management Server. Still, even the scaled-down version is a powerful and useful tool. It isn't installed by default, so you have to add this optional component to your installation of Windows NT Server or Windows 2000 Server.

Ethereal

Ethereal is a free protocol analyzer that is a good alternative to Network Monitor. We often use both tools. Depending on the task at hand, one may give us better results than the other, or one may be more easily accessible.

Ethereal has the advantage that it can capture all traffic on a network, without having to pay for the full-featured version of Network Monitor. It also runs on several Linux versions in addition to Windows. You can read more about Ethereal and download it at www.ethereal.com.

NetCat

NetCat has been described as the Swiss Army knife of network tools. You can use NetCat to send network packets and listen for incoming network packets using any port. Like many powerful tools available to network administrators, NetCat also has a number of uses for hackers, so it makes sense for you to familiarize yourself with all its features. After all, to defeat hackers, it helps to know their tools. NetCat is available for Windows, Linux, and UNIX. You can download it for free from www.atstake.com/research/tools/network_utilities/.

Chapter 20

Ten Web Sites to Visit

*A*lthough you use firewalls to protect your network from intrusion attempts from the Internet, you can also use the Internet to stay one step ahead of hackers. The Internet is full of useful information that you can use to learn about security issues and stay up-to-date on anything related to the firewall product that you are using. This chapter describes several sites that can help you to secure your network. Several of these sites also contain links to additional resources. Use them as a starting point when you are looking for answers about firewalls or other questions regarding computer system security.

www.sans.org

The SANS (System Administration, Networking, and Security) Institute homepage at www.sans.org provides many security-related resources. SANS concentrates on research and education and has earned a reputation for being a reliable and up-to-date source for security alerts and news summaries. SANS also offers a number of security training resources. In addition to providing conferences and a certification program, the SANS institute makes a number of valuable resources available on its Web site. Explore this site and see what SANS has to offer.

The homepage of SANS is filled with links that can seem overwhelming, so we look only at the most useful ones. You can explore the site further and see what else SANS has to offer. Here's what we recommend looking at first:

- **Security digests:** Weekly and biweekly publications that you can have sent to you by e-mail. Each of them deals with a different area, and each starts with a table of contents, so you can quickly scan each issue for news about a product you're using.

- **Top 20 vulnerabilities:** A list of the top 20 security vulnerabilities that exist on computers connected to the Internet. Do any of them apply to your computers and, if so, have you fixed them?

- **Conference presentations:** A number of security presentations from SANS-sponsored conferences. Where else can you read an FBI presentation about hunting the wily hacker?

- **Research papers:** Remember the term papers you had to write in school? SANS requires that their certification candidates submit research papers on security-related issues. These research papers are available via the Web site, and they are generally of very high quality.

- **Model Security policies:** You can use these to come up with ideas for your organization's Security polices.

- **Salary survey:** Find out how much money you can earn if you decide to make a career out of information security, or learn how much you should pay security professionals that you employ.

While you review the excellent free material on the SANS site, also check out some of the other offerings. The Step-by-Step guides to computer security are great resources and the frequent SANS conferences are more than worth the registration fee.

www.cert.org

CERT/CC started as the Computer Emergency Response Team, which is a federally chartered organization that operates out of Carnegie Mellon University. Today it's called the CERT Coordination Center (CERT/CC). CERT/CC employs over 50 security professionals. Its charter calls for working with other organizations and individuals to provide up-to-date information on security issues. Most importantly, CERT/CC issues advisories on newly discovered security threats, often including information on ways to meet them.

Here are the most valuable sections on the CERT/CC Web site, located at `www.cert.org`:

- ✔ **Quick fixes:** Sometimes you have to respond quickly and don't have the time to do a lot of research. Suppose you think that someone may have broken into your Web server. How should you respond? Whom should you contact? CERT/CC has detailed guides for what to do in this situation and several others.

- ✔ **Incident reporting:** We hope you don't get hacked. However, if it happens, you may be able to help others avoid the same fate or even get assistance as you respond to the incident by reporting a security-related incident. Keep in mind that CERT/CC has a priority for responding; life-threatening emergencies receive the most immediate attention while other activities, such as unsuccessful intrusion attempts, have a much lower priority. Review the reporting guidelines before reporting an incident.

- ✔ **Advisories and incident reports:** CERT/CC reports large-scale vulnerability risks, such as viruses that are spreading quickly. Often, this site also provides up-to-date fixes for such problems and advice on how to protect your systems.

CERT/CC is an organization that's based in the United States. Other countries have similar sites that may be of interest, such as `www.infosyssec.org` (described in the next paragraph), which has a list of many international CERT/CC sites.

www.infosyssec.org

If you regularly visit only one Internet site for security information, `www.infosyssec.org` should be the one. The InfoSysSec (Information System Security) bills itself as the "Security Portal for Information System Security Professionals," and this portal is indeed the best gateway to security information on the Internet. Sure, it can be overwhelming at first — after all, this site contains links to thousands of other resources. However, after you look around, you see the real value of this site. Not only does it contain links to any computer security resource on the Internet that you can imagine, but this site also does a great job organizing these resources into relevant categories and describing them for you. You can't find a better resource than InfoSysSec for starting your search for anything related to computer security, including firewalls.

Deciding which resources to highlight is almost impossible. This site contains so much information that a short list of highlights doesn't do it justice.

In addition to the following sections, take a close look at the homepage for this Web site, and make sure that you scroll to the bottom of the page to see all categories.

- ✔ **Research resources:** This is a long list of categories, including, of course, one on firewalls. Follow any of these links for an exhaustive list of resources including articles, links to vendor Web sites, research reports, and any other imaginable type of resource.

- ✔ **Security alerts:** Use this list of security alert sites to check out the latest security alerts that are either vendor-specific or independent of a specific product. After you've visited the Web site that contains these alerts, you can often subscribe to an e-mail newsletter that brings the latest warnings straight to your e-mail inbox every day. Be aware that signing up for some of these lists may result in a large amount of e-mail. Still, it is often the best way to get timely warnings.

- ✔ **Security news sources:** InfoSysSec has the best collection of security news sources anywhere on the Web. Don't try to view all the news sites that you can access from this site on a daily basis, though. It could easily turn into a full-time job! Instead, use this site to explore news sources that sound interesting, and then visit those that look most relevant to you.

- ✔ **Storm and severe weather warnings:** You may wonder how this is related to computer security. We included this link for two reasons. First, this link is somewhat hidden on the Web page and we really want to encourage you to review all the listings, from the top of the page to the bottom. Second, it's always a good idea to remember that network security depends on a number of factors, and you can't fix all of them with technology. A tornado disrupting your network operations and destroying your backup tapes is a good example.

www.microsoft.com/security

Considering Microsoft's role in the software industry, you likely have one or more computers that are running one of Microsoft's products. Microsoft has realized the importance for enabling its customers to learn about security issues related to its products and for them to stay informed about computer security issues, especially those related to the Internet. Because of this, Microsoft has created a Web site (www.microsoft.com/security) that acts as a clearinghouse for all kinds of network security-related issues. Keep in mind that other vendors maintain similar Web sites and that you can find links to them from the InfoSysSec Security Portal, which is covered earlier in this chapter.

Here are the sections of this Web site that you should look at first:

- **Bulletins:** If it's broken, fix it. Microsoft has been very good about creating fixes to security-related problems with its software. Because of the dominant role that Microsoft holds, its software has become a favorite target of hackers. On the other hand, because Microsoft sells a very large number of products, chances are good that vulnerabilities are discovered than if just a few were sold. Microsoft regularly releases security bulletins that outline what these issues are and how to fix them. The Bulletins section of this Web site allows you to quickly find bulletins that are relevant to you.

- **Best practices:** This link takes you to an extensive list of excellent documents that list best practices on securing your network. Best practices means that the practices outlined here are not required, but that it's a good idea to follow them. If you decide to ignore them, you only have yourself to blame for a security breach.

- **Tools and checklists:** Microsoft makes some tools and checklists available that can help you to configure servers running Microsoft operating systems very efficiently. If you don't need to configure servers, you should still go to this section just to download the security screen saver.

www.icsalabs.com

ICSA Labs is a division of TruSecure Corporation that evaluates and certifies firewalls. Among other services that this company provides, it sets standards for commercial security products. ICSA Labs is generally regarded as the ultimate authority on firewalls. All major firewall vendors have submitted their products to ICSA Labs for analysis. If you're planning to buy a firewall product, look for the ICSA certification as a seal of approval. ICSA Labs has a number of other firewall resources available on its Web site at `www.icsalabs.com/html/communities/firewalls`.

The ICSA Labs Web site has two sections that are interesting for anyone buying a firewall.

- **Certified firewalls:** If you want to buy a firewall product, this is the second place you should go. (The first resource to consult is this book, of course.) ICSA Labs has certified over 40 firewalls, and this section gives you product information and lab reports for each of them. See how the firewall that you're evaluating compares to others.

- **Buyer's guide:** This is one of the best online resources for learning about firewalls and their features. After you have mastered the basics (by reading this book, for example), you can find more details in the buyer's guide, which you can either peruse online or download. Don't be scared by the size. It's almost 100 pages, but you already know a lot of the information from reading this book, so you will be able to skip some sections.

www.securityfocus.com

SecurityFocus, a division of Symantec Corp., is a company that provides security information services. These services include maintaining an excellent Web site that provides you the latest information on security vulnerabilities in a variety of products. In addition, SecurityFocus also maintains a number of mailing lists on security-related issues.

The Web site for SecurityFocus at www.securityfocus.com is one of the best for getting timely information on vulnerabilities and for finding mailing lists that help you stay up-to-date on security issues. These are the most useful sections of the Web site:

- **Mailing lists:** This is what SecurityFocus.com is best known for. This section enables you to get information about and subscribe to a number of mailing lists. Some of these mailing lists cover newly discovered security vulnerabilities and fixes for them. Others deal with more specialized topics, such as intrusion detection. The best known of these lists is Bugtraq, which carries the largest number of reports on security vulnerabilities. Another great list is Security-Basics, which is intended to help beginners in the field learn the basics of computer security. Use this section to learn more about each list, search messages, and subscribe to receive regular messages via e-mail.

- **Vulnerabilities:** This is a searchable database of security vulnerabilities in all kinds of products. This database is one of the most comprehensive aids available to find out about security problems in almost any computer product.

- **Tools:** This is a comprehensive list of tools that you can use to improve the security of your network. For example, this Web site features a long, annotated list of intrusion-detection systems that you can use to assess whether your firewall is performing correctly and whether it sufficiently protects your network.

- **Multimedia:** Don't forget to check out the audio and video presentations, which include interviews and presentations by a list of contributors that reads like a virtual Who's Who of network security.

www.gocsi.com

Computer Security Institute (CSI) is a membership organization that provides a number of security-related resources. The memberships and the resources that are for sale on this site are useful, but you'll also find a lot of free information that makes this site well worth visiting.

CSI's Web site at `www.gocsi.com` has a section of interest to anyone working with firewalls. At the Firewall Product Resource Center link, you will find the Firewall Search Center, which allows you to quickly compare the features of several firewall products. You can also access the archives, which contain useful documents, such as one that explains how to test a firewall and one on how not to build a firewall.

www.isaserver.org

If you use ISA Server, you'll love the ISAserver.org site at `www.isaserver.org`. Even if you don't use ISA Server, you may want look at it to see an example of what an independently operated, product-specific Web site should look like. ISAserver.org is devoted to all things related to ISA Server, and the amount of information available and the links to resources make Microsoft's own ISA Server site look terribly incomplete. This is the best.

Where to start? This Web site has all information related to ISA Server that you can imagine, but here are the most useful ones:

- ✔ **Message boards:** The message boards enable you to ask questions about ISA Server and have them answered by other participants, who include a number of ISA Server experts. You can also learn quite a bit by reading what others have posted.

- ✔ **Learning Zone:** The Learning Zone contains a number of well-written tutorials that help you to configure several of ISA Server's features that are not as intuitive as they could be. The tutorials are illustrated with ample screen shots.

ISAserver.org is a great site, but if you are using FireWall-1, it won't help you much. Don't despair. You can find a good third-party support site at `www.phoneboy.com`. Check here for the latest information about FireWall-1.

www.interhack.net/pubs/fwfaq

Newsgroups have been part of the Internet for many years. These are forums where people post questions and receive helpful responses from others. As more and more people ask the same questions, volunteers compile lists of the most frequently asked questions (FAQs) with the corresponding answers. This helps the regulars avoid having to answer the same questions over and over, thus getting cranky in the process. At the same time, a FAQ is a great resource for anyone who needs to know an answer to many questions regarding a topic. Not surprisingly, such a FAQ for firewalls exists, and you can access it via the Web at `www.interhack.net/pubs/fwfaw`.

Much of the information in this FAQ forum is very basic, but it also contains some nuggets of excellent information, such as specific instructions on how to make particular protocols work through your firewall and descriptions of common attacks.

Firewall Lists

The last of our Top Ten resources is actually two separate links. By combining them, we can sneak in a bonus resource, and Top Ten sounds better than Top Eleven. Don't you agree?

A lot of information on the Internet is exchanged in mailing lists where people post questions and answers or announce new discoveries. The field of firewalls is no exception. If you sign up for one of these lists, you will receive periodic e-mail with firewall news and you can send your own questions to fellow list members.

The Firewall Wizards mailing list is a low-volume, moderated list that is hosted by the TruSecure Corporation, the same people who run ICSA Labs (see the Web site discussed previously). For more information about the list and how to sign up for it, go to `honor.trusecure.com/mailman/listinfo/firewall-wizards`.

The Internet Software Consortium's Firewalls mailing list covers all aspects of firewalls, with a special emphasis on open-source software. It has a high volume of messages, sometimes as many as 100 a day. If you don't want your e-mail inbox to overflow, you can subscribe to a digest version. You can find more information about this list, instructions for signing up, and list archives at `www.isc.org/services/public/lists/firewalls.html`.

Appendix

Protocol Listings and More

● ●

In This Appendix

▶ IP protocol numbers

▶ ICMP type numbers

▶ TCP and UDP port listing

● ●

*C*reating packet filters on a firewall requires knowledge about the different protocol numbers and port numbers used by the IP protocol suite.

This appendix summarizes the IP protocol numbers, ICMP type numbers, and TCP and UDP port numbers needed to configure the firewall.

IP Protocol Numbers

Different protocols can run in a layer above the IP protocol. They each have a different IP Protocol Number. The best-known IP Protocol Numbers are TCP (6) and UDP (17). A selection of common IP protocols is shown in Table A-1.

For a complete list, see `www.iana.org/assignments/protocol-numbers`.

Table A-1		IP Protocol Numbers
IP Protocol	*Name*	*Description*
1	ICMP	Internet Control Message Protocol
2	IGMP	Internet Group Management Protocol (multicast)
6	TCP	Transmission Control Protocol
17	UDP	User Datagram Protocol
47	GRE	General Routing Encapsulation (VPN-PPTP)
50	ESP	Encapsulating Security Payload (IPSec)

(continued)

Table A-1 (continued)

IP Protocol	Name	Description
51	AH	Authentication Header (IPSec)
89	OSPF	Open Shortest Path First

ICMP Type Numbers

ICMP messages are the housekeeping notices of the IP protocol. When a problem occurs with an IP packet being sent to its destination, an ICMP packet is returned to notify the sender of the problem. A selection of common ICMP type numbers is shown in Table A-2.

For a complete list see www.iana.org/assignments/icmp-parameters.

Table A-2	ICMP Type Numbers	
ICMP Type	**Name**	**Comment**
0	Echo Reply	Normal Ping reply
3	Destination Unreachable	
4	Source Quench	Router too busy
5	Redirect	Shorter route discovered
8	Echo Request	Normal Ping request
11	Time Exceeded	Too many hops to destination
12	Parameter Problem	

TCP and UDP Port Listing

The TCP and UDP protocols use a 16-bit number to indicate the port number. This means that possible port numbers range from 0 to 65535. The Internet Assigned Numbers Authority (IANA) maintains a list describing which port number is used by which application. It divides the port numbers into three ranges:

✔ **Well Known Ports (0–1023):** These ports are assigned by the IANA.

✔ **Registered Ports (1024–49151):** These ports are registered by the IANA merely as a convenience to the Internet community.

✔ **Dynamic or Private Ports (49152–65535):** The ports in this range are not registered. Any application can use these ports.

In case you only have ten fingers and wonder why the division is at the seemingly random number 49152, it's because this is the hexadecimal number C000.

Table A-3 contains a selection of the most common TCP and UDP ports, sorted by protocol name.

You'll often see references to RFC1700 as the source for the definitive list of port numbers. However, that document contains a list of ports from October 1994 and will never be updated. If you are interested in the latest version of the complete list of (currently) more than 7900 port registrations, sorted by port number, go to `www.iana.org/assignments/port-numbers`. That port numbers list is updated frequently.

Suspicious entries in the firewall log files may be caused by Trojan horse applications. Some of these applications are included in the list below. Note that most of these malicious applications can be configured to use different ports, so don't assume that they use the same port listed here.

Table A-3			Port Numbers (Sorted by Name)
Port	*TCP*	*UDP*	*Name (Sorted)*
1525		x	Archie
113	x		Auth (Ident)
31337	x	x	Back Orifice (BO)
54320	x		Back Orifice 2000 (BO2K)
54321		x	Back Orifice 2000 (BO2K)
179	x		BGP (Border Gateway Protocol)
512		x	Biff
1680	x		CarbonCopy
19	x	x	Chargen
2301	x		Compaq Insight Manager
531	x		Conference (chat)

(continued)

Table A-3 *(continued)*

Port	TCP	UDP	Name (Sorted)
	x		Conference (H.323) call setup
1167		x	Conference (phone)
1503	x		Conference server (T.120)
7648		x	CuSeeMe
7649	x	x	CuSeeMe
24032	x		CuSeeMe
26214	x	x	Dark Reign 2 (game)
13	x	x	Daytime
68		x	DHCP client
67		x	DHCP server
47624	x	x	DirectPlay
9	x	x	Discard
53		x	DNS name resolution
53	x		DNS zone transfer
666	x	x	Doom (game)
7	x	x	Echo
520	x		EFS (Extended File Name Server)
79	x		Finger
21	x		FTP (control)
20	x		FTP (data)
6346	x	x	GNUtella
70	x		Gopher
101	x		Hostname
80	x		HTTP
8008	x		HTTP alternate
8080	x		HTTP alternate (Web proxy)
443	x	x	HTTPS (SSL)
1494	x	x	ICA (Citrix)

Port	TCP	UDP	Name (Sorted)
1604		x	ICA (Citrix) browser
3130		x	ICP (Internet Cache Protocol)
3128	x		ICP HTTP
4000		x	ICQ (old)
5190	x		ICQ 2000/AOL Messenger
500		x	IKE (Internet Key Exchange)/IPSec NAT-D
220	x		IMAP3
143	x		IMAP4
993	x		IMAP4 (SSL)
585	x		IMAP4 (SSL) (old)
1524	x		Ingress
631	x		IPP (Internet Printing Protocol)
4500		x	IPSec NAT-T
213	x		IPX over IP
194	x		IRC
6667	x		IRC
7000	x		IRC
6665	x		IRC (Microsoft) load balancing
2998	x	x	ISS RealSecure
1214	x	x	Kazaa
88	x	x	Kerberos
750		x	Kerberos 4
749	x	x	Kerberos administration
2053	x		Kerberos de-multiplexor
543	x		Kerberos login
464	x	x	Kerberos password
1109	x		Kerberos pop
544	x		Kerberos remote shell

(continued)

Table A-3 *(continued)*

Port	TCP	UDP	Name (Sorted)
1701		x	L2TP
1547	x	x	Laplink
389	x	x	LDAP
636	x		LDAP (SSL)
3268	x		LDAP Global Catalog
3269	x		LDAP Global Catalog (SSL)
1352	x		Lotus Notes RPC
515	x		LPR (Printer spooler)
2535	x	x	MADCAP
9535	x		Man server
1755	x	x	MMS (Microsoft Media Streaming)
561		x	Monitor
560		x	Monitor (remote)
569	x		MSN Internet Access Protocol
1863	x		MSN Messenger
6901	x	x	MSN Messenger voice
3453	x		Myth (game)
6699	x		Napster
6801	x		Net2Phone protocol
6500	x		Net2Phone registration
138		x	NetBIOS Datagram Service
137		x	NetBIOS Name Service
139	x		NetBIOS Session Service
12345	x		NetBus
20034	x		NetBus 2.0
1731	x		Netmeeting audio control
49608	x	x	Netmeeting Remote Desktop

Port	TCP	UDP	Name (Sorted)
49609	x	x	Netmeeting Remote Desktop
522	x		Netmeeting ULS (old)
532	x		Netnews
533		x	Netwall
9100	x		Network printer (HP)
2049	x	x	NFS
1717		x	NLBS (Microsoft) remote control
2504		x	NLBS (Microsoft) remote control
119	x		NNTP
563	x		NNTP (SSL)
123		x	NTP (Network Time Protocol)
1600	x		Oracle Connection Manager
1526	x		Oracle Multiprotocol Interchange
1575	x		Oracle Names
1521	x		Oracle TNS Listener
22		x	pcAnywhere
65301	x		pcAnywhere
5631	x	x	pcAnywhere (data)
5632	x		pcAnywhere (status)
158	x		PCMail
109	x		POP2
110	x		POP3
995	x		POP3 (SSL)
1723	x		PPTP Control Channel
170	x		PrintSrv
27910		x	Quake II (game)
27970		x	Quake III (game)
545	x		QuickTime

(continued)

Table A-3 *(continued)*

Port	TCP	UDP	Name (Sorted)
17	x	x	Quote
1813		x	RADIUS Accounting
1646		x	RADIUS Accounting (old)
1812		x	RADIUS Authentication
1645		x	RADIUS Authentication (old)
3389	x		RDP (Remote Desktop Protocol)/Terminal Services
43188	x		ReachOut
7070	x		RealNetworks Streaming Media
556	x		Remotefs
2000	x		Remotely Anywhere
2001	x		Remotely Anywhere
799	x		Remotely Possible/ControlIT
800	x		Remotely Possible/ControlIT
512	x		RExec (Remote execution)
520		x	RIP
513	x		RLogin (Remote login)
39		x	RLP (Resource Location)
530	x		RPC (courier)
135	x	x	RPC (Microsoft)
111	x	x	RPC (Sun)
514	x		RSH
873	x		RSync (Remote Sync)
5005		x	RTCP (RTP Control Protocol)
24033		x	RTCP (RTP Control Protocol)
107	x		RTelnet (Remote Telnet)
5004		x	RTP (Real-time Transport Protocol)
24032		x	RTP (Real-time Transport Protocol)

Port	TCP	UDP	Name (Sorted)
554	x		RTSP (Real-time Streaming Protocol)
2233		x	Shiva VPN
445	x	x	SMB/CIFS
1761	x		SMS (Microsoft) remote control
25	x		SMTP
465	x		SMTP (SSL)
161		x	SNMP
162		x	SNMP trap
1080	x	x	SOCKS V4
1433	x	x	SQL Server (Microsoft)
1434	x	x	SQL Server (Microsoft) monitor
22	x		SSH (Secure Shell)
27374	x		SubSeven (S7S)
54283	x		SubSeven (S7S) application spying
2773	x		SubSeven (S7S) keystroke logger
7215	x		SubSeven (S7S) remote terminal
9000	x		Sybase IIOP
9001	x		Sybase IIOPS
9002	x		Sybase IIOPS
787	x		Sybase TDS
514		x	Syslog
11	x	x	Systat
49	x	x	TACACS
518		x	Talk
517		x	Talk (old)
23	x		Telnet
526	x		Tempo newdate
69		x	TFTP

(continued)

Table A-3 (continued)

Port	TCP	UDP	Name (Sorted)
1758		x	TFTP multicast
407	x	x	Timbuktu
525		x	Time Daemon
37	x	x	Time server
117	x		UUCP
540	x		UUCP Daemon
5500	x		VNC
5800	x		VNC
5801	x		VNC
5900	x		VNC
5901	x		VNC
210	x		WAIS
4103	x		WatchGuard control
2048		x	WCCP (Web Cache Coordination Protocol)
513		x	Who Daemon
550		x	Who Daemon (new)
43	x		Whois
5678	x		Windows CE Services
5679	x		Windows CE Services
137	x		WINS registration
1512	x	x	WINS replication (Windows 2000)
42	x		WINS replication (Windows NT 4)
102	x		X.400
6000	x		X11
177	x		X11 Display Manager
7100	x		X11 Font Server
82	x	x	XFER utility
5050	x		Yahoo Messenger

Index

• D •

Notes

FOR DUMMIES®

The easy way to get more done and have more fun

FOR DUMMIES®

A world of resources to help you grow

TRAVEL

0-7645-5453-0

Hawaii

0-7645-5438-7

Walt Disney World & Orlando

0-7645-5444-1

EDUCATION & TEST PREPARATION

Spanish

0-7645-5194-9

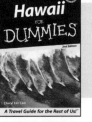

Algebra

0-7645-5325-9

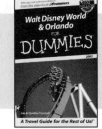

U.S. History

0-7645-5249-X

HEALTH, SELF-HELP & SPIRITUALITY

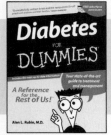

Diabetes

0-7645-5154-X

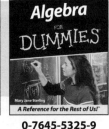

Sex

0-7645-5302-X

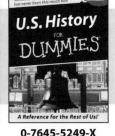

Parenting

0-7645-5418-2

FOR DUMMIES

Plain-English solutions for everyday challenges

FOR DUMMIES®

Helping you expand your horizons and realize your potential

GRAPHICS & WEB SITE DEVELOPMENT

Photoshop 7 FOR DUMMIES
A Reference for the Rest of Us!
Deke McClelland
Barbara Obermeier
0-7645-1651-5

Creating Web Pages FOR DUMMIES
A Reference for the Rest of Us!
Bud Smith
Arthur Bebak
0-7645-1643-4

Macromedia Flash MX FOR DUMMIES
A Reference for the Rest of Us!
Gurdy Leete
Ellen Finkelstein
0-7645-0895-4

Also available:

Adobe Acrobat 5 PDF For Dummies (0-7645-1652-3)

ASP.NET For Dummies (0-7645-0866-0)

ColdFusion MX For Dummies (0-7645-1672-8)

Dreamweaver MX For Dummies (0-7645-1630-2)

FrontPage 2002 For Dummies (0-7645-0821-0)

HTML 4 For Dummies (0-7645-0723-0)

Illustrator 10 For Dummies (0-7645-3636-2)

PowerPoint 2002 For Dummies (0-7645-0817-2)

Web Design For Dummies (0-7645-0823-7)

PROGRAMMING & DATABASES

C++ FOR DUMMIES
A Reference for the Rest of Us!
Stephen Randy Davis
0-7645-0746-X

Visual Studio .NET ALL-IN-ONE DESK REFERENCE FOR DUMMIES
7 BOOKS IN 1
0-7645-1626-4

XML FOR DUMMIES
A Reference for the Rest of Us!
Ed Tittel
Natanya Pitts
Frank Boumphrey
0-7645-1657-4

Also available:

Access 2002 For Dummies (0-7645-0818-0)

Beginning Programming For Dummies (0-7645-0835-0)

Crystal Reports 9 For Dummies (0-7645-1641-8)

Java & XML For Dummies (0-7645-1658-2)

Java 2 For Dummies (0-7645-0765-6)

JavaScript For Dummies (0-7645-0633-1)

Oracle9i For Dummies (0-7645-0880-6)

Perl For Dummies (0-7645-0776-1)

PHP and MySQL For Dummies (0-7645-1650-7)

SQL For Dummies (0-7645-0737-0)

Visual Basic .NET For Dummies (0-7645-0867-9)

LINUX, NETWORKING & CERTIFICATION

Red Hat Linux 7.3 FOR DUMMIES
A Reference for the Rest of Us!
Jon "maddog" Hall
Paul G. Sery
0-7645-1545-4

TCP/IP FOR DUMMIES
A Reference for the Rest of Us!
Candace Leiden
Marshall Wilensky
0-7645-1760-0

Networking FOR DUMMIES
A Reference for the Rest of Us!
Doug Lowe
0-7645-0772-9

Also available:

A+ Certification For Dummies (0-7645-0812-1)

CCNP All-in-One Certification For Dummies (0-7645-1648-5)

Cisco Networking For Dummies (0-7645-1668-X)

CISSP For Dummies (0-7645-1670-1)

CIW Foundations For Dummies (0-7645-1635-3)

Firewalls For Dummies (0-7645-0884-9)

Home Networking For Dummies (0-7645-0857-1)

Red Hat Linux All-in-One Desk Reference For Dummi (0-7645-2442-9)

UNIX For Dummies (0-7645-0419-3)

Available wherever books are sold.
Go to www.dummies.com or call 1-877-762-2974 to order direct

WILEY